A Brief History
of Japanese Civilization

Conrad Schirokauer
The City College of The City University of New York

Harcourt Brace College Publishers
Fort Worth Philadelphia San Diego New York Orlando Austin San Antonio
Toronto Montreal London Sydney Tokyo

Publisher	Ted Buchholz
Acquisitions Editor	Drake Bush
Project Editor	Angela Williams
Production Manager	Jane Tyndall Ponceti
Book Designer	Burl Sloan
Photo/Permissions Editor	Shirley Webster

Address for Editorial Correspondence
Harcourt Brace College Publishers, 301 Commerce Street, Suite 3700, Fort Worth, TX 76102

Address for Orders
Harcourt Brace & Company, 6277 Sea Harbor Drive, Orlando, FL 32887
1-800-782-4479, or 1-800-433-0001 (in Florida)

Credits and acknowledgments begin on p. 309.

ISBN: 0–15–500282–1

Library of Congress Catalogue Number: 92–71436

Printed in the United States of America

6 7 8 9 0 1 2 039 9 8 7 6 5 4 3

Preface

The reasons for studying Japan include the richness of its long historical record with all it can tell us about the human condition, the enduring value of Japanese cultural achievements, and the obvious importance of Japan in the world today. At a time when the roads are filled with Japanese cars and the bookstores with books on Zen, it is no longer necessary to argue the case for studying Japan. But setting aside Japan's contemporary prominence, surely some acquaintance with Japanese civilization is required of one who would be an educated person, for to be educated means to be able to see beyond the narrow geographic, temporal, and cultural bounds of one's immediate neighborhood. Indeed, to be educated entails the ability to see oneself in a broader perspective, including the perspective of history. And in this day and age, that means not only the history of one's own tribe or state or even civilization but ideally of all human history—for it is all our history.

That history is woven of many strands, and so we have economic and political history, the study of social structure, of thought, and of art. This text is based on the belief that an introduction to the history of a civilization requires consideration of all these facets of human activity, a general mapping out of the terrain so that the beginner may find his or her bearings and learn enough to consider in which direction to explore further, with some idea of the rewards to be gained for the effort. An introduction then is certainly not a catalog (although it should contain basic data) or a personal synthesis or summation, nor is it the proper vehicle for extending the expanding frontiers of present knowledge. Instead, it should, among other things, introduce the reader to the conventions of a field of study and attempt to convey the state of our present understanding.

History is the study of change and continuity, and both elements are always present, for no generation starts off with a blank slate, nor can even the most fervid traditionalist block changes wrought by the passage of time. In looking at a given segment of history, the scholar does not confront a choice between change and continuity but faces the more difficult task of weighing the change in the continuity, the continuity in the change. Such a determination requires, in the final analysis, as much art as science, and no assessment is ever final. This is so not only because of the continual discovery of new evidence or of new techniques (for example, in the dating of materials) but also because scholars' intellectual frameworks and analytic concepts change, and they learn to ask new questions. Even if that were not the case, history would still have to be rewritten at intervals, inasmuch as the ultimate significance of any individual historical episode depends in the final analysis on the whole story: as long as history itself is unfinished, so is its writing.

This is certainly true of Japanese history, about which scholars know a great deal more now than was the case just a generation ago. But, there remains much we do not understand. It is one of the attractions of this field of study that it offers many opportunities to the intellectually adventurous and hardy to work on major issues. Our hope is that the very inadequacies of a textbook will spur some readers on to these endeavors. Thus for this book to succeed, it must fail: some readers must come away hungry, their appetites whetted but not satiated.

Recent scholarship has been especially lively. Indeed scholarship has been so productive, as well as specialized, that it is extraordinarily difficult to keep up with all that is going on. Perhaps that is itself a sign that the field has come of age, but the effort to maintain a broad view is as rewarding as it is necessary. It is hoped that students will benefit from a book that speaks with a single voice and perhaps even from the temerity of a single author who tries to do it all!

A broad survey such as this is by necessity based on the studies of many scholars (indeed the author's pleasure in wide reading is matched only by his fear of inadvertent plagiarism). No attempt has been made to list all the works consulted. The suggested readings in the appendix have been drawn up in the hope of meeting some of the reader's needs, not of acknowledging the author's indebtedness, although there is considerable overlap. It is also impossible here to list all the individuals who have contributed by offering suggestions, criticism, and encouragement, or who helped by suggesting references, supplying a date or a translation for a term, and so forth, or to acknowledge individually the teachers, students, and colleagues who have influenced my thoughts about the broader problems of history, Japan, teaching, and writing. Similarly, I will refrain from any attempt to enumerate all those in Kyoto, Tokyo, Hirakata, and elsewhere who over the years have made Japan such a joy.

This book draws on my *Brief History of Chinese and Japanese Civilizations*, first published in 1978. My debt to the late William A. Pullin and Robert M. Somers, as well as the others acknowledged in various editions, continues. Mention should be made here of William F. Morton and H. Paul Varley for their help with the chapters on Japan in the first edition.

Special thanks for helping with the present volume go to Barbara Brooks for her careful reading of the whole manuscript, to Drake Bush, acquisitions editor, and to Angela Williams and her team at Harcourt Brace Jovanovich.

Japanese culture has from early times been profoundly visual, and arguably the highest art is calligraphy. It therefore gives me particular pleasure to thank Akira Fujieda, Professor Emeritus of the Institute of Humanistic Studies of Kyoto University, for gracing this book with the art of his brush.

My greatest debt goes to those closest to me for their forbearance during the writing of the original book and for all they contributed during the Kyoto years and after. In the case of David and Oliver, that included a child's eye view of Japan and continuing involvement ever since. Lore not only helped in innumerable direct and indirect ways but also contributed to the art work, which includes a number of her own photographs.

Notes on Calligraphy

The calligraphy which adorns this book (see cover, title page, dedication, and chapter-opening pages) is by Professor Akira Fujieda, an authority on East Asian history, whose numerous publications include a cultural history of Chinese style writing. A partial list of his publications emphasizing those on Dunhuang, the oasis in Northwest China at the crossroads between East Asia and points West, is found in *Cahier d'Extreme -Asie*, vol. 3, (1987), 1–7. Professor Fujieda is also famous as a calligrapher. One of his most prominent works is the inscription on the block of South American green granite at the entrance to the Museum of Ethnography in Osaka.

For Lore and our sons,
David and Oliver

Contents

PART THREE
LATE TRADITIONAL JAPAN

PART FOUR
JAPAN IN THE MODERN WORLD

Osaka Castle with Twin 21 Building. Although the castle goes back to Hideyoshi (1536–1598), it has been frequently and extensively rebuilt. The present version, complete with elevator, dates from 1931.

A Brief History
of Japanese Civilization

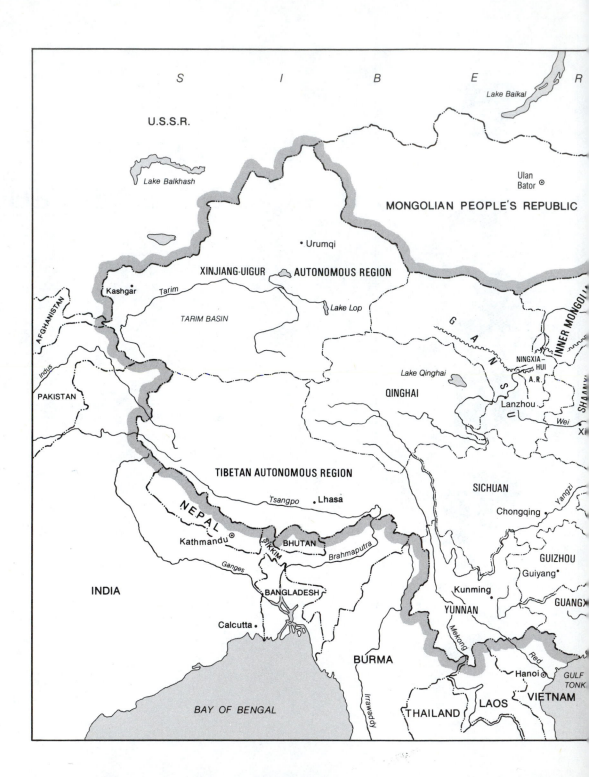

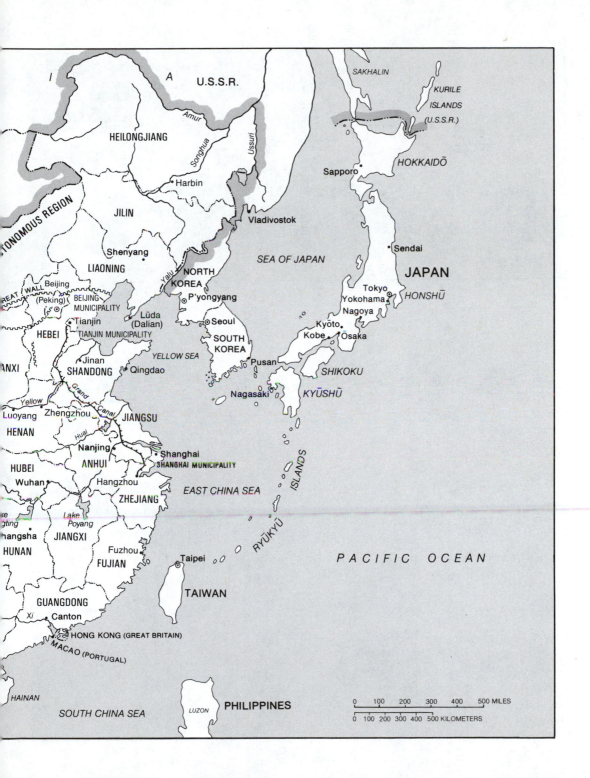

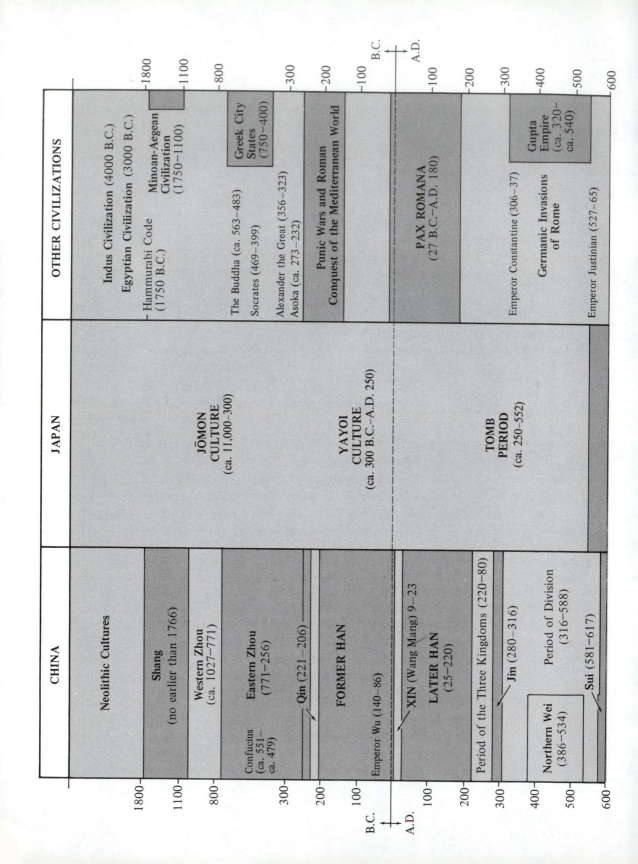

CHINA	JAPAN	OTHER CIVILIZATIONS
Neolithic Cultures		Indus Civilization (4000 B.C.) Egyptian Civilization (3000 B.C.)
Shang (no earlier than 1766)	JŌMON CULTURE (ca. 11,000–300)	Minoan-Aegean Civilization (1750–1100) Hammurabi Code (1750 B.C.)
Western Zhou (ca. 1027–771)		
Eastern Zhou (771–256) Confucius (ca. 551– ca. 479)		The Buddha (ca. 563–483) Socrates (469–399) Greek City States (750–400) Alexander the Great (356–323) Asoka (ca. 273–232)
Qin (221–206)	YAYOI CULTURE (ca. 300 B.C.–A.D. 250)	Punic Wars and Roman Conquest of the Mediterranean World
FORMER HAN Emperor Wu (140–86)		
XIN (Wang Mang) 9–23 LATER HAN (25–220)		PAX ROMANA (27 B.C.–A.D. 180)
Period of the Three Kingdoms (220–80) Jin (280–316)	TOMB PERIOD (ca. 250–552)	Emperor Constantine (306–37)
Period of Division (316–588) Northern Wei (386–534) Sui (581–617)		Germanic Invasions of Rome Gupta Empire (ca. 320– ca. 540) Emperor Justinian (527–65)

1800
1100
800
300
200
100
B.C.
A.D.
100
200
300
400
500
600

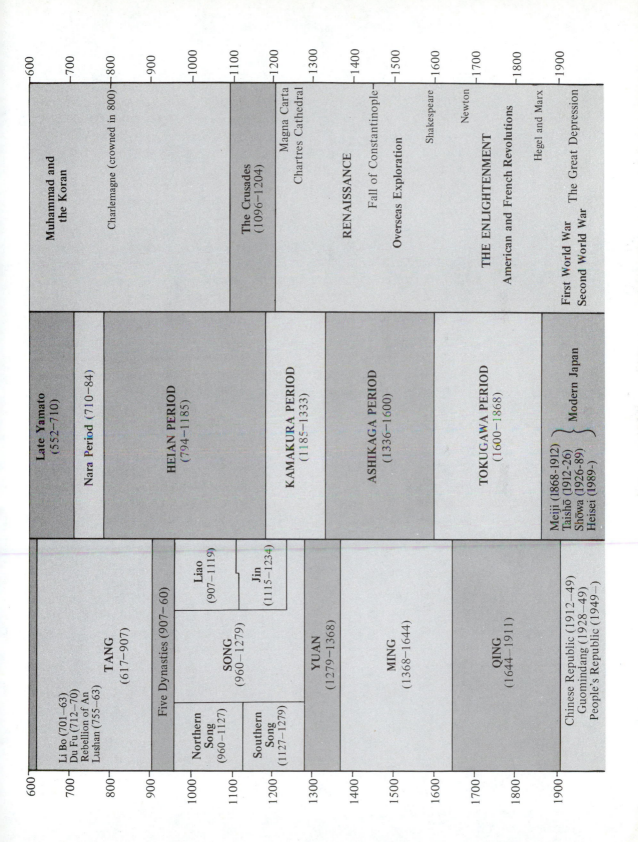

Late Yamato (552–710)		**Muhammad and the Koran**
Nara Period (710–84)		
		Charlemagne (crowned in 800)
HEIAN PERIOD (794–1185)	TANG (617–907)	
	Li Bo (701–63) Du Fu (712–70) Rebellion of An Lushan (755–63)	
	Five Dynasties (907–60)	
	Liao (907–1119)	
	Northern Song (960–1127)	
	SONG (960–1279)	
	Jin (1115–1234)	The Crusades (1096–1204)
	Southern Song (1127–1279)	Magna Carta Chartres Cathedral
KAMAKURA PERIOD (1185–1333)	YUAN (1279–1368)	
ASHIKAGA PERIOD (1336–1600)	MING (1368–1644)	RENAISSANCE Fall of Constantinople Overseas Exploration Shakespeare
TOKUGAWA PERIOD (1600–1868)	QING (1644–1911)	Newton THE ENLIGHTENMENT American and French Revolutions Hegel and Marx
Meiji (1868–1912) Taishō (1912–26) Shōwa (1926–89) Heisei (1989–) } Modern Japan	Chinese Republic (1912–49) Guomindang (1928–49) People's Republic (1949–)	First World War Second World War The Great Depression

600
700
800
900
1000
1100
1200
1300
1400
1500
1600
1700
1800
1900

PART ONE

Beginnings and Foundations

Figure 1   Dancing Couple.
Ht. left 56.6 cm; right
63.9 cm. Late tomb period.
Kōnan site, Osato, Saitama
Prefecture, Tokyo
National Museum.

一 上古ノ日本

1
Early Japan

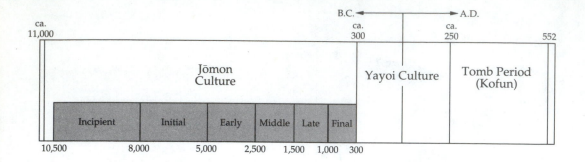

From the earliest times, Japan has been both part of a larger East Asian geographical and cultural complex and a world in itself. Japanese civilization was born out of the interaction between indigenous and imported elements in culture and institutions, and today the interplay between Japan and the world remains as vital, and as subtle, as ever.

The Beginning of the Beginning

Humans have lived in Japan for well over thirty thousand years. Early inhabitants may have arrived over land bridges that once linked Japan to Korea and the Northeast Asian mainland, but it is also very likely that people arrived from the same area by sea. There are clear biological and cultural affinities with Northeast Asia but many of the specifics remain in dispute.

Japanese is generally considered an Altaic language, and as such is related to Korean, Turkic and Mongolian, and linguistic evidence connects the Japanese people and the inhabitants of Northern Asia and the Amur region. In contrast to the Chinese or Sinitic languages, both Japanese and Korean are agglutinative. That is, they are languages in which words are formed primarily by a process of adding (or "gluing" together) words and word elements. Verbs and adjectives are highly inflected, with differences in tense, mood, level of formality, and so forth expressed by adding to the stem one element after another. The function of nouns in a sentence is indicated through the use of postpositions. These are somewhat similar to English prepositions except that they follow rather than precede nouns, and no noun can appear without one. These postpositions and various particles delineate the structure of sentences, which, in contrast to the compact mode of classical Chinese, tend to be long and rambling. Language then was a prime factor in preserving the integrity of Japanese culture even when Chinese influence was at its height. Japanese men of letters might immerse themselves in Chinese learning but continued to speak (and think) in the language they shared with their countrymen.

In Japan, during the long centuries of the Paleolithic, people lived by hunting and gathering and developed great skill in using flaked stones as tools. Without the benefit of written sources, our understanding of the way of life of the earliest inhabitants, as of all prehistory, is dependent on the work of archaeologists. Considering the difficulties, remarkable progress has been made, but many issues remain in doubt also for students of the ten-thousand-year-long Jōmon period. By then the essential geographic features of Japan were in place. Then as now, Japan was clearly separated from the continent and internally divided into four main islands (see Figure 1.1).

Geography

If geography may be said to provide a stage for history, it is not only a revolving stage following the rhythm of the seasons but an ever-changing stage. At times change has been sudden and violent, as when a typhoon strikes or the land is rocked by an earthquake or set afire by volcanic eruptions. At the same time change has been as slow and steady as the activity of the sea or the laborious toil of farmers patiently working away in and on a land so mountainous that about four-fifths of the land area does not permit cultivation. There are just three major plains, each ending in a bay. At 500 square miles the smallest in size but the earliest in historical importance is the Kinai plain at the head of Osaka Bay. This is where both Nara and Kyoto are located. Next comes the 600 square mile plain at the head of Ise Bay, home of Japan's most sacred shrine. In contrast, the Kantō Plain at the head of Tokyo Bay measures around 5,000 square miles.

Japan has a wide range of climates, but in much of the country, including all three plains, the weather is warm. Late spring and early summer bring abundant rainfall, allowing for the cultivation of rice. This was also the case in several smaller plains and numerous mountain valleys in all but Hokkaido and northern Honshū. Since rice yields more nourishment per land unit than any other staple, Japan, like other rice-growing areas, had the potential for sustaining a large population. In addition, Japan was also rich in fish and other seafood; from the beginning the sea has been a major source of protein. Poor in the natural resources required by modern industry, it was well endowed for an agricultural way of life.

Furthermore, at 142,707 square miles Japan was sufficiently large to sustain a varied and lively civilization. Smaller than the Chinese (or American) giant, it covered more ground than the British Isles (99,909 square miles).

Japan's mountains, covered with wood and bamboo, and its verdant valleys for centuries delighted the eyes and inspired the brushes of poets and painters. Mountains also affected politics and economics, for the ranges were large enough to impede transportation and communication in early times. This is significant on the main island of Honshū where transportation between the Inner Zone facing the continent and the Pacific side was difficult except for a single easy route from Wakasa Bay to the eastern end of the

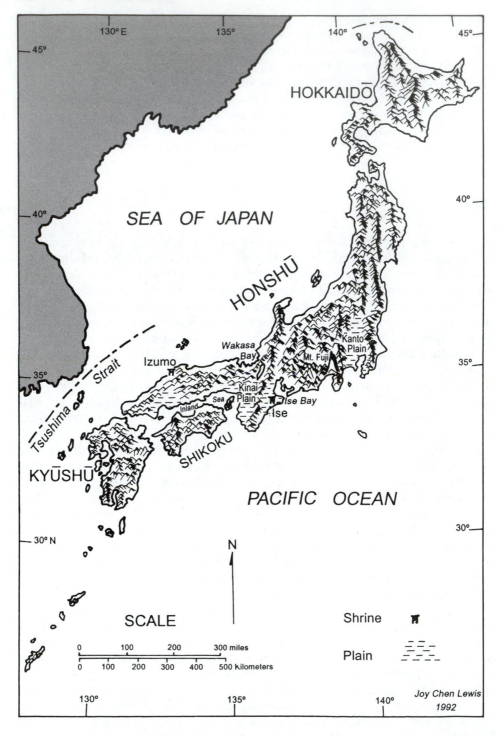

Inland Sea. In contrast, travel along the Inland Sea and on east was easy: Hakone Pass, the main barrier between the Kinai and Kantō plains is only 3,000 meters high. It was, however, to be of great strategic importance. The terms "Kantō" and "Kansai," designating respectively the areas east and west of the barrier, are still current in the age of the bullet train.

Endowed with an adequate physical base for the development of its own institutions and traditions, Japan was also profoundly affected by its location on the world map. At its closest point, the island of Kyūshū is about 120 miles from the continent, across the Korean Strait. It was over this route that continental influences entered Japan, for direct contact with China did not become general until late in the seventh century and, even then, remained hazardous. Although conquerors from the mainland may have played an important part in Japan's early history, Japan was too far away to be dominated by mainland powers. Foreign ideas, institutions, and techniques could be adapted to Japanese needs without military or political interference from abroad.

Jōmon Culture

Japan's first distinct Neolithic culture takes its name from the Jōmon or "rope pattern" pottery found near heaps of shells, the remains of consumed shellfish deposited near the seashore and on the banks of rivers and lakes. Archaeology also reveals that these people hunted wild deer and pigs as well as eating seeds and plant food. Richard Pearson has referred to them as "affluent foragers."[1] The Jōmon culture may have originated around the middle of the eleventh millennium B.C. and lasted until around 300 B.C. This vast period of time has been variously divided. Scholars have found the following six-part division useful:

Incipient	10,500–8,000 B.C.
Initial	8,000–5,000 B.C.
Early	5,000–2,500 B.C.
Middle	2,500–1,500 B.C.
Late	1,500–1,000 B.C.
Final	1,000–300 B.C.

Jōmon people lived in pit dwellings and quite likely in small villages, although village cemeteries appear only in late Jōmon. Beginning in the middle period, there was an increase in the consumption of vegetable food, and people fished the deep sea. Rice was not native to Japan, but there is evidence of the beginnings of its cultivation in Kyūshū in the final stage. However, it remained a supplementary source of food.

During these thousands of years, there were regional as well as temporal variations, and it may be that the basic culture was actually an amalgam of cultures developed by different peoples. Jōmon sites range from Hokkaido to the Ryūkyū islands in the far south. The two most important regions were northern Honshū and the southwest with the Kantō Plain providing linkage.

Figure 1.2   Pottery vessel.
Aomori, Middle Jōmon Period,
44.2 cm high. Osaka
University.

Figure 1.3   Jōmon figurine.

Linguistically the situation is also complex: the Japanese language may have been developed in Kyūshū around 5000 to 3500 B.C. and from there spread only slowly into the rest of Japan.

Figure 1.2 shows an example of the pottery from which the period takes its name. Lacking the potter's wheel, the Jōmon people made their ware by building up coils of clay (or perhaps simply kneading it into shape). They then decorated the vessel by pressing twisted rope into the wet clay to give the pottery its distinctive pattern. Also characteristic of the Jōmon period were clay figurines. The earliest of these frequently had animal subjects, which perhaps were totems. Later, human figures prevailed (see Figure 1.3). There are indications that they served as fertility symbols: one even had the bone of an infant baked into it, perhaps expressing hope for safe childbirth, or for a healthy child to take the place of one who had died. J. Edward Kidder has suggested that the figurines' strange eyes were associated with the belief that the "eye is the direct line of communication with the soul."[2] Surviving from prehistoric times, these images evoke a powerful world of primitive magic.

Phallic-shaped stones are another indication of the prevalence of fertility cults. Other discoveries of the Jōmon period include the remains of pit dwellings, various stone implements, and articles of personal ornamentation such as earrings and amulets. Among the latter are late Jōmon stone *magatama*, comma-shaped ornaments also found in early Korean sites. Skulls found at archaeological sites provide evidence of tooth extraction. The removal of certain teeth at initiation into the adult community or to mark other life passages was practiced in certain African, Southeast Asian, and African tribes into the twentieth century. The figurines also suggest that these people tattooed their bodies—a custom reported in early Chinese accounts of Japan.

Yayoi Culture

Beginning in the third century B.C. Jōmon culture was gradually displaced by a new culture, which spread from Kyūshū east to the Kantō Plain. It is called the Yayoi culture after the section of Tokyo where the first archaeological finds were made but got its start in northern Kyūshū. Large storage jars of a type found on the Korean peninsula suggest continental influence, but other early Yayoi pottery continued Jōmon styles. Most likely, Yayoi culture emerged from a combination of the old Jōmon culture and new elements from abroad. The old custom of tooth extraction did not disappear in Japan until toward the close of the Yayoi period. By then, however, a society had developed that was dramatically different from its predecessor.

A sense of the difference between the two cultures is suggested by the pottery illustrated in Figure 1.4. Yayoi ware is so even and graceful that for

Figure 1.4   Pottery jar. Miyagi, Late Yayoi period. 29.2 cm high. Tōhoku University, Sendai.

a long while the view prevailed that it was made on the potter's wheel. But it is clear now that pottery was made by coiling, though it may have then been paddled out and decorated on a turntable. Small at the base and thin at the neck, the vessel shown here is both functional and aesthetically pleasing. Indeed the shape was so pleasing and served so well that it was later developed into the standard form of the Japanese sake container, the form still in use today.

The most profound change that occurred during the Yayoi was the development of wet-field rice cultivation. Rice, introduced in late Jōmon (ca. 350 B.C.) was first cultivated in Kyūshū in fields created by draining coastal lowlands little used previously. It then spread east and up into higher ground where fields required irrigation rather than drainage. Both kinds of sites have yielded rich archaeological evidence. Excavations such as those of a community near Shizuoka show that Yayoi rice was grown on irrigated paddies, even some of the perforated steamers used for cooking the rice have been recovered. Perhaps some of the crop was stored in the warehouses built on raised posts, a building technique widespread in Southeast Asia. Since there is also ample evidence that fishing was an important source of food, it would seem that not only the sake container but the basic elements of the Japanese diet date back to this time.

These changes in fundamental economic activity must have affected most aspects of life. For example, we know that intensive rice cultivation results in an increase in the economic resources of a society, encouraging population growth and geographic expansion. But since we are still dealing with a preliterate period, the impact of these changes on the social, political, and intellectual character of society is largely a matter of speculation. Evidence of links to the continent at this time come from archaeological sites that have yielded glass beads, bracelets, and disks; iron and bronze weapons, bronze coins and mirrors. These objects reached Japan through the Chinese colony established by the Han in Korea and from native Korean tribes or states.

Various metal objects were also produced in Japan itself. Many locally made weapons have been found. Of particular interest are bronze bells, ranging in size from less than five inches to more than four feet, related in form to some Korean bells but, nevertheless, distinctly Japanese. Some are decorated in low relief, depicting various animals, or scenes that reveal something of daily life. For example, there are scenes of people pounding rice or using dogs to hunt a boar. The bells also portray the boats of the Yayoi and houses covered with thatched roofs. Iron also came into widespread use in agriculture as in warfare.

The Tomb Period

The existence of late Yayoi burial mounds linked to the later tombs suggests that there was no sharp break between the Yayoi and Tomb periods. Some of the tombs characteristic of the latter were very large. The most magnificent has been identified as that of "Emperor" Nintoku, the dates of whose reign have been calculated as about 395–427. It occupies 80 acres, is about 2,695 feet long, and is of the popular "keyhole" shape (see Figure 1.5). Other tombs were round or square, and all shapes may be found with or without moats. Although such tombs continued to be built into the seventh century, it is convenient for purposes of historical periodization to end the tomb period around the middle of the sixth century when Buddhism became officially acknowledged in Japan. It was under Buddhist influence that the construction of these tumuli was gradually abandoned.

The sheer scale of Nintoku's tomb indicates an ability to put a large number of people to work. Although there is a great deal about the organization of society that remains unknown, there is ample archaeological evidence for the presence at this time of warriors who wore armor and rode horses. To account for the appearance of these warriors, scholars have speculated about a possible invasion from Korea. These views gain plausibility in the light of large-scale shifts of peoples on the continent in the fourth century, but the nature of the available historical data makes all historical reconstruction highly speculative. What is clear is that there was an intensification of relations with Korea.

On the Korean side of the equation, we do know that from the fourth century until the state of Silla unified Korea in 668, three states dominated the area. The oldest of these was Koguryō, a state that later defeated the armies of the Sui and thereby helped to bring an end to that Chinese dynasty. Two other states, Paekche in the Southwest and Silla in the East,

Figure 1.5 Tomb of Emperor Nintoku, Mozu, Sakai City, Osaka. Middle Tomb Period, total length approx. 815.5 m.

shared the peninsula. Although each state had its own traditions, all three had been formed out of tribal confederations, which had coalesced into more permanent unions. Even though they were conversant with elements of Chinese civilization, the extent of Chinese influence on these Korean states should not be exaggerated, for this was a time when even at home, in a divided land, Chinese civilization was in retreat.

In the Southeast of the Korean Peninsula was an area identified as Kaya by the Koreans and Mimana by the Japanese. It is extremely difficult to reconstruct the history of this region, but it is clear that there was a close relationship between this area and people living in Southwest Japan, a relationship antedating the appearance of the mounted warriors in Japan and continuing until the last of the area was conquered by Silla in 562.

During the next two centuries, numerous Koreans came to Japan, bringing with them important aspects of mainland culture. One early contribution was the potter's wheel, and it is hardly surprising that Korean influence is visible in tomb period pottery. However, the period is best known for a uniquely Japanese kind of clay sculpture called *haniwa*, literally "clay circles," placed on the outside of the tombs. These *haniwa* included cylindrical representations of human figures, clay houses, boats, horses, and other animals. Figures of warriors dressed in armor and clay horses, along with bronze and iron military equipment found inside the tombs, provide evidence for the presence of mounted fighting men.

Most likely the *haniwa* were associated with ritual, but their origin and function is still ill understood. Archaeology does not bear out the tradition, recorded in the eighth century, that they originated as substitutes for live people buried up to their neck around an imperial tomb. Modern theories that they helped preserve the mound from erosion or that they demarcated the world of the living from that of the dead do not fit all cases. Their function, may, of course, have changed over time.

There is nothing grim or stern about the figures (see figure on the Part I title page). The overwhelming impression one gets from groups of *haniwa* is one of warmth and even of joy. They display no indication of pain, sorrow, or grief, such as one would expect to find on a tomb. Many of the figures seem to dance and sing. Others depict scenes of daily life: a poor peasant carrying a hoe, a figure offering a drink of sake, a mother with a baby on her back. Some were merely elongated cylinders with holes for eyes and mouth; and the features in others were often out of proportion.

The *haniwa* also provide evidence of the presence of female shamans, who apparently played a very important role in early Japanese culture. The earliest Chinese accounts of Japan describe an unmarried queen named Pimiko, who ruled the country of Yamatai with the help of a younger brother, and who "occupied herself with magic and sorcery, bewitching the people."[3] She lived in a grand palace and, when she died, was buried in a great mound. This calls to mind the tumuli of the tomb period. Unfortunately the location of Yamatai and the identity of Pimiko remain unclear. However, it seems increasingly probable that Yamatai was in northern

Kyūshū. Pimiko may mean "sun princess," in which case there would be a link to the origins of the Japanese ruling house, which claimed descent from the Sun Goddess.

In addition to the findings of archaeology and the accounts in Chinese texts, information concerning this period is found in the *Kojiki* (Record of Ancient Matters) and *Nihon Shoki* (Chronicle of Japan), which date from the eighth century but contain earlier materials. Incorporating a melange of legendary and semihistorical accounts, at times contradicting each other, and reflecting the political and intellectual needs of a later age, these books must be used with great care, but they do offer indispensable insights into Japanese antiquity and the Japanese conception of their own history. Here, for example, is found the first statement of the myth that Japanese emperors are of divine descent, a myth later used to sanctify the right to rule of the imperial house.

Shinto Legends and Beliefs

Later emperors claimed as their ancestor the legendary Emperor Jimmu, to whom they attributed the founding of the Japanese state in 660 B.C. The accounts reach back to an unsophisticated creation myth in which a divine brother and sister, Izanagi and Izanami, descend to earth and create the islands of Japan as well as a number of deities. Izanami died after giving birth to the god of fire, and Izanagi, like the Greek Orpheus, followed her to the world of the dead but was driven away by the putrifying condition of her body. When he then purified himself in a stream, a series of deities were born.

Most important among the new gods were Amaterasu, The Sun Goddess, and Susanoo, the storm god. The two deities in turn produced a third generation of gods, but their union was hardly tranquil. At one point the Sun Goddess was so offended by the conduct of her uncouth husband-brother, who had damaged her rice fields and even defecated in her palace, that she retreated into a cave and refused to reappear, plunging the whole world into darkness. Fortunately the other deities devised an entertainment (which featured a lewd dance) and managed to lure her back out. Susa-no-ō was then banished to Izumo, where he became the progenitor of a line of rulers who were in constant conflict with a line of rulers descended from the Sun Goddess herself. Ninigi, a grandson of the Sun Goddess, settled in northern Kyūshū, bringing with him the three sacred imperial regalia: the mirror (symbol of the sun); the "herb-quelling great sword," which Susa-no-ō had discovered in the body of a giant eight-headed serpent; and a jewel *magatama*. Ninigi's grandson, in turn, fought his way successfully to Yamato, where as Emperor Jimmu he founded the imperial line. His descendants finally defeated the rulers of Izumo and brought other parts of Japan under their rule, but they continued to allow worship at the great shrine at Izumo.

Figure 1.6   Ise:
The Inner Shrine

Of the three regions in which these legends are set, Northern Kyūshū and Yamato have yielded abundant evidence for the existence of the tomb culture, but archaeology has not revealed the presence of a major center at Izumo. Nevertheless, the current shrine at Izumo is considered second in holiness only to that of the Sun Goddess herself at Ise. The buildings standing there today are not very old, for both have been rebuilt repeatedly. The shrine at Ise is rebuilt every twenty years. But because they are regarded with great reverence, they preserve certain essential features of very early Japanese architecture: a pleasing simplicity of design; the subtle use of natural materials such as unpainted and undecorated wood and the thatched roof (see Figure 1.6); and the sensitive care shown for the natural setting. But the word "setting" is not quite appropriate: for nature does not play a subordinate role; it is as much a part of the shrine as the building itself. Religious ceremonies were, no doubt, performed outdoors at these sacred places before there were any buildings at all, and it is quite likely that the idea of housing the deities was a foreign import.

Such closeness to nature is a part of early Japanese religious life as expressed in the native animism later termed Shinto, or "the way of the gods" (or spirits, *kami*). In the legendary beginning even rocks and plants could move and speak, and although mythical heroes later put an end to these troublesome powers, the *kami* continued to be identified with nature. They could be found in a special stone, a stream, an old tree, a mountain or any object felt to be imbued with some extraordinary quality. Stories about the *kami* were numerous but they were not systematized, nor were these localized spirits clearly visualized. Just as the *haniwa* are apparently cheerful figures, the religion associated with the *kami* apparently expressed a positive and optimistic attitude toward life. In it the defilements encountered in life could be overcome through ritual purification. These defilements were conceived in physical not ethical terms. Blood was defiling, for example, whether it was spilled on purpose, or by accident, or occurred in menstruation. This concern for ritual cleanliness, noted by the Chinese chroniclers, probably explains the great importance the Japanese have always attached to the bath. This early religion was no match for Buddhism intellectually or in terms of grandeur of vision, but the *kami* were intrinsic to the spiritual life of the communities that looked after them. The very absence of theoretical elaboration or doctrinal demands may have helped to give Shinto its remarkable staying power.

Social Organization

In early Japan, as elsewhere, religion was deeply identified with the prevailing social structure. During the tomb period the elite was organized into lineage groups or clans called *uji*, the members of which traced their descent to an alleged common ancestor, often a deity. The members of an *uji* shared in the worship of their *kami* thereby sanctioning and confirming their sense of solidarity. Each *uji* was headed by a chief who, as a direct descendant of the deity, served both as a head priest and as the patriarchal ruler. Usually the members of an *uji* lived in a specific geographic area, which they dominated by combining political and military power. The horses, weapons, and armor they used have been found by archaeologists.

Subject to the *uji* elite were the commoners, most of whom lived in villages and tilled the land. Others wove cloth, made pottery, brewed sake, and generally did society's work. They were not completely free, for they were organized into occupational communities called *be* that were governed and protected by the *uji*. The *uji* in turn derived their wealth and manpower from the *be* under their authority. At the bottom of the social scale was a small class of household slaves.

The Yamato State

In the course of time some *uji* became more powerful than others and were able to exert a measure of control over lesser lineages, which accepted a subordinate status. In this way larger political units were formed, and these, in turn, interacted, peacefully or militarily, in a process of political agglomeration. Largely because Japan's mountainous geography worked to the advantage of local power holders, the process of creating a large state was both slow and incomplete. It is also difficult to date. While many scholars trace the development of the state to the fifth century, some date it earlier or later. Solid evidence is provided by two inscribed swords, one found about 35 miles from Tokyo and dated to 471 or possibly 531 and another from Kyūshū. Although so far apart, their owners are thought to have served "the great king," based on the Kinai (also called Yamato) plain. Chinese as well as later Japanese records speak of embassies to South China, and scientific analysis of one of the swords reveals that it was made of steel derived from iron ore available only in South China.

In the process of transforming a federation of chiefs into a single state, the lineage of the "great kings" came to occupy a position of authority. This was the lineage that claimed descent from the Sun Goddess.

The sun lineage acquired its status in part through the use of arms, but also by exploiting kinship ties and by forming marriage alliances. (The latter was facilitated by the practice of polygamy.) The Sun lineage enjoyed the services of other *uji*, some of whom rendered certain military or ritualistic services and others who provided support in outlying areas. This was a highly flexible political system, kept in balance as much by manipulation as by force. The power balance might shift or be disrupted (by a recalcitrant chief or a struggle for the succession) but, on the whole, the system proved resilient.

A powerful inducement for other *uji* to accept the primacy of the Sun lineage was religious, for it was natural for the *uji* to conceive of society in terms of lineage and descent and to give primacy to the descendants of the prime deity. Just as the local *kami* protected their regions, so the Sun Goddess looked after the entire country. By implication, therefore, so should the Yamato line. Government and religion were conceived as one. Even the same word *(matsurigoto)* was used for both.

During the fifth century the Yamato rulers increased in strength by subordinating the *uji* chiefs to the ruling house. One technique was to assign them places in an official hierarchy and gradually turn them into great ministers of state. However, this process did not proceed unchallenged. For not only the Yamato rulers but also the outlying *uji* were gaining economic and political strength. In the sixth century the power of the outlying *uji* threatened to get out of hand. Nevertheless, the long-term trend favored the center. Meanwhile Japan continued to benefit from the continental influences. Among the imports was the art of writing, most likely initially a skill limited to Korean or Chinese immigrants. Confucian texts too are said to have been introduced in the fifth century and Buddhism was not far behind.

NOTES

1. Richard Pearson in Erica H. Weeder, ed. *The Rise of a Great Tradition: Japanese Archaeological Ceramics from the Jōmon through Heian Periods* (Exhibition catalog, New York: Japan Society, 1990), p. 15.
2. J. Edward Kidder, *Japan Before Buddhism* (New York: Frederick A. Praeger, 1966), p. 73.
3. Ryusaku Tsunoda, *Japan in the Chinese Dynastic Histories* (Kyoto: Perkins Oriental Books, 1968), p. 20.

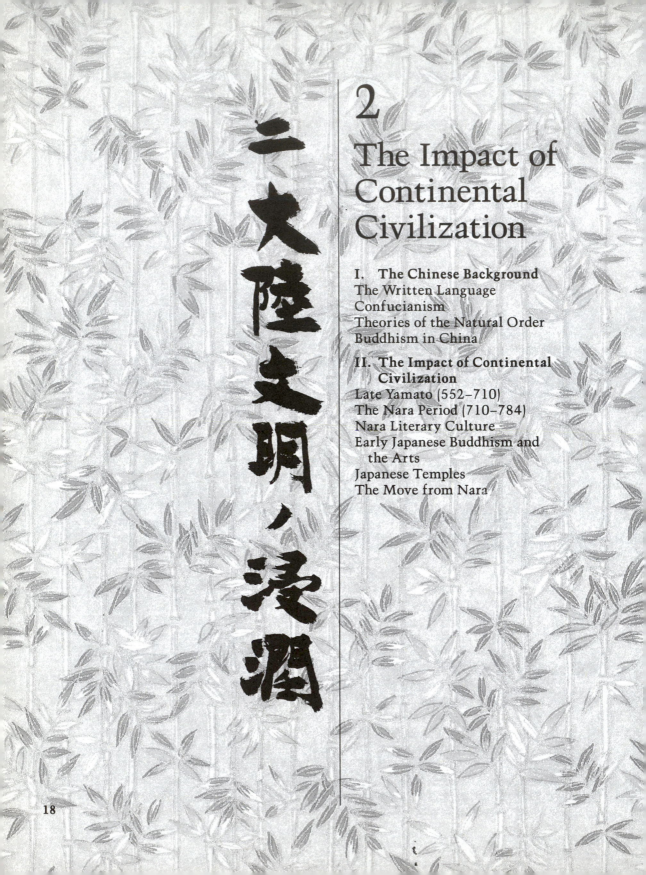

二大陸文明ノ浸潤

2
The Impact of Continental Civilization

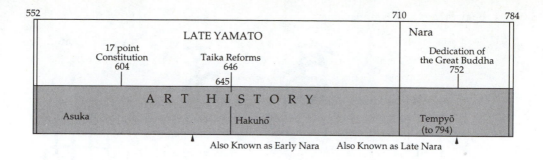

552		710	784
LATE YAMATO		Nara	
17 point Constitution 604	Taika Reforms 646	Dedication of the Great Buddha 752	
	645		
A R T H I S T O R Y			
Asuka	Hakuhō	Tempyō (to 794)	

Also Known as Early Nara   Also Known as Late Nara

Scholars generally define civilization by two primary characteristics: writing and cities. In those terms, we may say that it was the impact of Chinese civilization, as mediated through Korea, that stimulated Japanese culture to grow into a civilization. Japan's first cities were modeled on those of China, and the first texts read and written in Japan were in Chinese.

Part I. The Chinese Background

If China provided the classic background for civilization in Japan, we need to bear in mind that it was a vital, changing, developing background. Chinese influences had long entered Japan either directly or through Korea where there was a Chinese presence during and after the Han. But it greatly accelerated during the Late Yamato period, not only because Japan became more receptive but also because China itself became more impressive and attractive.

A new era began when the Sui reunified China late in the sixth century and laid the foundations for the much more long-lasting Tang. Once again China was ruled by an emperor who exercised power over a government structured on essentially bureaucratic lines and manned by officials of aristocratic background. In Sui and Tang some officials boasted a degree earned in the examination system first established by the Sui, but the time when this was to become the standard avenue to office was still in the future. Nevertheless, even members of the most lofty lineages owed much of their prestige to their command over classical learning transmitted in a written language whose basic principles go back to the second millennium B.C.

The Written Language

In its origins and fundamental orientation, Chinese writing was strongly visual (see Figure 2.1) and calligraphy became a highly prized art in Japan as in China. From early pictograms (stylized pictorial representations of things) and from ideograms (visual representations of a thing or concept

19

DRAGON

GOOD   BOOK

Figure 2.1   Early Chinese writing: inscriptions on bronze (heavy ink) and
bone (lighter ink). Drawn by Dr. Léon L. Y. Chang.

through association), the student can learn much about early Chinese culture. The pictogram for "book," for example, suggests that the first books
were made of slips of wood or bamboo held together by a thong. The symbol
also suggests that the written language, originally developed for communication with the gods in the form of burnt offerings, was now used for human
communication as well.

The interpretation of pictograms and ideograms, particularly those for
abstract terms like "good" (woman and child), is fascinating but fraught
with danger, for many etymologies accepted for centuries have conclusively
been shown to be false. Furthermore, many symbols or characters are neither pictograms nor ideograms, but phonograms. The simplest of these are
phonetic loans, symbols borrowed for their sound rather than for their meaning. An imaginary English counterpart might be the use of a symbol representing a bee to write the verb "to be," and we could go on and combine "bee"
and "leaf" to write "belief," but it would hardly do to conclude from this that
people in England conceived of "being" in terms of insect and vegetable life.

Most phonograms are more complex, and the majority of Chinese characters are composed of a combination of pictogramic and phonetic elements. The development of such compound characters was no doubt a response to the proliferation of phonetic loans, which must have caused great
confusion in a language that, like Japanese, has an unusually large number
of homonyms. In the compound characters, one element (the phonetic)

indicates the pronunciation of the word and another (the radical or signific) designates the general category to which the word refers. This principle is illustrated by the word for "black horse." The radical, "horse," is on the left; the phonetic, "li," on the right: together they inform the reader that the "li" under discussion has something to do with horses. The presupposition is, of course, that the reader already knows that there is a word in the language with this sound and meaning. Over the course of time the significs were standardized and their number reduced, finally resulting in the 214 that still provide the basic organization for most character dictionaries. However, the language has undergone numerous phonetic changes over time, with the result that in modern times the phonetic element is no longer a sure guide to pronunciation.

BLACK HORSE

The failure of the Chinese to develop a wholly phonetic script shows that the existing system, complex as it is, was adequate to their purposes. The consequences for Chinese thought of this written language are important. The average literate Chinese in later times were no more conscious of the etymology of the words they wrote than are modern English speakers writing about Oxford (where oxen ford the river). Yet the Chinese symbols, unlike their alphabetic counterparts, tended to acquire an identity and life of their own and to function as potent emblems.

The written language, furthermore, was a unifying element geographically in that people who spoke mutually unintelligible languages could and did read the same texts. Scholars in Vietnam and Korea as well as Japan were able to participate in Chinese literary culture although they usually did not learn to speak Chinese. Of the bodies of ideas introduced to Korea and Japan in Chinese texts, none have been of more lasting influence than Confucianism and Buddhism.

Confucianism

Confucius (ca. 552–ca. 479 B.C.) lived about a thousand years prior to the introduction of Confucianism to Japan. By that time the teachings of the Master had been amended and developed, but the core ideas proved to have great staying power. This core can be studied in *The Analects (Rongo, Lunyu),* * a collection of Confucius' words as passed on by his disciples and assembled after his death. The *Analects* do not consist of systematic philosophical treatises or even students' lecture notes. They are an unorganized collection of statements and conversations, open to varying interpretation. In their totality, however, they give a surprisingly full picture of the man and his ideas.

Confucius believed that his teachings merely transmitted the traditional wisdom and values of Chinese culture, but he was a creative transmitter, a man who understood the old traditions in terms suitable for his own age and

---

* Here and throughout we list the Japanese pronunciation first, followed by the Chinese in *pinyin* romanization and, when necessary to avoid confusion, also the Wade-Giles version.

thereby revitalized and transformed old values. A good example is his re-definition of nobility as something acquired through virtue and wisdom, not through birth. Confucius' ideal man or true gentleman is humane, wise, and brave. He is devoted to virtue in contrast to the petty man out for gain. His standard is righteousness. The ultimate virtue is *jin (ren, jen)*, which, like most of the central terms of Chinese philosophy, defies translation. It is the ground for all the other virtues, the condition of being fully human in dealing with others—the character for *jin* consists of "man" and "two."

For Confucius the interaction between men is governed by *rei (li)*, a term which encompasses the meaning of sacred ritual, ceremonial, propriety, and good manners. The *rei* (like all Chinese words it can be read either as a singular or as a plural) are traditional and, because of their religious associations, had been sanctified and imbued with a quality of magic that they retained even after literal belief in the old religious ideas faded away. For Confucius the *ri* themselves, when performed with true sincerity, are what make the individual human. Sacrifices should be performed as though the spirits were present. On the spirits themselves Confucius was noncommittal.

All dealings between people should accord with *rei* performed in perfect good faith. Then everyone would perform his role with genuine understanding and devotion. Harmony would result, and there would be no need for physical sanctions, no necessity for laws and punishments. Of crucial importance was the initiative of the ruler, who by following the advice of true gentlemen could initiate benevolent government and win over the people. The people's confidence was essential to the state, more important than arms or even food.

Among the virtues and *rei* most important for Confucius were those connected with the family, and he placed special emphasis on filiality, the wholehearted obedience child owes to parent. For Confucius obligations toward a father have priority over those to the state: a son should not turn his father in for stealing a sheep. The relationship between father and son formed one of the classic Five Relationships of Confucianism. The other four were between ruler and minister, husband and wife, elder brother and younger brother, and between friend and friend. They emphasize the importance of reciprocal obligations between people of superior and inferior status and illustrate the existence of these values at the family level, at the community level (friendship), and in state relationships (ruler and minister). The Confucian view of society was essentially hierarchical; while Confucians felt that the values expressed in the Five Relationships applied to all, that did not mean they favored an egalitarian polity. Quite the contrary. Similarly, the Way *(Tō, Dao, Tao)* to perfection was open to all, but only the morally and intellectually cultivated could understand it. The common people could only be made to follow.

For Confucius and his disciples there was only one, valid and true, eternal and universal way. The idea that there might be a number of equally legitimate ways or value systems was foreign to people who had no contact with any highly developed, literate civilization radically different from their own.

A potent force in Confucianism was the personality of the founder. Confucius appears in the *Analects* as a man of moderation, gentle but firm, dignified but not harsh, respectful but at ease. He displays a nice sense of balance, as when he warns both against learning without thinking and against thinking without learning. In one place Confucius gives an account of his own intellectual and spiritual progression, culminating when he reached 70 and was able to follow his heart's desires without transgressing against morality. Like the master of ceremony who has internalized every movement or the great musician who has become one with his instrument, the Confucian sage perfects his own moral wisdom until he reaches a point at which he no longer needs to worry about a wrong gesture, a missed note, an improper act. In all three cases the efficacy of the performance depends on the authenticity of the state of mind of the performer.

Confucius left many issues open, and his language permitted various interpretations. There was ample room for future elaboration and for disagreement among Confucians. A major issue in Confucian discourse was the nature of human nature. Prevalent during the Han were the views of Xunzi (Hsün Tzu, fl. 298–238 B.C.) who held that human beings are inherently selfish and antisocial but redeemable. However, ultimately the most influential was the theory of Mencius (371–289 B.C.) that people are basically good, as shown, for example, by the instantaneous, uncalculated compassion we feel when we see a child about to fall into a well. We are naturally endowed with a sense (or heart) of compassion that is the beginning, the germ, from which grows our benevolence or humanity *(jin)*. Similarly our sense of shame is the germ for dutifulness; our sense of courtesy, for modesty; our sense of right and wrong, for wisdom. These four senses are as much a part of the person as are his four limbs. Challenged with the proposition that human nature is neutral and can, like water, be channeled in any direction, Mencius retorted that the goodness of human nature was like the tendency of water to flow downward.

This view of human nature opened the way for a deepening of the philosophy of individual self-perfection, since "all things are already complete in oneself."[1] Everyone can become a sage by recovering his original nature or finding his lost mind, and thereby know Heaven itself. Mencius thus provided a source of inspiration for the development of Confucian theories of self-cultivation that stimulated later theorists, particularly those of the post-Buddhist age. Additional psychological and metaphysical depth was provided by the "Doctrine of the Mean," a chapter of the *Records of Rites* compiled around 100 B.C. Still another chapter of the same work, "The Great Learning," stressed the link between self-cultivation and government, viewing the perfection of the individual as the prerequisite for the perfection of society:

> when the personal life is cultivated, the family will be regulated; when the family is regulated, the state will be in order; and when the state is in order, there will be peace throughout the world. From the Son of Heaven down to the

common people, all must regard cultivation of the personal life as the root or foundation.[2]

For Confucians, sagehood was by definition expressed in society.

Mencius looked for a perfectly humane prince who would, by his acts and example, transform all with his benevolence. Such a prince was needed, according to Mencius, to bring out and nourish human goodness. Given his belief in human nature, Mencius needed to explain the all too obvious failure of individuals to be good in actual life. His solution was typically Confucian in its insistence that the germs of goodness must be cultivated if they are to grow and flourish. In an eloquent passage he compared the human heart to Ox Mountain. Once, in accordance with its original nature, Ox Mountain was green and covered with vegetation, but it became bald because of the abuse inflicted by man and beast, until anyone looking at it would conclude that its intrinsic nature was to be barren.

To Mencius, it was the function of government to provide the environment for the nurture of human goodness. He vigorously defended familial virtues against Mohist attack and, like Confucius, thought in terms of a political and social hierarchy based on virtue and ability. He made it explicit that those who work with their brains are to be supported by those who work with their hands. But he insisted that the government was responsible for the well-being of all its subjects, that it provide for their material as well as spiritual needs. Once the people's material wants were satisfied, schools should be established to educate them.

Drawing on such sources as *The Classic of History* and *The Book of Songs*, Mencius refined the concept that government is based on divine and moral sanctions by insisting that a dynasty rules by virtue of a Mandate of Heaven, which can be revoked if the ruler does not conduct himself as a ruler should. Heaven in making its judgment follows the voice of the people. Mencius quotes a now lost portion of *The Classic of History:* "Heaven sees with the eyes of its people. Heaven hears with the ears of its people."[3] This right of rebellion became a permanent part of Chinese political thought, used by reformers to frighten recalcitrant rulers as well as by those who took up arms against the government. "Removing the mandate" (*geming* or *ke-ming* in Chinese; *kakumei* in Japanese) became the modern word for revolution, but, as we shall see, this concept did not find acceptance in Japan.

Theories of the Natural Order

Chinese thought was not exclusively focused on the human world. In their scientific and philosophic speculations about the world, the Chinese thought of nature in dynamic rather than static terms and considered man a part of the natural process. Animating this process were *yin* and *yang*, paired, complementary opposites whose interaction keeps the world going. *Yin* is associated with the feminine, the passive, the negative, the weak;

yang, with the opposite qualities and forces: the masculine, the active, the positive, the strong. Perhaps reflecting the rhythm of agricultural life, *yin* is cold and winter, *yang* is hot and summer. *Yin* is response; *yang* is stimulus. The two terms range widely in application from the popular to the technical, from the concrete to the abstract, and if phenomena are conceived in terms of polarities, the list goes on endlessly. When Japan adopted a Chinese-style administrative system, it included a Bureau of Yin and Yang (Ommyōryō) in charge of astrology, the calendar, and unusual natural phenomena.

Another and in some ways similar concept was that of the Five Phases, Five Processes, or Five Agents: wood, fire, earth, metal, and water. Since this recalls the four elements of Greek philosophy, for a long time this was translated as the "Five Elements." This translation is misleading, for it implies inertia and passivity rather than the dynamism and self-movement inherent in the Chinese conception and also fails to reflect the point that the processes of nature occur in regular sequence. This perception was also reflected in the calendar. It was a view of the world informed by sensitivity to change as exemplified by the *Classic of Change (Ekikyō, Yi Jing, I Ching)* an ancient divination text incorporated into the Confucian canon. Nevertheless, some Confucians, including Xunzi, were hostile to such speculation.

Confucianism had its enemies. Prominent among them in earlier times were tough-minded Legalists who placed the needs of the state over all other concerns. Meanwhile, attacking from another direction, Daoists rejected whatever stood in the way of attaining harmony with the ineffable totality which is the Dao (Way). However, especially in our period, the overarching challenge to Confucianism came from Buddhism.

By the time Confucianism entered Japan, Buddhism prevailed but Confucian values continued to be fostered within the family, and Confucian theories and precedents remained important in government. In Japan Buddhism worked so powerfully that it was not until the seventeenth century that Confucianism became a recognizable independent school of thought. Yet its influence was deep and lasting. Martin Collcutt aptly summarized the place of Confucianism in Japanese history when he wrote, "At no time did Confucianism have the field to itself. On the other hand there has been no time since its introduction when Confucianism has not been an active player in the shaping of Japanese politics, intellect, and behavior."[4]

Buddhism in China

Gautama Siddhartha* (ca. 563–483 B.C.), the founder of Buddhism, was roughly contemporary with Confucius, but his teachings did not take hold in China until the collapse of the Han dynasty weakened faith in the imperial Confucian orthodoxy. By that time Buddhism, which had begun as a

---

* Gautama refers to his clan, and Siddhartha was the name he received at birth. He is also known as Sakyamuni (sage of the Sakya tribe). After he attained enlightenment, he was called the Buddha or the Tathagata.

teaching directed at satisfying the spiritual quest of a small group, had developed into a universal faith. Considerable time passed before this religion from India sank its roots into Chinese soil; but once it had, Buddhism came to pervade the cosmopolitan culture of the Tang (617–907). It was from China that it spread to Korea and Japan. In both lands Buddhist texts were read in Chinese, but we cannot afford to disregard its Indian roots. Accounts of the Buddha's life were not committed to writing until centuries after his death. These narratives were the work, not of dispassionate scholars, but of faithful believers whose aim was to extol the great founder. Yet, despite the accretions of the mythical and the miraculous in these accounts, the Buddha they reveal is essentially a humane man, not a god. Only later was he deified.

Tradition has it that Gautama Siddhartha was born a prince and brought up in luxury. He was shocked into a search for religious understanding, however, when on three successive outings from the palace he encountered an old man, a sick man, and a dead man—and learned that such is the fate of humankind. He abandoned worldly pleasures to seek religious truth. Initially he became an ascetic and practiced austerities so severe that they almost cost him his life; ultimately he found a middle way between self-deprivation and gratification. His subsequent enlightenment under the bodhi (wisdom) tree (at which time he became the Buddha, or "Enlightened One") was achieved despite the efforts of Mara, the evil one, who first sent demons to assail him, and then sent his daughters, (Discontent, Delight, and Desire) to tempt him, all equally in vain. The Buddha's success elicited a suitable cosmic response. The whole earth swayed, and blossoms rained from the heavens. After attaining enlightenment, he spent the remainder of his life teaching his disciples, a following whose growth led to the formation of communities of monks and nuns.

At the core of the Buddha's teachings are the Four Noble Truths. The first of these is that life is suffering. Like many religions throughout the world, Buddhism teaches that pain and unhappiness are unavoidable in life. The traditional response of Indian religions to this perception is to seek for ways to transcend life. Death is not the answer, for in the Indian view, living beings are subject to reincarnation in one painful life after another. According to the law of karma, for every action there is a moral reaction. A life of good deeds leads to reincarnation at a higher and more desirable level in the next cycle; evil deeds lead in the opposite direction. But the ultimate goal is not rebirth as an emperor or millionaire: it is to achieve Nirvana and never be born again. Legend has it that the Buddha himself gained merit in many reincarnations before his final rebirth, and stories of his previous lives have provided rich subject matter for the artist (see, for example, Figure 2.8).

The second Truth explains the first, stating that the cause of human suffering is craving, or desire. This in turn leads to the third Truth: that to stop suffering, desire must be stopped. The cause of suffering must be completely understood and halted. This is accomplished by living the ethical life and practicing religious contemplation and the spiritual exercises set out in the last of the Four Truths.

The fourth Truth proclaims the Eightfold Path: right views, right intention, right speech, right action, right livelihood, right effort, right mindfulness, and right concentration. The religious life involves vegetarianism, celibacy, and abstinence from alcoholic beverages, as well as positive religious practices. Carried to perfection it leads to release from reincarnation and to Nirvana: that is, to the absolute, the infinite, the ineffable.

There is much that is subtle in the elaboration of these ideas and in their explication by the Buddha and his followers. The explanation of the doctrine that there is no ego provides an example. That which we think of as the self is merely a temporary assemblage of the five aggregates (material body, sensation, perception, predisposition, and consciousness). At any point in time an individual is a momentary cluster of qualities without any underlying unity. It is a dangerous delusion to think that these qualities pertain to some kind of permanent entity or soul: only by understanding that all is change can Buddhahood be achieved. Transmigration is likened to the passing of a flame from one lamp to another until it is finally extinguished. "Extinguished" is the literal meaning of Nirvana.

Many problems of a doctrinal interpretation were left unanswered by the Buddha, for he was a religious teacher concerned with showing the way to salvation, not a philosopher interested in metaphysics for its own sake. The Buddha's concern for spreading the faith was carried on by later missionaries who undertook hazardous journeys to bring the message to distant lands. As in other religions, such as Christianity, later commentators worked out the philosophical implications of the founder's teachings, producing a mass of writings. These holy scriptures were compiled in the Tripitaka, or "three baskets," which consists of sermons attributed to the Buddha himself (sutras), later treatises (sastras), and monastic rules (vinayas). The enormity of this body of scripture indicates the vast breadth of Buddhism. It had no centralized organization or ecclesiastical hierarchy and developed in a generally tolerant atmosphere conducive to producing a rich variety of schools and sects.

The distinction between the Theravada sects, which still predominate in Sri Lanka and Southeast Asia, and the Mahayana schools, which played the major role in China and continue to do so in Japan, is the result of a major division in Buddhism that occurred early in its history. The word "Mahayana" literally means "greater vehicle," reflecting the claims of its followers to more inclusive and powerful teachings than those of their predecessors in the Hinayana, or "lesser vehicle"—a term generally resented by Theravada Buddhists. A branch of Mahayana Buddhism important for its development of doctrine was the Madhyamika (middle way) school, which taught that reality is empty or void *(sunya)*. Emptiness became an absolute, underlying all phenomena. In innermost essence, everything, including the world of appearances, is Nirvana and empty. If everything is emptiness, then what is it that perceives the emptiness? The Yogacara (yoga practice) school held that the ultimate reality is consciousness, that everything is produced by mind.

Mahayana Buddhism developed not only a metaphysical literature whose richness and subtlety are barely hinted at here; it also broadened the appeal of Buddhism to draw in those people who did not have the time, training, or inclination for abstract speculation. A significant development was the growth of devotionalism directed at the Buddha, deifying him and placing him at the head of an expanding pantheon. Other Buddhas also appeared and had their following, especially Maitreya, the Buddha of the future, who exerted a messianic appeal and was often adopted as a symbol by Chinese rebel movements. The three-body doctrine helped to accommodate and justify new forms of Buddhism, for it taught that Buddhahood can be considered under three aspects: the "transformation body," that is, the historical personage of the Buddha, the "enjoyment body," that is, the celestial Buddha as beheld by the devout, and the "truth body" as understood in the abstractions of the metaphysicians.

In addition to the Buddhas, there were numerous lesser gods, but more important than these were the celestial Bodhisattvas, who postponed their own entry into Nirvana in order to help other beings. Somewhat like the Virgin Mary and the saints of Christianity, the Bodhisattvas themselves became objects of veneration and worship, none more than Avalokitesvara (Kannon in Japanese, Guanyin or Kuan-yin in Chinese), famed for the shining quality of his mercy. In China this embodiment of the gentle virtues was gradually transformed into a feminine figure. Sometimes depicted with multiple hands and arms, Avalokitesvara is a favorite subject of Buddhist sculpture. Buddhist art was itself a significant development, dating from

Figure 2.2   Seated Bodhisattva. Stone, Longmen, Late Northern Wei. Museum of Fine Arts, Boston.

the first images of the Buddha that were sculpted in India in the first century A.D. in what was at the time a daring departure from tradition.

Buddhism appealed to people in China, and later to people throughout East Asia, because it addressed itself to human suffering with a directness unmatched in their native traditions. It also provided a well-developed body of doctrine, art, magic and medicine, music and ritual, even heavens and hells for those bewildered by the abstract quality of Nirvana. Because of the giant differences between the civilizations of India and China, it took a long period to fashion credible translations of Indian texts and generally acclimatize Buddhism to Chinese circumstances. The Bodhisattva from the caves at Longmen (see Figure 2.2), for example, shows how by the late Northern Wei Chinese artists had assimilated and transformed an art which, like the concept of creating temples in caves, was Indian in origin. In contrast to the lovingly sensuous modeling of the naked body in three dimensions that is the glory of the Indian sculptor, the essentially linear style of the figure, with its geometric composition and frontal orientation, is characteristically Chinese. At its best, this art reproduced in metal and stone the simple piety and sweet spirituality of a religious age.

The Bodhisattva was carved under the Northern Wei, a nomadic dynasty of conquest. Buddhism also advanced in China's south where quick-witted monks became experts in sophisticated repartee and engaged also in highly

Figure 2.3   Vimalakīrti. Clay, 45.2 cm high. Pagoda of the Hōryūji.

abstract metaphysical discussions in which they displayed their command of the Chinese as well as Buddhist intellectual heritage. Given new prominence as a model for the Buddhist as aristocrat was the figure of Vimalakīrti, a wealthy layman who enjoyed life to the full and displayed great powers of intellect and a pure and lofty personality. (See Figure 2.3.) This depiction of Vimalakīrti from Japan illustrates that Buddhism was not only for the poor and ignorant.

By Sui and Tang, Buddhism had entered deeply into the fabric of Chinese life. Chinese monks now were sufficiently confident to develop their own original interpretations and to establish independent sects which will enter our narrative as they become influential in Japan.

Part II. THE IMPACT OF CONTINENTAL CIVILIZATION

Late Yamato (552–710)*

Continental influences remained conspicuous during the Late Yamato age. A new element was Buddhism. Most likely the Japanese had been introduced to Buddhism before the middle of the sixth century, but in 552 the king of Paekche in Korea is said to have commended the religion to the Japanese and sent them some Buddhist texts and statues. By that time, Buddhism was well established in Paekche, which hoped for Japanese assistance in fighting neighboring Silla.

At the Yamato court the introduction of the new religion set off a bitter controversy. Opposing the acceptance of what they considered a powerful *kami* from abroad were two strong *uji:* the Nakatomi who served as Shinto ritualists and thus had a stake in the religious status quo, and the Mononobe, an *uji* with military responsibilities. Championing the cause of Buddhism were the Soga, who had come to prominence fairly late but enjoyed great influence because they intermarried with the Sun lineage. The Yamato ruler Kinmei (r. 540–71) had many children by his Soga consort to perpetuate the family's influence. The Soga's adoption of Buddhism may have been, in part, an effort to bolster and sanctify their power.

After consulting all sides, Kinmei presented a Buddhist image to the Soga, who established it in their home as their clan *kami*. Shortly afterward, however, an epidemic broke out. The Soga's enemies claimed that the epidemic was caused by the local *kami*, angered at the Buddhist intrusion. Buddhism suffered a setback, and the image itself was reportedly thrown into a canal. Both the clan and the religion recovered, however, and in 587 the Soga defeated the Mononobe in war.

The victorious Soga leader, Umako, was now the most powerful man in the land, but he did not seek to displace the Yamato line. Instead, he first had a

---

* This designation combines the periods known to art historians as Asuka (552–645) and Hakuhō (645–710).

nephew assume the rulership and then, when this man proved insufficiently pliable, replaced him with a niece, Suiko (r. 592–628). Actual government, however, was conducted by the regent, Prince Shōtoku (Shōtoku Taishi) who became one of Japan's most revered figures. It is impossible now to separate legend from fact in the accounts of his life, but he appears to have been a most remarkable man. Part of his fame came from his generous patronage of Buddhism. He has been credited with sponsoring many temples, including the famous Hōryūji, and staffing them with clergy from Korea. In Korea itself he tried to restore a Japanese client state (Mimana) but without success. He then opened direct relations with China, recently unified by the Sui. Chinese records indicate that the Sui emperor was not amused on receiving a communication addressed, "from the emperor of the sunrise country to the emperor of the sunset country"; nevertheless, during the short Sui period, four Japanese missions were sent to China.

Direct contact with China increased Japanese receptivity to continental imports such as new religious ideas, the Chinese calendar, and concepts of government that the Japanese found useful in their attempt to build a stronger state. The new court ranks introduced in 603 were based on Chinese practice, and Chinese influence is pronounced in the famous 17-point "constitution" traditionally ascribed to Prince Shōtoku and dated 604. Its first article is a Confucian discourse on harmony. This is followed by a second commanding reverence for the three treasures of Buddhism (the Buddha, the Law, and the Order). Other articles call on subordinate officials to obey their superiors, and the subordinates are admonished to behave with decorum, avoid greed, be suspicious of flatterers and so on. The "constitution" affirmed the primacy of the sovereign and asserted the monopoly role of government in collecting taxes. Unlike modern constitutions, its purpose was not to organize a form of government, but to promulgate certain moral precepts that *ought* to characterize the conduct of government. Nevertheless, its objectives were clearly political: to strengthen the political power and moral standing of the state.

This was by no means an easy matter. Although the trend in these years was toward adoption of Chinese institutions and an increase in the strength of the central government, the process was neither smooth nor uninterrupted. The death of Prince Shōtoku in 622 led to bloody struggles that culminated in a coup d'etat in 645 led by an imperial prince and by the head of the Nakatomi, which had opposed the Soga from the beginning. This man, Nakatomi no Kamatari, was given the surname Fujiwara and became the founder of a family that was to dominate Japanese government off and on for centuries to come. The anti-Soga group also included some men who had studied in China, and once in power, they not only continued the practice of sending missions to China but worked to further the adoption of Chinese practices. In 646 the new government proclaimed the Taika (Great Change) reforms. To effect greater control over outlying areas, a new system of provincial administration was announced and provisions were made for an extensive system of roads and post stations. Private ownership of land was abolished as were the *be*. Rice fields were now to be allotted on the model of the Chinese "equal field" system, with the fields reverting to the state for redistribution each generation. A new Tang-style tax system was also proclaimed and a census ordered, an essential component for the functioning of the new system. The crown prince himself gave up his land to the state, but the implementation of the program was gradual and incomplete. For example, the first census was not taken until 670.

The Nara Period (710–784)

The Late Yamato period came to an end with the establishment, in 710, of a capital at Nara, then called Heijō. Prior to 645 the capital had consisted simply of the ruler's palace, and its location changed with each ruler. (This may have been partly to avoid defilement, for according to Shinto belief a death polluted the place of its occurrence.) Changes in ruler, and hence changes in location, reflected the shifting political realities as rival *uji* maneuvered for power. The adoption of Chinese institutions of government required a more elaborate bureaucratic structure and more formal administrative procedures, however, and these in turn required government buildings: an audience hall, offices, and housing for officials and their staffs. Moving the capital became an increasingly complex business. Fujiwara, the last and largest of the seventh-century capitals, served three emperors before it was abandoned for Heijō.

Heijō was conceived and laid out as a miniature Changan, the capital of the Tang. The Japanese ruler now claimed to be an emperor in the Chinese sense, a virtuous "son of heaven." He ruled through a divine mandate, but unlike his Chinese counterpart, the Japanese emperor's mandate was irrevocable, entrusted for all time to the ruling house by virtue of divine descent. Chinese concepts were adopted to strengthen the throne, not to weaken it; and the Mencian idea that the mandate could be revoked was disregarded. Individual emperors might exercise a great deal of power, as did Emperor Temmu (r. 672–86) shortly before the Nara period and Emperor Kammu (r. 781–806) at its end, but even weak emperors continued to function as the country's chief priests. The continued importance of this native religious tradition in the Japanese concept of government and throne is also exemplified by the high prominence accorded the peculiarly Japanese Department of Deities, which looked after the imperial Shinto ritual.

Underlying the Nara system of government was the Taihō Code. Implemented in 702, this body of law further extended the work of the Taika reforms. The bureaucratic structure of government was more closely modeled on that of the Tang. The country was divided into three levels of administrative jurisdiction: provinces, districts, and villages. The peasantry was organized into village units whose members, as in China, were mutually responsible for each other's behavior. Emulating the Chinese equal field system, rice lands were now reorganized into square fields of standard size and redistributed every six years according to the number of males and females over five years old in each household. As in China, taxes were to be collected in kind: grain, textiles, and labor-service. In addition, men were liable to military conscription.

Also as in China, the land allotment system was not permitted to interfere with the wealth and status of aristocratic families or with the flourishing religious establishments, which enjoyed special privileges, such as immunity from taxation. Moreover, while the Taihō Code established civil service examinations that did offer career opportunities for minor aristocrats, the tendency was for government office to remain a prerogative of the wellborn. Government posts were filled by persons of appropriate rank, and rank was hereditary.

This ambitious, bureaucratic system was placed under enormous strain by the smallpox epidemic of 735–37 which devastated Japan since the people, previously not exposed to the disease, had not developed antibodies to combat the disease. Indeed, there is evidence of epidemics recurring roughly every thirty years until smallpox finally became presumably an endemic childhood disease in late Heian. Confronting the economic effects of an unprecedented disaster that may have reduced the population by 30 percent, the Nara government in 743 allowed newly opened rice paddies to be retained in perpetuity, and in 745 resorted to tax farming to refill depleted provincial granaries. Eventually these measures would help to undermine the centralized state.

Nara Literary Culture

During the eighth century Chinese influence and prestige reached a new high. Indicative of Japanese admiration for the civilization of Tang China were the seven missions of up to 500 or 600 men each sent on the long and dangerous journey to Changan between 701 and 777. Chinese cultural influence was paramount but was not allowed to drown out native traditions. Significantly, Japan's oldest literary works, the *Kojiki* and the *Nihon Shoki*, had as their subject matter the purported history of Japan.

In contrast to the completely mythological *Kojiki*, the *Nihon Shoki* includes as its second half an account of the sixth and seventh century that can be considered historical. Both books helped to preserve old legends, but the authors did more than just compile old traditions. The legends were arranged and presented in ways that would bolster claims of the imperial house to supernatural as well as historical legitimization. Genealogies of the leading aristocratic families were also incorporated in them for the same purpose. In this way, the characteristically Chinese practice of recording the past was adopted to serve Japanese ends.

Both works were written in the Chinese script, the only form of writing available in Japan during the Nara period, but they differ in that the *Nihon Shoki* is written in Chinese while the *Kojiki* is written in a very difficult mixed style that sometimes employs the Chinese characters for their meaning but at other times uses them merely to represent the sounds of eighth-century Japanese.

There are also two famous collections of poetry from this period: the *Man'yōshū (Collection of Ten Thousand Leaves,* or *of Ten Thousand*

Generations), a collection of roughly 4,500 poems, completed around the middle of the eighth century; and the *Kaifūsō,* an anthology completed about the same time. The *Man'yōshū* was written using Chinese symbols to transliterate the spoken Japanese, while the *Kaifūsō* contained Chinese poetry written by Japanese. It is hardly surprising that the poems written by Japanese in their own language are of superior literary merit.

The *Man'yōshū* poems range widely in form, authorship, and subject. However, the most commonly used poetic form is the *tanka,* a verse in which 31 syllables are arranged in five lines in a pattern of 5–7–5–7–7 syllables. Because the Japanese language has a relative absence of stresses while having a superabundance of rhyming possibilities, neither stress nor rhyme have played an important role in Japanese poetry. Hence the relatively greater emphasis on length and balance of lines. As Earl Miner has suggested, the language was so fluid and free that "for centuries only one form, the *tanka,* seemed able to contain it."[5] Already in the *Man'yōshū* the *tanka* prevails, but there are also poems of up to 149 lines. The finest poet included in the *Man'yōshū* is Kakinomoto Hitomaro. Although he also wrote *tanka,* his best poems are longer. Among them is his "On Seeing the Body of a Man Lying among the Stones on the Island of Samine in Sanuki Province." It begins:

> O the precious land of Sanuki,
> Resting where the seaweed glows like gems!
> Perhaps for its precious nature
> I never tire in my gazing on it,
> Perhaps for its holy name
> It is the most divine of sights.
> It will flourish and endure
> Together with the heaven and earth,
> With the shining sun and moon,
> For through successive ages it has come down
> That the landface is the face of a god.[6]

The poem reflects an abiding Japanese love of the land. This quality is an inherent aspect of the Shinto heritage, with its veneration for spirits of the local countryside *(kami).* It is important to bear in mind that the spread of Buddhism in seventh- and eighth-century Japan represented the overlay of one religion on the other, not the replacement of Shinto by Buddhism. The melding of Shinto sensibilities with Buddhist aesthetics was to create a highly refined, beautiful, and evocative artistic tradition.

Early Japanese Buddhism and the Arts

Through the Late Yamato and Nara periods Buddhism continued to exercise a varied appeal. The spiritual content of its religious message was only one, and by no means the dominant, element in this appeal. Many were drawn to Buddhism by the potency of its rituals and the reputed efficacy of its healing power, as is shown by the popularity of the Buddha of Healing (Yakushi). It is hardly surprising that the finest large surviving bronze sculpture of the

Nara period is a triad in which the figure of the Healing Buddha occupies the central place. The sculpture is housed in the "Temple of the Buddha of Healing" (Yakushiji), which was built by order of an emperor worried by the illness of his consort.

Within the temples, as in Western monasteries, monks and nuns, under the direction of an abbot or abbess, read and copied the scriptures and performed various solemn religious rites, including the chanting of the sutras. Thereby, they hoped to advance not only their own salvation but also to contribute to the welfare of their patrons, who frequently were members of the royal family. Indeed, it was common practice for the emperor to encourage Buddhism and to endow Buddhist temples in an effort to obtain divine protection and acquire religious merit. This is similar to the religious patronage practiced in China, or in Europe where Christian monarchs built cathedrals, endowed religious establishments, and went on crusades. In times of crisis, when the emperor was ill or the state in danger, men and women were even coerced into taking orders and entering a monastery or nunnery, in an act of forced piety.

Japanese Temples

There is no finer expression of the aesthetic impulse of Nara Japan than the emergence of its temple architecture and related arts. The oldest surviving temple, which, incidentally boasts the oldest wooden buildings in the world, is the Hōryūji, near Nara. The original structure, erected by Prince Shōtoku, was rebuilt after being destroyed by fire in 670. Figure 2.4 shows the nucleus of the temple, a quadrangle enclosed by a cloistered walk. Equal emphasis is accorded the pagoda and the Golden Hall, balanced against each other at opposite ends of the north-south axis. This layout was characteristic of the temples of the Nara region, but in subsequent temples the Golden Hall was given greater prominence, and there was some experimentation with alternate possible locations for the pagoda. As in China, some temples had double pagodas.

Other buildings commonly found in temples included a lecture hall, usually located to the north or back, a sutra repository to store the scriptures, a belfry, a refectory, and buildings to house monks in their cells. The major buildings stood on a stone base and were roofed in clay tile. Again as in China, these heavy roofs were supported by a system of bracketing that in itself contributed greatly to the aesthetics of the building. Large exterior wooden units were painted red, yellow paint covered the crosscut faces of the brackets, rafters, and so on, and other, intervening spaces were painted white. In their orientation, structure, and ornamentation these were basically continental buildings.

The art housed in these temples was also basically continental; frequently the work of Korean and Chinese artists and craftsmen. Indeed, Nara period temples in Japan are among our best sources for studying Chinese Buddhist art up through the Tang in its temporal and regional variations. The Hōryūji

Figure 2.4   The Hōryūji, Nara Prefecture.

itself is a great treasure house. Here we shall mention only two of its most famous sculptures. One is a triad that looks like a bronze version of a Northern Wei stone sculpture. It is signed by an artist whose grandfather came from China and is dedicated to Prince Shōtoku. As Robert Paine has noted, the flatness of this sculpture and its frontal approach are logical consequences of the techniques needed for rock carving but are unrelated to bronze casting, which begins with a model in clay. "An accepted traditionalism, not questions of material, directed these early sculptures in Japan."[7] Another major piece, surely one of the most lovely figures in the Hōryūji, is the Kudara Kannon (which, since "Kudara" is Japanese for "Paekche," is a reminder of the Korean provenance of so much in Japanese Buddhism). The overall effect of this elongated figure is one of great elegance and grace (see Figure 2.5).

Also representative of the best temple art of the period is the figure of Maitreya, the Buddha of the future (see Figures 2.6 and 2.7), with its shared Chinese and Korean ancestry, and its remarkable aesthetic fusion of piety and sensuousness. This figure belongs to a temple in Kyōto that traces its origins, although not its current buildings, to Prince Shōtoku. It is a visual reminder of the spiritual, philosophical, and artistic influence of Buddhism in East Asia and of the role of Buddhism in creating linked cultures throughout the region.

The Hōryūji also contains material for the study of painting. The earliest painting is found on the Tamamushi (Jade-Beetle) shrine, so named because it was decorated with iridescent beetle wings set into metal edging, a technique also practiced in Korea. The scene, shown in Figure 2.8, derives from a famous story concerning an earlier incarnation of Sakyamuni. It shows the future Buddha sacrificing himself to feed a starving mother tiger unable to feed her young. The painting, like the story, begins at the top where the future Buddha is shown hanging his clothes on a tree, and it ends at the bottom where the tigress is devouring him. Its linear effects and the elongation of the figure fit in nicely with the general style of the Asuka period. The Hōryūji also contained frescoes that were an important source for the study of Tang-style painting. They

Figure 2.5
Kudara Kannon.
Painted wood,
Asuka period,
204.8 cm high.
Hōryūji, Nara
Prefecture.

Figure 2.6
Maitreya
(Miroku). Wood,
Asuka period,
123.5 cm high.
Kōryūji, Kyoto.

were destroyed by fire in 1949 but can still be studied from photographs.

The Hōryūji was just one of the temples built before the construction of the capital at Nara, where during the eighth century Tang arts and Tang styles flourished. The spirit of Tang architecture is well illustrated by the Golden Hall of the Tōshōdaiji (see Figure 2.9) as seen when one enters the temple through the south gate. Although the original roof was more sloping and less steep than the

Figure 2.7   Detail of Maitreya
(Miroku). Wood, Asuka period.

present version, the illustration gives a good idea of the self-assured strength
of Tang building at its best. The careful symmetry of its proportions is
exemplified by the bays: the central bay measures sixteen *shaku* (about
25.29 centimeters); the next bay on each side is reduced to 15 *shaku*; the
third set of bays measures 13; the end bays (not visible in the illustration)
measure 11 *shaku*. The result is a handsome building with the emphasis on
the center. Similarly, whereas in the Golden Hall of the Hōryūji the altar was
square and therefore ideal for the rite of circumambulation (ritual walking
around an "altar"), in the Tōshōdaiji it has been replaced by a rectangular
platform affording the central Buddha a position of enhanced prominence.

The Tōshōdaiji was founded by the Chinese monk Ganjin (Jianzhen,
Chien-chen), who finally reached Japan on his sixth attempt, having earlier
been frustrated by storms, pirates, shipwrecks, and once by the Chinese
authorities. By the time he reached Japan, he had lost his sight. His portrait
(see Figure 2.10) is housed at Tōshōdaiji. It is constructed in the dry lacquer
technique in which layers of cloth and lacquer are alternately built up,
usually on a wooden frame. It is an important starting point for Japanese
portrait sculpture, as well as being a reminder of the courage and devotion
shown by the early Buddhist missionary monks and of the serenity that was
their earthly reward.

The main Buddha at Tōshōdaiji is Vairocana, the cosmic Buddha who
encompasses all. It was for this Buddha that the most ambitious Nara temple

Figure 2.8 *Tamamushi Shrine*. Lacquer on wood, seventh century, 233.7 cm high. Hōryūji, Nara Prefecture.

was built, the Tōdaiji. The casting of the Great Buddha, 53 feet high and requiring over one million pounds of metal, was a great technical achievement and a truly national undertaking requiring contributions from all quarters. The final act was the painting in of the pupils of the eyes by an Indian monk. This was the highlight of a great celebration, held in 752 amid universal rejoicing, at which 10,000 monks were presented with a vegetarian feast. It was surely one of the most magnificent spectacles in Japanese history. Unfortunately, the present figure in the Tōdaiji has been so much restored that it probably bears little resemblance to the original.

The Tōdaiji was the head temple of the land, for in Japan as in China Huayan doctrines appealed to centralizing rulers. The government was also the sponsor of Buddhism in the provinces. In 741 an edict was promulgated requiring that a Buddhist temple and pagoda be established in every province. Each temple was to have twenty monks and ten nuns who were to chant sutras and perform other religious ceremonies on behalf of the emperor and the state. At the same time, however, it was believed that the well-being of the country was impossible without the cooperation of the ancient *kami* as well. Efforts were

Figure 2.9   ABOVE: Tōshōdaiji, Nara. BELOW: Tōshōdaiji, side elevation.

Figure 2.10   *Portrait of Ganjin* (Jianzhen). Dry lacquer, mid-eighth century, 80.7 cm high. Tōshōdaiji, Nara.

made to assure the friendly coexistence of the old spirits with the divinities of the new religion. The consent of the Sun Goddess was duly obtained for the construction of the image of the Great Buddha himself as a form of the "Sun Buddha" (Dainichi). Meanwhile, Shinto shrines protected Buddhist temples by ensuring that the local *kami* would welcome them, and Buddhist altars extended their benefits to Shinto gods. Buddhist monks also found room for Shinto deities by treating them as avatars, or manifestations, of their own divinities. One major divinity, Hachiman, was both a Shinto *kami* and a Buddhist bodhisattva. This coexistence between the two religions began at a time when Buddhism itself was only just beginning to filter down to the common people, and probably hastened its acceptance.

Far removed from the eyes of the common people were the treasures housed in a remarkable building that was originally part of the Tōdaiji. Called the Shōsōin, it is a great repository of eighth-century secular art. Like other Japanese storehouses it stands on pillars and is built of logs. These logs expand when it is humid (keeping out moist air) and contract in dry weather (providing ventilation). Inside the Shōsōin are about 10,000 objects: books, weapons, mirrors, screens, silks, and objects of gold, lacquer, mother-of-pearl, and glass. Objects used in the dedication ceremonies of the Great Buddha are there. There are even goods from China, India, Persia, Greece, and Rome, testifying to Japanese participation in the cosmopolitan culture of the eighth century. A similar openness to the world is evident elsewhere, in court music for example, which shows Persian influence. Perhaps some of this music was played on the instruments preserved in the Shōsōin.

The Move from Nara

The Buddhist establishment had obtained such wealth and power that the decision to abandon Nara has often been interpreted as a measure to counteract Buddhist political influence after the notorious career of the priest Dōkyō and his relationship to the ex-empress Kōken (r. 749–58), who resumed the throne in 764 to rule as Empress Shōtoku until her death in 770. Seduced by the charms of the priest, this empress housed him in the palace, bestowed on him the highest office of the state, and in 769 even gave him a title used exclusively by abdicated emperors entering the priesthood. Then Dōkyō overreached himself by trying for the throne itself. He encountered strong resistance but was protected as long as the empress remained alive. When she died, however, his political enemies had their revenge and drove him into banishment.

After this episode, there were to be only two more empresses in Japanese history—one in the seventeenth and one in the eighteenth century. The move from Nara, however, had more to do with rivalry between competing royal lineages than with hostility to Buddhism. Even in the middle of the Nara period Emperor Shomu (r. 724–49) toyed with the idea of moving the capital. Nara was abandoned by Emperor Kammu in 784. After an unsuccessful attempt to establish the capital at another site, he moved it in 794 to

Heian, modern Kyoto, which was ritually associated with his line and close to the power base of his maternal relatives.

The emperor's motives may have been traditional. Furthermore the plan of the new capital, modeled like its predecessor on Changan, also suggests continuity. However, the move was epochal not only because the court was to remain in Kyoto until the nineteenth century, but also because in Kyoto the process of acquiring continental ideas gave way to that of transforming them into something Japanese. During the Heian period the divergence between Japan and the continent became increasingly marked.

NOTES

1. Wing-tsit Chan, *A Source Book In Chinese Philosophy* (Princeton: Princeton Univ. Press, 1963), p. 79.
2. Ibid., pp. 86–87.
3. *Mencius*, V, pt. A, Chap. 5, translated by D. C. Lau, *Mencius* (Baltimore: Penguin Books, 1970), p. 144.
4. Martin Collcutt, "The Legacy of Confucianism in Japan" in Gilbert Rozman, ed. *The East Asian Region: Confucian Heritage and Its Modern Adaptation* (Princeton: Princeton Univ. Press, 1991) p. 114.
5. Earl Miner, *An Introduction to Japanese Court Poetry* (Stanford: Stanford Univ. Press, 1968), p. 22.
6. Ibid., p. 48.
7. Robert Treat Paine and Alexander Soper, *The Art and Architecture of Japan* (Baltimore: Penguin Books, 1955), p. 12.

Aristocrats, Monks, and Samurai

Figure 3 *Pine Trees*. Six-fold screen; ink, color and gold on paper. Attributed to Tosa Mitsunobu, 1434–1522. Muromachi period. Tokyo National Museum.

3
The Heian Period

平安時代

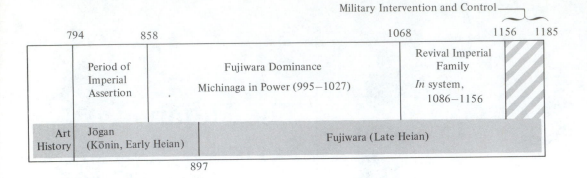

	794	858		1068	1156	1185
	Period of Imperial Assertion	Fujiwara Dominance Michinaga in Power (995–1027)		Revival Imperial Family *In* system, 1086–1156		
Art History	Jōgan (Kōnin, Early Heian)	Fujiwara (Late Heian)				

897

A s Japanese civilization grew to full maturity, it developed its own themes, institutions, and styles. Although not lacking in continuities, each of the three lengthy periods discussed in this part had its own highly distinct character, just as each helped to shape what it meant to be Japanese.

The Heian period began with a vigorous assertion of imperial power under Emperor Kammu. However, the long-term trend was in the opposite direction. The aristocracy, not the emperor, dominated the age and created a refined culture that left a permanent mark on Japanese life and perceptions of the world.

By keeping the temples out of the new capital of Kyoto and by patronizing the new Tendai and Shingon sects, which had their headquarters in the mountains, Emperor Kammu was able to evade the political influence of the old, city-based orders. Equally energetic and innovative in secular matters, he established new agencies to advise the throne and enforce its decisions, appointed inspectors to examine the books of retiring provincial governors, and replaced the ineffective conscript army with a militia system. In this way he and his immediate successors were able, for almost half a century, to rule in the spirit of the Taika Reforms and the Taihō Code.

This period of imperial assertion was followed by two centuries during which the Fujiwara family enjoyed political and economic ascendance, reducing the throne to an impotence reminiscent of the days of Soga domination. But the Fujiwara remained content to dominate emperors and did not seek to displace the imperial house. During most of subsequent Japanese history as well, emperors continued to function as titular heads of government, symbols of legitimization and objects of veneration, without actual political power. They were manipulated rather than removed, for the religious aura of the imperial person was based on his family's unique divine descent. There is nothing quite comparable to this phenomenon in Western history.

The Fujiwara

The Fujiwara house was founded by Nakatomi no Kamatari, head of the Nakatomi clan who played the leading role in the coup of 645. He was rewarded with the name Fujiwara, literally "wisteria plain," an apparent reference to the wisteria arbor where the anti-Soga plotters met. Kamatari's son Fuhito (659–720) continued the family's influence. He headed the committee that drew up the Taihō Code and became the father-in-law of two emperors and the grandfather of another. After that the family fortunes had their ups and downs, but the Fujiwara continued to be an important factor in Nara politics. For example, the opposition to the priest Dōkyō was led by a Fujiwara. The Fujiwara clan was itself divided into four main branches. It was a subbranch of one of these (the Northern, or "Hokke" branch) that gained power in the Heian period.

Intermarriage with the imperial family was one of the keys to Fujiwara power. In 858 Fujiwara Yoshifusa (804–72), Grand Minister since 857, placed his own eight-year-old grandson on the throne and assumed the title of Regent for a Minor (sesshō). This was the first time anyone outside the imperial family had filled this position. Yoshifusa was succeeded by his nephew Mototsune (836–91), who was the first to continue as regent even after the emperor was no longer a minor, assuming for that purpose the new title of kampaku, designating a regent for an adult emperor. It was as regents that the Fujiwara institutionalized their power.

The ambitions of this family did not go uncontested. After Mototsune died in 891, there was an interlude without a Fujiwara regent until Tadahira (sesshō, 939–41; kampaku, 941–49) resumed the tradition. Most famous of the opponents of the Fujiwara was Sugawara no Michizane (845–903). A noted scholar of Chinese studies and poet, he enjoyed great influence for a time but eventually could not withstand the Fujiwara political machinations and ended as a virtual exile in Kyūshū. There he died, but his ghost reputedly returned to punish his enemies, leading to a brilliant posthumous career. To put an end to a series of storms, floods, droughts, fires, and other calamities attributed to his angry spirit, he was promoted several times and finally became the patron god of letters and calligraphy, worshipped at the Kitano shrine erected in his honor in the capital.

Other rivals of the Fujiwara were considerably less successful, and in 967 the tradition of Fujiwara regents was reestablished. A high point in Fujiwara power was reached under Michinaga (966–1027) who demonstrated great skill in the intrigue and political infighting necessary to succeed at court. He was especially skilled at marriage politics, for he managed to marry four daughters to emperors, two of whom were also his grandsons. Emperors who were the sons of Fujiwara mothers and married to Fujiwara consorts were unlikely to resent the influence of the great family, let alone to resist it. Michinaga himself felt so secure that, although he did become a sesshō, he never assumed the title of kampaku, preferring the reality to the trappings of power. His successors, however, resumed the title while continuing to derive legitimacy and prestige from their close association with the imperial family. In the meantime, as the emperor's political power waned, his sacerdotal role grew even more important. Indeed, the ritual and ceremonial demands on the throne were so great that when the imperial family reasserted its power in the eleventh century, the lead was taken by abdicated emperors who by resigning had freed themselves from the burdensome routine of official observances.

The importance of marriage politics and control of the emperor should not be underestimated, but lasting political power usually is linked to some kind of economic power, and Heian Japan is no exception. In their heyday the Fujiwara were the wealthiest family in the land; their mansions outshone the imperial palace. To understand the source and nature of their wealth, it is necessary to examine changes in Japan's basic economic institutions, changes that had their origins in the Nara period but reached their fruition in Heian times. At the heart of these changes was the development of *shōen*, or estates.

The Shōen

The *shōen* were private landholdings essentially outside of government control. Since there is nothing quite like them in Western history, we are forced to use the Japanese term.

The origins of the *shōen* go back to the Nara period. Recall that Japan had adopted the Chinese "equal field" system for distributing land to peasant cultivators and redistributing the land again upon the proprietor's death. Certain lands were exempt, however: (1) those held by the imperial family and certain aristocratic families, (2) those granted to the great Buddhist temples and Shinto shrines, and (3) newly developed fields, which after 743 could be retained in perpetuity. Furthermore, there was a natural tendency for all land assignments to become hereditary. This was true of lands assigned to accompany certain ranks and offices and also of lands assigned to cultivators. The complicated and foreign system of land redistribution fell into abeyance. Perhaps it was not suited to Japanese conditions, but whether it was associated with failure to adjust to economic growth or, on the contrary, a response to decline brought on by recurrent epidemics, remains in dispute.

The development of private landholdings was accompanied by the growth of tax exemptions granted to influential aristocrats and temples. In the course of time, these tax exemptions were broadened to include other privileges such as immunity from inspection or interference by local provincial government officials, who were thus deprived of administrative authority over the *shōen*. They could not even enter the estates.

Landholdings of this type first appeared in the eighth century and grew thereafter largely by a process of commendation. Small landholders placed their fields under the protection of those powerful enough to enjoy tax exemption and immunities. Thus, a small relatively powerless local landholder might assign his land to a richer and more influential family or religious institution, retaining the right to cultivate the land in exchange for a small rent, less than he would have had to pay to the tax collector. In this way he secured an economic advantage and received protection from the exactions and pressures of the local officials. The new proprietor might in turn commend the land to one of the truly powerful families such as the Fujiwara with their high status at the capital. To obtain their protection, he would in his turn cede certain rights. Furthermore, since the proprietor was usually an absent landlord living in the capital area, he required the services of administrators, and these men too received certain rights to income from the land. These rights, called *shiki* and entitling the bearer to a certain portion or percentage of the income from the land, could be divided, passed on to one's heirs, or even sold without affecting the integrity of the estate. As a result the system became very complicated—one man might hold different kinds of *shiki* in one estate and/or hold *shiki* in several estates. Women too could hold these rights, and the most fortunate were able to enjoy an independent source of income not unlike the modern owners of stocks and bonds.

It was a complicated system, but essentially four levels of people were associated with an individual *shōen* in what Elizabeth Sato characterizes as a "hierarchy of tenures."[1] At the bottom of the scale were the cultivators *(shōmin)*. Above them were the "resident managers" known variously as "local lords" or "proprietors" *(ryōshu)*, members of influential families resident in the *shōen (shōke)*, or officials *(shōkan)*. Still another step up were the "central proprietors" *(ryōke)*, and at the top of the ladder were the patrons *(honke)*. Frequently the patrons lived, not in the *shōen*, but at court in the capital.

Government and Administration

The appearance and steady growth of large holdings outside government jurisdiction continued despite sporadic efforts by government to halt the process by decree, for those who controlled the government themselves profited from the growth of *shōen*. As a result, by the twelfth century more than half of Japan's rice land was incorporated into *shōen*. The growth of these lands naturally led to a decrease in government revenue and a decline in the power of government. Furthermore, administration of taxable land was entrusted to local officials. Even governors entrusted their responsibilities to deputies so that they themselves could remain in the capital.

In the capital, skill in intrigue, wealth, and good looks tended to be more important assets for the official than intellectual or administrative ability. The emphasis on form was consistent with the Confucian insistence on *ri* (propriety, rites, ceremony) and was reinforced by the ethos of the Heian aristocracy, which valued good taste above everything else. It was in keeping with the times that form was stressed at the expense of function, or indeed that form became function. There were officials who took their duties seriously, and the capital continued to provide the arena where the great families competed for status and its benefits, but the deterioration of the government machinery also took its toll. Not even the basic institutions for maintaining order were exempt. For example, pedigree, not ability, determined who was appointed chief of the Imperial Police. This agency had been established in the early ninth-century reassertion of imperial power and in its heyday exercised wide powers in the capital and even in the provinces. It was the only official source of armed support for the throne. But by the time of Michinaga it lacked the strength even to secure the capital against internal disruptions and disorders. Already in 981 unruly priests from the Tendai monastery on Mt. Hiei marched through the streets of the capital to press their demands without encountering effective resistance, and in 1040 robbers found their way into the imperial palace itself and made off with some of the emperor's clothes.

Clearly government was no longer functioning as it had in Nara or during the period of vigorous imperial rule in early Heian. The period of Fujiwara ascendancy can therefore be considered a time of deterioration in government, a view not inconsistent with possible economic growth produced by the opening of new lands, for not only in Japan have old political institutions often been undermined by positive economic developments, nor is there any necessary correlation between political centralization and economic growth. However, to focus on the decline of the imperial government may blur the part played by nonofficial but perfectly legal institutions in the de facto government, now largely in private lands.

What affected the lives of the people on the *shōen* were not the decisions reached at court but rather those made by the aristocratic families or temples that served as the *shōen*'s patrons. To administer their *shōen* holdings (and household affairs), these patrons had a *mandokoro*, translated by G. Cameron Hurst as "administrative council." He describes the Fujiwara *mandokoro* as having the following components:

A documents bureau *(fudono)* "for handling complaints and other types of correspondence"

A secretariat *(kurōdo-dokoro)*

A retainer's office *(samurai-dokoro)* "to coordinate the activities of the warriors in the service of the household"

A stable *(mimaya)*

An attendant's bureau *(zushin-dokoro)* "to control the attendants allotted by the court to high-ranking nobles"

An Office of Court Dress *(gofuku-dokoro)*

A provisions bureau *(shimmotsu-dokoro)*, which "handled the receipt and storage of rice and other grains, vegetables, fish, and other foods for the household's meals"

A cook's bureau *(zen-bu)* "in charge of the actual preparation of food"[2]

There was also a Judicial Office *(monchūjo)* for administering justice in those *shōen* where this right belonged to the patron.

Sato describes the administrative process by which the patrons governed the *shōen* as follows:

> Matters regarding the transmission, receipt, and distribution of income from the shōen were handled by the shōke's *mandokoro* (administrative office), which communicated directly with the managerial office of the shōen *(honjo)*. When the honjo was located on the shōen, the original ryōshu or his descendants as shōke, were responsible for the day-to-day affairs of the shōen. These included assignment of fields to cultivators, distribution of seed and implements, regulation of water supply, collection of revenues, and, if full immunity had been obtained, administration of justice. As one of the chief officials of the honjo of the shōen, the shōke was responsible for forwarding revenues to superior proprietors.

> When the honjo of the shōen was in the capital the shōke acted as agent of the absentee proprietor, working primarily as an overseer rather than as an administrator. In some cases, special agents were dispatched from the capital to serve as officials of the shōen.[3]

The Warriors

The Fujiwara were a family of civilian aristocrats who preferred intrigue to war and shared the disdain for the military that was prevalent among the Heian aristocracy. No society seems able to dispense with force entirely, however. Prior to the introduction of conscription and peasant armies, most fighting had been done by *uji* fighting men, that is, trained clan warriors. This class of fighters never disappeared. As less and less land was administered under the "equal field" system, raising conscript armies became less and less practical. In 792, two years before the move to Kyoto, the conscription system was abolished. The central government no longer had the means to raise armies—except as the emperor or his ministers raised fighting men in their own domains—and military power and responsibilities passed to government officials and great families in the provinces.

Since fighting involved costly equipment, such as horse and armor, and training in special techniques, such as archery and swordsmanship, it remained the profession of a rural elite established in both the political and the estate system. Some warrior leaders were originally provincial officials to whom the government had delegated military responsibilities. Others rising within the *shōen* system were entrusted with defense responsibilities on the estates. The pace of the development of local warrior organizations and their size varied according to local conditions. They were especially prominent in the eastern part of the Kantō region, still a rough frontier area, where formidable warrior leagues grew and clashed.

It was fighting men of this type who kept order in the provinces, performing police and military functions as well as fighting for various patrons as they jockeyed for power. For example, such warrior organizations fought on both sides during the rebellion led in 935 by Taira no Masakado, a fifth-generation descendant of Emperor Kammu. The practice was to keep the size of the imperial family within reasonable limits by cutting off collateral branches after a given number of generations. At that time they would be given a family name and endowed with rich official posts in the capital or the provinces where their prestige, wealth, and political connections were great assets in attracting local warrior followers. Two of the greatest warrior families had such imperial antecedents: the Taira (also called Heike) and the Minamoto (or Genji). The Masakado Rebellion was put down only with great difficulty. Concurrently, there was trouble also in the west: Fujiwara no Sumitomo (d. 941) had been sent to suppress piracy on the Inland Sea but, instead, turned outlaw himself. In the restoration of order, Minamoto no Tsunemoto (d. 961) played a leading role. Tsunemoto's son established an alliance between the Seiwa branch of the Minamoto (or Seiwa Genji) and the Fujiwara house.

In the eleventh century there was more fighting in the Kantō area, with wars from 1028 to 1031, smaller-scale fighting between 1051 and 1062, and another war from 1083 to 1087. These wars provided opportunities for building up the strength of local warrior houses and also of the Minamoto and Taira. While Minamoto's strength was based in eastern and northern Honshū, the Taira developed their power base in the Inland Sea and capital areas.

At the same time, in the second half of the eleventh century, the Fujiwara went into decline, their manipulation of marriage politics hampered by a shortage of daughters. Emperor Go-Sanjo (r. 1068–72) came to the throne because his brother's Fujiwara empress was childless. Although he was opposed by the Fujiwara regent, he enjoyed the support of another powerful Fujiwara noble, and this support insured his success.

Rule by "Cloistered Emperors"

The revival of the imperial family begun by Go-Sanjō was continued by his son Shirakawa, who became emperor in 1072. He abdicated in 1086 but continued to enjoy great power as retired emperor (In) until his death in 1129. Two more vigorous heads of the imperial line followed, Toba (r. 1107–23; In, 1129–56) and Go-Shirakawa (r. 1155–58; In, to 1192).

The role of the retired emperor (In) was not unlike that of the Fujiwara regent, except that in place of the paramountcy of the family of the emperor's mother, the paternal family now attained supremacy. The resemblance to the Fujiwara went still further, for, despite the ambivalence of Shirakawa, the general policy of the abdicated emperors was to acquire for the imperial family the same type of assets enjoyed by the Fujiwara. As a result the imperial house acquired a vast network of estates and was transformed into the largest landholder in Japan.

The political situation at this time could and did get very complicated when there was more than one retired emperor on the scene. The ambitions and machinations of the courts, the Fujiwara, and the temples (which had their own armed forces) all contributed to political instability and complicated the politics and the life of the capital. Much of the substance of power continued to shift to the provincial warrior organizations employed by both the imperial and the Fujiwara families to foster their causes.

The system came to an end under Go-Shirakawa. In 1156 military power was, for the first time, directly involved in capital political disputes; and once the warriors had been called in they could not readily be dismissed. By 1160 the Taira clan were in control of the government. Kyoto remained the political center until 1185, but the last 20 years or so do not really form part of the Heian period. Rather, they constitute an interlude that can be considered an overture to the Kamakura period. Yet, for another 700 years, until 1869, the imperial family and the Fujiwara remained in Kyoto, and the Fujiwara still provided most of the regents. Indeed, the Fujiwara family grew so large that men came to be called by the names of the branch families, and even in the twentieth century a member of one of these Fujiwara branches (Konoe) became a prime minister.

The Life of the Heian Aristrocracy

Literature is our best source for the study of Heian society, which produced some of Japan's greatest prose and poetry. Its art diaries and other literary works furnish details of the daily life of the upper classes and insights into their values and taste. Most Heian authors were court ladies, and their feminine view of life at the top is unique in the history of East Asia and perhaps the world. Japan's greatest prose work, *The Tale of Genji,* was composed by one such woman, Murasaki Shikibu (978–ca. 1016).

The literary eminence of Heian ladies itself suggests something of their social status. Obviously they had ample leisure for reading and writing; *The Tale of Genji* is twice as long as Tolstoy's *War and Peace.* Often they suffered from an excess of leisure. They became bored with long days of inactivity spent in the dimly lit interiors of their homes and welcomed the chance to exchange pleasantries and gossip with an occasional caller. If the caller was a man, he had to conduct the visit seated in front of a screen behind which the lady remained demurely hidden. Fortunately, there were numerous festivals to break up the monotony of the daily routine, and pilgrimages to temples provided further diversion.

Although there were also men who had literary inclinations and the means to pursue them, prose literature was considered the woman's domain; so much so that when Ki no Tsurayuki (869–945) composed the *Tosa Diary,* he pretended that it was written by a woman. Conversely, men continued to be educated in Chinese, which enjoyed undiminished prestige and remained the official language. This Chinese erudition constituted a male preserve from which women were excluded. For them it was not considered a respectable pastime, and those who nevertheless indulged in Chinese learning made it a point not to broadcast the fact. Nor was it proper for women to write in Chinese—instead they wrote Japanese using a mixture of Chinese characters and the *kana* syllabary, which now made its appearance. This was a system of phonetic symbols, originally derived from Chinese characters (see Figure 3.1). Each symbol represents a syllable. With this system there is no longer any need to employ Chinese characters to represent Japanese sounds, but they were retained nevertheless, since Japanese has numerous homonyms. In the modern language, the Chinese characters, used to write nouns and the stems of verbs and adjectives, float in a sea of *kana*, representing particles, endings, and certain other common words. (Foreign words, however, are today written in an alternate *kana* system.) In modern Japan everyone uses this mixed system of writing, but during the Heian period it was used by women. Excluded from writing in Chinese, they were left free to express themselves in their own native language, and in the process they composed the classic works of Japanese prose.

The world described in this literature is a small one for it concerns only a tiny fraction of the Japanese people, those at the pinnacle of society in the capital. Although there are descriptions of travel outside the capital area, the focus is very much on the capital itself. A provincial appointment, lucrative though it might be, was regarded as tantamount to exile. The provinces were viewed as an uncultured hinterland where even the governing classes were hopelessly vulgar. To these aristocratic ladies, the common people whose labor made society possible were so far removed in manners and

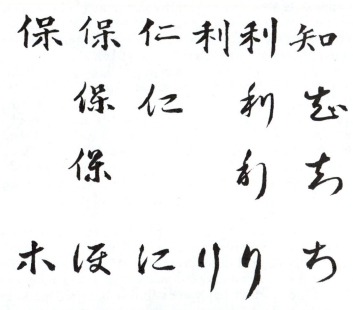

Figure 3.1   Development of *kana* syllabary. The top row contains Chinese characters and the bottom row shows the *kana* into which they eventually developed. Reading from right to left, the *kana* are pronounced *chi, ri, ri, ni, ho, ho.* All except the third and the last rows are in Hiragana, the most commonly used form; the third and last rows illustrate Katakana, the form used primarily for foreign terms and for emphasis. (Taken from G. B. Samsom, *Japan: A Short Cultural History* [Stanford: Stanford University Press, 1978], p. 238; calligraphy by Dr. Léon L. Y. Chang.)

appearance as to resemble the inhabitants of another world. At best, they seemed uncouth. At worst, they were regarded as not quite fully human, as when Sei Shōnagon encountered a group of commoners on a pilgrimage and noted in her famous *Pillow Book*, "They looked like so many basket-worms as they crowded together in their hideous clothes, leaving hardly an inch of space between themselves and me. I really felt like pushing them all over sideways."[4]

Geographically limited, constricted in social scope, the world of the Heian aristocracy was also narrow in its intellectual range. The last official Heian government mission to China was sent in 838, and when near the end of the ninth century it was proposed to send another and Sugawara no Michizane was chosen as ambassador, he successfully declined on the grounds that conditions in China were unsettled. Even after order had been restored in China with the establishment of the Song (Sung, 960–1279), relations were not resumed. The Japanese of the Heian period were steeped in the Chinese culture of the Tang and earlier but, except for some Buddhist monks, displayed a lack of concern for the China of their own time. Perhaps societies, like people, require a period of cultural digestion before they are ready for a new meal. Be that as it may, in the absence of stimuli from abroad, the Heian aristocrats also failed to respond creatively to the changes taking place at home. As we have seen, these changes were momentous, but they were also slow and did not stimulate a reexamination of the old or inspire new intellectual departures. Since the course of historical development went against the fortunes of the court aristocracy, their viewpoint became increasingly pessimistic. This pessimism found an echoing note in Heian Buddhism.

Refinement and Sensibility

What ultimately saved this small world from cultural sterility, and gave meaning to the lives of its inhabitants, was that these people developed the greatest subtlety of refinement within the range of their experience and concerns. At its best, as in the ideal of the perfect gentleman depicted by Murasaki's Genji ("the shining prince"), they sought to fuse life and art through the cultivation of human sensibilities. At its worst, their conduct smacked of effeminacy, and an aesthetic of good taste led to overrefinement.

In this world where aesthetics reigned supreme, great attention was paid to pleasing the eye. Ladies dressed in numerous robes, one over the other (twelve was standard), which they displayed at the wrist in overlapping layers, and the blending of their colors was of the utmost importance in revealing a lady's taste. Often all a man saw of a lady were her sleeves, left hanging outside her carriage or spread beyond a screen behind which she remained invisible. The men were by no means to be outdone in the care they took over their own attire. The following description is from Sei Shōnagon's *Pillow Book:*

> His resplendent, cherry-colored Court cloak was lined with material of the most delightful hue and lustre; he wore dark, grape-colored trousers, boldly splashed

with designs of wisteria branches; his crimson under-robe was so glossy that it seemed to sparkle, while underneath one could make out layer upon layer of white and light violet robes.[5]

This concern for appearance also extended to the features of the gentlemen and ladies. Both sexes used cosmetics, applying a white face powder, which in the case of the women was combined with a rosy tint. The ladies took great pride in their long, flowing, glossy hair but plucked their eyebrows and painted in a new set. Such customs are not unfamiliar to the modern world, but far more difficult for us to appreciate are the blackened teeth of the refined Heian beauty. Confined to the aristocracy during the Heian period, this practice, like so many features of Heian taste and sensibility, later spread to the lower classes of society. It became the sign of a married woman, and in the Tokugawa period was also adopted by courtesans.

Specific fashions change, but the concern for visual beauty remained a lasting legacy from the Heian period. Even today, for example, great care is taken over the appearance of food, and its impact on the eye is considered at least as important as its taste.

The emphasis on visual beauty did not mean the neglect of the other senses. Music played an important part in the lives of the Heian aristocracy, and aural and visual pleasure was often combined in courtly dances, at which Genji, of course, excelled. Nor was the sense of smell neglected. The Heian ladies and gentlemen went to great lengths to blend perfumes, and a sensitive nose was a social asset second only to a good eye and ear. Among the aesthetic party contests used to while away the time in polite society, there were even perfume blending competitions such as the one described in *The Tale of Genji*.

Ideals of Courtly Love

The ideal Heian aristocrat was as sensitive in personal relations as in matters of aesthetics: feelings should be as beautiful as dress. Nowhere was this more important than in the love affairs that gave Heian literature its dominant theme, and in this respect, too, literature often mirrored life. Marriages were arranged by and for the family in a game of marriage politics at which the Fujiwara excelled. But for a noble courtier to confine himself to one wife was the rare exception. He was much more likely to have, in addition, one or more secondary wives while conducting still other, more or less clandestine, love affairs. Nor were the ladies expected to remain true to one love for their whole lives either, although few were as amorous as Izumi Shikibu (generally considered the author of the love diary that bears her name). Nevertheless, jealousy posed a recurring problem for a lady of the Heian age who might have to bear long waits between visits from her lover. For the less fortunate and less hardy, waiting could become a torture. So unhappy was the author of *The Gossamer Diary* that her writing has been characterized by Ivan Morris as "one long wail of jealousy."[6]

The qualities most valued in a lover were quite similar regardless of sex: beauty and grace, talent and sensibility, and personal thoughtfulness. A gentleman is always considerate. The paragon, Genji, was ever gallant to one lady even though he discovered that she was very unattractive. He found himself in this predicament because Heian men often had no clear idea of the appearance of the women they were wooing, hidden as they were behind screens with only their sleeves showing. (Rare was the thoughtful consideration of a guardian like Genji who provided a lamp of fireflies to shed some illumination for the benefit of his ward's suitor.) Men fell in love with a woman's sense of beauty, her poetic talents, and her calligraphy. As in China, the latter was all-important, since it was thought to reveal a person's character. The Heian version of love at first sight was a gentleman falling hopelessly in love after catching a glimpse of a few beautifully drawn lines.

At every stage of a love affair, and in other social relationships too for that matter, the aesthetics of writing were stressed. At least as important as the literary merits of the poems that were exchanged on all occasions were such matters as the color and texture of the paper, the way it was folded, and the selection of a twig on which to tie the note. Most critical and most eagerly awaited of these poetic missives were the "morning after letters" sent by a lover immediately upon returning home from a night of love, from which he had torn himself away just before dawn with a proper show of reluctance. The first such letter was particularly important as it would provide a good indication of the seriousness and probable duration of the relationship.

In this world of sensitive people, men and women were expected to respond as readily to sadness as to joy. Both sexes cried freely and frequently, and neither felt any hesitation about expressing self-pity. Tears were a sign of depth of feeling and of a genuine awareness of the ephemeral nature of beauty, the transient nature of all that is good and beautiful. Sentiments such as these were expressed in a special vocabulary, using words so rich in their associations as to defy translation, words which became part of the subtle and shifting language of Japanese aesthetics.

Religion: Tendai

When Emperor Kammu turned his back on Nara and moved his capital to Heian-kyō in 794, he crippled the political power of the old sects, but Buddhism continued to grow and flourish. It also continued to enjoy imperial patronage. Kammu himself supported the priest Saichō (767–822) who, dissatisfied with the worldliness of the Nara priesthood, had founded a small temple in 788 on Mt. Hiei northeast of Kyoto. To gain for his temple the kind of prestige enjoyed by the Nara temples, Chinese sanction was a must, so in 804 Saichō traveled to China, the source of Japanese Buddhism. But after his return and throughout his life, his relationship with the Japanese court remained close. His writings show a reverence for the emperor and a love of country not found among the important monks of the Nara period, many of whom were Koreans or, like Saichō's own ancestors, Chinese.

Saichō originally moved to Mt. Hiei because he wanted to escape the corrupt atmosphere of Nara and not because he disagreed with the teachings of Nara Buddhism. However, in China he studied the doctrines of the Tendai (Tiantai, T'ien-t'ai) school which took its name from a mountain range in China. Its founder, Zhiyi (Chih-i, 538–97) combined the scholarly tradition of south China with northern pietism and meditation. The complete truth was contained in the Lotus Sutra, believed to have been preached by the Buddha to 12,000 arhats (saints), 6,000 nuns, 8,000 Bodhisattvas, and 60,000 gods. The great god Brahma attended, accompanied by 12,000 dragons, and there were hundreds of thousands of other supernatural beings. As he talked, a ray of light emanated from the Buddha's forehead revealing 18,000 worlds in each of which a Buddha is preaching. This text was enormously influential in East Asia, and its imagery inspired many artistic representations.

Tiantai doctrine centered on a tripartite truth: (1) the truth that all phenomena are empty, products of causation without a nature of their own; (2) the truth that they do, however, exist temporarily; (3) the truth that encompasses but transcends emptiness and temporariness. These three truths all involve and require each other—throughout Tiantai the whole and the parts are one. A rich but unified cosmology is built on this basis: temporariness consists of ten realms. Since each of these includes the other, a total of 1,000 results. Each of these in turn has three aspects—that of living beings, of aggregates, and of space. The result is 3,000 worlds interwoven so that all are present in each. Since, therefore, truth is immanent in everything, it follows that all beings contain the Buddha nature and can be saved. One eighth-century patriarch taught that this includes inanimate things, down to the tiniest grain of dust.

On his return from China Saichō established this sect in Japan, thereby removing himself doctrinally as well as geographically from the Nara temples. The latter resented him bitterly, and when Emperor Kammu died they fought back with some temporary success, as when they disputed the new sect's right to ordain priests, a right not granted to the Tendai temple on Mt. Hiei until 827, by which time Saichō was dead.

The doctrinal content of Saichō's Tendai, like that of its Chinese parent, was grounded in the Lotus Sutra. In contrast to the proponents of some of the older sects, Saichō preached the universal possibility of enlightenment. Everyone could realize his Buddha nature through a life of true religious devotion. On Mt. Hiei, Saichō insisted on strict monastic regimen.

Saichō was more skilled as an organizer than as a theoretician. He built well; and eventually his little temple grew to some 3,000 buildings. It flourished on Mt. Hiei until it was destroyed in the sixteenth century for political reasons. In keeping with the syncretic nature of Tiantai, the Buddhism propagated on Mt. Hiei was broad and accommodating; so much so that it remained the source of new developments in Japanese Buddhism even after the temple community had departed from the earnest religiosity of its founder.

After Saichō's death, a line of abbots succeeded him, among them Ennin, the famous traveler to China, whose diary is a major source of information about the Tang. Then late in the ninth century there developed a split between the followers of Ennin and those of his successor. This bitter rivalry, fueled as much by jealousy as by doctrinal differences, led to the introduction of force into religious politics and the appearance of bullies (akusō—"vicious monks") who engaged in brawls and combat. The use of violence increased, and by the eleventh century leading Shinto shrines as well as the Tendai temples maintained large standing armies. Particularly troublesome was the monastery of Mt. Hiei, which kept several thousand troops. They repeatedly descended on the capital, terrorizing its inhabitants, to demand ecclesiastical positions, titles, and land rights. Thus the temple on Mt. Hiei, founded and supported as an early Heian solution to problems of temple intervention in politics in Nara, became in the late Heian period itself a major source of widespread distress.

Esoteric Buddhism: Shingon

Contemporary with Saichō was Kūkai (774–835), founder of the other major sect of Heian Buddhism, Shingon. He too studied in China and benefited from imperial patronage, although in his case it came not from Emperor Kammu but from that emperor's successors. Like Saichō he established his main monastery on a mountain, choosing Mt. Kōya on the Kii Peninsula, far removed from the capital. When Kūkai returned from China, Saichō befriended him and showed genuine interest in the doctrines Kūkai brought back with him, but largely through Kūkai's doing, the cordial relations did not last. A year after Saichō's death, Kūkai moved closer to the center of Heian life when he was appointed abbot of Tōji, the great temple at the main (southern) gateway to the capital.

In contrast to Tendai, which flourished in China as it did in Japan, the type of Buddhism introduced by Kūkai was never prominent in China and failed to survive the mid-Tang persecution of Buddhism. Shingon (mantra, in the original Sanskrit, zhenyan, chen-yen in Chinese) literally means "True Word," thus conveying the importance of mystic verbal formulae in this sect and its insistence on a tradition of oral transmission of secret teachings from master to disciple. Since only the initiate were privy to the full truth, it is known as Esoteric Buddhism. Transmitted in addition to the sacred teachings and verbal utterances were complicated ritual observances involving the mudra (hand positions of the Buddha but also used by Shingon priests) and the use of ritual instruments.

Central to Shingon teachings and observances is Dainichi (Vairocana), the cosmic Buddha whose absolute truth is all encompassing and true everywhere and forever. In his *Ten Stages of Religious Consciousness*, Kūkai ranked the various levels of spiritual life. At the lowest level he ranked animal life, totally lacking in spiritual dimension. Confucianism he ranked as only the second step upwards, with Daoism third. Then came various sects of Hinayana and Mahayana Buddhism, including Tendai (eighth) and Kegon (ninth). At the top he placed Shingon. In this way Shingon incorporated and found a place for other schools of Buddhism, although the Tendai monks were hardly pleased with their place in the Shingon hierarchy. No provision was made in this schema for Shinto, but the name Dainichi (Great Sun) invited identification with the Sun Goddess, and Shingon also proved hospitable to Shinto deities through its concept of duality. This concept held that a single truth manifests itself under two aspects, the nomenal and the phenomenal, so in theory Dainichi and the Sun Goddess could be considered as two forms of one identical truth.

The teachings of Esoteric Buddhism were complex and difficult to understand; yet it was enormously popular during the Heian period, even overshadowing Tendai until Ennin introduced esoteric practices into Tendai itself. One reason for the appeal of Shingon was the mystery of its rites. From the beginning, people in Japan had been drawn to Buddhism at least in part by magical elements connected with Buddhist observances, for example, incantations, divination, exorcism, and the medicinal use of herbs. Now they were impressed by the mysterious elements in the secret rituals performed in the interior of Shingon temples, hidden from all but the most deeply initiated of the priests. The people of Heian Japan, with their taste for pageantry, were also attracted by the richness of the colorful Shingon rites.

Much of the prosperity of Shingon can be attributed to the genius of Kūkai (also known by his posthumous name Kōbō Daishi, Great Teacher Kōbō). He was an exceptional man, famed for his brilliance and learning, his artistic talents and, of course, his calligraphy. He is credited with the invention of the kana syllabary, and it is just possible that his exposure to a phonetic system of writing (he studied Sanskrit in China) helped influence the development of kana. Kūkai is also credited with the introduction of tea to Japan and the building of bridges. A cluster of miraculous stories grew up around his name. To this day, he lies in his grave on Mt. Kōya awaiting the coming of Maitreya (see Figure 3.2).

One of Kūkai's most lasting contributions to Shingon, and a major source of its appeal, was his emphasis on the arts. A gifted artist himself, he saw art as the ideal vehicle for transmitting religious truth. He once wrote that the truth cannot be conveyed in writing—only in art—reflecting the Heian tendency to equate truth and beauty. Unlike Tendai, Shingon did not give birth to many new schools of Buddhist thought, but it did leave a rich artistic heritage.

No society is composed entirely of the devout—certainly not that of Heian Japan! The degree of piety felt by those who attended religious observances ranged widely. Sei Shōnagon once remarked that a priest should be handsome, so that the audience will have no inducement to divert their eyes and thoughts. Frequently, then as now, a visit to a temple was primarily a pleasure trip. On the other hand, in the daily lives of all classes, religion and magic were inextricably interwoven with elements of Buddhism, Shinto, yin-yang theory, geomancy, and popular beliefs of all kinds. (Geomancy, fengshui in Chinese, is the Chinese pseudoscience for selecting sites for graves, buildings, or cities according to the topographical configuration of yin and yang.) The inhabitants of the capital were forever purifying

Figure 3.2   Mt. Kōya, Wakayama.

themselves, superstitiously avoided walking in certain directions on certain days, and when ill sought the services of a priest skilled in exorcism. The monastery on Mt. Hiei provides a good example of this fusion of beliefs. It was established northeast of the capital to guard the city against the evils that, according to Chinese beliefs, emanate from that direction. And before he built this Buddhist temple, Saichō was careful to pay his respect to the local Shinto deity. "Thus, by the friendly collaboration of Indian Buddhism, indigenous Shinto, and Chinese geomancy, the protection of the city was assured."[7]

Pietism

In the Later Heian period, revulsion at the worldly (and military) success of the established temples, and hope of rescuing a world falling into increasing disorder, stimulated a pietistic movement. This movement was led by the priests Kūya (903–72) and Genshin (942–1017) and centered around Amida (Amitābha, the Buddha of the Infinite Light, who presides over the Western Paradise). So disrupted was Japanese society in the tenth century that many people were convinced they were about to enter the last of the three Buddhist ages *(mappō)*, the degenerate age of the decline of the Buddha's law. The pietists taught that only faith in Amida could provide salvation in such dire times, and a famous statue of Kūya shows him with little Amidas issuing from his mouth (see Figure 4.4). In a spirit of evangelical zeal, he traveled through the countryside and even to the land of the Ainu bringing people his message of Buddhist salvation and leading them in dancing and chanting the name of Amida.

It is characteristic of the Heian period that Genshin propagated his teachings not only in writing but also in art. His work contains terrifying representations of hell. He is best known for a painting not actually his that depicts a *raigō*, that is, a descent by Amida mercifully coming down to a man's deathbed to gather his soul to paradise. One custom among the devout was for a dying man to hold on to a string attached to the figure of Amida in such a painting. For example, when Michinaga, the strong-minded Fujiwara who was de facto ruler of Japan, lay dying, he repeated the *nembutsu* (invocation to Amida) while holding on to such a cord, while a chorus of monks chanted the Lotus Sutra. This practice became as widespread as the *raigō* themselves.

Another deity worthy of mention is Jizō, who began as the bodhisattva who saved souls in hell but became popular as the embodiment of Amida's compassion. Eventually he merged with other gods, until in the course of time he came to be regarded as the protector of children who had died young. He still graces many a roadside shrine in Japan today.

Amidism continued to attract an increasing following and devoted apostles such as Ryōnin (1072–1132), a Tendai monk who placed additional emphasis on the *nembutsu*. As the Heian period neared its end, the veneration of Amida and the use of the *nembutsu* spread to all temples, but eventually the new religious force could no longer be contained in the established sects despite their syncretic tendencies. The break came when Hōnen (1133–1212) established Pure Land Buddhism as an independent sect in the Kamakura era.

Literature

> The poetry of Japan has its roots in the human heart and flourishes in the countless leaves of words. Because human beings possess interests of so many kinds, it is in poetry that they give expression to the meditations of their hearts in terms of sights appearing before their eyes and the sounds coming to their ears. Hearing the warbler sing among the blossoms and the frog in his fresh waters—is there any living being not given to song? It is poetry which, without exertion, moves heaven and earth, stirs the feelings of gods and spirits invisible to the eye, softens the relations between men and women, calms the hearts of fierce warriors.[8]

These famous lines are from the introduction to the *Kokinshū* (*Collection of Ancient and Modern Times*), an imperial anthology of poetry completed around 905, by Ki no Tsurayuki. They express the classic Japanese view of poetry. It is the spontaneous creation of the human heart giving rise to "countless leaves of words." It is a message from the heart to the heart: genuine feelings expressed in the right words. These words were purely Japanese, for although Heian poets also composed Chinese verse, Chinese loan-words were meticulously excluded from poetry written in the Japanese language. The greatest of these short poems are enriched by the resonance of their verbal music, suggestive overtones arising from a richness of shared associations, and by double meanings and plays on words. The result is a poetry which, even more than usual, defies translation.

Among the uses of poetry mentioned by Tsurayuki is that it "softens the relations between men and women." It should come as no surprise then that much of Japanese poetry was love poetry, and that court ladies were among its most outstanding practitioners. Much of this poetry is subtle and delicate, but it can also be strongly passionate. It is full of tears, but does not lack fire:

> On such a night like this
> When no moon lights your way to me,
> I wake my passion blazing,
> My breast a fire raging, exploding flame
> While within me my heart chars.[9]

The author of this poem was a court lady, Ono no Komachi (fl. ca. 850), but it was characteristic for Japanese poets of both sexes to think that love could best be understood from the woman's point of view.

One of the greatest male poets of the period was the great lover Ariwara no Narihira (823–880). Many of his poems are contained in *The Tales of Ise*, one of Japan's literary classics. This work consists of prose explanations of the occasions which gave rise to each verse, followed by that verse. For example:

Long ago a young man had an affair with a woman who was well experienced in love. Was he not perhaps a bit uneasy?

> If it is not me
> take care not to loosen your sash!
> Oh, morning glory,
> even though you are a flower
> that falls before the evening.

In reply:

> By the two of us
> was this sash tied at parting—
> One of us alone
> will not I think unloose it
> till we two are face to face[10]

Heian literature laid great stress on blending prose and poetry, life and art. Consequently, the art diary—a prose form to which poetry was central—was the favorite literary genre in this period. Some diaries, like Tsurayuki's *Tosa Diary*, were cast into the form of travel accounts while others dealt with life at court, but all contained large numbers of poems. Their attention to feeling and sensibility were shaped, in form and substance, by the requirements of art. Art as much as life determined their content; and in Heian diaries, as well as in Heian fiction, the distinction between art and life, fact and fiction, was not clearly delineated. Just as the diaries were shaped by art, it was demanded of novels that they remain true to life. The importance of the diary as a literary form and the close relationship between the diary and the novel may be a uniquely Japanese literary phenomenon, but it is not unique to the Heian period: like so many other aspects of Heian culture, it survived even into the twentieth century, helping to account for the popularity of autobiography thinly disguised as fiction, known as the "I novel."

The greatest Japanese novel is, of course, *The Tale of Genji* (ca. 1010) by Murasaki Shikibu. Its influence on Japanese culture was enormous and varied. References to *Genji* echo throughout Japanese literary history down to the present. To make this classic accessible to a modern audience it has been translated into modern Japanese by such outstanding novelists as Tanizaki Junichiro (1886–1965) and Enchi Fumiko (1905–1986). It has also provided subject matter for the arts (see Figure 3.7) and left its mark on the writing of history. One such history is *The Tale of Glory (Eiga monogatari)*, an eleventh century account focusing on the Fujiwara, particularly Michinaga. (The word *"monogatari"* appears alike in novels, histories, and compilations of stories.)

One reason for *The Tale of Genji's* enduring fascination and appeal is its psychological subtlety. It is, among other things, the world's first psychological novel, for Lady Murasaki was as interested in the thoughts and feelings of her characters as in their tastes and talents. She has been praised for her narrative skills, for creating "an art of life without lapsing into mere aestheticism" and for her moral intelligence.[11] Motoori Norinaga (1730–1801), the novel's greatest traditional interpreter, admired it above all for its expression of *mono-no-aware,* a word frequently used by Lady Murasaki for "that power inherent in things to make us respond not intellectually but with an involuntary gasp of emotion."[12] It could refer to joyous as well as sad experiences, but eventually the implication of melancholy predominated. It involves a realization of the ephemeral quality of beauty, of all that is best in life, indeed, of life itself. Clearly in this concept there are resonances of Buddhist teaching, which views life as an illusion, insubstantial as a dream. To the Japanese, it was a beautiful but fleeting dream, and sadness was itself a necessary dimension of beauty.

Of the other terms used in, and applied to, Heian literature, the word *"miyabi"* is particularly appropriate. Translatable as "elegance," "refinement," or "courtliness," it demanded the rejection of anything that was gross or vulgar and the polishing of manners, diction, and feelings to eliminate all roughness and crudity so as to achieve the highest grace. *Aware* and *miyabi* complement each other. In particular they share that sensitivity to beauty that was the hallmark of the Heian era and has been the hallmark of Japanese culture ever since.

The Visual Arts

In art also imported themes and forms were domesticated during the Heian period and were turned into something definitely Japanese. The period is readily divided into two parts for purposes of art history. "Early Heian," also

sometimes called the Kōnin or Jōgan period, designates roughly the first
century in Kyoto (794–897).

In architecture the reassertion of Japanese taste took a variety of forms. It
is particularly notable in the layout of the new temples, for when Saichō and
Kūkai turned from the Nara Plain to build their monasteries in the mountains, they abandoned the symmetrical temple plans that had been used
around Nara. Down on the plain, architecture could afford to ignore the
terrain; but in the mountains, temple styles and layouts had to accommodate
themselves to the physical features of the site. On Mount Hiei and elsewhere, the natural setting, rock outcroppings, and trees became integral
parts of the temple, as had long been the case with Shinto shrines. But it is
interesting to note that even on Mount Kōya, where there was enough space
to build a Nara-style temple complex, the traditional plans were abandoned.
Changes were also made in building materials and decoration.

During the Nara period the main buildings had been placed on stone
platforms; the wood was painted; and the roofs were made of tile. In the Nara
temples, only minor buildings had had their wood left unpainted and had
been fitted with roofs of thatch or bark shingles. Now, these techniques were
also used for the main halls. An excellent site at which to observe the resulting aesthetic is Murōji, set in the mountains some 40 miles from Nara,
among magnificent straight, cedarlike trees (cryptomeria) such as are also

Figure 3.3   Pagoda of
Murōji, Nara Prefecture.

found on Mt. Kōya and at other locations. Not only in material but also in the size of its buildings, Murōji is more modest than the Nara temples. Its pagoda (see Figure 3.3) is only half the size of that at the Hōryūji but makes up in charm and grace what it lacks in grandeur.

In the Early Heian period, wood replaced clay, bronze, dry lacquer, and stone as the material of choice for sculpture. Statues, and sometimes their pedestals as well, were carved out of a single block of wood. Frequently the finished sculpture was painted or lacquered, but this was never allowed to obscure the beauty of the wood grain, for that would have offended the artist's sense of respect for his material.

Although some statues of Shinto deities survive from this period, most Early Heian statuary concerned Buddhist themes. As a result, the art form reflects the demands of the new forms of that religion, particularly Esoteric Buddhism. Usually the statues are formal and symmetrical. The flesh is full and firm. The faces are cast in a serious mien, creating an aura of mystery without the hint of a smile or any indication of friendliness. A famous example of Early Heian art is the figure of Sakyamuni (the historic Buddha) at Murōji (see Figure 3.4). It is among other things, a fine example of "wave" drapery, so called because its lines flow like the sea. It has been suggested that the curious swirls at the bottom may be the result of copying in wood an original calligraphic drawing.

The Shingon sect demanded unusual iconographic exactitude in its art, just as it did in its rites. The result was an unwholesome tendency toward

Figure 3.4   Sakyamuni. Ninth century, 129.6 cm high. Murōji, Nara Prefecture.

sterile formalism, both in reciting the mantras and in religious art. This was especially true of Shingon mandalas, which became very complex as artists tried to represent the cosmos graphically, including all the various deities that were emanations of Dainichi. Some altars, for example, at Tōji in Kyōto, were arranged in mandala fashion, but more usual were painted mandalas, such as that shown in Figure 3.5. This is a depiction of the Womb Mandala, representing the world of phenomena. The red lotus at the center symbolizes the heart of the universe. Dainichi is seated on the seedpod of the lotus. Other Buddhas occupy the petals. Altogether there are 407 deities in the Womb Mandala. Its counterpart, the Diamond Mandala, centers on a white lotus and represents the world containing 1314 gods.

A frequent subject of painting and sculpture is Fudō, the Immovable, a ferocious deity bent on annihilating evil. In the Red Fudō at Mt. Kōya (see Figure 3.6), the red of the figure and the flames behind him dominate the color scheme and help to create a terrifying atmosphere. In his hand he holds a sword the handle of which is a thunderbolt (*vajra*), a symbol originating in India as the weapon of the god Indra, and in Esoteric Buddhism thought to cut through ignorance just as lightning pierces the clouds. A dragon coiled around the blade of the sword adds to the threat. The proportions of the

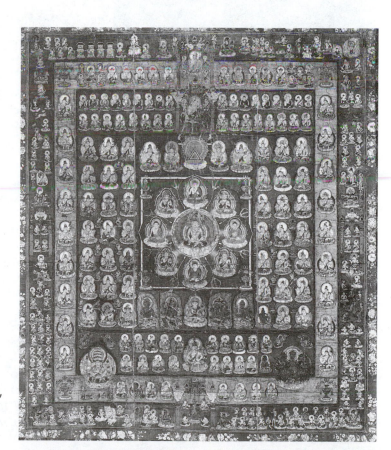

Figure 3.5   *Womb Mandala.* Painting on silk, ninth century. Tōji, Kyoto.

Figure 3.6 *Red Fudō.* Color on silk, Early Heian, 130.8 cm. Myōin, Mt. Kōya, Wakayama.

figures and the manner in which the picture fills the space produce a feeling of massiveness characteristic of the art of this age.

Early Heian art at its best achieved a certain majesty, but it has a forbidding quality about it that stands in striking contrast to the sweetness of Late Heian art. Shingon continued to produce art after the ninth century, but the period really belonged to Amida—and to the Fujiwara. Michinaga had a great temple built in the capital reproducing Amida's paradise, containing "columns with bases of ivory, roof ridges of red gold, gilded doors, platforms of crystal."[13] This temple and a similar one built by Emperor Shirakawa are no longer extant. They have to be reconstructed from texts to give us some idea of what Heian Kyoto looked like.

The historical and artistic origins of such temples go back to Chinese images of the Western Paradise and to its closest terrestrial approximation, the Tang palace garden systematically laid out with its lake and bridges. Similarly, a major feature of the Heian mansion *(shinden)* was a garden with one or two artificial hills, carefully placed trees and bamboo, and a pond in which a tiny island was reached by a bridge. A small stream fed the pond and was used to float wine cups at banquets in the Chinese manner. To the north of the garden were the living quarters: rectangular buildings joined by roofed corridors. Like all Japanese-style buildings, these structures were raised a few feet off the ground, and usually a little stream ran under a part of the mansion. Inside, the floors were of polished wood. Flexibility was provided by sliding paper screens, and shutters could be moved to combine small rooms into a larger one. Several kinds of screens (see Figure 3.7) provided some privacy. Sparsely furnished, the Heian *shinden* reflected the Japanese appreciation for aesthetic restraint.

Painting

Sliding doors in the Heian *shinden* were frequently decorated with landscapes, such as the picture within a picture in Figure 3.7. In painting, as in the other arts, after serving a period of apprenticeship to continental masters, the Japanese went their own way. Japanese-style paintings *(Yamato-e)* depicted native, not Chinese, subjects, including views of the Japanese landscape. The greatest of such paintings still extant illustrate *The Tale of Genji*. In the Genji Scroll, unlike later narrative scrolls, the individual scenes are separated by passages of text. The scene reproduced in Figure 3.7 shows a lady (upper left) looking at pictures while one of her attendants

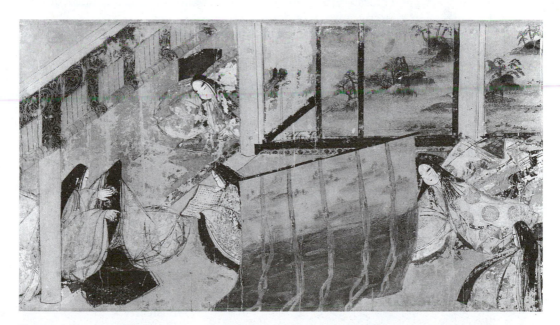

Figure 3.7   *Genji Monogatari*, section of hand-scroll. Color on paper, twelfth century, 21.6 cm high. Tokugawa Museum, Nagoya.

Figure 3.8 *Animal Caricatures* (Chōjū Giga), section of hand-scroll. Attributed to Kakuyū (Toba Sōjō). Late twelfth century, 30.5 cm high. Kozanji, Kyoto.

reads aloud the story they illustrate. At the lower left, another lady is having her hair combed. In the foreground is a screen such as was used by a lady when receiving a gentleman caller. In this and similar paintings, the roofs are removed to afford a view from above into the rooms. The treatment of human features is conventionalized with "straight lines for eyes and hooks for noses." The colors were applied quite thickly to produce a richly decorative effect in keeping with aristocratic taste.

Late in the Heian period there also appeared scrolls *(emaki)* in which no text interrupted the flow of pictorial narrative. Some represent Buddhist

Figure 3.9   Cosmetic box. Lacquered wood, Late Heian, 22.5 × 30.5 cm, h. 13 cm. Hōryūji, Nara Prefecture.

hells, but others display a gift for comic caricature. Particularly well known are the animal scrolls attributed to Kakuyū (Sōjō, 1053–1140) but probably completed near the end of the twelfth century. Here frog-priests and rabbit-nobles gambol and disport themselves. In Figure 3.8, a monkey is worshipping not a Buddha but a frog.

The minor arts also illustrate the taste of the Heian aristocrats. See, for example, the cosmetic box shown in Figure 3.9. It is decorated with cart wheels, made of mother-of-pearl and gold, half immersed in water. The asymmetry of the design and the unifying flow and rhythm, here supplied by the water, are characteristic of the Japanese achievements in decoration.

The Phoenix Pavilion

Sometimes a single site offers a summary of a whole era; for Late Heian art this is true of the Phoenix Pavilion (Byōdōin) (see Figure 3.10). It is located in Uji, a locale some ten miles from Kyoto that figures prominently in *The Tale of Genji*. The building is associated with the Fujiwaras: it was built by Michinaga's son. And it was built for Amida who occupied the center of a *raigō* in sculpture. Other versions of the *raigō*, painted on the doors and inner walls, show Amida and his entourage descending onto a purely Japanese landscape. Mother-of-pearl insets in the main dais and in some of the columns contribute to the overall richness of effect.

Figure 3.10   Byōdōin (Phoenix Pavilion). Uji. Kyoto Prefecture.

Amida himself is the work of the sculptor Jōchō. He is fashioned in the joined-wood technique, which affords greater freedom of expression than the early Heian process of carving from a single piece of wood. It also allows for a greater and more varied exploitation of the grain. The halo, alive with angels, clouds, and flames, contrasts with the calm of Amida himself. As Robert Paine so eloquently expressed it, "the tranquility of the Absolute is made to harmonize with the Buddha's sympathy for the finite."[14]

The design of the buildings suggests a bird coming in for a landing or ready for flight. Two bronze phoenixes grace its highest roof. It may be considered a mansion for the Buddha himself. And to assure that Amida, too, will enjoy the beauty of the setting and the lovely sight of his hall reflected in the pond, the architect has thoughtfully provided an opening so that he can look out. Here is another example of the unity of building and site that was such a key feature of Heian architecture and which suggests the acceptance of man and nature as one.

NOTES

1. Elizabeth Sato, "The Early Development of the Shōen," in John W. Hall and Jeffrey P. Mass, *Medieval Japan: Essays in Institutional History* (New Haven: Yale Univ. Press, 1974), p. 105.

2. G. Cameron Hurst, Jr., "The Structure of the Heian Court," in Hall and Mass, *Medieval Japan*, p. 52.

3. Sato, "The Early Development of the Shōen," p. 105.

4. Ivan Morris, *The Pillow Book of Sei Shōnagon* (New York: Columbia Univ. Press, 1967), p. 258.

5. Ibid., p. 76.

6. Ivan Morris, *The World of the Shining Prince* (New York: Alfred A. Knopf, 1964), p. 244.

7. Sir George Sansom, *A History of Japan to 1334* (Stanford: Stanford Univ. Press, 1958), p. 118.

8. Earl Miner, *An Introduction to Japanese Court Poetry* (Stanford: Stanford Univ. Press, 1968), p. 18.

9. Ibid., p. 82.

10. H. Jay Harris, trans., *The Tales of Ise* (Rutland, Vt. and Tokyo: Charles E. Tuttle, 1972), p. 76.

11. Earl Miner, Hiroko Odagiri, and Robert E. Morrell, *The Princeton Companion to Classical Japanese Literature* (Princeton: Princeton Univ. Press, 1985), p. 37.

12. David Pollack, *The Fracture of Meaning: Japan's Synthesis of China from the Eighth through the Eighteenth Centuries* (Princeton: Princeton Univ. Press, 1986), p. 44.

13. Robert Treat Paine and Alexander Soper, *The Art and Architecture of Japan* (Baltimore: Penguin Books, 1955), p. 212.

14. Ibid., p. 45.

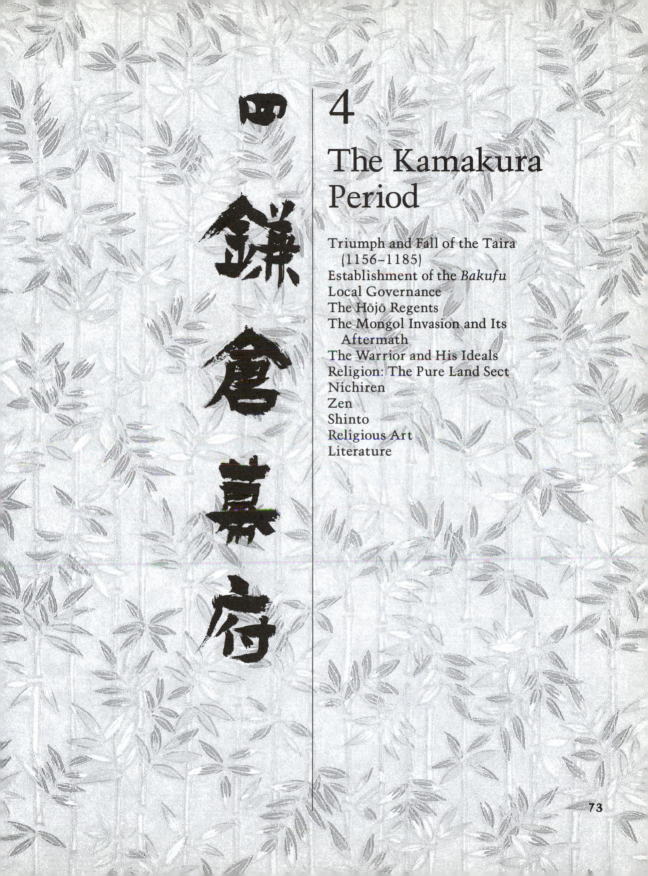

四鎌倉幕府

4

The Kamakura Period

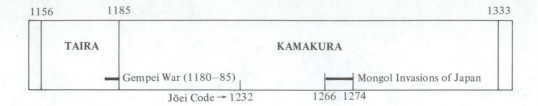

TAIRA   KAMAKURA

Gempei War (1180–85)

Mongol Invasions of Japan

Jōei Code → 1232   1266 1274

T he ascent of the Japanese warrior was a slow process that began well
before the Kamakura period and his dominance remained incomplete.
Although the period gets its name from the seat of warrior power at Kamakura in Eastern Japan (Kantō), it was a time of shared power. The sanctity
of the throne as the ultimate source of authority remained unchallenged.
Furthermore, the leaders of both the Minamoto and Taira groupings were
not just commanders of warriors pure and simple, but, to quote Jeffrey Mass,
"bridging figures—military nobles in the truest sense—between the great
central aristocrats, who were their patrons, and the great provincial warriors, who were their followers." This helps to explain the slow development
of warrior power and "the incompleteness of the warrior revolution."[1]

Rivalries among the provincial fighting men overshadowed any potential
ties of common class interests or feelings of solidarity. The same was true of
the civilian court. The political intrigues and fighting that marked this
harsh transitional period pitted not only warriors and aristocrats against
each other but also warriors against warriors, court nobles against court
nobles, and even fathers against sons, in a complicated and treacherous
struggle for power.

Triumph and Fall of the Taira (1156–1185)

In 1156 open conflict broke out between the cloistered (retired) emperor and
the reigning emperor, and military men were called in on both sides. On one
side, supporting the cloistered emperor, was a force led by Minamoto no
Tameyoshi (1096–1156); on the other side, the emperor, Go-Shirakawa, had
the backing of a coalition led by Taira no Kiyomori (1118–81), which also
included among its leaders Tameyoshi's own son, Yoshitomo (1123–60).
Military victory in what is known as the Hōgen Conflict went to Kiyomori's
coalition, but the real losers were the court and the old civil nobility.

The outcome left Kiyomori in a position of great power, but the victorious
coalition was soon dissolved, and further fighting ensued in the Heiji War
(1159–60). Once again Kiyomori won, this time defeating his former ally
Yoshitomo. These Hōgen and Heiji conflicts were brief and localized, but
extremely bitter. They were followed by manhunts and executions, for warriors did not share the civilian aristocrats' qualms about taking life. Gone

were the days when the usual penalty for being on the wrong side politically was exile.

These military victories made Kiyomori the de facto ruler. The basis of his power was new, but he used it in the old way, dominating the court and government machinery in the capital and marrying his daughters into the imperial line and also to Fujiwara regents. And in 1180 he placed his grandson on the throne. In his personal deportment, too, he conformed to the standards of taste set by the court. But to the grand Kyoto aristocrats, he remained an arrogant provincial parvenu, worthy only of contempt. An attempt to exert greater control over the court by transferring it to a site near modern Kobe failed. More successful was Kiyomori's handling of the troublesome temple armies. He attacked and burned two of the worst offenders, both in Nara: the great Tōdaiji, and Kōfukuji, the prime temple of the Fujiwara family.

Conditions in the capital were unusually harsh during these years. Storms, earthquakes, and disease afflicted the city, which, as always, was also very susceptible to the ravages of fire. A major conflagration destroyed a third of the city in 1177; in one two-month period after the fire over 40,000 corpses were found in the streets of the capital.

Kiyomori's most serious problem was that in ruling through the old institutions, his regime shared their weaknesses. He could no more exercise real control over the provinces, where the sources of actual power now lay, than could the cloistered emperor. Led by Yoshitomo's son Yoritomo (1147–99), the Minamoto took advantage of this situation to rebuild their power. With the support of many eastern Taira as well as Minamoto families, Yoritomo initiated the Gempei War (1180–85), which culminated in the permanent defeat of the Taira. Contributing to this outcome was the brilliant generalship of Yoshitsune (1159–89), Yoritomo's younger brother, who defeated the Taira at sea as well as on land. Later Yoshitsune himself incurred the suspicion of his powerful brother, who, in the end, turned his armed might against him and brought about his death.

The extent of the fighting, the style of combat that placed a premium on personal valor, the contrast between the Taira (who had adopted many of the ways of Kyoto) and the rougher Eastern warriors, and the impact of the war on subsequent developments have assured the war a lasting place in the Japanese imagination and in literature. It generated one major literary work, The Tale of the Heike (Heike monogatari), and a host of minor romances, including many which embellished the tale of Yoshitsune and transformed it into a heroic legend.

Establishment of the *Bakufu*

Yoritomo was not himself a great general, but he was a good judge of men, a consummate politician, and an effective organizer. Carefully he consolidated his position in the East. With his headquarters in the small fishing village of Kamakura, he built a secure base for warrior power (see Figure 4.1). There he established his *bakufu*, literally "tent government," a term

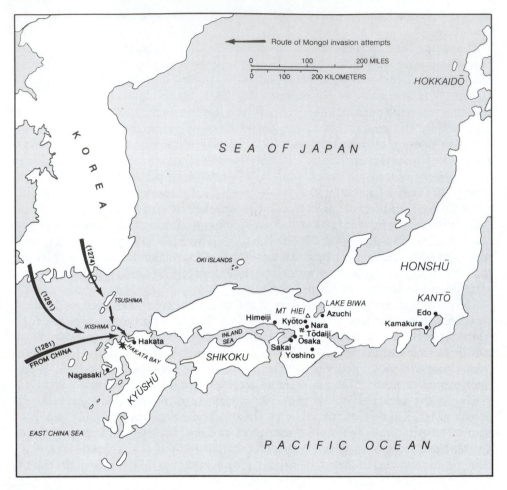

Figure 4.1   Japan, 1200–1600.

which evokes the military origins of his power. Legitimization for the new order came from the emperor, who in 1192 "appointed" Yoritomo shogun, or to use the full term, "Seii Taishōgun ("Barbarian Suppressing General"). Under the theoretical sovereignty of the emperor, the shogun's government exercised substantial "delegated" power. This was the beginning of an institution (the shogunate) that lasted until 1868.

At the heart of Yoritomo's power in Eastern Japan were ties of vassalage, aptly defined by Peter Duus as "a personal bond of loyalty and obedience by which a warrior promised service to a lord or chieftain in return for military protection, security, and assistance."[2] The ties of vassalage were more inclusive and expandable than the old kinship bonds, which, however, did not disappear. Vassalage was contractual in the sense that there was at least a tacit understanding of mutual obligations, but these were never spelled out or incorporated in legal documents. Nor were there legal mechanisms for altering or dissolving the arrangement. Ideally it called for deep personal devotion of vassal to lord rather than the more abstract loyalty demanded in an impersonal bureaucratic state; but in practice, especially in turbulent and unsettled times, much depended on the individuals involved.

From his vassals (gokenin, "honorable housemen") Yoritomo demanded and expected absolute loyalty. Such loyalty was granted him partly as a result of the confidence he inspired in his men, some of whose families had served the Minamoto for generations. Others, particularly in Western Japan, cast their lot with Yoritomo only after they had been impressed with his visible accomplishments. Calculations of military and political advantage on the part of the lesser lords played a role in augmenting Yoritomo's strength, which after the defeat of the Taira, surpassed that of any possible rival, military or civil. Economic inducements also provided powerful motivation. Those who served him could expect confirmation of land rights (shiki) they already held; and they could hope for further rewards in the form of rights over land confiscated from the enemies of the Minamoto. Economic self-interest reinforced the bonds of personal vassalage in Japan just as in feudal Europe; it was the cement that ensured the cohesiveness of the system.

There are certain striking resemblances between Kamakura Japan and feudal Europe. Both featured rule by a military aristocracy that held predominant local power, a system of vassalage, and land as a source of wealth. However, the Kamakura system functioned in uneasy tandem with the political and economic system centered on Kyoto. Yoritomo had neither the power nor the intent to eliminate the old order but used it to his own advantage in consolidating his power. His vassals received land rights, not land, and at least until the early thirteenth century the old Kyoto nobility and religious establishments retained much of their political influence and wealth.

Local Governance

The most important power "delegated" to Yoritomo was legal control over the staffing of provincial posts, which enabled him to appoint his own men to administrative positions in the provinces. He was also authorized to appoint his men to the newly created position of Land Steward or Overseer (jitō) and Military Protector or Constable (shugo).

Land stewards were appointed to shōen and given official responsibility for the collection of rents and the forwarding of dues to the absentee holders of rights in the shōen, that is, the court aristocracy, the imperial family, and the great religious establishments. The stewards also received considerable police and judicial authority over the estates and were rewarded by grants of rights (shiki) to a portion of the estate income. The function of the Military Protectors, appointed to most provinces, was to provide liaison between the bakufu and its retainers and to maintain security. They were responsible for suppressing rebels and punishing major crimes. The appointment of jitō and *shugo* thus served both the cause of *bakufu* power and that of public order, but it left the old system basically intact.

The restoration of order benefited everyone, and the new system recognized the economic prerogatives as well as the legitimacy of the Kyoto establishment. However, tensions inevitably resulted from the intrusion of a lord-vassal system into the old *shōen* proprietary structure, as well as between the continued coexistence of *shōen* and the non-*shōen* land that remained under public administration (*kokugaryo*). Disputes between *jitō* and central proprietors were endemic. In the long run, the advantage clearly lay with the local warriors, but the *bakufu*, determined to uphold the system, frequently ruled against *jitō* attempts to extend their powers at the expense of proprietors or peasants. The latter ranged widely in status and wealth. At the top were the *myoshu*, managers and later owners of some land with responsibilities for tax collection, while down at the bottom were transient laborers. Peasants were free to leave but when they did, they lost any claim to the land.

The coexistence between Kamakura and Kyoto was put to the test in 1221, when Emperor Go-Toba (1190–1229) used imperial *shōen* and Buddhist monasteries to raise a force of dissatisfied warriors in an attempt to restore imperial power. He was soundly defeated, and the end result was to increase the strength of the shogunate, which used the occasion to confiscate 3,000 *shōen*, appoint additional stewards in Central and Western Japan, and establish its own deputies in Kyoto. However, faced with widespread general disorder, the *bakufu* sought to strengthen its own place within the system rather than to devise a new system.

The Hōjō Regents

Yoritomo established the shogunate on firm foundations, but did not succeed in founding a dynasty of shoguns. During his life he killed off rivals within his own family, and when he died he left only two sons, one aged 11 and the other a wild 17-year-old without political judgment. Consequently, Yoritomo's death in 1199 was followed by a struggle for power.

Emerging victorious was the Hōjō, the family of Yoritomo's remarkable, strong-minded widow, Masako (1157–1225). Her father now assumed domination over the shogunal government and became the first in line of de facto Hōjō rulers, although they never assumed the title of "shogun." That was held by a puppet, who after 1219 was not even a Minamoto, for in that year a Fujiwara infant received the appointment. Meanwhile the Hōjō, by placing family members in key posts, exercised actual control over the *bakufu*. In this way real power was doubly divorced from apparent authority: in theory Japan was ruled by an emperor, but this emperor was actually under the control of his abdicated father (the cloistered emperor); meanwhile, in Kamakura, the power ostensibly "delegated" to the shogun was actually exercised by Hōjō ministers.

Although the overall structure seems complex, organization of the Kamakura *bakufu* remained relatively simple, in keeping with the more modest scope of government itself. An Office of Samurai looked after the affairs of the shogunate's vassals *(gokenin)* and generally supervised military and police matters. A Board of Inquiry *(monchūjo)* dealt with various judicial matters and under the Hōjō handled cases arising outside of Kamakura itself. General administration was under the jurisdiction of an Office of Administration similar to the household offices used by the great Heian families. Yoritomo, in the end, designated it the *mandokoro*, the usual name for such a household bureau. The heads of these three bureaus participated in a council that advised Yoritomo, who made the final decisions himself. The council was led by the chief of the *mandokoro*, and it was in this capacity that the Hōjō exercised their power. In 1225 an innovative Hōjō statesman created a Council of State to allow for broader warrior participation in government, but the Hōjō soon dominated this body.

The Hōjō concept of government is reflected in the law code of 1232, the Jōei Code, the first codification of warrior law. One of its purposes was to define the duties of stewards and constables. Another major concern was to clarify matters of land tenure and succession. Included among the latter were the property rights of women. For example, divorced women could retain the land they had originally brought into the marriage.

The code emphasized the impartial administration of justice in settling disputes between warriors, disputes which usually concerned land rights. The adjudication of such matters was one of the shogunate's prime functions, and much of its power and prestige rested on samurai confidence in the equity of its decisions. The Jōei formulary sought to achieve this by setting forth its provisions in a simple and direct manner and by restricting itself to a small number of regulations, for according to later copies (the original is not extant) it consisted of only 51 articles (actually model cases) plus a short preamble and an oath. For cases not covered by precedent, it advised recourse to common sense. When the need arose, additional articles were added. The code's reputation as a symbol of justice was so strong that it outlasted the Kamakura shogunate.

Another indication of Hōjō effectiveness and the resilience of the *bakufu's* institutions was the ability of the regime to withstand a most formidable military challenge and to survive the strains it produced in the body politic.

The Mongol Invasion and Its Aftermath

The Mongol conquest of East Asia was in full swing at the time the Jōei Code was issued, but it was another third of a century before the momentum of the Mongol conquests was felt in Japan. Before they were faced with the need to defend themselves against the Mongols, the Kamakura statesmen had successfully avoided political or military entanglement in continental affairs, although they did nothing to discourage trade with the Song, which flourished both before and after the founding of the shogunate. Although this trade consisted mostly of luxury items, it brought on a drain of copper coinage, which posed a problem for Song finances. Its primary effect in Japan was to stimulate a renewed interest in Chinese culture. The shogunate also maintained cordial relations with Korea: when, in 1227, the depredations of Japanese pirates off the Korean coast prompted Korean complaints, the *bakufu* ordered the offenders arrested and executed.

The Mongols changed all that. In 1266, even before the conquest of the Southern Song had been completed, Khubilai Khan dispatched his first messenger to Japan demanding submission. This threat produced great consternation at court in Kyoto, but the shogunate remained calm, determined to resist. It took the Mongols until 1274 to organize a military expedition, but in that year a force of about 30,000 Mongols and Koreans was sent to Japan. They landed near Hakata, in North Kyūshū, and fought with a Japanese force assembled by the *bakufu*. Fortunately for the Japanese, a great storm destroyed this expedition. Heavy casualties did not deter Khubilai Khan from trying again. He renewed his demands, only to meet with rebuff; the Japanese showed their determination to resist by executing his envoys. In 1281 Khubilai sent a much larger force, estimated at 140,000 men, to crush the Japanese. But the shogunate, too, had used the intervening years in military preparation: they built a stone wall along Hakata Bay, amassed troops, and trained them in the techniques of group fighting employed by the Mongols, which contrasted with the individual combat customary in Japanese warfare. They fought for seven weeks before nature intervened once more; another great storm, called the *kamikaze* ("divine wind") by the Japanese, settled the issue. About half the men sent by Khubilai perished in this fruitless attempt to add Japan to his empire.

Still the Great Khan did not give up. Preparations for a third attempt were in progress when he died in 1294. Only then was the project abandoned. But the *bakufu* did not know that: it continued the policy of military preparedness until 1312.

In repulsing these attacks, the shogunate achieved a great success and further increased its power vis-à-vis the civilian court. But it had to share the glory of victory with temples and shrines, which claimed credit for securing divine intervention, while it alone bore the burden of paying for the wars. This was especially onerous because fighting the Mongol invaders, unlike internal warfare, brought in no new lands or booty with which to meet the expectations of warriors demanding their just rewards. And the long thirty years of preparation for defense did not even bring military glory. When the shogunate proved unable to satisfy warrior claims, the *bushi* lost confidence in the regime. Their loyalty was weakened, and as they turned for support increasingly to local authorities (Military Protectors and the stronger stewards), centrifugal forces came to the fore. The characteristic Hōjō response was to draw more power into their own hands, a policy not designed to deal with the underlying causes of their deteriorating situation. At the same time, economic pressures and the realities of power also worked against aristocratic civilian interests, as military stewards proved increasingly reluctant to forward payments to Kyoto. Vis-à-vis the cultivators too, the stewards were assuming ever greater powers. If a steward departed too far from custom in his demands, the cultivators could appeal to higher authority (including Kamakura), or they could negotiate with the *jitō* himself. However, the stewards' local authority was so extensive that increasingly they treated the estates as though they were their own property. The policy of excluding the military from interfering with civilian prerogatives was breaking down, and as the shogunate declined, the peculiar Kamakura relationship between court and *bakufu*, aristocrat and warrior, was also coming to an end.

The Warrior and His Ideals

By background and training, the *bushi* was a man very different in kind from the Heian aristocrat. As a fighting man he was called upon to exhibit martial skills and to demonstrate virtues recalling those attributed to the ideal knight of the European Middle Ages: valor, manly pride, vigor, and undying loyalty were among the qualities most highly prized in both societies. For the sake of his lord and the honor of his family name, a samurai should be prepared to face every hardship and make every sacrifice. He was expected to be completely reliable, earnest and sincere, to live a frugal and strenuous life, to care nothing for wealth or luxury, and to treat with contempt considerations of personal gain or calculations of profit or loss. Of course, just as the "refined" Heian period had had its wellborn but uncouth boors utterly incapable of turning out acceptable verse or writing a decent hand, so the "martial" Kamakura period had its full complement of cowards and turncoats: many *bushi* fell far short of the ideal. But in both ages, the widely accepted ideal did serve as a model and as a basis for judging men.

In some ways the demands on the Japanese warrior were harsher than those on his European counterpart, for the Japanese code was not softened by considerations of chivalry toward ladies nor did the rules of warfare provide for the taking of prisoners to be held for ransom. Instead the *bushi* defeated in personal combat expected to lose his head, for it was the practice of the victor to decapitate his enemy and present the head as proof of his triumph.

The complete elaboration of the code of the samurai did not take place until the seventeenth century, but its essential features are evident in the Kamakura period. Virile, selfless, and incorruptible, the ideal samurai gains added mystique through his disdain for death—and not just on the battlefield. To avoid dishonor or demonstrate his sincerity or underline a protest, he should be ready to commit ritual suicide by disembowelment *(seppuku)*:

> With that very dagger he stabbed himself below the left nipple, plunging the blade so deep that it almost emerged through his back. Then he stretched the incision in three directions, pulled out his intestines, and wiped the dagger on the sleeve of his cloak. He draped the cloak over his body and leaned heavily on an arm rest; then he summoned his wife . . . [3]

Thus begins the description of Yoshitsune's death recounted in a fourteenth-
or fifteenth-century text, and such was the death proper to a noble *bushi*—a
death still valued by latter day followers of the samurai ideal.

Like the cherry blossom which falls from the tree in its prime, the samurai
must have no regrets when his life is cut off. The cherry blossom became the
stock symbol of the samurai, suggesting his outlook on life and conveying
an aesthetic dimension peculiarly Japanese in flavor. Another important
component of the Kamakura view of life was religious, and it is to religion
that we now turn.

Religion: The Pure Land Sect

The turbulence and uncertainties accompanying the transition from aristocratic to warrior rule tended to confirm the belief that history had indeed
entered its final phase of degeneracy *(mappō)* and made people all the more
receptive to the solace of religion. One result was the continuing growth and
development of the popularizing and pietistic trends exemplified earlier by
the activities and teachings of Kūya and Genshin. A major leader in this
tradition was Hōnen who established in Japan the Pure Land sect (Jōdo,
Qingdu, Ch'ing-tu), named after the paradise in the West over which
presides Amida (Amitābha), the Buddha of Infinite Light. To the faithful it
offered the hope of rebirth in the land of bliss. In practice it stressed the
nembutsu. Hōnen carried the invocation of Amida further than his predecessors by teaching that the *nembutsu* was not just one method for attaining
salvation but that it was the best and indeed the only method suitable for
the age.

When Hōnen expressed his ideas in writing, his book was burned by the
monks on Mt. Hiei. He remained a controversial person, suffering in his
seventies an exile of four years from which he was allowed to return only a
year before he died. Underlying the emphasis on the invocation of Amida
was a belief in salvation through faith rather than through works or religious
observances—Hōnen himself, on his deathbed, declined to hold the usual
cord connected to an Amida to draw him to paradise. His persistent rejection of traditional ritual and scholasticism helps to explain the hostility of
the older sects.

Pure Land Amidism was further developed by Hōnen's greatest and most
renowned disciple, Shinran (1173–1262), founder of the True Pure Land
sect (Jōdo Shinshū). Shinran has been compared to the founders of Christian
Protestantism, for, like them, he insisted that humans were so debased that
they could not possibly gain salvation through their own efforts or "self-
power" but must depend on the "other power" of Amida. Specifically, salvation comes through faith—frequently experienced by the individual in an
act of conversion. The boundless compassion of Amida embraces the bad
man or woman as well as the good. Indeed the bad individual, conscious of a
lack of worth, may be closer to salvation than good individuals who are
incapable of resisting self-congratulation on their merits and who rely on

their own efforts to attain rebirth in paradise. Once converted and granted faith, each person will naturally bring the message to others, repeating the *nembutsu*, not out of a desire to be saved or for reassurance, but out of gratitude and joy.

Shinran was himself filled with a sense of his own sinfulness. "A bald-headed old fool" is the name he adopted for himself. He also carried rejection of the old monastic observances further than any of his predecessors; he ate meat, and, like Luther, he married a nun. Exiled in consequence, he spent his life proclaiming his religious message among the common people as one of themselves.

Shinran did not intend to found a new sect, nor did he acknowledge having disciples. But he left many followers who developed the True Pure Land sect. One of the best known Kamakura Pure Land evangelists was Ippen (1239–89) who, like Kūya, practiced the dancing *nembutsu* and became the subject of a famous narrative picture scroll. Meanwhile, Shinran's True Pure Land continued to attract followers. In the fifteenth century, during the Ashikaga period, Rennyo (1415–99) organized the community of believers into a disciplined body, ready and able to fight for their beliefs. The True Pure Land Sect is still one of the largest religious organizations in Japan, now divided into two branches, each headed by descendants of Shinran. This tradition of hereditary leadership was, of course, made possible by the abandonment of celibacy. It is also consistent with Japanese familism and with Jōdo faith in the benign "other power" of Amida.

Nichiren

Many of the older sects also practiced invocation of the Buddha of the Western Paradise without, however, abandoning their older rituals or beliefs. But not all were tolerant. A vociferous and vehement opponent of Pure Land teachings, as of the doctrines of all the other rival sects new and old, was Nichiren (1222–82), one of Japan's most remarkable religious leaders. Like Hōnen and Shinran, he too was exiled for his advocacy of unacceptable beliefs, but, unlike the others, he was almost put to death; he was saved, according to his followers, only by a miracle, as lightning struck the poised executioner's sword. Nichiren's conviction of the correctness of his teachings was buttressed by his belief that he was a reincarnation of a Bodhisattva specially entrusted with the Lotus Sutra, the one and only text incorporating Buddha's teachings in all their dimensions.

Nichiren, although born into a family of poor fishermen, was a learned man. But like Hōnen and Shinran, his message was simple: faith in the Lotus Sutra, rather than a mastery of its contents, was the requirement for salvation. In place of the invocation of Amida practiced by Pure Land Buddhists, he substituted "*namu myōhō renge-kyō*"—Hail to the Lotus Sutra of the Wonderful Law—usually chanted to the beat of a drum.

In adversity Nichiren demonstrated a depth of conviction and strength of character readily appreciated by warriors who valued similar virtues.

Perhaps Nichiren's origins in Eastern Japan also enhanced his standing among the *bushi* who had established the shogunate. Furthermore, he was greatly attached to the land and was Japan-centered to an unusual degree, envisioning Japan as the headquarters for his faith, which from there would spread throughout the world. The very name he chose for himself, Nichiren (*nichi* = sun, *ren* = lotus), indicated his dual devotion to the Land of the Rising Sun and the Lotus Sutra. In his view, the one required the other. Repeatedly he warned that the Lotus was essential for Japan and predicted dire consequences if other sects remained in favor. He prophesied the Mongol invasions, thereby increasing his credibility. Nichiren's concern for state and country, his courage, and his zeal remained an inspiration for his followers in later times. One man is even said to have journeyed to Siberia as a missionary. Nichiren, the man and the faith, have retained their magnetism to the present. Today he is venerated not only in the traditional Lotus sect but also by the Sōka Gakkai (Value Creation Society), a religious body whose membership has burgeoned since the Second World War.

Zen

Zen (Chan or Ch'an) originated in China although it was supposedly founded by Bodhidharma, an Indian monk frequently depicted in Zen art. It was a form of Buddhism with strong affinities with Daoism (Taoism), a philosophy and way of looking at the world that found its classic expression in the *Daodejing (Tao Te Ching)* attributed to Laozi (Lao Tzu, ca. 3rd century B.C.). Suspicious of language because words make distinctions and thereby do violence to the all-inclusive Way (or *Dao*), Daoists advocated apprehension of the truth through an incommunicable intuitive identification. Zen, for its part, centered on meditation as the way to pierce through the world of illusion and recognize the Buddha nature within oneself. Whereas for other schools meditation was only one among a number of techniques, Zen originally rejected all other practices, such as performance of meritorious deeds or the study of scriptures.

The so-called Northern branch of Zen emphasized sitting in silent meditation and attaining enlightenment gradually. In contrast, Southern Zen maintained that illumination comes in a sudden flash, although only after long and arduous searching. A Western analogy might be Newton's experience under the apple tree: he discovered the law of gravity in a sudden flash, but he would never have done so had he not been constantly thinking about the problem, searching for a solution.

Southern Zen teachers often employed unorthodox methods to prod their disciples on the road to illumination. Their methods included irreverent or irrelevant answers to questions, contradictory remarks, nonsense syllables—anything to jar the mind out of its ordinary rut. Some masters would strike their disciples in the belief (as with Newton) that enlightenment might come as the result of a sudden physical shock. One widely practiced technique was for the master to assign his pupils a kōan (gongan, kung-an), an enigmatic statement to be pondered until the pupil attained an understanding that transcended everyday reasoning. One famous kōan asks: "what is the sound of one hand clapping?"

Pure Land Buddhism and the teachings of Nichiren appealed widely to warriors, but Zen, with a more limited following, enjoyed official favor and bakufu support. Zen practices were not unknown in Japan before the Kamakura period, but it was established only through the efforts of two monks, Eisai (1141–1215) and Dōgen (1200–53), who reintroduced Zen directly from China, then under the Song Dynasty (Sung, 960–1279; more precisely, Southern Song as the dynasty is called after it lost the North in 1127). Eisai made two trips and brought back not only religious ideas but a great enthusiasm for tea, thus initiating the long association between that beverage and Japanese Zen. He was a follower of the Rinzai (Chinese, Linji, Lin-chi) school, practicing the use of the kōan riddles. Eisai found support in Kamakura, but in Kyoto he accommodated himself to the religious life of the old capital by observing Tendai and Shingon practices as well as Zen rules. He even recommended the nembutsu and allowed chants and prayers.

Dōgen, in contrast, was uncompromising in his attitude toward secular authority. He eventually settled in the mountains remote from Kamakura and Kyoto. He consistently declined worldly honors and built a small temple, which later grew into the great monastery of Eiheiji. Dōgen differed from Eisai also in the type of Zen he preached, for he brought back from China the doctrines of the Sōtō (Chinese, Caodao, Ts'ao-tao) school, which emphasized sitting in silent meditation (zazen) without a specific object or goal in mind, a gradual process of realizing the Buddha nature through the body as well as the mind. In his attitude toward the transmission of the truth, Dōgen was a moderate, accepting scriptural authority as well as the authority of the personal transmission from patriarch to patriarch. The influence enjoyed by the Sōtō school in Japan was much greater than that accorded Caodao in China.

The proper practice of Zen made very great demands on its practitioners, demands no less severe than those encountered in military training. Seekers after illumination did not, like the second patriarch, have to sever an arm to demonstrate their seriousness of purpose, but they did have to endure a period of waiting and abuse before they were admitted to the spartan life of the temple. Even now the average day of the Zen Buddhist monk in Japan may run from 3 A.M. to 9 P.M., and is filled with a steady round of religious observances, manual labor, and zazen. The latter is itself a rigorous discipline, a period of formal meditation in which no bodily movement is allowed (see Figure 4.2). A senior monk makes the rounds with a long flat stick to strike those who show signs of becoming drowsy. Some Zen temples also make provisions for members of the laity who wish to practice meditation without submitting themselves to the full religious life. Ultimately, enlightenment is a personal quest.

The fortunes of Zen were furthered not only by native Japanese monks but also by Chinese masters who traveled to Japan and won considerable influence in Kamakura, where they were favored by the Hōjō regents. For

Figure 4.2   Zazen.

example, the Kenchōji, one of the great Kamakura temples, was built by a Hōjō regent, who invited a Chinese monk to become its abbot. Several of the regents became deeply versed in Zen. Along with Zen these monks brought from China a variety of artistic and cultural influences of which the interest in tea is only one example. The secular influence of Zen became even more marked in the succeeding Ashikaga period. The continuity of Zen influence is reflected in the career of Musō Soseki (1275–1351), also known as Musō Kokushi (Musō the National Master), who successively enjoyed the favor of the Hōjō regent, the emperor Go-Daigo, and the Ashikaga shogun.

Shinto

No account of the religious scene in the Kamakura period is complete without mentioning the continuing appeal of the native spirits, or *kami* (Shintoism). Old patterns of coexistence between Shinto and Buddhism, and tendencies toward some amalgamation of the two, remained vigorous. Ippen, for example, identified individual Buddhas and bodhisattvas with *kami*; Tendai and Shingon remained hospitable to the old gods, and Shinto in turn borrowed freely from Buddhism. The Inner and Outer shrines at Ise were regarded as Shingon mandalas. It may well be that there was a special affinity between Shingon and Shinto; indeed the major Shinto writer and champion of the imperial house, Kitabatake Chikafusa (1293–1354), ascribed the success of Shingon in Japan, as opposed to China, to its compatibility with Shinto. Another syncretic religion was preached by mountain priests *(yamabushi)*, who were themselves combinations of shamans, monks, and Daoist mountain ascetics. They identified mountain *kami* with

Buddhist incarnations and emphasized the role of religious retreats in the mountains. In their ceremonials and incantations they blended Shinto and Buddhist elements. This mountain religion (Shugendō) had enjoyed aristocratic patronage during the Heian period but in feudal times turned increasingly toward the common people for support. In the process it furthered the spread of Buddhism to Northern Japan.

Similar recourse to popular support when previous sources of income dried up led to the development of Ise Shinto. The priests at Ise successfully encouraged people to go on pilgrimages to the sacred shrine, which came to rely largely on the offerings of the pious for revenue.

Religious Art

When the Taira destroyed the Tōdaiji and Kōfukuji temples in Nara, they inadvertently prepared the way for a great revival of Buddhist sculpture,

Figure 4.3   Niō (Guardian Figure), Great South Gate. Wood, approx. 808 cm high. Tōdaiji, Nara.

stimulated by a happy conjunction of artistic talent and generous patronage. Old works that were damaged or destroyed had to be restored or replaced. Patronage for this effort came both from the *bakufu* and the Court, giving rise to a school of highly talented artists (all of whom chose names ending in "kei"). Artistic inspiration came in part from the sculpture in the old capital area, but the best Kamakura sculptures also convey a new realism and robust vigor, reflecting the martial values of the warrior class in the East. The leading figure of the new school was Unkei (active 1163–1223), whose own career exemplified the blending of the old and the new. He participated in the restoration of some traditional Nara sculptures, but he also traveled and worked in Eastern Japan, where he was exposed to the values and tastes of the warrior class. Both experiences influenced his work.

A good example of the new style is provided by the guardian figures flanking the main entrance of Tōdaiji (see Figure 4.3). This was a joint enterprise in which Unkei, along with others, participated. Almost 30 feet tall, these figures are constructed of many pieces of wood carefully fitted together; Kamakura sculptors rejected the delicate serenity of late Heian sculpture but not its new technique. In the Tōdaiji figures, the wood is

Figure 4.4   Kōshō, *Kūya*, Wood, Kamakura, approx. 117 cm high. Rokuharamitsuji, Kyoto.

undercut to emphasize tendons and muscle, thereby giving an effect of virility and strength appropriate to martial figures, and to a martial society.

In such guardian figures, ferocity tends to take precedence over realism, but this is not the case in sculpture portraits of milder Buddhist saints and monks. A new device that appears at this time is the use of crystal for the eyes to give them a lifelike sparkle. The figure of Kūya (see Figure 4.4) goes beyond realism: even the words of the priest have to be portrayed.

The figure of Kūya is an example of the influence of Amidism in the arts. A still more impressive symbol of the popularity of Amida in the religious life of this period is the giant, 49-foot figure completed in 1252 and paid for by funds raised from the common people (see Figure 4.5). In his compassionate benevolence, the massive Amida leans forward and looks down on pilgrim and sightseer alike. Artistically the figure compares favorably with the badly restored giant Buddha at Nara, but its effectiveness is probably more a function of its dimensions than of any inherent artistic excellence. Originally housed in its own temple, it now stands outside under the open sky. The figure is partially hollow; inside, steps lead to a little window in Amida's back, through which visitors may look out.

Along with Amida, Kannon continued to enjoy great popularity. Dating from around the middle of the thirteenth century, and thus roughly contemporary with the Kamakura Amida, are the contents of the Sanjūsangendō (Rengeōin) in Kyoto. It features a seated "thousand-armed" Kannon, which is flanked by a thousand standing statues of the same Kannon neatly formed

Figure 4.5   *Amida.* Bronze, Kamakura, approx. 1138 cm high.

in ranks, a Kamakura reminder of the Buddhist proclivity for repetition. Of greater artistic appeal are some of the realistic Kamakura sculptures also kept in this hall.

The vitality of early Kamakura sculpture gradually waned and the resulting decline in the quality of Buddhist sculpture turned out to be permanent. Craftsmen continued to produce Buddhist figures in imitation of older styles, but there was a dearth of new departures or even creative revivals. The Buddhist religion and the visual arts continued to enrich each other, but after the Kamakura period the relationship between them took a new form.

Chinese influence is visible in some fourteenth-century religious sculpture and can also be studied in Kamakura architecture, which drew on at least two distinctive Chinese traditions. One style of great power was known in Japan as the "Indian Style" (Tenjikuyō), although it was actually imported from Fujian. Its outstanding feature is bracketing constructed along a single, transverse axis and inserted through, rather than mounted on, the supporting columns. The best example of this style is the gate of Tōdaiji (see Figure 4.6), which shelters the two guardian figures discussed previously. Like these figures it is an effective expression of some of the qualities associated with the Kamakura period. As Sherman Lee observes, "the gate structure is logical but simple, almost heavy rather than lucid, with a brute strength that overpowers memories of the refined Heian architectural style and which finds no later repetition."[4] This style was short-lived in Japan but survived in Fujian. A later version was reintroduced to Japan from Fujian in the seventeenth century, along with the Ōbakusan (Huangboshan) sect of Chan Buddhism.

Perhaps the Japanese called this style "Indian" because it ran counter to the prevailing fashions of Song architecture and taste. In any case, they reserved the term "Chinese Style" (Karayō) for buildings modeled on the prevailing continental style. In Kamakura, the Kenchōji (1253) was supposed to be a copy of a famous Chan temple in Hangzhou and the Engakuji (see Figure 4.7) is said to have been built by an architect who had traveled to Hangzhou to study the Chinese model. Unfortunately the Chinese prototypes have not survived, and the Engakuji building is now covered with an incongruous Japanese-style thatched roof. Another important Kamakura-period building in the Chinese manner is the Kaisandō of the Eihōji, a Zen temple near Nagoya (see Figure 4.8). Along with its general air of elegance, a particularly Chinese feature is its relative verticality when compared to similar buildings in the native Japanese style, which tend to hug the ground. As usual in the Chinese style, the Kaisandō stands on a stone platform, but its roof too has been restored in a Japanese manner, for it should really be of tile. In addition to these two imported architectural styles, the Japanese built many religious as well as secular buildings in the native Japanese style. Also influential was a mixed style combining Japanese and Chinese elements.

Along with architecture and sculpture, painting also continued to serve religious purposes or to depict religious themes such as gruesome hells watched over by terrifying, grotesque demons, as raging fires threaten the sinners and the blood of the damned gushes and flows in screaming reds.

Figure 4.6   LEFT, The Great South Gate, Tōdaiji, Nara. ABOVE, The Great South Gate, Tōdaiji: bracketing.

Like their European counterparts, these paintings require no subtle understanding of doctrine or connoisseur's eye. Even the most obtuse will get the message. A secular equivalent may be found in the horrors of war depicted in scenes illustrating battle accounts from such works as the *Tales of the Heiji Period (Heiji monogatari)*, which provided the subject matter for a famous scroll now in the Museum of Fine Arts, Boston. The Kamakura ethos did not allow for pacifism.

Kamakura paintings combine representations of the secular and the sacred. What looks like a landscape may also be an icon. This is true of a

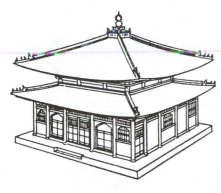

Figure 4.7   RIGHT, Engakuji Relic Hall. Thirteenth century. Kamakura. ABOVE, Drawing of Engakuji Relic Hall showing original roof.

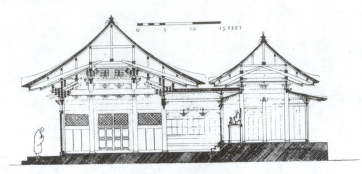

Figure 4.8   BELOW, Front View, Kaisandō of Eihōji, Tajimi, Nagoya. RIGHT, Kaisandō: side elevation.

famous painting of the Nachi waterfall, which actually represents the *kami* who resides in this, the largest and most revered waterfall in Japan. In an original way this painting combines the Buddhist mandala tradition with the native Japanese religion and the deep love for nature that is intrinsic to it. In the narrative scrolls also, there are scenes showing the beauties of the Japanese landscape rendered in a Japanese manner, although Chinese influence is visible in the Ippen scroll, an influence which was to lead to the development of Chinese-style landscape in the following period.

Both art and craftsmanship are combined in the beautiful and lethal products of the Kamakura sword maker. The attention lavished on swords and richly decorated armor is reminiscent of similar developments in Europe when these were the prized possessions of a warrior class.

Literature

The crosscurrents of Kamakura history and the styles of life prevalent at court, in the military, and in the temple found expression in a rich and varigated literature, much of it of the highest quality. The *Confessions of Lady Nijō*, completed in the first decade of the fourteenth century and thus quite late in the Kamakura period, takes us back to the familiar world of the Heian court lady. In the early chapters we find her conducting her love affairs and paying attention to the fine points of aesthetics against a general background of melancholy awareness that reminds us of *The Tale of Genji*. The last two sections, however, are an account of her life as a Buddhist nun, fulfilling vows to copy the sutras, and traveling to holy sites (including Ise). She also travels to Kamakura, where her advice on dress and decoration is eagerly sought, for in these matters the prestige of the court remained paramount.

Poetry too remained an integral part of court life. Some very fine poetry was produced in the late twelfth and early thirteenth centuries under the auspices of two great poets, father and son: Fujiwara Shunzei (1114–1204) and Fujiwara Teika (1162–1241). The name itself echoes the past; they were descendants of Michinaga, although poetry, not politics, was their world.

In addition to his fame as a poet, Shunzei was recognized by his contemporaries as an arbiter of poetic taste and was influential in developing a new aesthetic, which sought to deepen the expression of melancholy *(aware)* by adding to it a new dimension of profound mystery *(yūgen)*. A mood of sadness also colors the word *sabi*, first used as a term of praise by Shunzei, for whom it basically meant "loneliness." These qualities permeated the aesthetic climate of the subsequent Ashikaga period and will be encountered again in our discussion of the characteristic achievements of that era.

Teika presided over the committee that compiled the Shinkokinshū (New Kokinshū, 1205), one of the great collections of Japanese verse and often considered the last of the great imperial anthologies. The following poem by the priest Saigyō (1118–90) is an example of the poetic qualities to be found in the best court poetry:

> While denying his heart,
> Even a priest cannot but know
> The depths of a sad beauty:
> From the marsh a longbill
> Flies off in the autumn dusk.[5]

Buddhism demands that a devout man give up the feelings of his own heart even when they are humbly aesthetic.

The opening lines of the poem convey the dilemma in subjective, human terms, as the closing lines do in sensuous natural terms. The beginning suggests tragedy, as the priest is drawn back to the lovely but illusory phenomenal world; the end gives something like consolation in the fact that even such a humble sight, which seems almost an aesthetic and human void, affords such beauty and significance. And yet in the balance of the two parts and in the countercurrents within each there is the creative polarity that I have termed celebration and desolation. Beauty is found at the very abyss of human darkness, and yet even the humblest scenes of the illusory world touch the ascetic heart to its depths with mingled suffering and affirmation.[6]

One of Teika's poems included in the anthology is from a series of 100 poems on the moon. (The composition of such series was one way Japanese poets transcended the limitations of the *tanka*.)

> On her straw-mat bedding
> The Lady of the Bridge of Uji
> Spreads the moonlight out,
> And in the waiting autumn night
> She lies there in the darkening wind.[7]

Even in translation the beauty of the original imagery remains untarnished.

In contrast the following is just one example of a poem which dispenses with imagery altogether—a practice not unusual in *tanka*. It was written by Lady Jūsammi Chikaku who lived around 1300 (after the great age of Saigyō, Shunzei, and Teika). It is included here to remind us that poetry did not end with them and that ladies as well as gentlemen continued to excel in this medium. It deals with one of the recurrent motifs in statements of the woman's side of love, the breaking of love's promises.

> In recent days
> I can no longer say of wretchedness
> That it is wretched,
> For I feel my grief has made me
> No longer truly capable of grief.[8]

The theme is ageless. The private, delicate yet resilient, world of the court poet is far removed from the hurly-burly of politics and warfare; it did not deign to notice the intrigue and the fighting.

A literary man who wrote excellent prose as well as fine poetry was Kamo no Chōmei (1153–1216), who withdrew from the turbulent world to live quietly in a hut on a mountainside near Kyoto. In his *An Account of My Hut*, he wrote about the calamities such as fire, famine, and earthquake suffered by those who remained behind in the world, and about the simplicity and solitude of his own life. Deeply religious, he fell short of the complete detachment taught by Buddhism but found consolation in repeating the *nembutsu*.

Less sophisticated were the stories in *Tales from the Uji Collection*, which in simple and direct language describe the morals and miracles of Buddhism. One story, made famous by a twelfth-century narrative scroll, concerns the holy man of Mt. Shigi who obtained his daily food by sending his begging bowl flying down from his mountain to be filled. When one day the bowl was disdained by a wealthy man, it flew back up the mountain with his entire rice-filled warehouse. The artist had great fun depicting the consternation of the rich man as his storehouse goes flying off. The episode ends happily when the holy man decides to return the rice, and the bowl goes flying back down the mountain carrying one bag, followed by all the other bags flying through the air in single file.

Kamakura literature is also an important source of information about the world of the warrior, as reflected in the military tales and romances. We have already mentioned the tales which grew up around Yoshitsune. Often retold were accounts of his heroic exploits and those of his right-hand man, the stout monk and formidable fighter Benkei, who became his lifelong follower after the young Yoshitsune bested him in a sword fight on a bridge. Stories extolling bravery in battle, engaging accounts of clever stratagems, and celebrations of victory were as appreciated by the Kamakura warrior as by warriors everywhere, but the ultimate tone of the tales is somber. Yoshitsune was, in the end, vanquished (even if one legend has him fleeing to the continent to become Chinggis Khan). Defeat is also the fate of the Taira in *The Tale of the Heike*, an oratorio given its final, classic form after the Kamakura *bakufu* had passed away, by the blind musician-priest Akashi no Kakuichi (d. 1371), praised by Barbara Ruch as "one of the greatest composer-performers in history."[9] The main theme of his work is the fall of Taira pride, not the glory of the victorious Minamoto.

Underlying *The Tale of the Heike* is a sense of the transience of victory, the ultimate emptiness of success. Buddhist consciousness of the fleeting nature of all that is best in life saved the age of the Heian courtier from sinking into mere shallow hedonism, and likewise rescued the world of the Kamakura warrior from the futile pomposity of the vainglorious. The sweetness of the warrior's triumph is just as ephemeral as the joy of lovers. The opening words of *The Tale of the Heike* sound a note that reverberates throughout the feudal period:

> In the sound of the bell of the Gion Temple echoes the impermanence of all things. The pale hue of the flowers of the teak-tree show the truth that they who prosper must fall. The proud do not last long, but vanish like a spring-night's dream. And the mighty ones too will perish in the end, like dust before the wind.[10]

NOTES

1. Jeffrey Mass in Kozo Yamamura, ed., *The Cambridge History of Japan*, Vol. 3: Medieval Japan (Cambridge: Cambridge Univ. Press, 1990), p. 49.

2. Peter Duus, *Feudalism in Japan* (New York: Alfred A. Knopf, 1969), p. 8.

3. Helen Craig McCullough, trans., *Yoshitsune: A Fifteenth Century Japanese Chronicle* (Stanford: Stanford Univ. Press, 1971), p. 290.

4. Sherman Lee, *A History of Far Eastern Art* (New York: Harry N. Abrams, 1964), p. 324.

5. Earl Miner, *An Introduction to Japanese Court Poetry* (Stanford: Stanford Univ. Press, 1968), p. 103.

6. Ibid., pp. 106–107.

7. Ibid., p. 113.

8. Ibid., p. 133.

9. Barbara Ruch in *Cambridge History*, 3, p. 531.

10. Donald Keene, *Japanese Literature* (New York: Grove Press, 1955), p. 78.

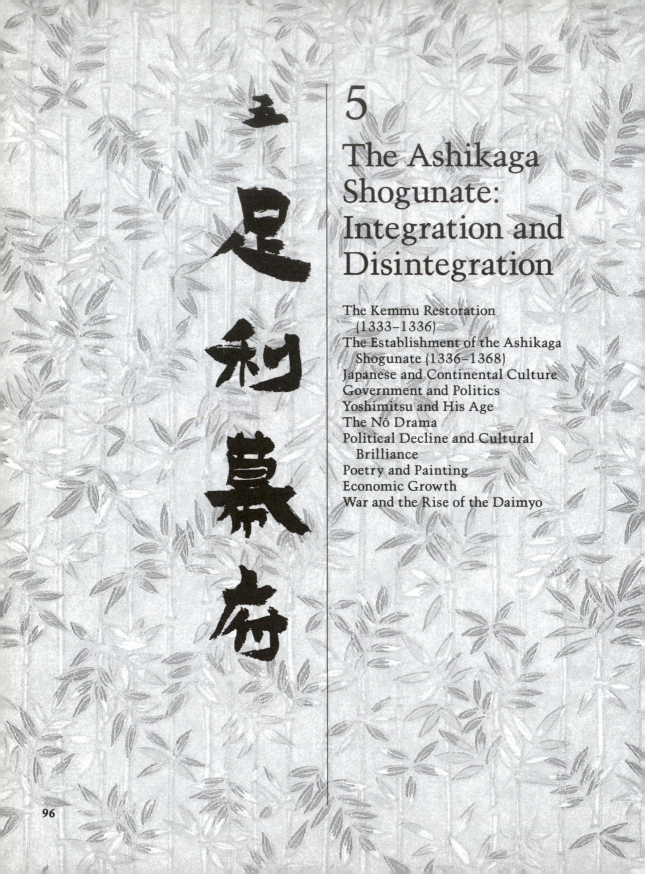

足利幕府

5
The Ashikaga Shogunate: Integration and Disintegration

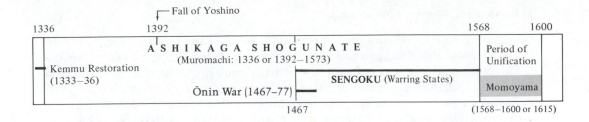

Culturally and politically the more than two centuries discussed in this chapter were an unusually rich and complex time in the history of Japan. The political ascendancy of warriors, so long in the making, was now completed, but the period's cultural efflorescence owed much to the heritage of aristocratic culture as the *bakufu* itself took up residence in Kyoto. Yet, as suggested by this chapter's title, after 1477 the Ashikaga *bakufu* virtually ceased to exist, even if in name a "shogun" continued to play a minor role until 1573.

The Kemmu Restoration (1333–1336)

Between the Kamakura and Ashikaga shogunates, as earlier between the Heian and Kamakura periods, there was a brief interlude. The Kemmu Restoration of Emperor Go-Daigo (1288–1339) was an attempt to reassert the prerogatives of the throne similar to the earlier efforts of Emperor Go-Toba. Since it confronted a much weakened shogunate, the restoration had considerable initial success. Even after Kyoto was lost, there was sufficient momentum to sustain a government in exile in the mountains of Yoshino, south of Nara, which for over half a century provided at least a potential rallying point for those opposed to the Ashikaga. Not until 1392 did it come to an end.*

The origins of the restoration go back to the middle of the thirteenth century. Two branches of the imperial family disputed succession to the throne. After the reluctant intervention of the *bakufu*, a compromise was reached whereby the two branches occupied the throne in alternation. It was Go-Daigo's determination to break this agreement and retain the succession in his own line that precipitated the split with the shogunate.

Fighting began in 1331 when the shogunate tried to force Go-Daigo to abdicate. He defied Kamakura and at first suffered setbacks, including capture and exile to the Oki Islands in the Sea of Japan. But the *bakufu* was unable

---

* The Ashikaga period is also frequently called the Muromachi period after the section of northeast Kyoto where the shoguns resided, although this term is sometimes applied only to the time after 1392.

to suppress all those who rose in rebellion. In 1332 the emperor escaped from Oki and was able to return to Kyoto in triumph after Ashikaga Takauji (1305–58), commander of a *bakufu* force sent to destroy him, changed sides. Behind Takauji was the wealth and prestige of the Ashikaga family, which, like Yoritomo, the founder of the shogunate, belonged to the Seiwa Minamoto lineage. Of similarly imposing descent was Nitta Yoshisada (1301–38), who now seized Kamakura in the name of Go-Daigo and put an end to the power of the Hōjō family and to the Kamakura *bakufu*.

The coalition that destroyed the Kamakura shogunate did not last long because the participants had no common program or interests. Moreover, few of the military leaders were attracted by the emperor's vision of a return to rule by the throne, since a genuine imperial restoration would necessarily lead to a reduction of warrior power. Many warriors were alienated and developed a sense of personal grievance when the throne failed to give them what they considered just reward for their services, and imperial justice turned out no better than that dispensed by the Later Hōjō. They were further dismayed by the emperor's adoption of a policy for merging provincial military and civil power and placing it in the hands of civil governors. When Go-Daigo appointed his own son shogun, it disappointed Takauji and did so without any compensatory increase in the new regime's military strength.

The throne's policies cost it the military support required for its survival. But the men who had the military power were themselves divided by conflicting interests and ambitions that could turn brother against brother, as happened in the case of Takauji himself and his brother Tadayoshi (1306–52). A common thread running through the shifting pattern of the political and military history in these years was the rivalry between Takauji and Nitta Yoshisada. The Kemmu Restoration came to an end when Takauji defeated Nitta and then dethroned Go-Daigo. But this did not bring peace, even to the capital. Four times the city was seized by forces of the southern court, the last in 1361, but each time they were forced to relinquish it. The prime motive of the participants in these various campaigns was to strengthen the fortunes of their own families; sometimes a family made certain that it would be on the winning side by having branches fight on both sides of the conflict. Ironically, a major casualty of the military turbulence was the not inconsiderable sector of civil provincial administration that had survived the Kamakura period, for now the *shugo* more and more assumed control of public land. The emperor's attempt to turn the clock back had misfired badly.

The Establishment of the Ashikaga Shogunate (1336–1368)

The power of the Ashikaga, enhanced after the defeat of Nitta Yoshisada, was legitimated in 1338 when Takauji received the coveted title of shogun from the new emperor he had installed in Kyoto. Takauji, however, did not live to see the reunification of the imperial family. Indeed, the southern court continued for another twenty-two years under Yoshimitsu, the third and very vigorous shogun. After a period of desultory conflict, the Ashikaga eventually did come to an agreement with the emperor of the southern court (1392). By that time, his position had become hopeless, and he agreed to a resumption of the old arrangement for alternate succession to the throne. Once firmly in control, however, the Ashikaga declined to honor the agreement. Since many historians treat the time of division as a single period (Nambuku-chō, 1336–92), we have marked it in the timeline, but by 1392 the basic foundations of the shogunate were in place.

Although the southern court was defeated, later historians did not side with the winner, for the traditional Japanese view accepted the claims of Go-Daigo. The genealogical as well as theoretical basis for these claims was supplied by Kitabatake Chikafusa. In his *The Records of the Legitimate Succession of the Divine Sovereigns*, Chikafusa argued not only for the legitimacy of Go-Daigo but for the sanctity of the correct imperial succession, which ultimately led back to the Sun Goddess. It was this, he claimed, which set Japan apart from other lands and made Japan uniquely divine. The *Taiheiki*, a military romance, supplied stirring accounts of the feats of imperial loyalists, such as Kusonoki Masahige (d. 1336), an early and faithful adherent to Go-Daigo's cause, and Nitta Yoshisada. It turned these men into popular heroes, shedding luster on the cause they served. One of the legacies of the Kemmu Restoration and the Yoshino court was an embellished and fortified imperial myth.

By contrast, Takauji was cast as the villain of this historical drama. This is an ungenerous view, for the shogun wanted to preserve the status of the throne and protected its dignity, even while denying its occupant any real power. The throne was, after all, the theoretical source of Takauji's own "delegated" authority, and Takauji sought to protect the dignity of the emperor. That the court needed a defender, that it was in disrepute among some of the rough-and-ready warriors newly risen to prominence, is suggested by a number of recorded incidents. One for example, tells of a warrior, probably under the influence of alcohol, who refused to dismount when he encountered the procession of the abdicated emperor. He is quoted as saying, "Did you say 'cloistered emperor' *(In)* or 'dog' *(inu)*? If it's a dog, perhaps I'd better shoot it." Adding injury to insult, he then hit the retired emperor's carriage with an arrow, and the upshot was that the carriage overturned and the *In* tumbled into the street. Takauji promptly had the warrior beheaded.[1]

Japanese and Continental Culture

As mentioned in the last chapter, the life of Zen Master Musō Soseki is an indication that the vicissitudes of political and military fortune did not disrupt all careers, for he enjoyed in turn the favor and patronage of the Hōjō, Go-Daigo, and Takauji. Of the latter it is said that he often practiced Zen before going to sleep after a heavy dinner party.

Musō was responsible for the fine garden at Tenryūji, the great Zen monastery built by Takauji for Musō and dedicated to the memory of

Go-Daigo. Its building and grounds covered almost 100 acres west of the capital. Musō also deserves much of the credit for the Saihōji, popularly known as the "moss garden." He also persuaded Takauji to have Zen temples erected throughout the country.

Musō's role extended beyond that of spiritual mentor: it was on his advice that Go-Daigo in 1325 sent an official embassy to China, resuming relations broken off almost 500 years earlier. Similarly his influence is seen in Takauji's decision to send another mission in 1339. In the latter case, the ship was named after the Tenryūji, and afterwards the monastery continued to be involved in lucrative voyages to China, while Zen monks were the major source for renewed interest in Chinese culture.

By this time the Song had given way to the Mongol Yuan Dynasty, but Song artistic and literary culture had great appeal for sophisticated Japanese who, on the other hand, evinced little interest in Song secular institutions. Furthermore, the impact of Song philosophy on Japan came only in the seventeenth century. However, the story was different in poetry and painting, which were linked gentlemanly arts in China. For Su Shi (Su Shih, 1037–1101, also known as Su Dongpo or Su Tung-p'o), poetry was "pictures without form" and paintings were "unspoken poems."[2]

In the arts, as elsewhere, the Japanese selected what appealed to them. They ignored the monumental Northern Song landscapes, preferring the more intimate Southern Song painting of Ma Yuan and Xia Gui (Hsia Kuei) and especially the vigorous brushwork and bold imagery in the paintings by Zen monks such as Muqi (Mu Ch'i). Even though the Zen artists never traveled to Japan, much of their work has been preserved only there. For

Figure 5.1   Muqi, *Six Persimmons*. Ink on paper, 36 cm wide. Daitokuji, Kyoto.

Muqi six persimmons mirrored the truth as faithfully as any portrait of the Buddha. (See Figure 5.1.) The painting is still owned by the Daitokuji temple, founded in 1326 with the backing of the retired emperor and Go-Daigo.

Monasteries and nunneries continued to provide a haven for those seeking to retire from the trials and tribulations of an unstable world. Among them was Yoshida Kenkō (1283–1350), poet, court official, and author of *The Essays in Idleness (Tsurezuregusa)*, a prose collection long admired in Japan as a repository of good taste, in social conduct as in art. As in the case of Sei Shōnagon's *Pillow Book* and Kamo no Chōmei's *An Account of My Hut*, and despite the randomness of its organization, Kenkō's work is held together by certain recurrent themes. Particularly significant is his celebration of the aesthetics of the impermanent, for to Kenkō perishability is an essential component and a necessary precondition for beauty. And he voices aesthetic judgments that have become closely associated with Japanese taste, displaying a preference for objects which bear the signs of wear and have acquired the patina of age *(sabi)*. He loves the old literature and reiterates the value of *yūgen*. His antiquarianism is pervasive: he admires the old whether it be in poetry, carpentry, or even torture racks for criminals.

Government and Politics

Unlike their predecessors, the Ashikaga shoguns did not attempt to establish a new center of power but conducted their affairs from Kyoto and appointed a deputy to look after their interests in the Kantō region. Other deputies were established in Kyūshū, west-central Japan, and in the North. Although the shoguns held the highest civil offices, their actual power depended on their control over their vassals. But the recent disorders had weakened old bonds, and the system of loyalties on which the Ashikaga depended proved to be highly unstable.

The Military Protectors of the Kamakura period now developed into military governors, although their title, *shugo*, remained the same. In the days of its vigor, the Kamakura *bakufu* had limited the power of the *shugo* by assigning men to provinces where they had no family roots or property, by asserting its right to dismiss and confirm the *shugo*, even though the positions eventually became hereditary, and by maintaining direct control over lesser vassals. However, the steady whittling down of the *shiki* of absentee proprietors, appropriated by local authority, worked to the advantage of the men who controlled the provinces. Furthermore, the Ashikaga, eager to obtain support, played into the hands of the military governors by assigning them virtually unlimited rights to taxation and adjudication. Increasingly the *shugo* were able to turn local warriors into vassals. Frequently the term *shugo-daimyo* is applied to these provincial powerholders who, like the later full-fledged daimyo, held extensive territory, but, unlike the later lords, still participated in central government.

The Ashikaga depended on the *shugo* families for support and appointed some of their leaders to important positions in their own *bakufu* organization.

Both *bakufu* and *shugo* were involved in a complicated balance of power, which all parties tried to manipulate to their own advantage. Until the Ōnin War, the fulcrum of this balance remained in Kyoto. Accordingly, the powerful provincial families established themselves in the capital and assigned deputies to manage the provinces on their behalf.

The situation offered military governors and their deputies opportunities but also posed dangers. They might be able to recruit local warriors as vassals to augment their own military power, but, in the absence of significant moral authority, they could not count on the loyalty of these men, who were concerned about their own family interests and were no more reluctant to switch sides than were their superiors.

On a lower level too the trend favored the warriors. Instead of retaining *shiki* in scattered areas, *jitō* now consolidated their holdings. They became strong enough to turn peasant leaders into vassals and took on the character of local overlords. The *shōen* system, badly battered by the fighting associated with the rivalry between the two courts, was severely damaged but did not disappear completely until the period of reunification discussed in the next chapter.

To complicate matters still further, the military families, *shugo* as well as *jitō*, themselves lost stability when a practice designed to strengthen families created as many problems as it solved. This happened when families abandoned the old tradition of dividing an estate equitably among a man's heirs. Feasible in times of peace and security, such fragmentation was too dangerous in a period of constant fighting when force alone restrained men in pursuit of wealth and power, and families needed to muster all their economic and human resources to survive. Therefore, to secure the family's future, the property was left intact and passed on to a single heir designated by the family head. This was not necessarily the eldest son, but it was always a son: a daughter would be unable to protect the property militarily. Far from functioning smoothly, however, this system frequently led to bitter rivalries and hard fought succession disputes. These, like all serious conflicts in this period, were settled by force of arms.

John Whitney Hall succinctly defined the ailment of the Ashikaga body politic when he wrote, "The imperial system was now in effect dead, but the system of military allegiances and feudal controls had not fully matured."[3] It was an inherently unstable government, and yet for a while under Yoshimitsu (1358–1408), it worked at least to a degree, and it neither hampered considerable economic growth nor inhibited fine cultural achievements.

Yoshimitsu and His Age

In 1368 Yoshimitsu, not yet ten, became the third shogun. Initially, however, the shogunate was controlled by the capable Hosokawa Yoriyuki, a member of one of the Ashikaga collateral families powerful in Kyoto and the provinces. Yoriyuki's official appointment was as Chief Administrator (*kanrei*), the top position in the *bakufu*, which was always assigned to one of the three most powerful vassal families (Hosokawa, Shiba, or Hatakeyama). His services to the *bakufu* included administrative reform, settlement of conflicting land claims, and a strengthening of the shogunate's finances. Spending was reduced and new sources of revenue were opened by taxing the wealth of sake breweries and pawnshops. These establishments frequently belonged to the same proprietor, since the original capital of the pawnshops often came from the profits of the sake trade. Indeed, taxes paid by commercial ventures in the capital were crucial to the Ashikaga *bakufu*, as they provided both a large and a reliable source of income.

When Yoshimitsu took power into his own hands, he continued efforts to strengthen the shogunate. He successfully met several military challenges, and in 1392 he secured the reunification of the two imperial courts. One further campaign (1399) was needed to assure a workable balance of power in the country. Through a series of tours to religious sites, such as Mt. Kōya and Ise, on which he was accompanied by an impressive retinue, Yoshimitsu further displayed his power and was also able to inspect local conditions in person. Lavish patronage of religious establishments no doubt helped to win him support in those quarters as well.

Yoshimitsu, unlike his father and grandfather, the first two Ashikaga shoguns, was born and raised in Kyoto and sought to combine his warrior heritage with the values long cherished in the capital. In gratifying his taste for fine architecture and beautiful gardens, he spared no expense. Unfortunately, his "Palace of Flowers" (Hana no Gosho) has not survived. Politically he demonstrated his dual legacy by assuming the title of Chancellor as well as shogun, and he even managed to have his wife made empress dowager! Yoshimitsu believed in doing things in truly royal style: once he entertained the emperor with twenty days of banqueting, music, and theatrical performances.

This entertainment took place on Yoshimitsu's estate in the northern hills (Kitayama) just beyond Kyoto, graced by the Golden Pavilion (Kinkakuji), a symbol of his good taste as well as of affluence. Although the roof line and parts of the building were covered with gold leaf, the plain surfaces of natural wood, the pavilion's shingled roofs, and the grilled shutters and solid doors of the second floor preserved the Japanese tradition of natural simplicity. On the other hand, the paneled doors and arched windows of the top story derive from the standard repertoire of Chinese Zen architecture. With artful casualness, the building is set on an artificial platform in a pond. It combined Chinese and native elements blended harmoniously and in good taste.

Chinese elements in the Golden Pavilion are but one facet of Song influence on Ashikaga art. Indeed, without the patronage of such men as Yoshimitsu, many valuable Chinese paintings would have been lost. The shogun's fondness for things Chinese extended also to Chinese dress, for he liked to wear Chinese clothes. He reported that the emperor of China visited him in his sleep. When awake, he made an effort to cultivate good relations with the Ming, phrasing his diplomatic communiqués in the properly humble language expected by the Chinese court, which recognized him as the "king" of

Japan. As usual, the Chinese responded to foreign tribute by giving even more impressive gifts in return. A lucrative trade ensued in which the officially patronized Five Zen Temples of Kyoto *(gozan)* played a leading role and from which they derived much wealth. Along with the Tenryūji, a Zen temple founded by Yoshimitsu, the Shōkokuji, played a prominent part in these undertakings. Here communications intended for the Ming were drafted by monks in Chinese. At Chinese request, Yoshimitsu took measures against Japanese pirates who infested East Asian waters.

It is characteristic of the age that Zen monks were welcomed not only for their religious insights but also for their managerial abilities, their command of Chinese learning, their poetic talents, and their expertise in the various arts. For example, the Zen monk Josetsu of the Shōkokuji was famous as an ink painter, and was patronized by both Yoshimitsu and his successor. His "Patriarchs of the Three Creeds" (Figure 5.2) reflects the religious, cultural, and artistic ambiance of the period. In it the three great teachers Sakyamuni, Confucius, and Lao Zi are shown in harmonious agreement. The "abbreviated" brushwork is in the manner beloved by Zen artists. Each figure is rendered in its own style, and every stroke, every line, counts. The style of this painting is Chinese, and its subject also inspired Song artists, although none of their paintings survive. It is a theme that reflects the Chinese trend toward religious and philosophical syncretism. Such syncretism was readily accepted in Japan, which had never experienced an

Figure 5.2 *Patriarchs of the Three Creeds.* Attributed to Josetsu. Hanging Scroll, ink on paper, 98.3 cm × 21.8 cm.

institutionalized Daoism competing with a Buddhist establishment and where Buddhism had from the first been mixed with Confucianism. The close relationship between Daoism and Zen has already been discussed. Josetsu's own name is a case in point. It was given to him by a great priest of the Shōkokuji and was derived from the *Daodejing* passage, "the greatest skill is *like clumsiness (josetsu)*."[4] This was his artistic ideal; and his achievement.

The Nō Drama

When Yoshimitsu hosted the emperor for twenty days, among the entertainments offered were performances of Nō, the classic drama of Japan. The roots of Nō go far back into the history of singing and dancing, music and mime, but its developed form was truly the creation of a remarkable father and son. Kan'ami (1333–84), a Shinto priest, and Zeami (or Seami, 1363–1443) developed this highly sophisticated theater out of a tradition of mimetic dance known as "monkey music" *(sarugaku)*. Father and son both composed plays and acted in them, and Zeami also formulated the critical and aesthetic criteria of the art. When Yoshimitsu first saw them perform, he was especially captivated by Zeami, then a good-looking boy of eleven, for the shogun was eclectic in his sexual as well as artistic preferences.

A performance of Nō is presented on a highly polished square wood stage open to the audience on three sides. A raised passageway leads from the actors' dressing room through the audience to the stage. Both stage and passageway are roofed. Three small pine trees placed in front of the passageway and a band of pebbles in front of the stage replicate the drainage area surrounding gutterless buildings, symbolic reminders that Nō performances were originally held out of doors. The stage is bare or almost bare. Occasionally there are symbolic representations of scenery, an outline of a boat, a cube to suggest a well. Likewise, stage properties are few and generally symbolic.

The Nō is often compared to the Greek drama, but the differences are as important as the similarities. For example, both use a chorus, but the chorus in Nō does not participate in the dramatic action. Seated at the side of the stage, the chorus expresses what is in the actor's mind and sings his lines when he dances. The music, produced by a flute and some drums, provides accompaniment and accent.

The actors and the chorus are all male. Some, but not all, of the actors wear highly stylized and exquisitely fashioned masks. The carving of these masks is itself a prized art. The one reproduced in Figure 5.3 represents a young woman. It illustrates the characteristic features of a classic Heian beauty, with her powdered complexion, artificial eyebrows, and blackened teeth. By subtle body movements and just the right tilt of the head, a great actor can suggest remarkable nuances of mood and emotion, while the frozen faces of the unmasked actors attain a mask-like effect. Attired in all

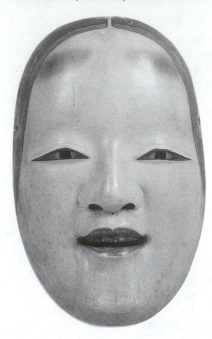

Figure 5.3
Nō Mask.

the elegance of Heian courtier costumes, the actors move with deliberate grace, unfolding gestures as full of meaning to the cognoscenti as those employed in the religious observances of esoteric Buddhism.

Nō plays are classified by the Japanese according to subject matter, that is, plays about a god, a warrior, a woman, a mad person, or a demon. It later became customary to include one of each type, in the order listed, in a full program that would take about six hours. The texts are short, and although they contain some fine poetry, they were always meant for the stage. The plots draw heavily on the literary tradition, recreating some of the best-loved and most poignant scenes from earlier literature, such as *The Tale of Genji*, *The Tale of the Heike*, and *The Tales of Ise*. As one might expect, there are plays about Yoshitsune and other notable figures, including the great poetess Komachi, who is portrayed as an old woman suffering because she had caused others to suffer when she was young and beautiful. Others deal with legends; the story of the fishermen who stole the angel's cloak (*Hagomoro*) is a favorite.

The tone is serious; the presentation symbolic. The typical Nō play is not an enactment of a dramatic episode nor a dramatic rendition of a historical or mythological occurrence; it is a retelling after the event. Consider the play based on the death of young Atsumori, reluctantly slain in battle by Kumagai as recounted in *The Tale of the Heike*. The main actors in Zeami's play on this theme are the priest who was once Kumagai and a young reaper who is actually the ghost of Atsumori. Here the purpose of art is not to mirror life but to transform it; setting the action in the play's own past creates the requisite artistic distance. It is an art which eschews realism and aspires to convey a sense of profound meaning beyond the words and scenes on stage. The ultimate criterion, according to Zeami himself, is a play's success in creating *yūgen*, the sense of underlying mystery.

A tone of grave sadness is hard to sustain for hours on end. Even a refined Kyoto aristocrat with his penchant for melancholy must have welcomed the comic relief provided by *kyōgen* (mad or wild words) performed in the interlude between Nō plays. Often in the nature of farce, they show a fondness for broad humor and foolery: servants outwitting their master, a dull country bumpkin sent out to purchase a sculpture of the Buddha and taken in by the trickery of an apprentice posing as a statue, and so on. Livelier than the Nō, the *kyōgen* are less demanding of the audience, but they lack the aura of poetic mystery that has sustained the Nō tradition in Japan.

Political Decline and Cultural Brilliance

When Yoshimitsu died in 1408 and was succeeded by his son, there was no radical discontinuity in shogunal politics nor even in cultural policies, although his death did bring to an end the favor shown to Zeami. Under the fifth shogun there were signs of fiscal and political weakness, but the following shogun, the sixth in line, Yoshinori (r. 1428–41), was able to rally the Ashikaga fortunes. However, Yoshinori's policy of strengthening the *bakufu* necessarily involved checking the power of strong military governors (*shugo*), and this turned out to be a dangerous as well as difficult game. It cost Yoshinori his life, when he was lured to a mansion by a military governor and assassinated.

Yoshinori turned out to be the last strong and vigorous Ashikaga shogun. His son was 8 when he inherited the office and died two years later. He was followed by another child, Yoshimasa (1436–90). Yoshimasa remained shogun for 30 years (1443–73) and then retired, having presided over the political collapse of the regime. From Yoshinori's assassination in 1441 to the outbreak of the Ōnin War in 1467, the government went through a process of disintegration. But the Ashikaga shogunate benefited from its historical momentum and the absence of a viable alternative, since the power of the provincial families, afflicted by succession disputes, was also declining. It is characteristic of the age that the Ashikaga downfall came not at the hands of a more powerful family or coalition but as the result of disputes within its own ranks. In 1464 Yoshimasa, still without an heir, designated his brother as next in line, but the following year his ambitious and strongminded wife bore him a son. Anxious to have her son be the next shogun, she found support in a powerful provincial governor's family, while another family backed the older claimant. Thus the ground was prepared for the succession struggle that produced the disastrous Ōnin War. The outcome of the war did not lead to the triumph of either family, but it did destroy the authority of the Ashikaga as well as half of the city of Kyoto, and it wreaked havoc on much of the surrounding country. During these violent years, Yoshimasa continued to emulate Yoshimitsu in patronizing the arts, for he had the exquisite aesthetic sensibilities long cultivated in Kyoto. But he completely lacked the qualities of command and decisiveness required of a shogun, a holder of what was, after all, a military office.

Yoshimasa was as lavish as Yoshimitsu in financing building projects and in giving entertainments. He too was a great patron of Nō and an admirer of Heian as well as Song aesthetics. Like Yoshimitsu his name is associated with a district in (what were then) the outskirts of Kyoto and to which he retired (Higashiyama). As a counterpart to Yoshimitsu's Golden Pavilion, there is Yoshimasa's Silver Pavilion (Ginkakuji), somewhat smaller, more intimate and more subdued than its predecessor, having two stories instead of three (see Figure 5.4). It too combines, or at least juxtaposes, Chinese and native elements, featuring a continental second story placed on a Japanese first story.

A Chinese theme is also echoed in the Ginkakuji's sand garden, identified as a rendition of the West Lake, outside Hangzhou, frequented by Song painters and poets like Su Shi on their pleasure outings. Near one bank, however, stands a volcano, also of sand—a miniature Mt. Fuji. Such gardens were the objects of much care and careful planning. Wealthy patrons like Yoshimasa went to great expense to obtain just the right effect. Transportation costs were disregarded when a stone was discovered precisely right in shape and texture and presenting the exact contrast between its rough and smooth surfaces required for the composition of the garden. As in China, stones themselves were objects of connoisseurship. Similar care went into the selection and pruning of plants and into performing the myriad chores necessary for maintaining a garden at its aesthetic best.

A story is told of a Chinese gentleman who painted the area around a window in his house to resemble the border of a hanging scroll, thus framing the view of his garden, which replaced the usual painted landscape. In Japan, too, the aesthetics of garden design and landscape painting were closely related. The garden artist also could choose rich, colorful landscapes, using tree and shrub, rivulet and waterfall, pond and bridge; or he could confine himself to stone and carefully raked sand, much like the ink painter who rejected color. Such sand and stone gardens can be viewed as three-dimensional monochrome landscapes, the sand representing water, the rocks functioning as mountains; or they can be enjoyed as abstract sculptures inviting the viewer to exercise his or her imagination. Like Zen they concentrate on the essentials. The finest are found in the Zen temples of Kyoto (see Figure 5.5). Not all of the Ryōanji's fifteen stones are visible in this photograph, since the garden is designed so that there is no single point from which they can all be seen at once.

The compound of the Silver Pavilion also contains a small hall, the interior of which is divided between a Buddhist chapel and a new element: a room for the performance of the tea ceremony. Tea grew in popularity after its enthusiastic advocacy by Eisai, the Zen monk who introduced Rinzai to Japan, but it was not until the time of Yoshimasa that the formal consumption of this beverage was developed into a ritual art with its own strict rules and regulations. The accent in the classic tea ceremony is on simplicity and tranquility.

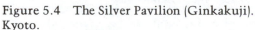

Figure 5.4   The Silver Pavilion (Ginkakuji). Kyoto.

Figure 5.5   Sand and Stone Garden. Ryōanji, Kyoto.

Through a small doorway no bigger than a window, the guests crawl into a room about nine feet square, there to enjoy in silent calm the movements of their host as he prepares the tea with motions as deliberate as those of an actor on the Nō stage. After they have drunk the deep green tea, they may exchange a few remarks about the bowl or the flower arrangement prepared for the ceremony. Among the unrefined, the ceremony may be exaggerated into ostentation; in incapable hands it easily degenerates into an empty and pedantic formalism; but when performed with an easy grace by a master, it can convey Japanese good taste at its best. The cult of tea—for such it was—reached perhaps its greatest height during the Momoyama period (1568–1600).

The tea ceremony influenced secular architecture, which during the Ashikaga period adopted many of the features of the tea room. Rush matting (*tatami*) now covered the whole floor—previously individual mats had been placed on wooden floors as needed to provide a place for people to sit. Sliding doors consisting of paper pasted on a wooden frame (*shoji*) came into common use, supplementing the earlier sliding partitions (*fusuma*) with their painted surfaces. Another standard feature is the alcove (*tokonoma*) with its hanging scroll and flower arrangement. Flower arrangement, like the tea service, became an art, with its own rules and styles passed on through the generations by the masters of distinct schools. It became one of the polite accomplishments expected of those with a claim to refinement.

In all the arts the influence of Zen aesthetics remained strong even after the Ōnin War disrupted the network centered on the Five Kyoto Temples, which by then included some 300 monasteries or several thousand institutions if sub- and branch-temple affiliates are counted separately.

Poetry and Painting

In Yoshimasa's time poetry continued to be an important part of Kyoto life. In the Heian period it was not uncommon for one poet to supply the first three lines of a *tanka*, leaving it to his companion to complete the poem with a suitable couplet. From such origins grew the linked verse *(renga)* which became a favorite Muromachi pastime. Its instability was an important part of its appeal. Nijō Yoshimoto (1320–88), a champion of *renga*, put it this way:

> The poet of *renga* does not seek to tie the idea of one moment in with that of the next but, like this fleeting world, shifts through phases of both waxing and waning, of sadness and joy. No sooner does he reflect on yesterday than today has passed; while thinking about spring it becomes autumn, and even as he admires a scene of new blossoms it turns into one of crimson leaves. Is this not proof that everything is impermanent, like scattered flowers and fallen leaves?[5]

Reflecting its social nature, the composition of *renga* came to be governed by complicated rules:

> Of the opening verse (the *hokku*) it was said, "The *hokku* should not be at variance with the topography of the place, whether the mountains or the sea dominate, with the flying flowers or falling leaves of the grasses and trees of the season, with the wind, clouds, mist, fog, rain, dew, frost, snow, heat, cold or quarter of the moon. Objects which excite a ready response possess the greatest interest for inclusion in a *hokku*, such as spring birds or autumn insects. But the *hokku* is not of merit if it looks as though it had been previously prepared." The requirements for the second verse were somewhat less demanding; it had to be closely related to the first and to end in a noun. The third verse was more independent and ended in a particle; the fourth had to be "smooth"; the moon had to occur in a certain verse; cherry-blossoms could not be mentioned before a certain point; autumn and spring had to be repeated in at least three but not more than five successive verses, while summer and winter could be dropped after one mention, etc.[6]

A master like the Zen monk Sōgi (1421–1502), the greatest of the *renga* poets, was able to create fine poetry within this framework. Sōgi also composed *tanka* in the old tradition of court poetry, now coming to an end. The last imperial anthology was compiled in the fifteenth century. The *renga* may not have been a great poetic form itself, but it pointed in new directions.

In painting as in poetry, Zen monks continued to contribute greatly. Josetsu's style of monochrome painting was continued by two Zen monks, Shūbun (d. 1450) and Sesshū (1420–1506), both trained at the Shōkokuji.

In their work the influence of Song painting remains clearly visible. The fifteenth-century painter-monks in the great Zen temples could draw on Japanese ink paintings in the Chinese manner going back to the Kamakura period, and the more eminent or fortunate among them might also see the Chinese paintings kept in Japan. The prime source for these was the shogunal collection systematized and cataloged for the first time under Yoshimasa. Most fortunate were those who were able to travel abroad. Thus Shubun drew inspiration from a journey to Korea, and Sesshū was able to travel to and in China. There was no need for him to paint Chinese landscapes from imagination alone.

Sesshū's versatile genius expressed itself in a variety of styles. One of his greatest paintings shows the man who was to become the second Zen patriarch offering his severed arm as a token of religious commitment to Bodhidharma, the reputed Indian founder of Zen in China. Another is a long landscape scroll (over 52 feet long) guiding the viewer on a leisurely trip through scenery and seasons. Reproduced in Figure 5.6 is his painting of a reknowned beauty spot on the Sea of Japan, Ama-no-Hashidate (the Bridge of Heaven). It was evidently painted on the basis of personal observation in the period shortly before his death. The written identification of the various localities confirms the realism of this solidly constructed painting, while the softness of the painter's brush techniques is appropriate for the gentle Japanese landscape.

Although Zen monks and temples had the greatest influence on the arts, some major contributions were also made by believers in the *nembutsu*, who

Figure 5.6   Sesshū, *Ama-no-Hashidate.* Hanging scroll, ink and light color on paper, 177.8 cm long.

demonstrated their faith in Amida by incorporating his name in theirs. The aesthetics of Nō may well be compatible with the teachings of Zen, but the greatest names in this theater were, as we have seen, Kan'ami and Zeami. And among the main painters in the monochrome style imported from the continent were the three Ami: Nōami (ca. 1394–1471), Geiami (1431–85), and Sōami (d. 1525), father, son, and grandson. These three men were not only fine painters but also served as the shogun's advisers in aesthetic matters, cataloging and evaluating his art collection and passing as masters in the whole gamut of Ashikaga art from flower arranging, tea, and incense to music and the stage.

Also part of the artistic scene were professional painters. Two names that were to remain important as major schools of painting enjoying official favor first appear in the fifteenth century. These schools, like the schools of Nō and other arts, were continued from father to son or, if necessary, to adopted son, perpetuating their traditions much like warrior or merchant families. Their secrets were just as carefully guarded as the formulae of sake brewers or pharmacists. Painting in the old native style (Yamato-e), Tosa Mitsunobu (1434–1525) became official painter to both the imperial court and the *bakufu*. Provided with a generous grant of land, he was able to establish the social and economic position of his family. Meanwhile his contemporary Kanō Masanobu (1434–1530) painted in the Chinese manner, although without all of the religious and literary associations found in the work of the nonprofessional artists. Of the two, the Kanō line was the more creative. Masanobu's son Motonobu (1476–1559) added color to his paintings. In this he was very likely influenced by the Tosa school.

It is the blending of the imported and the native that produced the characteristic Muromachi taste, a taste common to the aesthetic of the Nō mask, the sand garden, the tea ceremony, and a Sesshū landscape, a taste for the old *(sabi)*, the solitary and poor *(wabi)*, the astringent *(shibui)*, and the profound *(yūgen)*. The prestige of Chinese culture was enormous, and Sinophiles versified and painted in Chinese. But, unlike their predecessors of the Nara period, they were selective in their borrowing and rapidly assimilated the new. In later ages Muromachi aesthetic sensibility was challenged, assailed, and even displaced, but it never disappeared completely.

Economic Growth

The economy grew during the Kamakura epoch and even more spectacularly in Ashikaga times. Frequently developments that originated in the earlier period reached fruition in the later. The basis of the economy remained agricultural, and an increasing agricultural yield provided the means for growth. Improvements in farm technology employing better tools and devices such as the water wheel, new crops and new strains of rice, and a greater use of draft animals, were some of the major developments that increased the productivity of the land. This in turn had a positive impact on commerce and manufacturing. Technical progress in such endeavors as mining, sake brewing, and paper production, to mention just a few, further contributed to this process.

An added stimulus came from trade with China and Korea. Initiated by Yoshimitsu, it continued, with minor interruptions, to grow and flourish. To control this commerce and keep the number of ships within agreed-upon limits, the Ming issued official tallies valid for trading at a specified port. This system also helped control piracy by restricting the pirates' ability to trade stolen goods; it lasted until the middle of the sixteenth century. Japanese imports included cotton from Korea, and from China came great quantities of copper coins as well as porcelain, paintings, medicine, and books. A major Japanese export was fine swords. Japan also exported copper, sulphur, folding fans (a Japanese invention), screens, and so forth. The ability to trade products of sophisticated craftsmanship is another index of Japanese accomplishments during this period.

With the growth of commerce, of markets, and of market towns, there appeared guilds (za) formed by merchants and artisans to exercise monopoly rights over the exchange and production of various commodities. To safeguard their rights and privileges, and to obtain protection, these guilds turned to the great religious institutions and powerful families. The pawnbrokers of Kyoto, for example, enjoyed the protection of the Tendai monastery on Mt. Hiei, which on more than one occasion sent armed monks into the capital on behalf of its clients. Temples and shrines, the great families, and the bakufu itself welcomed the guilds as an additional source of revenue and became increasingly dependent on income from this source. As noted earlier, already under Yoshimitsu, the Ashikaga shogun relied heavily on income from these quarters, and this trend continued. The prosperity of the pawnbrokers is only one of several signs of the increasing use of money, a development which was both a product of and a stimulus to commercial growth. To facilitate transactions between places distant from each other, bills of exchange came into use.

Around ports and markets, cities grew. The most impressive was Sakai, near modern Osaka, which became an autonomous political unit governed by a group of elders who were mostly merchants. Hakata in Kyūshū, the center for trade with Korea, also flourished, as did a number of other well-placed cities.

The growth of cities and similar economic developments suggest parallels with European history, but such parallels hold only to a limited degree. Japanese merchants and cities did not achieve sufficient power to threaten the prevailing order; rather the merchants provided a source of revenue for feudal lords. Social and political institutions were not shattered, but society was enriched by the emergence of a new urban population. One result of political decentralization combined with economic growth was the diffusion of higher culture to the provinces. Conversely, students of Nō and linked verse have pointed out that these arts owe much to popular culture. Sōgi, the great master of linked verse, was himself of obscure parentage. Many more opportunities for men of low birth were created during the warfare that marked the last phase of the Ashikaga period.

War and the Rise of the Daimyo

The Ōnin War (1467–77) was a major turning point in Japanese history. It not only destroyed the power of the Ashikaga *bakufu* but also put an end to the system on which it was precariously based. The *shugo*, who had been drawn into Kyoto, were replaced by local deputies. Not only was the old balance of power demolished; its very constituents were eliminated. The Ōnin War became merely the first decade of a century of warfare. During this period, the shogun, unable to control even the provinces near Kyoto, was reduced to a symbol preserving the idea and the ideal of a unified state, even as the last vestiges of centralized government were swept away. Meanwhile, beneath the troubled, chaotic surface of events, new developments were at work reshaping the Japanese state and society.

With the collapse of effective central government, what had been a decentralized state gave way to radical fragmentation as Japan was divided into many separate principalities, directed by feudal lords known as daimyo. These lords competed with each other to preserve their territories and, if possible, to expand them. The sizes of these principalities varied widely; some were no larger than a small castle town while others might be as large as one of the old provinces. Regardless of the size of his holdings, the daimyo's fate depended entirely on his success in the field of battle. What counted was power. Although some of the mid-sixteenth-century daimyo belonged to the old families, many emerged out of the class of local warriors. In these strenuous, difficult times, capable, ambitious, and unscrupulous men struggled to the top using any means at hand; frequently, betrayal was the price of upward mobility. The introduction of formal oaths, unnecessary in an older and simpler age, did not change the situation. Vassals could be counted on for their loyalty only as long as it was in their own best interests to be loyal.

To obtain and hold their vassals, the daimyo granted or confirmed landholdings, much like European fiefs, thereby bringing to a final end the old and complicated system of *shōen* and *shiki*. In return for their grants, the vassals were obliged to render military service to their lord and provide the services of a set number of their own fighting men. Without the support of the now defunct system of political centralization, the remnants of the old *shōen* system could not survive.

Disruption and uncertainty affected the people at the bottom of society at least as much as the elite. This was a period of great popular unrest. During the middle of the fifteenth century, there were extensive peasant uprisings demanding debt cancellation. In one case in Yamashiro province, near Kyoto, peasants were able to hold power for eight years (1485–93). Also powerful were uprisings led by religious sects, particularly the well-organized Ikkō sect, whose members followed Shinran's True Pure Land Buddhism. These sectarians were able to obtain control of the province of Kaga, on the Sea of Japan, and extend their power into neighboring Echizen, as well as holding a strategic stronghold in the Kyoto-Osaka area.

The future, however, was to belong to warriors, not peasants or religious institutions. In the long run, success in this precarious age went to those daimyo who could most effectively mobilize the resources of their domains, turning them into small states. The ultimate consequence of the breakdown of central unity was the creation of smaller but more highly integrated political entities. Daimyo normally asserted their authority over the succession of their vassals and, since political combinations were involved, they also had a say concerning their vassals' marriages. Some daimyo, in their house laws, asserted rights to tax the land in their territory and to regulate economic activities. Frequently, spies were employed to keep the lord informed of the activities and plans of his vassals.

A potent force for integration was the changing nature of warfare. It was found that massed foot soldiers, recruited from the peasantry and armed with spears and the like, were an effective force against the traditional, proud, and expensive mounted warriors. Armies grew larger, and vassals tended to serve as officers commanding troops of commoners.

Sixteenth-century Japan was no exception to the rule that change in offense sooner or later stimulates new developments in defense. The Japanese answer to the new armies was the castle. It was often built on a hill, crowned with a tower, protected by walls, and surrounded by a moat or a natural body of water. These castles often served as the centers of daimyo-states, and there appeared a tendency for warriors to be gathered there removed from the land.

An added impetus to the use of the new type of armies came after the Portuguese introduced European firearms to Japan in 1543. Within ten years the daimyo of Western Japan were using imported and domestic muskets in their armies. In response, bigger and more elaborate castles became necessary, so that in defense as well as in offense the larger daimyo with ample means had a decisive advantage.

By the middle of the sixteenth century, trends toward political consolidation were apparent, but that did not come quickly or easily.

NOTES

1. H. Paul Varley, *Imperial Restoration in Medieval Japan* (New York: Columbia Univ. Press, 1971), p. 131.

2. Susan Bush, *The Chinese Literati on Painting: Su Shih (1037–1101) to Tung Ch'i–ch'ang (1555–1636)* (Cambridge: Harvard Univ. Press, 1971), p. 25.

3. John Whitney Hall, *Japan from Prehistory to Modern Times* (New York: Dell Publishing, 1970), p. 110.

4. Jan Fontein and Money L. Hickman, *Zen Painting and Calligraphy* (Boston: Museum of Fine Arts, 1970), p. 93.

5. Quoted by H. Paul Varley in Kozo Yamamura, ed. *The Cambridge History of Japan*, Vol. 3: *Medieval Japan* (Cambridge: Cambridge Univ. Press, 1990), p. 475.

6. Donald Keene, *Japanese Literature* (New York: Grove Press, 1955), pp. 34–35.

PART THREE

Late Traditional Japan

Figure 6   Harunobu, *Boy Water Vendor*. Calendar Print. 1765. Tokyo National Museum.

六　新秩序・形成

6
The Formation of a New Order

I. Unification and Consolidation (1573–1651)
Oda Nobunaga
Toyotomi Hideyoshi
The Invasion of Korea
Grand Castles and the Arts
The Tokugawa Political
  Consolidation

II. Japan and Europe: First Encounters (1543–1630)
The Portuguese in East Asia
The Jesuits in Japan: Initial Success
Persecution and Closure to the West

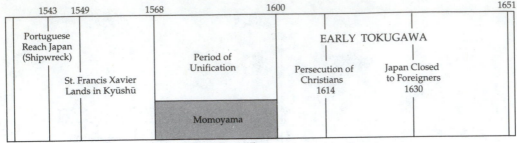

1543	1549	1568	1600	1651

Portuguese Reach Japan (Shipwreck)

St. Francis Xavier Lands in Kyūshū

Period of Unification

Momoyama

(1568 - 1600 or 1615)

EARLY TOKUGAWA

Persecution of Christians 1614

Japan Closed to Foreigners 1630

*I*n this part, we will consider Japan during the period of unification and the first two centuries of the Tokugawa shogunate. During these momentous years in world history, European civilization was transformed in ways which were to have profound effect all over the globe. But that came later. For now Japan was left free to deal with overseas challenges on its own terms and to develop according to its own internal dynamics. In the process, Japan underwent changes so deep that some scholars have described this period as "early modern," (*kinsei*) comparable to the European Renaissance. This designation is useful in that it highlights continuities with what was to come as well as the very considerable discontinuities with earlier history. Conversely, however, it may distract from what the Tokugawa shared with its past or cause us to overestimate its links to the future.

During the last thirty years of the sixteenth century, Japan was reunified, and the foundations were laid for an orderly political and social system as well as for economic growth. This was also a time of vigorous interaction between Japan and the outside world. We begin with internal developments.

PART I. UNIFICATION AND CONSOLIDATION (1573–1651)

The restoration of central authority was accomplished under three leaders. It was a cumulative process, each man building on the work of his predecessors. Begun by Oda Nobunaga (1534–82), it was virtually completed by Toyotomi Hideyoshi (1542–1616), but the final consolidation and grounding were left to Tokugawa Ieyasu (1542–1616). Ieyasu was appointed shogun in 1603, but this merely confirmed the hegemony he had established at the decisive battle of Sekigahara in 1600, a victory marking the effective beginning of the Tokugawa shogunate. Following in Ieyasu's footsteps, the second and third shoguns continued to strengthen and solidify the Tokugawa order.

Oda Nobunaga

Nobunaga inherited control of Owari, not one of the great territories but of strategic importance because it was located in central Honshū between the

Kantō and the capital region. From this base, he embarked on a ruthless drive for supremacy carried out with great military and political skill. In 1560 he won one of the key battles of his career by defeating an enemy army of some 25,000 with only 2,000 men of his own. In 1568 he entered Kyoto. For another five years the last Ashikaga shogun precariously retained his title, but then for thirty years, from 1573 to 1603, there was no shogun.

An important element in his military success was Nobunaga's effective use of firearms. As already noted, after their introduction by the Portuguese in 1543, daimyo were using imported and homemade muskets in their armies. Nobunaga was quick to employ the new weapons and techniques; he had the will as well as the means to do so with great effectiveness. Thus, in 1575 he won a crucial battle through the superior firepower of his 3,000 musketeers. For defense he built a great castle at Azuchi on the shore of Lake Biwa.

Secular opponents were not alone in feeling the full force of Nobunaga's wrath. After he seized Kyoto, he turned his attention to the monks on Mt. Hiei and put an end once and for all to the military proclivities of the great Tendai monastery. He did this by destroying its buildings, slaughtering its monks, and eliminating the unfortunate inhabitants of nearby villages. "The roar of the huge burning monastery, magnified by the cries of countless numbers of the old and young, sounded and resounded to the ends of heaven and earth."[1] An estimated 1,600 people lost their lives in this terrible bloodletting. Nobunaga was similarly set in his hostility toward the Ikkō sect. In Echizen province, he was responsible for the death of 30,000–40,000 Ikkō adherents, although he did not eradicate the sect completely. Even Mt. Kōya only narrowly escaped Nobunaga's wrath. His hostility to organized Buddhism was one of the factors influencing the friendly reception he accorded the first Jesuit missionaries to enter Japan.

Nobunaga was politically adroit. He forged valuable alliances through his marriage policies, managed to keep his enemies divided, and retained his followers and allies. A major element in his growing power was his ability to attract new vassals, frequently men who had been the vassals of his rivals. By going over to Nobunaga they could secure their own positions and hope to participate in future gains. Thus success fed on success.

By opening markets, breaking up guild monopolies, destroying toll stations, and encouraging road construction and shipbuilding, Nobunaga fostered trade. He also reorganized the administration of his lands, introducing a new system of tax collection and initiating a land survey. And he began to disarm the peasantry. Both were in full swing when Nobunaga died, betrayed by one of his own generals avenging a wrong. At the time of his death, he controlled about a third of Japan but clearly indicated his intent to be master of all.

Toyotomi Hideyoshi

Hideyoshi was born a peasant but rose to become one of Nobunaga's foremost generals. After Nobunaga's death, he defeated other contenders for the succession and then continued to increase his power much in the manner of Nobunaga, inducing daimyo to acknowledge his supremacy. Hideyoshi continued to increase his power by diplomacy. Unable to subdue the strongest daimyo, Tokugawa Ieyasu, he gave his sister to Ieyasu in marriage and assigned him very substantial holdings in the Kantō in exchange for domains of less value in central Japan. In this way he saw to it that Ieyasu was both content and at a distance.

Hideyoshi also relocated his own vassals to assure maximum security. Those he trusted most were placed in strategic positions, while those thought to harbor territorial ambitions were provided with hostile neighbors to discourage them. To demonstrate their loyalty, vassals were sometimes required to leave wives and children with Hideyoshi as virtual hostages. Feudal bonds were further strengthened through marriage alliances. Thus, through conquest, diplomacy, and manipulation Hideyoshi became, in effect, overlord of all Japan. By 1590 all daimyo swore oaths of loyalty to him. Since he did not belong to the Minamoto lineage, he was ineligible to become shogun. He did have himself adopted into the Fujiwara family, and in 1585 he was appointed regent *(kampaku)*. This association with the imperial throne gave added legitimacy to his place at the apex of a system of feudal loyalties.

Hideyoshi was intent to keep the daimyo in their places but not to eliminate them. On the contrary, his policies strengthened the daimyo locally vis-à-vis their warriors and farmers even as he took steps to assure their subordination. When a daimyo was relocated, he took many of his vassals with him into his new domain where they had no hereditary links to the land. This accelerated a tendency, already visible earlier, for samurai to be concentrated in castle towns where they received stipends collected from land but were divorced from direct supervision of the land. On the one hand, this severed the samurai from an independent power base and made them dependent on the daimyo. On the other, villages were left to provide their own leadership and to run their own affairs with little outside interference as long as they fulfilled their tax obligations. The village was freed from samurai control even as it was deprived of warrior leadership in case of conflict.

One of Hideyoshi's most important acts was the great "sword hunt" of 1588, when all peasants who had not already done so were ordered to surrender their weapons, the metal to be used in building a great statue of the Buddha. By depriving peasants of their weapons he did more than discourage them from rioting or rebelling—although he did that too. A major, and intentional, consequence of the measure was to draw a sharp line between peasant and samurai, to create an unbridgeable gulf between the tiller of the soil and the bearer of arms, where hitherto there had been low-ranking samurai who had also worked the land.

By this time Hideyoshi's land survey, begun in 1582 but not completed for all of Japan until 1598, was well under way. In this great survey the value of cultivated land was assessed in terms of average annual productivity, measured in *koku* of rice, a *koku* being equal to 4.96 bushels. The resulting listings were used to assess the taxes due from each village, and the holdings of the daimyo were also calculated in terms of the assessed value rather than acreage. From this time on, a daimyo, by definition, held land assessed at a minimum of 10,000 *koku.* Large daimyo held much more than that. Some of the greatest had several hundred thousand *koku,* and there were a few with over a million. Hideyoshi personally held 2 million, not including the lands of his major most trustworthy vassals. Tokugawa Ieyasu held 2,557,000. Like the confiscation of weapons, the land survey, which listed the names of the peasant proprietors, effectively separated farmers and fighters.

An edict of 1591 carried the process still further. The first of its three articles prohibited fighting men from becoming peasants or townsmen, and the second forbade peasants to leave their fields and become merchants or artisans and prohibited the latter from becoming farmers. The third prohibited anyone from employing a samurai who had left his master without permission. If discovered, the offender was to be returned to his master. If this was not done and the culprit was knowingly allowed to go free, then the edict declared that "three persons shall be beheaded in place of the one, and their heads sent to the offender's original master. If this threefold substitution is not effected, then there is no alternative but to punish the new master."[2] In this way, Hideyoshi, who had himself risen from the peasantry to the greatest heights, did his best to make sure that henceforth everyone would remain within his hereditary social status.

The Invasion of Korea

Hideyoshi's vision of the world and his own place in it extended well beyond Japan. He took an active interest in overseas trade. After he subjugated the Kyūshū daimyo, he undertook to suppress the pirates and freebooters who had long plagued the Chinese and Korean coasts. In East Asia as elsewhere the line between trade and piracy was often obscure as was the actual nationality of the so-called "Japanese pirates" *(wakō),* many of whom were Chinese. Hideyoshi undertook other measures to encourage international commerce. One of his two great castles was at Osaka, which soon eclipsed Sakai as a trading center and remains today the second largest city in Japan.

But Hideyoshi looked abroad for more than trade: he thought in terms of empire. In the 1590s, he demanded the submission of the Philippines by their Spanish governor, although no steps were ever taken to enforce the demand. He also made plans to conquer China, which he then intended to divide among his vassals, much in the same way he had dealt with his Japanese conquests. After China would come India and indeed the rest of the world as he knew it. Hideyoshi's invasion of the continent can partially be seen as an attempt to satisfy the perpetual land hunger of his vassals or, at least, to find employment for restive samurai. It would also convince the Japanese as well as the rest of the world of Hideyoshi's power and glory. Another factor surely was his personality, but Jurgis Elisonas has suggested that "not so much megalomania as ignorance moved the entire enterprise."[3]

Whatever Hideyoshi's motivation, he dispatched a force of 150,000 men to Korea in 1592, after Korea had refused free passage for his troops to march to China. The Japanese force had great initial success and captured Seoul within a month. But they ran into difficulties further north and were bested at sea by the superior ships and seamanship of the Korean fleet under Admiral Yi Sun-sin, famous for his armed "turtle ships." Chinese military intervention and Korean guerrilla fighting also took their toll, and in 1593 peace negotiations were under way. These talks were fruitless, however, and in 1597 Hideyoshi sent another force of 140,000 men to Korea. This time they met with stronger resistance. The whole attempt was suddenly abandoned when Hideyoshi died in 1598, and the Japanese forces immediately returned home.

The expense of the campaign helped undermine the Ming dynasty in China, but the real losers were the Korean people who suffered pillage and rape at the hands of their Chinese allies as well as the Japanese. In the second campaign, the Japanese announced that all Korean officials along with their wives and children would be killed, as would any farmer who did not return to his house and land. Following through, the Japanese conducted manhunts, and as proof of their exploits commanders sent back to Hideyoshi in Japan casks filled with noses preserved in salt. Careful records were kept, and nose counts figured in determining promotions and rewards. Other Koreans were brought back to Japan in bondage. One result was an infusion of Korean influence on Japanese pottery and printing.

Hideyoshi himself never joined the Korean campaigns but left command to his vassals, several of whom were seriously weakened as a result. As it turned out, not only his continental ambitions but also his hopes to found a lasting dynasty at home came to naught. Before he died, he made his most powerful vassals solemnly swear allegiance to his five-year-old son, Hideyori, whom he left in their care as regents. But this proved useless, and in the ensuing struggle for power Ieyasu emerged the winner. His victory at Sekigahara in 1600 was followed by his designation as shogun in 1603, after he had acquired a suitable Minamoto ancestry. Final confirmation of Ieyasu's triumph came with the fall of Osaka Castle and the death of Hideyori in 1615. Ieyasu inherited Hideyoshi's power, but unlike Hideyoshi, he concentrated on building a lasting state at home.

Grand Castles and the Arts

The period of unification is usually called the Azuchi-Momoyama epoch (or Momoyama for short) after Nobunaga's Azuchi Castle near Lake Biwa and Hideyoshi's Momoyama Castle in Fushimi, close to Kyoto. In many ways, these castles, along with those of the daimyo, are fitting representatives of the age. Dominating the surrounding countryside, they featured massive keeps and strong fortifications designed to withstand the new armies and weapons. Their great size was made possible by the wealth obtained by the unifiers and the daimyo as they achieved greater local control. The castles formed nuclei around which grew new cities, as first samurai and then merchants and artisans were attracted to castle towns. The most grandiose of all the castles was built by Hideyoshi in Osaka and boasted forty-eight towers. Unfortunately, Hideyoshi's castles and Nobunaga's were all destroyed, although the Osaka Castle was later rebuilt (see p. xi).

Most admired among Japan's castles is that at Himeji, which dates essentially from the early seventeenth century. In recognition of its suggestive white silhouette, it is commonly known as the "Heron Castle" (see Figure 6.1). Like European castles, it is a stronghold surrounded by moat and wall and protected by massive foundations. But the gracefulness of its higher reaches is reminiscent of a chateau rather than a fortress. Aesthetics were an important consideration in building a castle, and not only to please its owner, for "its purpose was to impress rivals by its elegant interiors as well as to frighten them by its strength."[4] One way to impress people was through richness of decor. The dark interiors of the castle were "lavish to the point of absurdity."[5] Hideyoshi's castle even had locks and bolts of gold and columns and ceilings covered with the precious metal.

Paintings on walls, sliding doors, and screens decorated and brightened the castle interiors. To meet new needs and tastes, the paintings were frequently large and used striking colors. Gold leaf was employed to create a flat background with the result that "its unreality reinforces the assertive substance of painted objects."[6] The artist Kano Eitoku (1543–90) epitomized the new style and spirit. Generously patronized by both Nobunaga and Hideyoshi, Eitoku worked at both the Azuchi and Momoyama castles. The Eitoku screen shown in Figure 6.2 was originally one of a pair, but its companion is now lost. It is about 20 feet long and 8 feet high and was

Figure 6.1   Himeji Castle. Himeji, Hyōgo.

Figure 6.2   Kanō Eitoku, *Chinese Lions* (Kara-shiki). Section of six-fold screen, 225 cm high. Imperial Household Collection, Tokyo.

obviously intended for use in a large room. Two "Chinese lions" are depicted against a gold background:

> Contour lines in ink are dashed on with sure twists and thrusts of the brush, alive and tense in each curve and linear opposition, to form the bodies of the two beasts as an incarnation of controlled ferocity. The flamelike treatment of the manes and tails gives a curvilinear lift, as an upward pull against the bulky weight. Massive and yet with a coiled spring of inner power . . . Eitoku has found the exact pictorial equivalent for the inner threat under a coating of dignity and majesty, such as a Hideyoshi would want to exert over the rebellious feudal barons.[7]

The Kanō school was continued by Eitoku's adopted son, Sanraku (1559–1653), in a trend which culminated in the great decorative screens of the early Tokugawa period. In another medium, Momoyama fondness for rich decoration produced elaborate wood carvings such as those on the Kara Gate of the Nishi Honganji in Kyoto, popularly known as the gate which requires a whole day to be properly seen.

Ostentatious and profuse, the Momoyama aesthetic is far removed from Ashikaga restraint. Nothing could be more alien to the aesthetics of the tea ceremony than the monster tea party given by Hideyoshi in 1587, to which literally everyone was invited for ten days of music, theater, and art viewing. This was not the only occasion on which Hideyoshi displayed a penchant for great gatherings and lavish entertainment. Yet the old values also survived, especially in the tea ceremony, although admittedly the fantastic prices paid by wealthy daimyo competing for ownership of a famous bowl or jar were not exactly in keeping with the intended spirit of tea. Sen no Rikyū (1522–91), greatest of the tea masters, stressed harmony, respect, purity, and tranquility in his writings on tea. Patronized by Hideyoshi, he was widely influential until, for reasons unknown, Hideyoshi ordered him to commit suicide. A story told about the great tea master and his son has them visiting another practitioner of the art. When they entered the garden, the son admired the wooden gate, covered with moss, at the end of the path leading to the tea hut, but the father disagreed: "That gate must have been brought from some distant mountain at obvious expense. A rough wicket made by the local farmer

Figure 6.3   Chōjirō, *Tea Bowl Named "Shobu."* Raku ware, sixteenth century, 8.9 cm high. Hakone Art Museum.

would give the place a really quiet and lonely look, and not offend us by bringing up thoughts of difficulty and expense. I doubt if we shall find here any very sensitive or interesting tea ceremony."[8]

Sen no Rikyū is said to have influenced the potter Chōjirō (1576–92), originator of Raku ware, illustrated by the tea bowl (see Figure 6.3). Eschewing the technical virtuosity of Chinese ceramics, the Japanese potter delights in bringing out the qualities of the clay. Another Momoyama tea master, Furuta Oribe (1544–1615), originated a ceramic tradition characterized by thick glazes and rough brushwork, and Korean-influenced Shino ware exhibited a traditionally Japanese freedom of decoration.

As in China, artists in Japan often worked in more than one style. Both Eitoku and his great contemporary Hasegawa Tōhaku (1539–1610) worked in monochrome as well as in color. In scale, Tōhaku's masterly *Pine Grove* (see Figure 6.4) is typically Momoyama, for it occupies two screens over five feet (61 inches) high; but it is ink on paper. By his subtle gradations in

Figure 6.4   Hasegawa Tōhaku, *Pine Grove.* Section of six-fold screen, 155.6 cm × 346.9 cm.

ink-tone and the fine work of his brush, the artist has created the effect of pines seen through the mist. The placing of the trees and the marvelous use of empty space imbue the painting with rhythm and create a poetry that goes beyond decoration.

The Tokugawa Political Consolidation

The essential structure of the Tokugawa political system was devised by Ieyasu and completed by his two immediate successors, Hidetada (1616–23) and Iemitsu (1623–51). By the middle of the seventeenth century, the system was in full operation.

Ieyasu rose to supremacy as the leader of a group of daimyo, each of whom was backed by his own vassals and supported by his independent power base. The daimyo were by no means all deeply committed to the Tokugawa. Hideyoshi's recent failure to establish a dynasty had demonstrated, if any demonstration was needed, the folly of relying solely on the loyalty of such men, especially when passing on the succession to a minor. Ieyasu himself assured the smooth transfer of power to his son by resigning from the office of shogun, in 1605, after holding it for only two years. But he continued in actual control until his death, working to ensure the continuity of Tokugawa rule.

All the daimyo were the shogun's vassals, bound to him by solemn oath, and when a daimyo's heir succeeded to his domain, the new daimyo had to sign his pledge of vassalage to the shogun in blood. Still, some vassals were more reliable than others, and the Tokugawa classified them into three groups. Least trusted and potentially the most dangerous were the "outside," or allied, daimyo (tozama), who were too powerful to be considered Tokugawa subordinates. Virtually all of these, like Ieyasu, had been vassals of Hideyoshi. Some had supported Ieyasu at the battle of Sekigahara, but others came over to the Tokugawa only after the outcome of that battle left them no other choice. More trustworthy were the "house daimyo" (fudai), most of whom had been Tokugawa family vassals raised to daimyo status by the Tokugawa and thus, unlike the outside daimyo, they were indebted to the bakufu for their status and domains. The third group, the "collateral daimyo" (shimpan), were daimyo belonging to Tokugawa branch families. The Tokugawa also held its own lands, which supported its direct retainers. Some of these held fiefs of less than the 10,000 koku required for daimyo status, but many of them received stipends directly from the bakufu.

When Ieyasu was transferred to the Kantō region by Hideyoshi, he chose as his headquarters the centrally located village of Edo (modern Tokyo), then consisting of about a hundred houses but destined to become one of the world's great cities. The shogunate also maintained castles at Osaka and Shizuoka (then called Sumpu) as well as the Nijō Castle in Kyoto, residence of a bakufu deputy responsible for the government of the capital city and serving concurrently as the shogun's representative at the Imperial court.

To secure itself militarily, the Tokugawa placed its house daimyo in strategic areas. It dominated the Kantō, central Japan, and Kyoto-Osaka regions, while the outside daimyo had their territories in the outer areas. A number of policies were initiated to keep the daimyo from acquiring too much strength. They were restricted to one castle each and had to secure *bakufu* permission before they could repair this castle. They were allowed to maintain only a fixed number of men at arms, and, in line with the seclusion policy, were forbidden to build large ships. To keep the daimyo from forming political alliances that might threaten the *bakufu*, they were required to obtain *bakufu* assent for their marriage plans.

During the first half of the seventeenth century the shogunate enacted a vigorous policy of increasing its own strength at the expense of the daimyo. In this period there were 281 cases in which daimyo were transferred from one fief to another, shuffles which strengthened some and weakened others. Another 213 domains were confiscated outright. This happened sometimes as a disciplinary measure, as when a lord proved incompetent or the domain was torn by a succession dispute. More often confiscation resulted from failure to produce an heir. Deathbed adoptions of an heir were not recognized. By such means the Tokugawa more than tripled the size of its holdings, until its own domain was calculated as worth 6.8 million *koku* of rice. The distribution of their holdings also favored the Tokugawa economically, as it did militarily, since they were in possession of many of Japan's mines and most of the important cities such as Osaka, Kyoto, and Nagasaki. In the mid-Tokugawa period collateral daimyo held land worth 2.6 million *koku*; house daimyo, 6.7 million; and outside daimyo, 9.8 million. It is indicative of the decline of their economic and political power that religious institutions held only around 600,000 *koku*, and the emperor and the court nobility could draw on land worth only 187,000 *koku*.

To see to it that the daimyo obeyed *bakufu* orders, the shogunate sent out its own inspectors. It also devised a highly effective system of strengthening itself politically (while at the same time draining the daimyo financially) by requiring them to spend alternate years in residence in Edo, where the *bakufu* could keep them under surveillance. When they did go back home to their domains, they had to leave their wives and children behind as hostages. This system of alternate attendance *(sankin kōtai)* forced the daimyo to spend large sums traveling back and forth with their retinues. The maintenance of suitably elaborate residences in Edo was a further strain on daimyo resources. The daimyo were also called upon to support public projects such as waterworks or the repair of the shogun's castle at Edo, but such exactions were not as burdensome as the constant expense of alternate attendance. The residence requirement had the additional effect of turning Edo into a capital not only of the *bakufu* but of all Japan.

In theory the shogun was the emperor's deputy as well as the feudal overlord of all the daimyo. Thus he had political legitimacy as well as standing at the apex of the military hierarchy. This dual role made him, in effect, responsible for the conduct of foreign affairs. The early *bakufu* also asserted its financial predominance when it reserved for itself the right to issue paper currency. Its regulations extended even to the dress of the daimyo. The final provision of a code issued in 1635 declared, "all matters are to be carried out in accordance with the laws of Edo."[9] The *bakufu's* own domain comprised about a fourth of Japan.

PART II.   JAPAN AND EUROPE: FIRST ENCOUNTERS (1543–1630)

The early contacts between post-Renaissance Europe and East Asia had nothing like the impact of those which were to follow in the nineteenth century. Even the introduction of firearms merely hastened the unification of Japan, accelerating but not changing the course of history. Yet these early relations form more than just an overture introducing themes to be developed in later history. For one, they provide an opportunity for comparisons of how different civilizations responded to similar foreign stimuli. More significantly for our purposes, the ultimate failure of the Catholic missionaries and the reduction of Western influence to a trickle left Japan, like China, comparatively isolated from Europe. This occurred just before developments in Europe that, for the first time in world history, were inexorably to affect all humanity.

The Portuguese in East Asia

The pioneers of European expansion in East Asia, as elsewhere at this time, were the Portuguese, who reached India in 1498, China in 1514, and Japan in 1543. Having wrested control of the seas from their Arab rivals, they established their Asian headquarters at Goa (1510), a small island off the coast of West India. They then went on to capture Malacca (1511), a vital center for the lucrative spice trade, located on the straits which separate the Malay Peninsula from Sumatra (see Figure 6.5). It was the desire to break the Arab spice monopoly that supplied the economic motive for this initial European expansion. Spices were highly valuable relative to their bulk and weight. Easily transported and fetching a high price, they formed an attractive cargo. And there was an assured market for them in Europe, where they added flavor to an otherwise dull diet and made meat palatable in an age when animals were slaughtered in the fall for want of sufficient fodder to sustain them through the winter. They were also used in medicine and in religious ceremonies.

Prospects for trade were hampered, however, by the fact that Europe, needing pepper and other spices from Asia, had no European commodities of equal importance to offer in return. Initially, therefore, Portuguese adventurers in East Asia supported themselves by a mixture of trade and piracy— like their Japanese predecessors in these waters. They were able to do this successfully because they had superior ships and weapons and were better seamen. Eventually, however, they became the primary carriers of goods in the East Asian trade, taking goods from one Asian country to another—

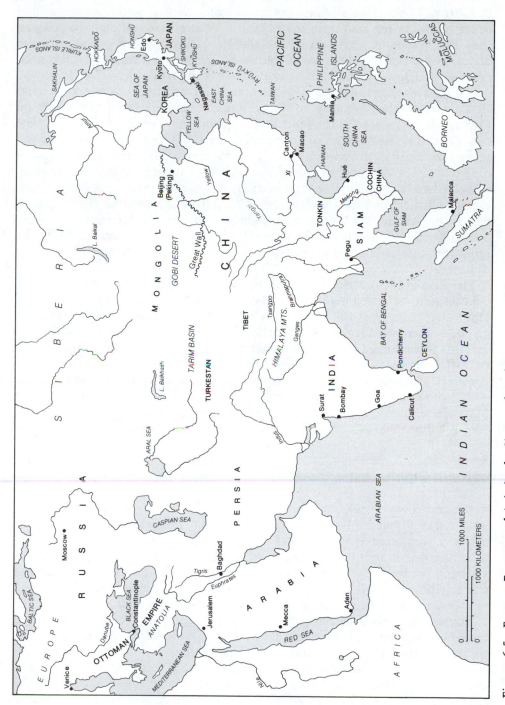

Figure 6.5 Eastern Europe and Asia in the Sixteenth and Seventeenth Centuries.

Southeast Asian wares to China, Chinese silk to Japan, and Japanese silver to China. Their profits from this trade were used to purchase spices and other products for European markets. But before this trade could prosper, they had to secure entry to China and Japan. This posed problems quite different from those they had encountered in seizing a small island off the coast of politically divided India or in driving the Arabs from Malacca.

In China they got off to a very bad start. Not waiting for official permission to trade, they engaged in illegal commerce and even built a fort on Lintin Island, located at the mouth of the river that connects Canton to the sea. Their unruly behavior did not endear them to the Ming authorities and served to confirm the opinion that these "ocean devils" were a new kind of barbarian. The outrageous behavior of the Portuguese traders was further embellished by the Chinese imagination. When the Portuguese bought kidnapped Chinese children as slaves, the Chinese concluded that their purpose was to eat them. They long continued in the firm belief that they were dealing with barbarous child eaters. Not just a popular rumor held by the ignorant, this belief found its way into the official history of the Ming dynasty.

The first Portuguese envoy to China not only failed to obtain commercial concessions; he ended his life in a Cantonese prison. It was a most inauspicious beginning. But the Portuguese would not leave, and their superiority on the seas made it impossible for the Chinese to drive them out. A *modus vivendi* was reached in 1557 when the Portuguese were permitted to establish themselves in Macao in exchange for an annual payment. There the Portuguese administered their own affairs, but the territory remained under Chinese jurisdiction until Macao was ceded to Portugal in 1887. Today Macao and nearby Hong Kong still remain under European control, but are scheduled to revert to China in 1997.

The Jesuits in Japan: Initial Success

Trade and booty were not the only objectives of the Europeans who ventured into Asian waters. Missionary work was also important: mid-sixteenth-century Goa boasted some eighty churches and convents. From the beginning, the missionary impulse provided a strong incentive as well as religious sanction for European expansion; and it was the missionary rather than the trader who served as prime intermediary between the civilizations of East Asia and the West from the sixteenth to the twentieth centuries.

Among the early missionaries, the great pioneers and the most impressive leaders were members of the Society of Jesus (Jesuits). Founded in 1540, this tightly organized and rigorously disciplined religious order formed the vanguard of the Catholic Counter-Reformation. They were the "cavalry of the church," prepared to do battle with Protestant heretics in Europe or the heathen in the world beyond. Along with its stress on martial discipline and intensive religious training, the Society was noted for its insistence on intellectual vigor and depth of learning. The latter included secular as well as sacred studies, and the ideal Jesuit was as learned as he was disciplined and devout.

In 1549, less than ten years after the founding of the Jesuit order, St. Francis Xavier (1506–52), one of the original members of the Society, landed in Kyūshū on a vessel captained by a Chinese wakō. This was just six years after the Japanese had encountered their first Europeans, some shipwrecked Portuguese who landed on the island of Tanegashima. Xavier was well received and was soon able to establish cordial relations with important men in Kyūshū. First impressions on both sides were favorable. Xavier and his successors liked the Japanese; he himself referred to them as "the best [people] who have yet been discovered."[10] Likewise, the Japanese were impressed by the strong character and dignified bearing of the European priests. The Jesuit combination of martial pride, stern self-discipline, and religious piety fitted well with the ethos of sixteenth-century Japan. Nor did the Christian religion seem altogether strange. On the contrary, initially Christianity, brought to Japan from Goa, seemed just another type of Buddhism. It was similar in some of its ceremonies to those found in Buddhism, and it was difficult for the early priests to convey the subtleties of theology, to explain the difference between God and the cosmic Buddha, for example, or to distinguish Paradise from the Pure Land. At last, the Jesuit fathers concluded that the devil, in all of his malicious cleverness, had deliberately fashioned Buddhism to resemble the true faith so as to confound and confuse the people.

The initial meeting of the Jesuits and the Japanese was facilitated by the similarities in their feudal backgrounds. In Japan, Xavier and other Europeans found a society that resembled their own far more than did any other outside Europe. "The people," wrote Alessandro Valignano (1539–1606), "are all white, courteous, and highly civilized, so much so that they surpass all the other known races of the world."[11] Only the Chinese were to receive similar praise—and, indeed, to be regarded as "white." Donald Lach has summarized the qualities the Jesuits found to admire in the Japanese: "their courtesy, propriety, dignity, endurance, frugality, equanimity, industriousness, sagaciousness, cleanliness, simplicity, discipline, and rationality."[12] On the negative side, besides paganism, the Jesuits were appalled at the prevalence of sodomy among the military aristocracy and the monks. They criticized the Japanese propensity to suicide and also found fault with the "disloyalty of vassal to master, their dissimulation, ambiguity, and lack of openness in their dealings, their bellicose nature, their inhuman treatment of enemies and unwanted children, their failure to respect the rule of law, and finally their unwillingness to give up the system of concubinage."[13] Nevertheless, the similarities between Japanese culture and their own gave the Jesuits high hopes for the success of their mission.

In their everyday behavior the Jesuits tried to win acceptance by adapting themselves to local manners and customs, as long as these did not run counter to their own creed. "Thus," Valignano observed, "we who come hither from

Europe find ourselves as veritable children who have to learn to eat, sit, converse, dress, act politely, and so on."[14] They learned how to squat Japanese style, learned to employ the Japanese language with its various levels of politeness, and mastered the art of tea—the Jesuit dwelling was usually equipped with a tea room so that their guests could be properly entertained. C. R. Boxer has pointed out that the Christian monks came from a land with rather different standards of personal cleanliness: "Physical dirt and religious poverty tended to be closely associated in Catholic Europe where lice were regarded as the inseparable companions of monks and soldiers."[15] But in Japan the devoted monks even learned to wash, a major concession to Japanese sensibilities. Still there were limits: Valignano could not bring himself to endorse the Japanese custom of taking a hot bath every day. That would really be going too far!

Careful attention to the niceties of etiquette was required of the Jesuit fathers in their strategy of working from the top down. It was their hope to transform Japan into a Christian land by first converting the rulers and then allowing the faith to seep down to the populace at large. The purpose of their labors was not to Europeanize Japan or China, but to save souls. They realized that the enthusiastic support of the ruling authority would be an invaluable asset, while without at least the ruler's tacit approval they could do nothing.

This approach met with considerable success in Kyūshū, where they converted important local daimyo, who ordered their people to adopt the foreign faith. Although there were numerous cases of genuine conversion, some daimyo simply saw the light of commerce, adopting a Christian stance in the hope of attracting the Portuguese trade to their ports. On at least one occasion it happened that when the great Portuguese ship did not appear, they promptly turned their backs on the new faith. In the end, Christianity did gain an impressive number of genuine converts, but the strategy of steering trade to friendly daimyo had grave political consequences. Since it strengthened some daimyo at the expense of others, the Jesuits inevitably became embroiled in the complicated and often bloody power struggles that continued in Kyūshū until Hideyoshi put an end to them. Nor was the Jesuit involvement always indirect. For seven years Nagasaki, which had developed into the major port for the Portuguese trade, was ruled by the Jesuits, overlords by virtue of a grant from an embattled Christian daimyo. Thus the Jesuits became minor players in a deadly secular game.

From the beginning the Jesuits had realized that real progress for their mission depended on the good will not only of local Kyūshū daimyo but of the central government. Xavier's initial trip to Kyoto came at an unpropitious time—the city was in disorder. But Nobunaga soon became a friend of the Jesuits. Attracted by their character and interested in hearing about foreign lands, perhaps he was also happy to talk with someone not part of the hierarchical order which he himself headed. This personal predilection also coincided nicely with reasons of state. It was consistent with his hostility toward the Buddhist orders and with his desire to keep up the flow of overseas trade.

Hideyoshi, sharing Nobunaga's desire for trade as well as his hostility toward militant Buddhism, was similarly well-disposed toward the new foreigners and curious about their religion. He liked dressing up in Portuguese clothes, complete with rosary, and he once said that the only thing that kept him from converting was the Christian insistence on monogamy.

The political and economic success of the Jesuits helped the spread of Christianity, but power, or the semblance of power, always entails risks. There was the danger that the ruler might perceive the activities of the monks not as assets bolstering his own position but as liabilities, actual or potential threats to his authority. Why should a man who had stringently suppressed Buddhist religious organizations exercising military and political power have been any more favorable to a Christian society engaged in similar activities? Initially Hideyoshi may have seemed to welcome a Jesuit Vice Provincial's promise of help in subduing Kyūshū and in the subsequent conquest of the mainland, but such political maneuvers proved harmful in the long run. Even if Jesuit plans for a coalition of Christian daimyo never materialized, Hideyoshi came to view them as a danger. In 1587 he issued an order expelling the monks. Soon thereafter he seized Nagasaki. Yet, since he did not really feel threatened and continued to want trade, he did not enforce the expulsion decree.

There was, instead, a surge of popularity for things Western such as "Southern Barbarian Screens" (Namban byōbu), showing the giant black ships of the foreigners. The barbarians themselves were depicted as exceedingly tall and rather ungainly, with sharp, long noses and red hair, wearing the ballooning pantaloons which formed the standard fashion in the Portuguese empire (see Figure 6.6). Other scenes, based on paintings from Europe, depicted various barbarian topics: the battle of Lepanto, an Italian court, European cities, maps of the world, not to mention religious subjects. While some artists painted European subjects in Japanese style, others experimented with Western perspective and techniques of shading to produce three-dimensional effects. Nor were Western motifs limited to painting. Western symbols were widely used in decoration, a cross on a bowl, a few words of Latin on a saddle, and so forth. In a letter written in 1594 a missionary described the foreign fad. Writing of non-Christian daimyo he stated:

> They wear rosaries of driftwood on their breasts, hang a crucifix from their shoulder or waist, and sometimes even a handkerchief. Some, who are especially kindly disposed, have memorized the Our Father and the Hail Mary, and recite them as they walk in the streets. This is not done in ridicule of the Christians, but simply to show off their familiarity with the latest fashion, or because they think it good and effective in bringing success in daily life. This has led them to spend no small sums in ordering oval earrings bearing the likeness of Our Lord and the Holy Mother.[16]

This was a passing fashion, but some new products entered Japan to stay, and new words were added to the language, for instance *tabako* (tobacco), *pan* (bread), and *karuta* (playing cards). Another Portuguese contribution was tempura, the popular Japanese dish prepared by deep fat frying vegetables

Figure 6.6 Namban screen. Section of a six-fold screen, 164 cm × 365.6 cm. Kano Mitsonobu school, ca. 1610. Namban Bunkakan, Osaka.

and seafood dipped in batter. The Japanese word is derived from *temporas* (meatless Friday).

Persecution and Closure to the West

Despite the order of 1587, Western influences continued to enter Japan: religious, commercial, cultural. The situation was complicated, however, by the arrival of other Europeans. The first Spaniards arrived from the Philippines, headquarters of the Spanish in Asia, in 1587; and the first Franciscans came from Manila in 1592. By the early 1600s, representatives of the Protestant Dutch and English had also arrived. Although the prospects for trade were attractive, the proliferation of foreigners was disturbing. The various nations competed with each other for Japanese trade. The Dutch and English sought to encourage Japanese suspicions of their Catholic rivals. Moreover, the Japanese were not unaware that the Spanish role in the Philippines was that of colonial master, and that the Spaniards might harbor imperial ambitions with regard to Japan as well. Finally, the Japanese became increasingly concerned that growing Catholic influence might prove subversive of internal stability. The Jesuits had been unable to avoid a degree of involvement in Japanese politics; now the Franciscans, working among the poor, seemed to threaten the traditional social order.

The Jesuits had sought to carry out their missionary activities within the framework of Japanese society and social values. They associated primarily with the upper classes, with a view to working their way down. The Franciscans were suspicious of the Jesuit approach. They were much less well informed concerning conditions in Japan and also much less discreet in their work. Instead of associating with the samurai, the Franciscans worked among the poor and forgotten, the sick and miserable, those at the very bottom of society. The Jesuits did not disguise their contempt for the ignorance and poverty of the Franciscans, the "crazy friars" *(frailes idiotas)* as they called them, and these sentiments were heartily reciprocated by the friars, who scoffed at Jesuit pretensions.

Rivalry between the Portuguese and the Spanish, between Goa and Manila, compounded the instability of the situation. On the one hand, Manila presented the possibility of a new source of profitable trade; on the other, the colonization of the Philippines demonstrated the imperialistic ambitions of the Europeans and the connection between Christian evangelism and colonialism. It was an omen of things to come when Hideyoshi, in 1597, crucified six Franciscan missionaries and eighteen of their Japanese converts after the pilot of a Spanish ship driven ashore in Japan reportedly boasted about the power and ambitions of his king. Ieyasu was at first friendly to the Christians, but he too turned against them. In 1606 Christianity was declared illegal, and in 1614 he undertook a serious campaign to expel the missionaries.

By 1614 there were over 300,000 converts in Japan. The destruction of Christianity was long and painful. Tortures, such as hanging a man upside down with his head in a pit filled with excrement, were used to induce people to renounce their faith. Before it was all over, there were more than 3,000 recognized martyrs, of whom less than seventy were Europeans. Others died without achieving martyrdom. In 1637–38 there was a rebellion in Shimabara, near Nagasaki, against a daimyo who combined merciless taxation with cruel suppression of Christianity. Fought under banners on which Christian slogans were written in Portuguese, and led by some masterless samurai, it was a Christian version of the rural uprisings characteristic of the century of warfare before Nobunaga. In its suppression, some 37,000 Christians lost their lives.

Persuasion as well as violence was employed in the campaign against Christianity. Opponents of Christian dogma argued that the idea of a personal creator was absurd and asked why, if God was both omnipotent and good, he should have tempted Adam and Eve and devised eternal punishment in Hell for non-Christians even though they led exemplary lives.

According to Christian teaching, even the sage emperors Yao and Shun would end in hell. The First Commandment was attacked as leading to disobedience of parents and lord; a loyal retainer should accompany his lord even into hell.

Such arguments suggest that the Japanese saw Christianity as potentially subversive, not only of the political order, but of the basic social structure, for it challenged accepted values and beliefs and demanded a radical reappraisal of long-revered traditions. Its association with European expansionism posed a threat from abroad, and, as exemplified by the Shimabara Rebellion, it also harbored the seeds of radical disruption at home. Thus the motivation for the government's suppression of Christianity was secular not religious. The shogunate was not worried over the state of its subjects' souls, but it was determined to wipe out a dangerous doctrine. An indication that the government's concerns were secular is provided by the oath of apostasy demanded of all former Christians. In it the recanters had to swear that if they had the slightest thought of renouncing their apostasy, "then let us be punished by God the Father, God the Son, and God the Holy Ghost, St. Mary, and all the Angels and Saints."[17] Thus they had to take a Christian oath that they no longer believed in Christianity! The persecutions succeeded in destroying all but a small underground group of secret Christians, who passed from generation to generation a faith increasingly infused with native elements. Meanwhile every Japanese family was registered with a Buddhist temple, and once a year the family head had to swear that there were no Christians in his household. Incidentally, the resulting demographic data, the most complete for any premodern society, constitutes an invaluable resource for modern scholars.

Not only Christianity but all foreign influences were potentially subversive, including trade that would tend to the advantage of the Kyūshū daimyo rather than the Tokugawa. Gradually the *bakufu* further restricted foreign contacts. The Spaniards were expelled in 1624, one year after the English had left voluntarily. In 1630 Japanese were forbidden to go overseas or to return from there or to build ships capable of long voyages. The Portuguese were expelled after the Shimabara Rebellion on the grounds of complicity with that uprising. When they sent an embassy in 1640, its members were executed. The only Europeans left were the Dutch (see Figure 6.7), who kept other Europeans from trying their luck in Japan until the English and Russians challenged Dutch naval supremacy in the late eighteenth and early nineteenth centuries. The Dutch themselves were in 1641 moved to Deshima, a tiny artificial island in Nagasaki Harbor, where they were virtually confined as in a prison. The annual Dutch vessel to Deshima was all that remained of Japan's contact with Europe, but an annual average of almost twenty-six Chinese ships came to Nagasaki, and Japan also maintained indirect diplomatic links with Korea. The "closing" was by no means complete.

The story of early contacts with Europe is one of promise unfulfilled. Neither the West nor the Japanese turned out to have been ready for fruitful discourse or exchange. In terms of world history, opportunities were missed. In terms of Japanese history, the exclusion of disruptive forces from abroad

Figure 6.7 *A Dutch Dinner Party.* Nagasaki, color print, 22 cm × 33 cm.

can be seen as an integral part of a broader effort by Ieyasu and his immediate successors to achieve stability in a land that had suffered a surfeit of warfare and disorder.

NOTES

1. Ryusaku Tsunoda, Wm. Theodore de Bary, and Donald Keene, comps., *Sources of Japanese Tradition* (New York: Columbia Univ. Press, 1958), p. 316.

2. David John Lu, *Sources of Japanese History* (New York: McGraw-Hill, 1974), 1:189. Trans. from Ōkubo Toshiaki et al., eds., *Shiryō ni yoru Nihon no Ayumi* (Japanese History Through Documents) *Kinseihen* (Early Modern Period) (Tokyo: Toshikawa Kōbunkan, 1955), pp. 40–41.

3. Jurgis Elisonas, "The Inseparable Trinity: Japan's Relation with China and Korea," in John W. Hall, ed., *The Cambridge History of Japan*, Vol. 4: *Early Modern Japan* (New York: Cambridge Univ. Press, 1991), p. 271.

4. Sir George Sansom, *A History of Japan, 1334–1615* (Stanford: Stanford Univ. Press, 1961), p. 380.

5. Sir George Sansom, *Japan: A Short Cultural History* (New York: Appleton-Century-Crofts, 1931), p. 437.

6. Carolyn Wheelwright, "A Visualization of Eitoku's Lost Paintings at Azuchi Castle," in George Ellison and Bardwell L. Smith, eds., *Warlords, Artists, & Commoners: Japan in the Sixteenth Century* (Honolulu: Univ. of Hawaii Press, 1981), p. 99.

7. Elise Grilli, *The Art of the Japanese Screen* (Tokyo and New York: John Weatherhill, 1970), p. 171.

8. Langdon Warner, *The Enduring Art of Japan* (Cambridge: Harvard Univ. Press, 1958), p. 95.

9. Harold Bolitho, *Treasures among Men: The Fudai Daimyo in Tokugawa Japan* (New Haven: Yale Univ. Press, 1974), p. 17.

10. C. R. Boxer, *The Christian Century in Japan* (Berkeley: Univ. of California Press, 1951), Appendix I, p. 401. Also quoted in Donald F. Lach, *Asia in the Making of Europe*, Vol. I: *The Century of Discovery* (Chicago: Univ. of Chicago Press, 1965), p. 284, also pp. 663–64.

11. Boxer, *The Christian Century in Japan*, p. 74.

12. Lach, *Asia in the Making of Europe*, 1:728.

13. Ibid.

14. Quoted in Boxer, *The Christian Century in Japan*, p. 75.

15. Ibid., p. 214.

16. Yoshitomo Okamoto, *The Namban Art of Japan* (Tokyo and New York: John Weatherhill, 1972), p. 77.

17. Boxer, *The Christian Century in Japan*, p. 441.

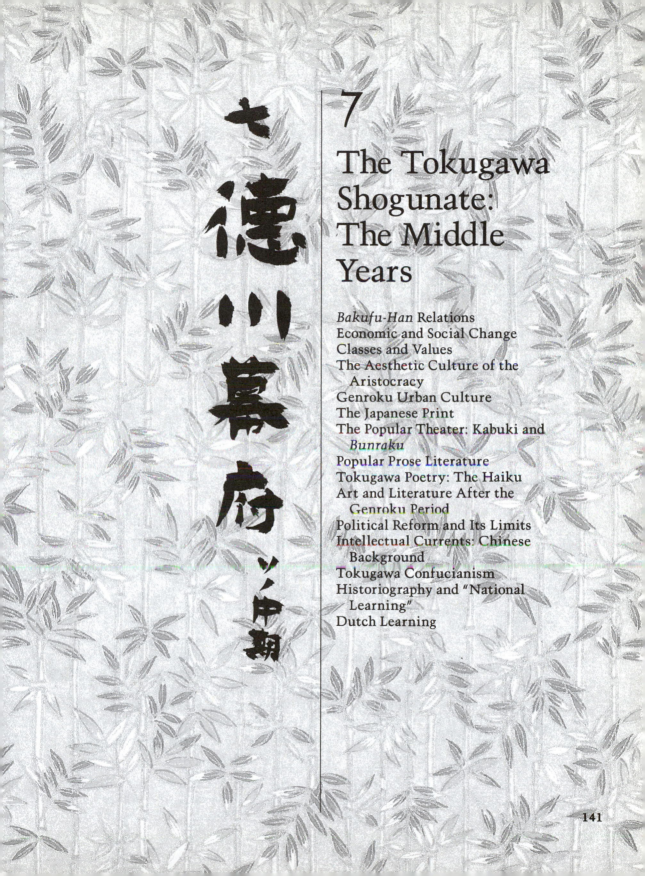

徳川幕府〈江戸期〉

7

The Tokugawa Shogunate: The Middle Years

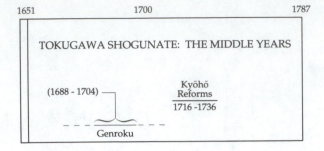

1651   1700   1787

TOKUGAWA SHOGUNATE: THE MIDDLE YEARS

(1688 - 1704)   Kyōhō
Reforms
1716 -1736

Genroku

*H*istory did not end with the achievement of order: the new stability itself generated change. Under the Tokugawa, Japan enjoyed peace, experienced economic growth, and developed a flourishing urban culture. At the same time, there were stresses inherent in the system itself, and, with the passage of time, new conditions arose to strain the body politic.

Bakufu-Han Relations

Despite the tendency of the shogunate to establish its preeminence as the central power, the daimyo remained largely free to manage affairs in their own domains or *han*. The *bakufu* usually interfered only when the daimyo proved themselves incapable of managing their *han*, or when problems involving more than one *han* arose. The daimyo themselves were naturally concerned to develop the strength of their own domains while keeping *bakufu* interference to a minimum. Even while tightening the administration of their *han*, their self-interest lay in preserving the decentralized aspect of the larger political system, thereby retaining their own feudal autonomy. Tokugawa government is sometimes described as a "centralized feudalism." Using this terminology, we may say that it was to the daimyo's advantage to keep the system feudal. Their ability to accomplish this is suggested by another expression used by scholars, "*baku-han*," signifying a system composed of the *bakufu* and the *han*. Both formulations allude to the mixed composition of the Tokugawa system.

Under the fourth shogun, Ietsuna (1651–80), the daimyo regained much of the ground they had lost under his three predecessors. *Bakufu* policy was reversed. There was a drastic decline in the number of daimyo transferred and *han* confiscated. Deathbed adoptions were recognized as legitimate. The shogunate even began permitting *han* to issue their own paper money, a policy which led to the proliferation of local currencies. Anxious to protect their own money, some *han* in the eighteenth century prohibited the use of outside currencies—including the *bakufu's* money!

The vigorous but eccentric fifth shogun, Tsunayoshi (1680–1709) presided over a reassertion of *bakufu* power, which earned him the enmity of the daimyo and lasting ignominy. A scant five years after his death, Tsunayoshi was satirized in a puppet play by Chikamatsu. He was an easy target, for he carried to an extreme his Buddhist devotion to the preservation of animal life and especially his solicitude for dogs. His exaggerated concern for these animals was often expressed at the expense of human well-being and sometimes at the cost of human life; this earned him the epithet "dog shogun." Despite the shogun's personality quirks, his period saw a great flowering of culture as well as a significant return to the policies of the early Tokugawa. However, this resurgence of centralizing activity did not lead to a permanent shift in the power balance nor did it initiate a long-term trend toward greater *bakufu* control. If it had, the shogun's historical image would have been rather different.

Until the end of the Tokugawa, the pendulum continued to swing between the *bakufu* and the *han*. The history and dynamics of this process have been analyzed by Harold Bolitho, who has shown that periods of *bakufu* assertiveness tended to occur under vigorous shoguns working in conjunction with trusted advisers drawn from among the shogunate's low-ranking retainers. Unencumbered by fief or vassals, totally dependent on the shogun, they became his men, free from potential conflicts of interest. Under such regimes, the high-ranking Senior Councilors, always selected from among the house daimyo *(fudai)*, were treated with an outward show of respect, but in actual practice they were bypassed and disregarded. Little love was lost between the *fudai* and the new men.

When the shogun was a minor or an incompetent, control over the *bakufu* reverted back to the Senior Councilors, descendants of the Tokugawa's most favored and highly trusted vassals. The service of these vassals had formed the core of Ieyasu's strength, and accordingly he relied on their descendants for continued loyal service to his house. While these men were conscious of their heritage of special obligations toward the shogunate, they also had to consider their particular responsibilities and opportunities as daimyo. The tensions between shogunate and *han*, characteristic of the system, were mirrored in their own persons as they faced the demands of *bakufu* and *han*, demands often in conflict with each other. The usual pattern was for them to act more as daimyo than as *bakufu* officials. It was they who were responsible for the relaxation of *bakufu* policies. Such Senior Councilors did not work to strengthen the shogunate at the expense of the *han* nor were they prepared to sacrifice *han* privileges for the sake of the larger body politic. There were even cases of *han* held by incumbent Senior Councilors prohibiting the export of grain badly needed to combat famine elsewhere in Japan. Thus there were periodic shifts in the balance of power between the *bakufu* and the *han*, but the issue was never resolved completely in favor of one or the other.

The more than 250 *han* varied widely in size, local conditions, and prosperity, nor were all the lands held by a daimyo necessarily contiguous. Some domains were more easily organized than others. In general, the daimyo tended to centralize the administration of their *han* even while guarding their independence vis-à-vis Edo. Operating on a smaller scale than the *bakufu*, the *han* governments were generally more successful in controlling their lord's retainers. Accordingly, the sixteenth-century trend for samurai to be divorced from the land and concentrated in the *han* capitals continued strong under the Tokugawa. By the last decade of the seventeenth century over 80 percent of the daimyo were paying stipends to their samurai. Looking at the system in terms of the samurai rather than their lords, it is significant that by the end of the eighteenth century 90 percent of the samurai were entirely dependent on their stipends. Only 10 percent still retained local roots in the country districts.

Assigned to various administrative, financial, and military duties, the samurai staffed the increasingly bureaucratized administrative machinery of the domains and the *bakufu*. Many of them were now occupied more with government than with military affairs, and numerous samurai followed the urgings of the Tokugawa that in times of peace samurai should devote themselves to study. In this respect as in others, Ieyasu had shown the way when he showed special favor to the Confucian scholar Hayashi Razan (1583–1657), whose family continued to supply the heads of the *bakufu's* Confucian Academy. Song Confucianism meshed with Ieyasu's anti-Buddhist proclivities. Furthermore, in Japan as in China it proved entirely compatible with bureaucratic government. Intellectually as well as professionally, the samurai of 1800 was quite different from his ancestor of two centuries earlier. In other ways also, Japan experienced great changes during this period.

Economic and Social Change

Peace made economic growth possible and stimulated a rise in demand created by the need to support the roughly 7 percent of the population that enjoyed samurai status and to meet the growing expenses of the daimyo.

Agricultural productivity increased very substantially, especially in the seventeenth century. Cultivated acreage doubled thanks to vigorous irrigation and land reclamation. Also contributing to increased output were improvements in technology, the practice of multiple cropping, better seed strains, and improved fertilizers. Useful knowledge was disseminated through agricultural handbooks and manuals. The development of a market network was accompanied by regional specialization in cash crops such as cotton, mulberry trees for the rearing of silk worms, indigo, tobacco, sugar cane, and so forth, but grain continued to be grown in all parts of Japan. Population rose from about 18 million at the beginning of the Tokugawa to around 30 million by the middle of the period. Afterwards there were fluctuations in population, but there was no major long-term increase for, in 1872 the population stood at only 33.1 million. Although famine and disease took their toll, mortality rates were comparatively low, and the average life span was very likely longer than in premodern Europe, since Japan was free from war and less susceptible to epidemics. Late marriage, the custom of having only one son marry, as well as abortion and female infanticide kept population growth under control. Family planning was widespread even when times were good. Life was by no means easy. Japanese peasants remained at the mercy of the elements, and there were many poor people, but it is clear that in the long term for most of the period, there was a rise in the standard of living.

With the samurai now largely removed from the land, the villages were left virtually autonomous units. They were responsible for the payment of taxes to the *han* government or, in the case of those held directly by the Tokugawa, to the *bakufu*. Within the village, neither the benefits of agricultural growth nor the burdens of taxation were shared equally: there were wide gradations in wealth and power in the countryside. Since tax reassessments were infrequent, wealthy peasants who were able to open new lands and otherwise increase their yields found their incomes rising and were able to accumulate funds with which to acquire still more land.

An increased use of money brought with it a decline in the traditional village social-economic order, under which the economic functions and relations of a household were determined by its standing within the extended family to which it belonged. Traditionally the main house of the extended family had claims on the services of the lesser households as well as some obligations to look after the poorer members. Furthermore, the heads of the main houses formed the traditional village leadership. During the Tokugawa, wealthy villagers turned more and more to hired labor or tenant farmers to work their land. They also put their money to work in rural commerce and industry, and engaged in money lending, the processing of vegetable oils, the production of soya sauce, and sake brewing. Since these wealthy villagers did not necessarily belong to the old main-house families, there were considerable tensions in the village.

These tensions were accentuated by economic disparities. In contrast to those who profited from the commercialization of agriculture were the poorer villagers and the landless, who shared little, if at all, in the prosperity of the countryside. They, in particular, suffered the dislocations caused by economic and social change as contractual relationships replaced those based on family. Most often they endured in silence, but there were also times when they gave vent to their resentment in uprisings. Peasant unrest was on the increase in the late Tokugawa. An indication of this change is the contrast between early Tokugawa rural uprisings, which were often led by village headmen, and those of the late period, which were frequently directed in the first place against those wealthy and powerful village leaders. However, neither the uprisings nor the changes in agricultural technology seriously threatened the basic stability of the village. Violence was a form of protest, not a means toward revolution. Changes in agriculture increased yield but did not alter the basic pattern of rice farming with its need for intensive labor and community cooperation.

The official Confucian theory recognized only four social classes and thus failed to reflect the more complex social stratification of the countryside. Nor did moral admonitions and sumptuary laws directed at wealthy peasants (laws defining who could own what) change matters. Still less acceptable in Confucian eyes was the growing wealth of the merchant class, theoretically considered economic parasites and relegated to the bottom of society. The authorities found that they could control the merchants politically and keep them in their place socially, but they were too dependent on their services to do them permanent harm as a class economically. By the beginning of the eighteenth century, Edo, with a population of about a million, may have been the largest city in the world, a little over half of them townspeople (chōnin). Osaka too developed as a prosperous commercial and shipping center while Kyoto also remained a major city. The capitals of the han, like Edo originally founded as political and military centers, also became foci for marketing systems and centers of trade, with merchants and artisans playing an active role in shaping the character of each city. The most prominent merchants, as City Elders, Ward Representatives, and the like, had a role in administration. And it was such merchants who supplied an economic link between the cities and the rural hinterlands, and between the local centers and the capital.

Merchants also handled the warehousing of rice and other commodities and were licensed to operate the han monopolies. Brokers converted rice into cash or credit for the sellers. Important merchants acted as financial and forwarding agents for the daimyo, handling shipments to Osaka for exchange or to Edo for the daimyo's consumption. They supplied banking services, dealing in the manifold han currencies, transferring funds, and repeatedly issuing loans to the political authorities and to hard-pressed samurai. The position of individual commercial establishments could be precarious, and in extreme cases a wealthy merchant with heavy loans out to the powerful might suffer confiscation so that the loans could go unpaid, as happened to a great Osaka merchant in 1705. However, these were exceptions, and government measures to force creditors to settle for less than full repayment or for the cancellation of loans simply had the effect of raising the cost of new loans, since the authorities never found a way to eliminate the need for such borrowing. The bakufu, daimyo, and samurai depended on the merchants as fiscal agents, and the merchants prospered; so much so, indeed, that in the second half of the eighteenth century there were over 200 mercantile establishments valued at over 200,000 gold ryo, a monetary unit worth roughly a koku of rice. Such merchants were fully the economic equals of daimyo. Some of the great modern commercial and financial empires go back to the early Tokugawa, most notably the largest of them all, the house of Mitsui founded in 1620.

As in the villages, there were also great differences in status and wealth among the town dwellers, and for every great merchant there were many more humble shopkeepers and artisans producing and repairing the various utensils required for everyday life. At the very bottom of society were people who did not belong even theoretically in the four Confucian classes. Bearing the designation "hinin" (non-people) were beggars, traveling performers, prostitutes, scavengers, and so forth. These were outcasts by occupation. Still worse off were pariahs* whose position beyond the pale of ordinary society was hereditary. Their origins are unknown but go back

* Formerly they were known as the eta, but this term has become pejorative, and at present the term burakumin is commonly used.

into much earlier Japanese history. Some were people engaged in butchering and tanning, tasks considered unclean. Others were simple artisans working in straw and reed (for example, making baskets, straw sandals, mats, and the like) or rural families who farmed. Considered unclean, they were discriminated against in law and kept in enforced segregation. The number of people falling into these categories is estimated at around 380,000 for the closing years of the Tokugawa.

Classes and Values

As part of his efforts to create an enduring order, Ieyasu followed Hideyoshi's example in drawing a clear line between samurai and commoner, using all the weight of the law and official ideology. On the surface at least, there was no conflict with the four classes of Confucian theory, for the character read *shi (shih)* in Chinese and designating the scholar (at the top of the social hierarchy) was in Japanese pronounced *samurai*. There were, to be sure, exceptions here and there to the rigid maintenance of hereditary class identity. It did happen that destitute *rōnin*, masterless samurai, dropped out of their own class, and that through marriage or adoption an alliance was sometimes formed between the family of an affluent commoner and that of an impoverished samurai, but such cases of social mobility remained uncommon. Members of the warrior class proudly cherished their status while most urbanites contented themselves with the pursuit of wealth and its attendant pleasures.

The most visible sign of the samurai's privilege was his sole right to wear swords, symbols of the samurai even after they had ceased to be his major tools. In an era of peace, when his duties were largely civil, the samurai was sent to school to attain a certain minimal mastery of Chinese learning and, more importantly, to absorb the Confucian ethic of dutiful obedience to superiors and conscientious concern for those below him on the social scale. He was also expected to acquire a degree of proficiency in at least one of the martial arts, although during the long years of peace these became "a matter of formal gymnastics and disciplined choreography"[1] rather than practical military techniques. Ideally the samurai was supposed to combine the virtues of the Confucian scholar and those of the old time *bushi*, to serve as both the moral leader and the defender of society, totally devoted to his moral duty *(giri)* even at the expense of his life.

This combination of Confucian and warrior values is apparent in the writings of Yamaga Sokō (1622–95). A student of Hayashi Razan and a devotee of the martial arts, he is considered a founding father of modern *bushidō*, a more systematized and Confucianized version of the old code of the warrior. One of his followers became the leader of the famed forty-seven *rōnin* who persevered in seeking vengeance for the wrong done their dead lord. In 1703 their carefully nurtured plans were rewarded with success as they stormed into the Kyoto mansion of the offending daimyo and killed him. They immediately achieved the status of heroes and have remained popular exemplars of the ideal of loyalty. Theirs was an act of warrior courage and devotion, but it was also illegal. For a time the shogunate debated what should be done. Then the shogun (Tsunayoshi) decided to uphold the substance of the civil law while preserving the warrior's honor: they were ordered to commit ritual suicide. Playwrights lost no time in adapting their story for the puppet theater and kabuki stage. It has remained a Japanese favorite; in the twentieth century both the cinema and the television versions were enormously popular.

The puppet theater and kabuki belonged to the world of the town dweller and not to that of the samurai proper, for whom the aristocratic Nō drama was considered more suitable. Nevertheless, the popularity of *Chūshingura* (Treasury of Royal Retainers), to give the drama of the forty-seven *rōnin* its proper title, shows that commoners could appreciate this aspect of samurai culture. And there was a good deal more on which samurai and commoners, urban and rural, could agree. The official morality was presented through periodic lectures, and was spread by the many schools that came into existence during the Tokugawa period. (By 1800, 40 to 50 percent of all Japanese males were literate to some degree.) As in China, the official Confucian values gave support to the hierarchical order within the family as well as in society at large, although the overriding emphasis on filial piety was somewhat relaxed among urban commoners.

Hierarchical principles of organization operated throughout the society as did a tendency to rank people in grades. Like samurai, even the inhabitants of the demimonde of the pleasure quarters in the great cities were carefully ranked. The great merchant establishments resembled feudal fiefs not only in their wealth but also in their expectation of lifelong loyal service from their employees, who in turn, were entitled to be treated with due paternalistic solicitude. A similar relationship survives in Japanese industry to this day.

Merchant and samurai held many values in common, but there were also major differences in their mores and norms. It was a mark of samurai pride to regard considerations of financial benefit as beneath contempt. Fukuzawa Yukichi (1853–1901) in his famous autobiography tells how his father took his children out of school when, much to his horror, their teacher began to instruct them in arithmetic; a subject fit only for merchants and their offspring. Merchants perceived the distinction in much the same way:

> A samurai's child is reared by samurai parents and becomes a samurai himself because they teach him the warrior's code. A merchant's child is reared by merchant parents and becomes a merchant because they teach him the way of commerce. A samurai seeks a fair name in disregard for profit, but a merchant, with no thought to his reputation, gathers profit and amasses a fortune. This is the way of life proper to each.[2]

The speaker is a rich merchant in a puppet play whose son has married the daughter of a samurai. They are addressed to his son's father-in-law, who now regrets having married his daughter outside her class.

A source of theoretical support for the merchant's occupation was provided by the Kaitokudo academy of Osaka where the sons of merchants were taught the importance of trade and of those who engage in it. Also legitimizing the merchants' calling was the strain of Buddhism that considered all occupations as legitimate forms of devotion and, especially, by "Heart Learning" (Shingaku), a religion founded by a Kyoto merchant and philosopher, Ishida Baigan (1685–1744). Heart Learning combined elements of Shinto, Confucianism, and Buddhism to create an ethic for the artisan and merchant, reinforcing a traditional morality that stressed honesty, frugality, and devotion to one's trade. Long years of training and supervision in the system of craft and business apprenticeships helped to perpetuate values as well as skills.

Meanwhile, a different ethos developed in the urban pleasure quarters officially designated by the *bakufu* as the sole areas where courtesans were permitted to ply their trade. Here a new theater and new arts flourished. However, the older aristocratic traditions also remained very much alive. Thus the distinctive character of the classes of Tokugawa Japan as well as their influence on each other is evidenced by developments in the arts.

The Aesthetic Culture of the Aristocracy

The upper classes of the Tokugawa period inherited and perpetuated much of the Ashikaga cultural tradition. Such arts as the tea ceremony and flower arranging were continued without major change. Government officials still patronized schools of Sino-Japanese painting in the Kano line and the native style of painting produced by Tosa artists. The Nō theater continued to receive enthusiastic support; indeed, the shogun Tsunayoshi was so enamored of the art that he himself performed in Nō plays. Although new plays were written for the Nō stage, there were few fresh departures or new themes.

The variety of Tokugawa architectural styles reminds us, however, that aristocratic taste was by no means uniform, that the simple aesthetics of the tea ceremony could coexist with a love for the ornate that would have delighted the men and women of Hideyoshi's time. The detached imperial villa at Katsura, outside Kyoto, is an exquisite example of studied simplicity in the use of natural materials. It is famed, not only for its architectural excellence, but equally for the subtle composition of its garden and tea houses. In striking contrast to the calculated restraint shown at Katsura is the profuse display at Nikkō, the mausoleum where Ieyasu's remains are interred. In chaotic flamboyance, its brightly painted and gilded decorations luxuriate in endless variety, free of any restraining notions of functional or aesthetic logic. A similar indulgence in decoration at the expense of form marks the final phase of the Gothic style in Europe, but the structures at Nikkō are ultimately saved from empty vulgarity by their setting in a magnificent forest, creating as Alexander Soper said, "a serene depth of shadow into which their tumult sinks without an echo."[3]

In Kyoto the aristocratic aesthetic tradition, going back to court circles in the Heian period, was given new life in a final surge of vitality. The movement was led by Hon'ami Kōetsu (1558–1637), descendant of a family of professional sword repairers and sword connoisseurs, and was tinged with elements of artistic defiance, for Kōetsu and his group rejected the values of the new military class, especially their continued patronage of Chinese styles in art and philosophy. Kōetsu's movement was practical, not merely intellectual. On a site north of Kyoto, granted him by Ieyasu in recognition of his prominence as a member of that city's Nichiren Buddhist community, Kōetsu established an artistic and religious colony of fifty-five houses. Here a new group of artists and craftsmen sought to carry on the artistic traditions of Heian Japan. Their success is indicated by the fact that Kōetsu became the arbiter of taste for his generation in the old imperial capital.

Kōetsu had, of course, been trained in his family's traditional art: sword repair and connoisseurship, but his talents were far-ranging. His tea bowls are considered among the very finest achievements in Raku ware; he made new departures in lacquer inlay work and was equally accomplished in the medium of cast metal vessels. He excelled in painting and, above all, in calligraphy. Frequently he worked in collaboration with other artists. An example is the handscroll *Thousand Cranes* painted by Tawaraya Sōtatsu

Figure 7.1 *Thousand Cranes.* Section of a hand-scroll. Painting by Tawaraya Sōtatsu, calligraphy by Hon'ami Kōetsu. Gold and silver underpainting on paper, 341 cm × 1460 cm.

(d. 1643?) with Kōetsu contributing the bold and free calligraphy. The result is a decorative elegance that does honor to the old tradition (see Figure 7.1).

Sōtatsu was a younger contemporary of Koetsu and apparently related to him by marriage. Tawaraya was the name of Sōtatsu's fan and painting atelier (that is, workshop) in Kyoto. Although influenced by Koetsu, Sōtatsu did not actually move out of town to the former's arts village. Both men were consciously influenced by the Heian tradition, which, among other things, originated the art of painting on fans. Also characteristically native in inspiration is the softness of Sōtatsu's "boneless" technique, which avoids the strong ink lines found in the work of the Kano painters. This style, as well as a gift for composition, he carried over to his work on large screens. Hiroshi Mizuo[4] has pointed out the influence of fan-painting techniques on such masterpieces as Sōtatsu's pair of screens *The God of Wind and the God of Thunder* (see Figure 7.2). The two screens form a single composition, with the pivot in the empty center pulling the swirling gods in and preventing them from spinning right off the painted surface. In this and in his *bugaku* (court dance) screen pair, Sōtatsu reveals his greatness as a master of dynamic movement.

A third great pair of screens, *Waves at Matsushima*, shows Sōtatsu as a daring stylist. It is this quality of decorative stylization that is most characteristic of the third great artist in this tradition, Ogata Kōrin (1658–1716), who studied and copied Sōtatsu's works. It is from the last syllable of his name, Kōrin, that there was derived the term "Rimpa" ("Rin school") designating the entire school of artists. A perennial favorite is Kōrin's pair of iris screens. Elise Grilli compares this pair to Mozart's variations on a musical

Figure 7.2   Tawaraya Sōtatsu, *God of Wind.* One of a pair of two-fold screens. Color on foil, 153.7 cm × 171 cm.

theme; the painter, like the composer "first stating his motif, then adding variations, shifts, repetitions, pauses, leaps, intervals, changes of tempo, accents, chords, rise and fall, with changes of mood from major to minor."[5] The iris theme derives from a poem by Narihira in *The Tales of Ise*, but it is not the literary reference but Kōrin's color orchestration and his superb eye for the decorative that link him most clearly to the native Japanese tradition (see Figure 7.3).

Genroku Urban Culture

Equally Japanese but drawing its nourishment from different roots was the urban culture of Edo, which reached a high point during the Genroku Era. Technically this era name applies to a period of only sixteen years, 1688–1704, but more broadly it designates the cultural life of the last quarter of the seventeenth century and the first quarter of the eighteenth. It was a remarkable period during which some of Japan's most creative artists were at work. These include the foremost playwright, Chikamatsu (1653–1724); the most gifted traditional short story writer, Saikaku (1642–93); Moronobu (1618–94), generally credited with developing the Japanese print; and Bashō (1644–94), the Tokugawa period's finest poet, master of the haiku.

Most large cities of the world have "pleasure districts," which are more or less tolerated by the political authorities, that is, sections of town devoted to bohemian life, erotic activities, entertainment, and gambling. The cities of Tokugawa Japan were no exception. But rarely, if ever, have such quarters produced a first-rate aesthetic as they did in seventeenth-century Yoshiwara, the home of Edo's "floating world." Here, and in similar quarters in the other large towns, the Japanese tradition of aesthetic discrimination

Figure 7.3   Ogata Kōrin, *Irises*. One of a pair of six-fold screens. Color on gold foil over paper, 151.2 cm × 360.7 cm.

once more led to keen appreciation of stylistic excellence in dress and coiffure, in gesture and perfume, and in life itself. The worldly flair of the man-about-town was greatly admired; the spirit and elegant chic of the great courtesans who presided over this world were particularly appreciated. There was nothing but disdain for the country boor, for the gaudy or gauche.

The Japanese Print

The life and values of this "floating world" left their imprint on Japanese culture: on fiction, and the stage, and particularly on the visual arts. A unique achievement is the *ukiyo-e*, "pictures of the floating world," perhaps the last major accomplishment of the native tradition of Japanese art.

Among the precursors of the *ukiyo-e* were genre paintings such as early seventeenth-century screens depicting kabuki performances in the dry river bed in Kyoto or spring excursions to picnic under blossoming cherry trees, and *ukiyo-e* painting remained an important art even after the full development of the color woodcut. The immediate antecedents of the prints were illustrations for books such as the *Yoshiwara Pillow* (1660), a combination sex manual and "courtesan critique," combining two of the perpetually popular themes of the prints. The production of erotica, much of it unpublishable even today, and of portraits of courtesans remained two of the mainstays of the *ukiyo-e* artist.

The fullest expression of *ukiyo-e* was the Japanese print. Portraits of courtesans, theater scenes, nature subjects, or scenes from urban life were carved in wood blocks. These were then inked and printed on paper. First efforts were highly experimental. Hishikawa Moronobu, sometimes considered the founder of the Japanese print, consolidated these early efforts. His work represents the establishment of the genre.

At the beginning the prints were in black and white, but then color was added, first by hand, then by developing techniques of multicolor printing. The early prints were limited first to basic red and green, but by the middle of the eighteenth century three- or four-color prints were produced. A versatile master who contributed importantly to the development of the print was Okumura Masanobu (1686–1764). Figure 7.4 shows an eighteenth-century beauty dressed in a characteristically sumptuous kimono. In the center of the stamp at the bottom is a gourd, colored red. The text to the right of the gourd reads, "The genuine brush of the Japanese painter Okumura Masanobu. Torishio Street Picture Wholesale Shop." To the left, the text resumes, "Sale of red pictures and illustrated books. The red gourd seal is enclosed. Okumura."[6] The lower part of the kimono is in bright red *(beni)* while the upper part is yellowish, with the obi (sash) decorated with a brown design painted in lacquer.

Masanobu was a many-sided master whose virtuosity extended to a variety of styles and who himself influenced other artists such as the creator of the hand-colored print illustrated in Figure 7.5. This print depicts the interior of a house in Yoshiwara and features a game of backgammon. The

Figure 7.4   Okumura Masanobu, *Girl in Transparent Dress Tying Her Obi.* Woodcut print.

composition experiments with the receding perspective of European painting. The print also shows such standard features of Japanese interior architecture as rooms separated by sliding partitions, the *tatami* floor, and that sense of spaciousness created by the virtual absence of furniture.

Masanobu was a publisher as well as an artist, but usually these functions were separate, carried out by different people. Indeed, numerous people had a hand in the creation of a print. The publisher was very important. He not only distributed and sold the block prints but also commissioned them from the artist with more or less explicit instructions on subject and style, with an eye on what would sell. The artist drew the picture and designed the print, but then turned it over to the engraver and the printer. The craftsmanship of these men did much to determine the quality of the finished product. However, the artist's contribution remained central. The essential vision was his.

Figure 7.5   *Game of Backgammon in the Yoshiwara.* Attributed to Torii Kiyotada (fl. ca. 1720–50). Hand-colored woodcut print.

The Popular Theater: Kabuki and *Bunraku*

A favorite pastime of the Genroku man-about-town, and an unceasing source of inspiration for the print-artist, was the popular kabuki theater, whose celebrated actors enjoyed as much acclaim and attracted as avid a group of admirers as did the most elegant of Yoshiwara courtesans. A similarly enthusiastic audience was drawn to *bunraku*, the puppet theater.

Important in the evolution of kabuki were the dances and skits presented in Kyoto during the early years of the seventeenth century by a troupe of female performers led by a priestess named Okuni. But this women's kabuki lasted only until 1629, when it was banned by the authorities. This action was not prompted by the *bakufu's* disapproval of the offstage behavior of the actress-courtesans, but by its desire to put an end to the periodic outbursts of violence that erupted as rivals competed for the favors of these ladies. Then, for two decades, young men's kabuki flourished, until it too ran into similar difficulties and was prohibited in 1652, after which date all actors were mature men. Even then kabuki continued to be under government restrictions, tolerated as a form of plebeian amusement, licensed and controlled, since, like other indecorous pleasures, it could not be suppressed.

Kabuki theater was wildly popular during the Tokugawa period, pleasing its audience with its spectacular scenery, gorgeous costumes, and expressions of violent passion. It was very much an actor's art, dominated by dynasties of actors who felt quite free to take liberties with the texts of the plays. The virtuoso performances of the great actors were greeted by shouts of approval from the audience. The raised walkway on which the actors made their way to the stage through the audience also provided a link between performers and spectators. Particularly esteemed was the artistry of the men who played the female roles. These masters devoted their lives to achieving stylizations of posture, gesture, and voice, conveying the quintessence of femininity, always operating in that "slender margin between the real and unreal,"[7] which Chikamatsu defined as the true province of art. In this sense, the bakufu's prohibition against female performers enriched kabuki artistically.

Chikamatsu wrote for the kabuki stage but preferred the puppet theater (bunraku) where his lines were not at the mercy of the actors. In bunraku large wooden puppets, each manipulated by a three-man team, enacted a story told by a group of chanters, accompanied by three-stringed samisen. This theater achieved such popularity that live actors even imitated the movements of the puppets. Even after kabuki carried the day in Edo, bunraku continued to flourish in Osaka. The puppets, like the masks employed in Nō, assured that the action on stage would not be a mere mirror of ordinary life but would have a more stylized and symbolic aspect. For the playwright, bunraku held an added attraction in that the puppets, unlike their flesh and blood counterparts, did not meddle with his text. There are also scenes of violence and fantastic stage business which, impossible for live actors, pose no problems for figures that do not bleed and are not bound by the usual limits of human physiology. Spectacular elements helped to attract a wide audience to this theater and are used frequently by Chikamatsu in his plays on historical subjects, such as The Battle of Coxinga, his most famous work in this genre.

Chikamatsu also wrote more subtle domestic plays set in his own contemporary world. These center on conflicts between moral obligations (giri) and human emotions (ninjō), the irreconcilable tensions between duty and feeling. One, for example, tells of the tragic love of a small shopkeeper and a lovely courtesan whom he cannot ransom from her house for lack of funds. A frequent solution is the lovers' flight to death, a trip which provides the poetic high point of the play. Often the ladies exhibit greater strength of character than the men, but both are turned into romantic heroes through the purity and intensity of their emotions. Art imitates life, but life also imitates art: the plays produced such a rash of love suicides that the government finally banned all plays with the words "love suicide" in the title.

Popular Prose Literature

In prose the life and mentality of the townspeople were best expressed in the writing of Saikaku, Chikamatsu's senior by eleven years. Both writers chronicled as well as molded the urban culture of the Genroku period.

The life of Saikaku's typical urbanite was centered on love and money. Although he also wrote about samurai, his best work deals with recognizable city types: the miser and money grubber, the playboy who squanders his patrimony, the young beauty mismatched to an elderly husband, the fan maker, and men and women in love with love. His erotic works, exuberant and witty, mixing humor and sex, were in keeping with the times and are of a robust directness far removed from the subtle delicacy of Heian sensibility even when, as in his later works, he recounted the darker aspects of his subject matter. In his writing, too, can be seen the conflict between duty and feeling that animated the plays of Chikamatsu. Saikaku was not only the finest of prose writers but also a prolific composer of *haikai* (light verse), a poetic genre widely popular among the townspeople.

Tokugawa Poetry: The Haiku

A haiku is a poem with 17 syllables arranged in three lines 5/7/5. Its antecedents are very old, for this is the form of the opening lines of the old 31 syllable *tanka*. It was also the usual form for the opening lines of the *renga* (linked verse). From the Ashikaga on, linked verse remained highly popular, and in the sixteenth and seventeenth centuries this was especially true of *haikai*, or light verse, enlivened by infusions of everyday speech and of humor. That some of the resulting verse departed considerably from the refined taste of the aristocracy is shown by a famous pair of links in a sixteenth-century anthology:

> Bitter, bitter it was
> And yet somehow funny.
>
> Even when
> My father lay dying
> I went on farting.[8]

Vulgar as it is, the second verse does contrast sharply with the first, as required in this poetic form. The popularity of *haikai* is attested by the appearance of several seventeenth-century anthologies, one of which contained verses by over 650 contributors.

The haiku came into its own thanks to the work of Matsuo Bashō, an almost exact contemporary of Saikaku. Bashō was born a samurai but gave up his rank to live the life of a commoner, earning his living as a master poet. His own pupils came from all strata of society from wealthy samurai to beggars. His finest poetry was written in the last decade of his life and shows the influence of Zen, which he began studying in 1681, but few of his haiku are overtly religious.

Not every 17-syllable poem is a true haiku, for the real measure of a haiku lies not in its formal structure or surface meaning but in its resonance, not in what it says but in what is left unsaid. It invites, indeed demands, that the reader himself become an artist, entering into its spirit and exploring (even creating) its manifold shades of meaning.

The essence of haiku is that rather than describe a scene or feeling, it presents the reader with a series of images, which when connected in the imagination, yield a wealth of associations, visions, and emotions. Consider, for example, Bashō's best known haiku:

> An old pond
> Frog jumps in
> Sound of water.

The inner spring of the poem is the juxtaposition of two contrasting natural elements, a juxtaposition that (like the frog in the water) sets off waves in the reader's mind. The old pond not only supplies the setting but also implies a condition—the stillness of water and of long years—that contrasts with the sudden action, and results in a delightful image. It raises the question, "How does one explain the relationship between the pond which has been there for centuries and a tiny splash that disappears in a moment?" This formulation is by the contemporary scholar Makoto Ueda, who responds, "Different people will give different answers, though they will all experience the same sort of 'loneliness' when they try to give an explanation. It seems that Bashō was more concerned with the loneliness than with the answers."[9]

Some of Bashō's finest poems were composed on his travels and are contained in his *The Narrow Road of Oku*. One such haiku reads:

> At Yoshino
> I'll show you cherry blossoms—
> Cypress umbrella.[10]

He wrote the poem on his umbrella, and there is a gentle whimsy in Bashō's idea of sharing the beauty of the cherry blossoms with his umbrella. The word translated "umbrella" can also mean "hat." Figure 7.6 shows Bashō, with his traveling hat, ready to begin his trip.

The painting itself is an example of the genre known as *haiga* in which a *haiku* and a painting *(ga)* were integrated. It is by Yokoi Kinkoku (1761–1832) and exemplifies "literati painting" *(bunjinga;* Chinese, *wenrenhua, wen-jen-hua)* in the general manner of Yosa Buson (1716–83), the most eminent artist in this mode. These artists looked to China for basic inspiration, although they did not limit themselves to Chinese subjects in their art. Like their Chinese models, Buson and other *bunjin* wrote poetry as well as painting pictures, but they represent only one of several trends during the post-Genroku period.

Art and Literature After the Genroku Period

After the Genroku period artists continued to work in the Genroku genres, but the classic age of the popular theater, the print, and haiku was past. Notable among the *ukiyo-e* artists of this time was the strikingly original Tōshūsai Sharaku (dates unknown), famous for the prints of actors that he

Figure 7.6 Yokoi Kinkoku, *Portrait of Bashō*. Ink and color on paper.

turned out during a ten-month outburst of creativity in 1794–95. His prints, theatrical, psychologically penetrating, and bitterly satirical, ran counter to the tastes of his time. More appreciated in his own day was Suzuki Harunobu (1724–70), who excelled in the subtle use of color and in the freshness of his young beauties. Controversial and uneven was the prolific Kitagawa Utamaro (1754–1806), who achieved great popularity with his prints of the ladies of the "floating world." Reproduced in Figure 7.7 is one of a series on the physiognomies of women, this one illustrating the "wanton" type.

With the end of the eighteenth century, there was a falling off in the artistic quality of the figure prints, but the *ukiyo-e* tradition retained enough vigor to achieve excellence in another form—the landscape print. A master of this art was the "old man mad with painting," Katsushika Hokusai (1760–1849), an eclectic genius. He is represented here by one of his depictions of the scenery along the Tōkaidō, the great road leading to Edo traveled by the daimyo and their retinues (see Figure 7.8). Less versatile but at his best producing works imbued with a delicate lyricism was Andō Hiroshige (1797–1858), who was still alive when Commodore Perry arrived in Japan (1853).

In the course of two centuries the Japanese artists and craftsmen achieved a level of artistic and technical excellence unrivaled anywhere in the world. They developed styles appropriate to their medium, creating an art of colors and planes and of crisp lines, with only a hint of the old calligraphic tradition. It was an art of great immediate appeal, not only to the Tokugawa townspeople and country folk looking for a souvenir of their trip to the

Figure 7.7   Kitagawa Utamaro, *Beauty Wringing Out a Towel.* Woodcut print, 37.8 cm × 25.1 cm.

great city, but also to European artists who found they had much to learn from this art.

Prose and poetry continued to be produced and enjoyed by a wide audience, although they did not again reach the quality attained by Saikaku or Bashō. Perhaps the best loved of the later haiku poets was Kobayashi Issa (1763–1827). He achieved a wide identification with nature and showed sympathy for even the humblest of animals and insects.

> Lean frog,
> don't give up the fight!
> Issa is here![11]

Political Reform and Its Limits

The underlying discrepancy between official theory and socioeconomic reality was brought home to the *bakufu* in a series of financial crises, some aggravated by poor harvests due to natural causes. In any case, something had to be done when government revenues failed to keep up with its needs.

Figure 7.8   Katsushika Hokusai, *The Station Hodogaya on the Tōkaidō*. Woodcut print, 25.9 × 28.8 cm.

Retrenchment was one standard response. Often, as in the Kyōhō Reforms (1716–36), a spending cut was seen as morally desirable as well as fiscally necessary. Calls for reduction in government spending were accompanied by admonitions for samurai to revive warrior morality, and detailed laws were designed to limit merchant expenditure. More lasting in effect was the licensing of merchant organizations which were granted monopolies and paid an annual fee. This system was widely adopted also by the daimyo.

The shogun also made it easier to employ capable samurai of low inherited rank in high office. Previously this had been difficult since such men were customarily granted high permanent hereditary rank, but now their stipend was raised only during their tenure of office.

Among the sources of needed revenue were special payments imposed on the daimyo, programs of land reclamation, and campaigns to squeeze more taxes out of the peasantry, but in the long run these yielded diminishing returns. The same can be said of the *bakufu's* attempts to set prices of essential commodities. Some initially successful measures eventually backfired. For example, monetary deflation did put an end to a destructive inflation but brought on a deflation so severe that it provoked Japan's first urban rice riots (1733).

Later in the century, the *bakufu* made some additions to its reform reper-toire as when under the leadership Tanuma Okitsugu (1719–88) it encour-aged foreign trade, tried to develop mines, created new monopolies and imposed new merchant licenses, and showed interest in developing Hok-kaido. Tanuma, however, was resented for favoring the *bakufu* vis-à-vis the *han*, and his enemies emphasized his corruption. He ended in disgrace, his initiatives abandoned.

The next reform wave, 1787–93, named after the Kansei Period (1789–1801) showed the *bakufu* still capable of vigorous action but brought no lasting solutions to endemic fiscal problems, samurai demoralization, shrinking finances, or suffering in the countryside. The reforms are dis-cussed more in the next chapter. What we need to note here is that there was cause for concern and, though the system still functioned, it was apparent to all thoughtful observers that all was not well.

Intellectual Currents: Chinese Background

Tokugawa Confucianism owes much to the continent, where a reinvigo-rated Confucianism had spread from Song Dynasty China (960–1279) to Korea. One facet of renewed Confucian vitality was an upsurge in the study and writing of history. Another was an intense concern with education and the spread of academies.

There were also developments in doctrine, forming what in the West is often called Neo-Confucianism. In Japan, as in China, many found in Neo-Confucianism religious fulfillment, intellectual stimulation, and moral in-spiration, for this was at one and the same time a creed that gave meaning to the life of the individual, a philosophy that provided a convincing frame-work for understanding the world, and an ideology supporting and sup-ported by state and society. It conceived of the world as an organic whole and itself constituted an organic system in which each aspect was seen as rein-forcing the others.

In China the new Confucianism received its classical formulation by Zhu Xi (Chu Hsi, 1130–1200). Zhu was a prolific scholar, but most influential of all his works were his commentaries on what became the core texts of Neo-Confucianism: *The Analects, Mencius, The Great Learning*, and *The Doc-trine of the Mean* (the last two are chapters from the *Records of Rites*). Zhu Xi and other East Asian thinkers did not present their ideas in systematic philosophical treatises but as commentaries on the classics, in miscella-neous writings (including letters), and in conversations that were recorded by disciples. This made the study of their ideas very demanding but also encouraged successive generations of scholars to reinterpret Confucianism in their own way. Neither in China nor in Japan was this a monolithic phi-losophy. Indeed the range is so broad that scholars disagree on its boundaries.

To explain the physical and metaphysical world, Chinese and Japanese thinkers still employed ancient *yin* and *yang* and five processes theory but stressed the conceptual pair *ri (li)* and *ki (qi, ch'i)*. This *ri*, not to be confused with the term meaning "ritual" (written with a different character), is usually translated as "principle." Because Chinese and Japanese nouns do not distinguish between singular and plural, *ri* can designate a single principle or a myriad of principles forming one network or pattern. According to Song scholars, the word originally signified veins running through jade. Each individual *ri* thus forms part of the entire system. For Zhu Xi, this network or system constitutes the underlying pattern of reality encompassing both the realm of proper human conduct and that of the physical world. No distinction in kind is made between society and nature, between ethics and physics: the *ri* of fatherhood is as much a part of the ultimate scheme of things as the *ri* of stones or mountains. Both are comprehensible and both are equally "natural."

For Zhu Xi nothing can exist if there is no *ri* for it, but *ri* never occurs apart from *ki*, the vital force and substance of which man and the universe are made. It can be conceived of as energy, but energy that occupies space. In its most refined form it occurs as a kind of rarefied ether but condensed it becomes the most solid metal or rock. In his cosmology Zhu Xi envisioned the world as a sphere in constant rotation, so that the heaviest *ki* is held in the center by the centripetal force of the motion. The *ki* then becomes progressively lighter and thinner as one moves away from the center. This way he explained why, for instance, the air at high altitude is thinner than that at sea level.

It was theoretically possible to construct a philosophy based on the priority of either *ri* or *ki*, but for Zhu Xi they are both irreducible, with *ri* holding logical and ontological but not temporal priority over *ki*. A major consequence of this philosophy was that it enabled Song philosophers to accept and strengthen Mencius' theory of the essential goodness of human beings even though we so often stray: people are good because everyone has good *ri*, but this exists in conjunction with more or less impure *ki*. The ancient sages were born with *ki* that was perfectly pure: they were born perfect. But ordinary folk have to cope with impure, more or less turgid *ki*: they must work to attain perfection.

For ordinary people, the way to attain perfection is by truly grasping the *ri*, but because these are found within everyone as well as out in the world, there was disagreement over the proper method of self-cultivation. Zhu Xi generally stressed the "investigation of things," by which he meant primarily the study of moral conduct and especially the timeless lessons contained in the classics. Consequently his school was associated with an emphasis on scholarly learning, even though it by no means ruled out more inner-directed endeavors such as silent meditation and reflection.

There were a number of thinkers who reduced everything to *ki*, but the most influential challenge came in the late Ming from Wang Yangming (Wang Shouren, 1472–1529) and his followers for whom only *ri* ultimately exists. Wang identified human nature with the heart/mind and taught that everyone has an innate capacity to know the good and to attain sagehood. From the beginning Confucians had been concerned less with abstract truth than with practical conduct, but Wang went a step further in insisting that truth cannot be grasped by abstract intellectualization but must be lived. What is true of sensory knowledge holds for all knowledge: a person can no more know filial piety without practicing it than he can know the smell of an odor or understand pain without experiencing them. Knowing and acting are not only inseparable, they are two dimensions of a single process: "Knowledge in its genuine and earnest aspect is action, and action in its intelligent and discriminating aspect is knowledge."[12]

Although emphasizing texts less than Zhu Xi, Wang Yangming too claimed a correct understanding of the classics, but in eighteenth-century China all the earlier Neo-Confucians were challenged by scholars who turned to philology in an attempt to get back to the original classics.

Tokugawa Confucianism

Tokugawa Confucian thinkers were deeply influenced by developments originating in China, but their writings also reflect the vast differences between the societies, institutions, and traditions of the two countries. There was no equivalent in Japan to the civil service examination system, based on Confucian texts, that, beginning in the Song, molded the Chinese political and social elite. In Japan, to be a Confucian was no guarantee of high status. On the contrary, most of Japan's notable thinkers came from lower samurai or commoner ranks and made a livelihood as teachers or doctors. Indeed, one of the attractions of Confucianism to such men was its advocacy of government by the meritorious rather than the well-born. At the same time, even the sinophiles among them took pride in Japan. Some argued that Japan came closer to Confucian ideals than Qing Dynasty China, while others played quite an ingenious "game of oneupmanship."[13]

Neo-Confucianism enjoyed *bakufu* support ever since the first shoguns patronized Hayashi Razan (1583–1657), founder of what became Edo's premier Confucian academy; but, given the *baku-han* system, Edo did not dominate Tokugawa thought. Even when the shogunate, in 1790 during its most restrictive period, officially prohibited heterodox doctrines, it had little effect on intellectual life.

Merchants and soldiers were not highly regarded in Chinese Confucianism, but in Japan samurai and merchant Confucianism flourished. The aristocratic Fujiwara Seika (1561–1619) did not find it beneath his dignity to write a letter for a trade mission or to draw up a ship's oath, the first article of which began by saying, "Commerce is the business of selling and buying in order to bring profit to both parties," defined profit as "the outcome of righteousness," and admonished merchants not to be greedy.[14]

An outstanding seventeenth-century exponent of Zhu Xi's Confucianism was Yamazaki Ansai (1618–82), a stern and forceful teacher who stressed "devotion within, righteousness without" and was so dedicated to Zhu Xi that he said he would follow the master even into error. When asked the supremely hypothetical question: what should be done were Confucius and Mencius to lead a Chinese invasion of Japan, he answered that he would capture the two sages and put them at the service of his own land. Deeply interested in Shinto, Ansai attempted to fuse Confucian ethics with Shinto religion. Another major orthodox thinker was Muro Kyūsō (1658–1734). Most Confucians justified the shogunate by incorporating it into the hierarchy of loyalty, but Kyūsō argued that the Tokugawa ruled by virtue of a heavenly mandate. He found it necessary to defend Song philosophy against increasingly vigorous challenges from other schools, the Japanese counterparts of the varieties of Confucianism that developed on the continent after the Song.

The man considered the founder of the Wang Yangming school in Japan was Nakae Tōju (1608–48). Like the Chinese philosopher, he stressed the inner light of man and insisted on the importance of action. It was his lofty and unselfish character especially that attracted the admiration of contemporaries and of later activist intellectuals. His best-known disciple, Kumazawa Banzan (1619–91) ran into political difficulties, not because of his unorthodox philosophic ideas, but for unconventional policy recommendations, including a relaxation of the daimyo's attendance requirements in Edo to save expenses. He was traditionally Confucian in his concern for the well-being of the peasantry and in his lack of sympathy for the merchant class, as reflected in his advocacy of a return to a barter economy using rice in place of money.

Like Yamazaki Ansai and Kumazawa Banzan, Kaibara Ekken (1630–1714) found much of value in Shinto, but his philosophy of nature was based on *ki*. The writings of this remarkable man range from botany to ethics, from farming to philology, and include precepts for daily life as well as a primer for women. They express his breadth of mind, commitment to the welfare of society, and his faith in the unity and value of knowledge. Miura Baien (1723–1789) like Ekken, was from Kyūshū. He too developed a philosophy of *ki* in a complex binary system based on "dynamic flux and static form."[15]

In Japan, as in China, there were thinkers who denied the authority of the Song scholars and insisted on going back to the classical sources. This was the stance of Yamaga Sokō, whose connection with *bushidō* was noted earlier in this chapter. Others who decided that the Song thinkers had distorted the authentic Confucian message differed on the contents of that message. A great teacher and moralist known for his benign view of the human emotions, stress on individual self-cultivation, and his emphasis on *jin* (ren, loving benevolence) was Itō Jinsai (1627–1705), who drew inspiration from the *Analects*:

> The *Analects* is like the boundless universe which men live in without comprehending its full magnitude. Enduring and immutable throughout the ages; in every part of the world it serves as an infallible guide. Is it not, indeed, great![16]

Philosophically Itō rejected the Neo-Confucian distinction between *ri* and *ki*, two concepts by then as much at home in Japan as in China.

Another attack on the Song philosophy of principle (*ri*) was made by Ogyū Sorai (1666–1728), who insisted on going back not just to the *Analects* but to the earlier Six Classics, according to him the genuine repositories of true doctrine. A complex, many-sided thinker, in his political thought he represented the tough-minded pole of Confucianism with its emphasis on rites and institutions. Like some of the seventeenth-century Chinese critics of Song philosophy, Ogyū Sorai was interested in practical as well as theoretical subjects. A prolific writer, he dealt with many topics: philosophy and politics; literature, linguistics, and music; military science; and economics.

Sorai too had his critics, including a remarkable series of thinkers from the Osaka merchant community who, like Itō Jinsai, taught that virtue was accessible to all. Also, like Jinsai, Goi Ranshū (1697–1762) insisted that knowledge was not complete, but Ranshū envisioned intellectual progress. Goi was the first of a series of distinguished thinkers to head the Kaitokudō Academy in Osaka. One who studied there was Tominaga Nakamoto (1715–46), a skeptic who argued that all historical texts were unreliable. In the work of these and several other men were the roots for ideas which exceeded the confines of the Tokugawa order and, indeed, the normal bounds of Confucian thought. But Confucian thought too could take men's minds in unanticipated directions.

Historiography and "National Learning"

A perennial field of Confucian scholarship was the study of history, but in the Tokugawa period it was not only Confucian scholars who were interested in the Japanese past. Hayashi Razan, himself, began work on a history of Japan that was completed by his son and accepted as the official history of the shogunate. Among those who made major contributions to scholarship was the statesman and scholar Arai Hakuseki (1657–1725), noted for his careful attention to the evidence and a willingness to reexamine traditional beliefs.

A different emphasis appeared in *The Great History of Japan (Dainihonshi)*, which was begun in the seventeenth century under the sponsorship of the Lord of Mito, Tokugawa Mitsukuni (1628–1700), but not completed until the twentieth century. Mitsukuni, a grandson of Ieyasu, enlisted the services of a Chinese emigree Ming loyalist, Zhu Shunshui (Chu Shun-shui, 1600–82). The resulting history was highly moralistic and loyalist in tone, exalting the Japanese imperial house. Since, in theory, the shogun himself derived his authority from this source, there was nothing inherently anti-*bakufu* in Mito historiography. That its focus on the emperor rather than on the shogun was potentially subversive, however, was shown later when it provided an emperor-centered source for nationalistic sentiments, and eventually it supplied ammunition for the anti-*bakufu* arguments of the movement to "restore the emperor," which culminated in the Meiji Restoration of 1868.

Interest in Japan's past often went hand in hand with a new appreciation of native traditions. Tokugawa Mitsukuni commissioned the Shingon priest Keichū (1640–1701), a great philologist, to write a commentary on the *Man'yoshu*, and Yamazaki Ansai expounded Shinto along with Confucianism.

First to advocate return to a Shinto purified of Confucian elements was Kada no Azumamaro (1669–1736). Rejection of Confucianism and celebration of the native tradition as morally superior became a persistent theme in nativist thought.

Motoori Norinaga (1730–1801) brought "national studies" to a new level of philological excellence and enjoyed wide influence as a teacher and political adviser. His views on *The Tale of Genji* have already been mentioned, for Motoori was a fine literary scholar with a keen appreciation for the old Heian aesthetic and the feminine sensibility of that age. However, his life's work was the study of the *Kojiki* which he believed contained the literal truth. Motoori thought it arrogant not to recognize the limitations of the human intellect and wrong to attempt to understand the *kami* rationally. Indeed the irrationality of the old legends was a sign of their truth, for "who would fabricate such shallow sounding, incredible things?"[17] For Motoori, the *kami* are the starting point: "People try to explain matters in the age of *kami* by referring to human affairs whereas I have understood human affairs by referring to the matters in the age of *kami*."[18] Supreme among the *kami* was the Sun Goddess, and though she spread her favor everywhere, foremost among the countries of the world was the land of her birth. Motoori left a dual heritage, academic philology and ideological nativism. Among those who drew on the latter aspect of Motoori's thought the most influential was Hirata Atsutane (1776–1843), an ultranationalist whose narrow Japanism proved attractive to many in the nineteenth and twentieth centuries.

Dutch Learning

In Tokugawa Japan, European learning equaled "Dutch Learning," for the Dutch remained the only Westerners allowed even limited access to Japan. Their annual audience with the shogun provided an occasion for the Japanese to satisfy their curiosity about the exotic:

> He [the shogun, mistaken for the emperor by the Dutch chronicler] order'd us to take off our Cappa, or Cloak, being our Garment of Ceremony, then to stand upright, that he might have a full view of us; again to walk, to stand still, to compliment each other, to dance, to jump, to play the drunkard, to speak broken Japanese, to read Dutch, to paint, to sing, to put our cloaks on and off. Meanwhile we obey'd the Emperor's commands in the best manner we could. I join'd to my dance a lovesong in High German. In this manner, and with innumerable such other apish tricks, we must suffer ourselves to contribute to the Emperor's and Court's diversion.[19]

This is from a report of the embassy of 1691 or 1692. The "Red-haired Barbarians," as the Dutch were commonly known, continued to be objects of wild rumor. But they also drew the attention of serious scholars after the *bakufu*, in 1720, permitted the importation of books on all subjects except Christianity. One result was the influence of Western art, which we have already noted in the discussion of the *ukiyo-e*, and in the eighteenth century, there were also Japanese painters who produced reputable Western-style works in oil.

Most remarkable were the achievements of a small group of truly dedicated scholars who wrestled with the difficulties of the Dutch language and laboriously made the first translations, compiled the early dictionaries, and wrote the first treatises on Western subjects, initially concerning geography, astronomy, medicine, and other sciences. Thus Shiba Kōkan (1738–1818), the first in Japan to produce copper engravings, was fascinated by the realistic aspect of Western art, by its ability to portray objects as they appear to the eye. The practical, scientific value of Western studies had already been recognized by Arai Hakuseki, and to Shiba, too, this is what was of value in the Western tradition. For spiritual nourishment the Japanese continued to turn to their own heritage, thus foreshadowing the nineteenth-century formula "Eastern ethics—Western science." Thanks to *bakufu* policy, they knew little about Western political, philosophical, or religious thought.

By the end of the eighteenth century, there were also scholars of Dutch Learning who, alarmed by Western expansionism, discussed political, military, and economic matters at considerable personal risk. Hayashi Shihei (1738–93) was arrested for defying a *bakufu* prohibition by publishing a book dealing with political issues: he advocated defense preparations against the threat he saw impending from abroad. Honda Toshiaki (1744–1821), who wanted to turn Japan into the England of the East, complete with mercantile empire, escaped persecution by not publishing his ideas.

Implicit in the views of the scholars of Dutch Learning was dissatisfaction with the Tokugawa seclusion policy, which stood in the way of their learning more about Western civilization and prevented them from traveling overseas. Meanwhile, by stressing the royal line, Mito Confucians and National Learning scholars also helped to weaken the *bakufu* ideologically. And even orthodox Confucianism did not really require a shogun or a *bakufu*.

Thus, by 1800 there were fissures in the Tokugawa's intellectual as well as political and economic foundations, but it was a new challenge from abroad that eventually destroyed them.

NOTES

1. Ronald P. Dore, *Education in Tokugawa Japan* (Berkeley: Univ. of California Press, 1965), p. 151.

2. Donald Keene, *Four Major Plays of Chikamatsu* (New York: Columbia Univ. Press, 1961), p. 151.

3. Robert Treat Paine and Alexander Soper, *The Art and Architecture of Japan* (Baltimore: Penguin Books, 1955), p. 274.

4. See Hiroshi Mizuo, *Edo Painting: Sōtatsu and Kōrin*, trans. John M. Shields (New York and Tokyo: Weatherhill/Heibonsha, 1974), pp. 40–41.

5. Elise Grilli, *The Art of the Japanese Screen* (Tokyo and New York: John Weatherhill, 1970), pp. 111–12.

6. Willy Boller, *Masterpieces of the Japanese Color Woodcut; Collection W. Boller*. Photo. by R. Spreng (Boston: Boston Book and Art Shop, [1950?]), p. 20.

7. Attributed to Chikamatsu by his friend Hozumi Ikan. Hozumi's account of Chikamatsu's views has been translated by Donald Keene as "Chikamatsu on the Art of the Puppet Stage," in Donald Keene, ed., *Anthology of Japanese Literature* (New York: Grove Press, 1955), p. 389.

8. Ryusaku Tsunoda, Wm. Theodore de Bary, and Donald Keene, comps., *Sources of Japanese Tradition* (New York: Columbia Univ. Press, 1958), p. 454.

9. Makoto Ueda, *Matsuo Bashō* (New York: Twayne, 1970), p. 53.

10. Calvin French, *The Poet-Painters: Buson and His Followers*, exhibition catalog (Ann Arbor: Univ. of Michigan Museum of Art, 1974), p. 132.

11. Henderson, *An Introduction to Haiku*, p. 133.

12. Wing-tsit Chan, *A Source Book in Chinese Philosophy* (Princeton: Princeton Univ. Press, 1963), p. 681.

13. See Kate Wildman Nakai, "The Naturalization of Confucianism in Tokugawa Japan: The Problem of Sinocentrism." *Harvard Journal of Asiatic Studies*, 40 (1980): 157–199.

14. Tsunoda, Ryusaku et al., *Sources of Japanese Tradition* (New York: Columbia Univ. Press, 1958), p. 349.

15. Rosemary Mercer, *Deep Words: Miura Baien's System of Natural Philosophy* (Leiden: E.J. Brill, 1991), p. 14.

16. Tsunoda et al., *Sources of Japanese Tradition*, p. 419.

17. Ibid., p. 524.

18. Shigeru Matsumoto, *Motoori Norinaga, 1730–1801* (Cambridge: Harvard Univ. Press, 1970), p. 81.

19. E. Kaempfer, quoted in Donald Keene, *The Japanese Discovery of Europe*, rev. ed. (Stanford: Stanford Univ. Press, 1969), p. 4.

PART FOUR

Japan in the
Modern World

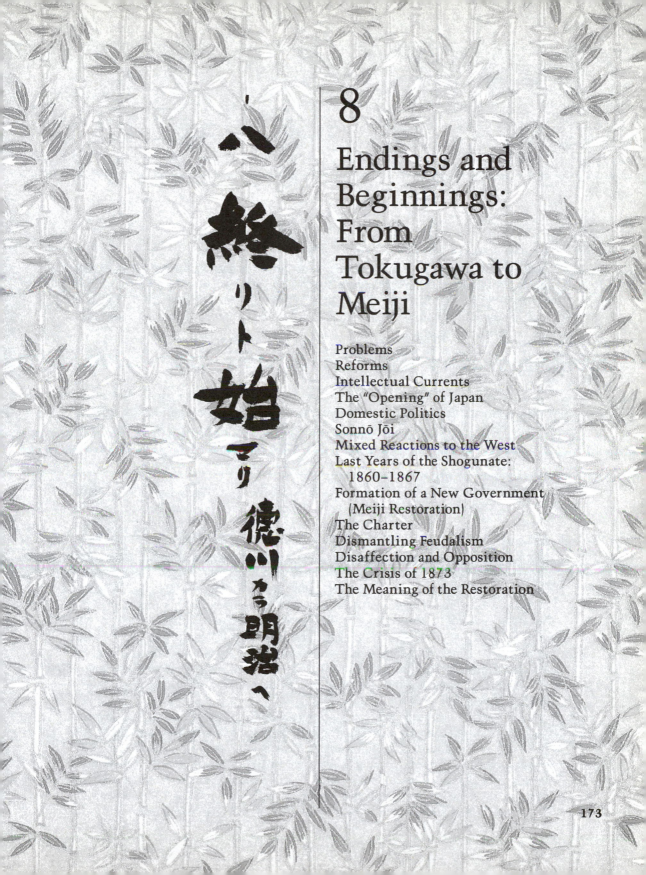

八　終リと始マり　徳川から明治へ

8
Endings and Beginnings: From Tokugawa to Meiji

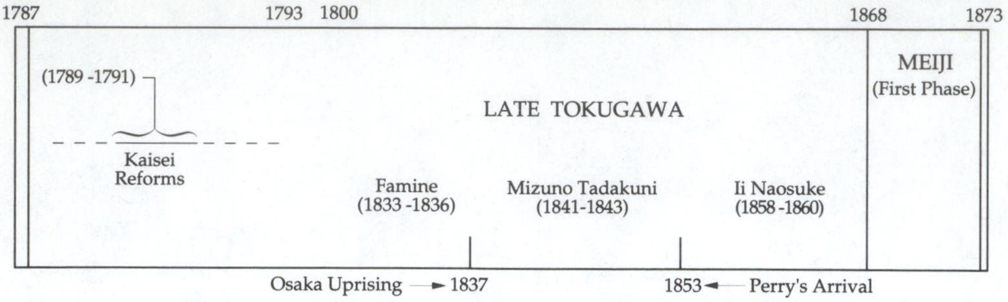
1787
1793 1800
1868
1873
(1789 -1791)
Kaisei
Reforms
LATE TOKUGAWA
MEIJI
(First Phase)
Famine
(1833 -1836)
Mizuno Tadakuni
(1841-1843)
Ii Naosuke
(1858 -1860)
Osaka Uprising → 1837
1853 ← Perry's Arrival

By 1800 the Tokugawa system was showing many symptoms of stress even before challenges from abroad put the old order to a test which it ultimately failed. But the dynamism of the forces subverting Tokugawa state and society contributed much that helped Japan to develop ultimately into a modern country.

Problems

Structurally, the Tokugawa political and economic systems pulled in different directions. The economic unity brought about by a national market was not matched by political centralization, and the political elite lacked the economic savy to deal with the new forces. Too often the *bakufu* sought to deal with new problems in old ways.

That at least seems largely the case with the ambitious Kansei Reforms (1787–93) carried out by Matsudaira Sadanobu, an earnest Confucian who launched a campaign against corruption and tried to put the system back on a sound fiscal and economic basis by edicts mandating lower prices for rice, restrictions on merchant guilds, cancellation of some samurai loans, rent control, as well as improved public services in Edo. He reduced contact with the Dutch and favored leaving Hokkaido undeveloped as a buffer to foreign intervention. To improve administration he not only sought "men of ability" but also proscribed heterodoxy from the official *bakufu* school, turning the Neo-Confucianism of Zhu Xi for the first time into official doctrine. At the same time, there was a hardening of censorship. All told, as summarized by Marius Jansen, these measures "institutionalized and hardened tradition . . . and left a regime less flexible and more concerned with preserving a tradition that had now been defined."[1]

In any case, systemic ills soon reappeared. By 1800 the *bakufu's* annual budget showed a small deficit, the beginning of a trend. Once again, it resorted to forced loans and currency devaluations. Between 1819 and 1837 it devalued the currency nineteen times, but this brought only temporary relief. The political authorities remained dependent on the market and the merchants who understood and manipulated the market. There was in Tokugawa Japan no system or theory of regular deficit financing.

Especially hard hit by the financial crisis were lower ranking samurai who had to convert a substantial portion of their rice stipend into cash and were constantly at the mercy of a fluctuating market which they could not understand and would not study. Even the daimyo, burdened with the heavy expenses of periodic attendance in Edo, and required to maintain separate establishments in the *bakufu* and *han* capitals, found themselves in financial difficulty. One way for a daimyo to improve his finances was to cut stipends, further aggravating the situation of the samurai. This hurt even the small minority of high-ranking men, but the effects were most serious, even devastating, on the bulk of samurai who ranked low in status and stipend.

Some samurai married daughters of wealthy merchants, but many lived in desperate circumstances. They pawned their swords, worked at humble crafts, such as umbrella making and sandal weaving, and tried to hide their misery from the world. A samurai was taught that he should use a toothpick even when he had not eaten.

The samurai were not dissatisfied with the basic social system in which, after all, they formed the ruling class. But they were enraged by the discrepancy between the theoretical elevation of their status and the reality of their poverty. Not only was their poverty demeaning, but the spectacle of contrasting merchant wealth hurt their pride. It seemed the height of injustice that society should reward the selfish money-making trader and condemn to indigence the warrior whose life was one of service.

The immediate focus of samurai discontent was not with the Tokugawa order but with the character and abilities of the men in power. There was deep resentment against incompetence and corruption in high places, and it was felt that government could be reformed by putting into office more capable men, including able men from the lower ranks of the samurai class. In staffing the *bakufu* and *han* bureaucracies, ability and competence should take precedence over family.

City merchants and rural entrepreneurs flourished economically and were acquiescent politically, but below them the rural and urban poor included many who earned barely enough to keep themselves alive. Crop failures in the 1820s and a severe national famine which began in 1833 and reached a crescendo in 1836 caused great misery and brought masses of desperate peasants into the cities. The government did supply relief but not enough to forestall violence. The best estimate has it that during the Tempō era (1830–44) there were 465 rural disputes, 445 peasant uprisings, and 101 urban riots.[2] A great impression was made by the 1837 uprising in Osaka. It was led by Ōshio Heihachirō (1793–1837), a low-ranking *bakufu* official and follower of Wang Yangming's philosophy of action, but it was poorly planned and quickly suppressed. Peasant discontent also found expression in the rise of messianic movements. There was a general sense of malaise and of the disintegration of authority. In earlier conflicts with domainal lords, villagers had united behind their headmen but differentiation between the rich and poor had now reached the point where interests diverged too widely for the village to speak with a single voice.

Reforms

In response to the financial and social crises, there was one more concerted effort at reform both by the domains and by the *bakufu*. On both levels, large doses of antiquated remedies such as economic retrenchment, bureaucratic reform, and moral rearmament were administered, but there were also some innovative economic and social policies. In the *bakufu*, reform began in 1841, after the death of Ienari, shogun since 1787. Under the leadership of Mizuno Tadakuni (1793–1851) they included recoinage and forced loans, dismissal of officials to reduce costs, and sumptuary laws intended to preserve morals and save money. Censorship became stricter. An effort (by no means the *bakufu's* first) was made to force peasants to return to their lands. This was in keeping with the Confucian view of the primacy of agriculture as well as with the Tokugawa's policy of strict class separation but hardly solved any problems. A program to create solid areas of *bakufu* control around Edo and Osaka proved too ambitious. It called for the creation of a *bakufu*-controlled zone of 25 square miles around Edo and 12 square miles around Osaka by moving certain daimyo and housemen out of these areas, but the plan was never carried out. In the hope of fighting inflation, merchant monopolies were broken up, and an attempt was made to bar the daimyo from engaging in commercial monopolies. Despite the retrenchment policy, an expensive and ostentatious formal procession to the Tokugawa mausoleum at Nikko was organized in an effort to reassert the *bakufu's* preeminence. But the daimyo were not easily bridled, and the reform lasted only two years.

The various domains, faced with similar problems, attempted local reform programs of their own. Here and there *han* government machinery was reformed, stipends and other costs were cut, and some domains even rewarded the expert assistance of outstanding members of the merchant community by promoting them to samurai status. To deal with the economy, agriculture was encouraged and commercial policies were changed. Generally, in the *han* as in the *bakufu*, the Tempō era reforms ended, "some whimpering their way into oblivion, others culminating in an explosion in which the reformers were dismissed . . . and sometimes thrown into prison as well . . . Whatever the end, they were ignored until their resurrection as models for fresh reforms in the 1850s and 1860s."[3]

A major domain in which the reforms did take hold was Satsuma in Kyūshū. Subsequently Chōshū in Southwest Honshū (see Figure 8.1) enjoyed a similar success. In interesting and important ways these were untypical domains. For one thing, they were both large, outside *han (tozama)*, that is, *han* that had arisen independently of the Tokugawa, which prior to 1600 they sometimes opposed and sometimes supported, but as equals not subordinates. In the seventeenth century they accepted Tokugawa supremacy since they had no other alternative, but their commitment to the Tokugawa order was not beyond question. In line with Tokugawa policy, Satsuma and Chōshū had their domains transferred and reduced in size in the seventeenth century. One consequence was that they kept alive an anti-Tokugawa feudal tradition. Another

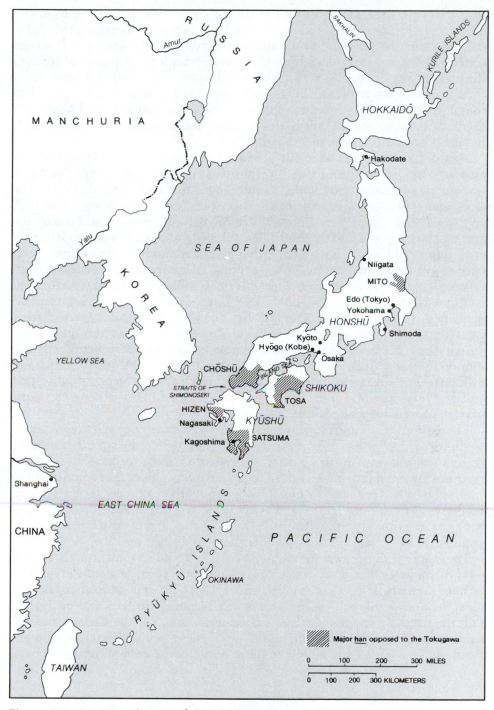

Figure 8.1   Japan on the Eve of the Meiji Restoration.

result was that the reduction in the size of their domains left them with a much higher than average ratio of samurai to the land. In Satsuma this led to the formation of a class of samurai who worked the land *(goshi)* and a tight control of the countryside, which experienced not a single peasant uprising throughout the Tokugawa period. Satsuma backwardness was also an asset to the domain in the sense that it worked against the erosion of samurai values found in economically more advanced and urbane regions. Both Chōshū and Satsuma also had special family ties with the court in Kyoto, the most likely focus for any anti-*bakufu* movement.

In both *han*, finances were put in order and a budget surplus was built up, although by different methods. In Chōshū a rigorous cost-cutting program was initiated, major improvements were made in *han* financial administration, and there was a reform of the land tax. Most *han* monopolies were abolished, since they were unprofitable for the government and unpopular among the people. Only the profitable shipping and warehouse monopolies at Shimonoseki were continued. Otherwise, commodity transactions were turned over to merchants for a fee. Satsuma, in contrast, derived much of its income from its monopolies, especially the monopoly on sugar from the Ryūkyū Islands (Liuqiu, Liu-ch'iu, in Chinese), which were a Satsuma dependency. At the same time Satsuma directed the Ryūkyūs to continue sending tribute to China in order to foster trade between China and the islands, which thus became a source of Chinese goods for Satsuma. The sugar monopoly was strictly enforced: private sale of sugar was a crime punishable by death. The sugar was brought to market in Osaka in the *han's* own ships, and at every stage from production to sale everything was done to insure maximum profit for the Satsuma treasury.

These programs required vigorous leadership, since they naturally ran up against the opposition of merchants and others who benefited from doing things the old way. Both Chōshū and Satsuma were fortunate in having reform-minded daimyo who raised to power young samurai of middle or low rank, men who tended to be much more innovative and energetic than conservative samurai of high rank. Particularly in Chōshū such differences in background and outlook within the samurai class led to bitter political antagonisms and produced a period of turbulence in *han* politics.

The fact that reform was more successful in Chōshū and Satsuma than in the *bakufu* suggests that it was easier to implement reform in a well-organized, remote domain than in the central region where the economic changes were most advanced and political pressures and responsibilities were far greater. Reform attempts in the other *han* varied in success, but the Chōshū and Satsuma cases are particularly important, since these two large and wealthy domains were to play a crucial role in the eventual overthrow of the Tokugawa.

Intellectual Currents

Economic, social, and political changes were accompanied by intellectual restiveness. Perceptions and ideas advanced by Shinto Revivalists of the

School of National Learning, the Mito school with its emphasis on the centrality of the emperor, followers of "Dutch Learning," and advocates of social restructuring all ate away at the intellectual foundations of *bakufu* rule.

From the world of Osaka merchants came not only the history of money by Kusama Naokata (1753–1831) but also the bold ideas of Yamagata Bantō (1748–1821) who, as a great Osaka financier, had a well-established place in society. Yamagata, basing his ideas on the findings of astronomy, formulated a view of the world that allowed for achievements to occur anywhere on the globe. He had great regard for utility and trust. One of his recommendations was to make written Japanese more accessible by using only the phonetic *kana* script and eliminating all Chinese characters.

One of the most interesting thinkers was Kaihō Seiryō (1748–1821) who spent his life traveling all over Japan free from encumbrances of status or family and who saw all relations, including that of lord and samurai, in economic terms: the samurai sells his service to the lord in exchange for a stipend. For him this was merely accommodating to *ri*. Here a key Neo-Confucian concept is employed to structure a new theory of social conduct.

In the realm of political thought, Mito scholars developed the idea that the emperor ruled by virtue of his unique descent, but that the shogun's legitimacy came from the mandate he derived from the emperor. Aizawa Seishisai (1782–1863), a leading Mito thinker, combined the values of Confucianism and *bushidō* with Shinto mythology in discussing Japan's unique polity *(kokutai)*. In 1825 he tried to use the emperor to create in Japan the kind of unity that he saw as the basis for the strength of Western states and he attributed to (iniquitous) Christianity. As Bob Wakayabashi has pointed out, in 1825, Aizawa's "argument for using the emperor's religious authority to bolster *bakufu* political supremacy was sensible and compelling."[4] Thirty years later it would have been inconceivable.

An example of an influential writer who combined advocacy of an irrational and frequently naive nativism with a good understanding of, and appreciation for, Western medicine was Hirata Atsutane (1776–1843), whose life straddled the eighteenth and nineteenth centuries. Hirata was himself a physician and had studied Dutch medical texts in translation. To reconcile his adulation of Japan with his appreciation for the foreign science, Hirata maintained that Japan had originally been pure and free of disease: the need for a powerful medical science arose only after Japan was infected by foreign contacts.

During the first half of the nineteenth century, interest in such practical Western sciences as astronomy, medicine, and mathematics continued to grow. The *bakufu* itself, in 1811, set up a bureau to translate Dutch books into Japanese even while it maintained its closed door policies. Takano Chōei (1804–50) and Watanabe Kazan (1795–1841) were persecuted for disagreeing with the *bakufu's* seclusion policy and ended as suicides. Outstanding among the students of Western science was the Confucian scholar Sakuma Shōzan (1811–64), who conducted experiments in chemistry and glassmaking and later became an expert in the casting of guns; he was a serious thinker about the principles as well as products of Western technology. There was ample room in his thought for both: he was a firm believer in the ultimate unity of *ri* as taught by Zhu Xi. His formula, "Eastern ethics and Western science," became a very influential slogan after the Meiji Restoration, but Sakuma did not live to see the day, for he was murdered by an antiforeign extremist from Chōshū in 1864.

Sakuma's intellectual strategy was essentially one of compartmentalization: the native and foreign traditions were assigned different functions. Each had its distinct role. Most students of Dutch painting would have agreed, for they valued Western techniques more for their practical results than for any aesthetic merit. Yet, like all generalizations, this demands qualification. Hokusai, who lived until 1849, once contrasted the use of shading for decorative purposes in Chinese and Japanese art with its employment to create an effect of three-dimensionality in the West. He concluded, "One must understand both methods: there must be life and death in everything one paints."[5]

The "Opening" of Japan

The "opening" of China to the West was a result of the Opium War and subsequent treaties with the European powers. In Japan, the "opening" resulted from an armed mission by Commodore Matthew C. Perry of the United States Navy in 1853 (see Figure 8.2). The treaties which followed that momentous event ended the Tokugawa policy of seclusion. They thus contributed to the growing instability of the Tokugawa system and helped to pave the way for a very different future.

Before 1853 there were a number of Western attempts to induce the Japanese to broaden their foreign policy, but these efforts were sporadic since they were not supported by substantial economic and political interests of the kind at work in China. Regarded as poor and remote, Japan was considered an area of relatively low priority by the great powers. The first approaches came from Japan's nearest Eurasian neighbor, the Russian empire, and took place in the North, in the Kurile Islands, Sakhalin, and Hokkaidō. In 1778 and again in 1792 the Russians requested trade relations in Hokkaidō, and in 1804 a similar request was made in Nagasaki. All were refused. British ships seeking trade or ship's stores were also turned away. British whaling ships sometimes requested supplies, but in 1825 the *bakufu* ordered that all foreign ships should be driven from Japanese waters. In 1837 a private American-British attempt to open relations with Japan fared no better. But in 1842 the shogunate relaxed the edicts of 1825 and ordered that foreign ships accidentally arriving in Japan were to be provided with water, food, and fuel. China's defeat in the Opium War and the opening of new ports increased the number of Western vessels in East Asia and hence the pressure on Japan.

This changing situation could not be ignored. To begin with, the lessons of Chinese weakness and Western strength were not lost on Japanese

Figure 8.2 *Commodore Perry.* Artist unknown. Woodcut print, nineteenth century, 26 cm × 24.5 cm.

observers. Information concerning Western science, industry, and military capabilities continued to be provided by scholars of "Dutch Learning." Information also came from China: Wei Yuan's *Illustrated Treatise on the Sea Kingdoms* was widely read after it appeared in a Japanese edition in 1847. Furthermore, the Japanese were making progress in mastering Western technology. By the 1840s the domains of Mito, Hizen, and Satsuma were casting guns using Western methods. In 1850 Hizen possessed the first reverberatory furnace needed to produce iron suitable for making modern cannons. As we have already noted, a few courageous students of the West had suggested abandoning the policy of seclusion well before the arrival of Perry. The Dutch, too, had warned the *bakufu* of the designs of the stronger Western nations.

In 1846 an American mission to Japan ended in failure, but with the acquisition of California in 1848 the interest of the United States in Japan increased, since Nagasaki, 500 miles from Shanghai, was a convenient fueling stop for ships bound from San Francisco to that port. Accordingly it was the United States, rather than Britain or Russia whose interest in Japan remained marginal, that took the lead, sending out Commodore Perry with eleven ships, three of them steam frigates. Perry and his fleet reached Japan in July 1853, forced the Japanese to accept a letter from the American president to the emperor, and announced that he would return for an answer the following spring.

No match militarily for the American fleet, the *bakufu* realized that it would have to accede at least in part to American demands. In preparation for that unpopular move, it took the unprecedented step of soliciting the opinions of even the "outside" daimyo. This turned out to be a serious miscalculation, for instead of the hoped-for support, the *bakufu* received only divided and unhelpful advice while seriously undermining its exclusive right to determine foreign policy.

When Perry returned in February 1854, an initial treaty was signed that provided for the opening of Shimoda and Hakodate to ships seeking provisions, assured that the shipwrecked would receive good treatment, and permitted the United States later to send a consul to Japan. Similar treaties with Britain and France followed in 1855, and the Dutch and Russians negotiated broader agreements in 1857. Still, there was no commercial treaty satisfactory to Western mercantile interests. The task of negotiating such an agreement was left to the first American consul, Townsend Harris, who arrived in Japan in 1856 and gradually succeeded in persuading the shogunate to make concessions (see Figure 8.3). The resulting treaty was signed in 1858,

Figure 8.3 *Harris's Procession on the Way to Edo.* Artist unknown. Watercolor, 53.5 cm × 38.8 cm. Peabody Museum, Salem.

and another round of treaties with the Dutch, Russians, British, and French followed.

At the end of this process, Japan's international situation was similar to that of China. First there was the matter of opening ports. This began with Shimoda on the Izu Peninsula and Hakodate in Hokkaidō; it was extended to Nagasaki and Kanagawa (for which Yokohama was substituted); and dates were set for the opening of Niigata, Hyōgo (modern Kobe), and the admission of foreign merchants to reside in Osaka and Edo. As in the case of China, the treaties provided for the right of citizens of the foreign countries to be tried by their own consular courts under their own laws (extraterritoriality). Japan lost her tariff autonomy and was limited to relatively low import duties. Furthermore, "most favored nation treatment" obliged Japan to grant to one power any concession it granted to any of the others. Thereby Japan was prevented from playing off the powers against each other.

Domestic Politics

For the *bakufu* these were very difficult years, for it was forced to accede to the foreign powers without enjoying support at home. Each failure in foreign affairs provided additional ammunition to its domestic enemies. The *bakufu* was itself divided by factionalism and policy differences. An attempt was made after Perry's arrival to broaden the shogunate's political base by drawing on the advice of nonhouse daimyo. The Lord of Mito, Tokugawa Nariaki (1800–1860), a persistent advocate of resistance to the West, was placed in charge of national defense. These measures, however, failed to strengthen the *bakufu*—too many men were pulling in opposite directions.

When the shogun died without an heir in 1858, a bitter dispute took place over the rival claims of two candidates for the succession. One of these was still a boy, but he had the strongest claim by descent. He also had the backing of most of the house daimyo *(fudai)* including that of Ii Naosuke, the greatest of the *fudai*. The other candidate was Tokugawa Yoshinobu (then known as Hitotsubashi Keiki), the capable son of the Lord of Mito. It will be recalled that Mito was a collateral house of the Tokugawa, eligible to supply shoguns if the main line failed to produce an heir.

The immediate issue in the succession dispute concerned control over the *bakufu*, for Keiki's accession was seen as a threat to the continued control over the shogunate by the *fudai*. At the same time, foreign policy was also involved, for the *bakufu* officials, as men on the spot, were more inclined to make concessions to the foreigners. The great lords, on the other hand, demanded a vigorous defense policy against the intruders from the West. Furthermore, the Lord of Mito and some of his peers envisioned their own *han* as playing important roles in building up military strength against the West. Thus his advocacy of a strong foreign policy was consistent with his desire to strengthen his own *han* at the expense of the center.

The split in the *bakufu* increased the political importance of the imperial court. Nariaki even appealed to Kyoto for support for his son's candidacy. And when the shogun tried to obtain imperial approval for the treaty negotiated with Harris, he failed.

The crisis of 1858 was temporarily resolved when Ii Naosuke took charge of the *bakufu*. He did so as Grand Councilor *(tairō)*, a high post more often than not left vacant, and one that had previously been held by several members of the Ii family. The effective power of this position depended on the authority of the incumbent, and the strong-minded Ii Naosuke used it to dominate the shogunate. He proceeded to sign the treaty with the United States without prior imperial approval, vigorously reasserted *bakufu* power, purged his enemies, forced into retirement or house arrest the daimyo who had opposed him and were on the losing side in the succession dispute, including the Lord of Mito, and punished some of the court nobles and Mito loyalists. For a moment the *bakufu* was revitalized. But it was only for a moment: in March 1860 Ii was assassinated by a group of samurai, mostly from Mito.

Before committing suicide Ii's assassins drew up a document expressing their devotion to the cause for which they had killed and for which they were about to die. It can be summed up in the two phrases that became the slogans for the movement against the Tokugawa: *Sonnō* —"Revere the Emperor"—and *Jōi* —"Expel the Barbarians."

Sonnō Jōi

As we observed earlier, Mito was the home of an emperor-centered school of historiography and political thought, and its lord was one of the most fervent advocates of a strong military policy to "expel the barbarians." It is therefore not surprising that Mito thought influenced the passionate and brilliant young man who became the main spokesman and hero of the *Sonnō Jōi* movement. This was Yoshida Shōin (1830–59), the son of a low-ranking Chōshū samurai. Yoshida was influenced by *bushidō* in the tradition of Yamaga Sokō, by books on military science, and by Confucianism. From Sakuma Shōzan he learned about the West. Then he became acquainted with Mito ideas on a study trip to northern Japan, which, since it was unauthorized, cost him his samurai rank. Apprehensive of the West and convinced of the importance of knowing one's enemy, he tried to stow away on one of Commodore Perry's ships but was caught and placed under house arrest in Chōshū. After his release he started a school there and attracted disciples, including Kido Kōin, one of the three leading statesmen of the Meiji Restoration, and the future Meiji leaders Itō Hirobumi and Yamagata Aritomo.

Yoshida condemned the *bakufu* for its handling of the foreign problem. He charged that its failure to expel the barbarians reflected incompetence, dereliction of duty, and a lack of proper reverence for the throne. Like many men of lower samurai origins, he resented a system that rewarded birth more than ability or talent, and blamed the *bakufu's* inability to eject the foreigner on this system. What was needed to redress the situation were pure and selfless officials who would act out of true loyalty rather than mindless obedience. Thus Yoshida's teaching combined elements of moral revival at home, opposition to the foreigner, and championship of the throne.

Initially Yoshida favored the appointment of new men to the *bakufu*, but after the signing of the treaty with the United States in 1858, he concluded that the *bakufu* must be overthrown. Both personal fulfillment and national salvation required an act of unselfish self-sacrifice by a national hero. Yoshida sought to achieve both aims himself. In 1858 he plotted the assassination of the emissary sent by the shogun to the imperial court to persuade the emperor to agree to the commercial treaty with the United States. Word leaked out. Yoshida was arrested and sent to Edo where he was beheaded the following year.

Mixed Reactions to the West

In this turbulent era Japanese reactions to the West varied widely. Some Japanese, like the Confucian Shinoya Tōin (1810–67), had an absolute hatred of everything Western. He even belittled the script in which the foreigners wrote, describing it as

> confused and irregular, wriggling like snakes or larvae of mosquitoes. The straight ones are like dog's teeth, the round ones are like worms. The crooked ones are like the forelegs of a mantis, the stretched ones are like slime lines left by snails. They resemble dried bones or decaying skulls, rotten bellies of dead snakes or parched vipers.[6]

It is not surprising that a culture which prized calligraphy on the Chinese model should find the strictly utilitarian Western script aesthetically unappetizing, but Shinoya's invective goes beyond mere distaste. Every word betrays, indeed is meant to express, horror and disgust at the beast that had now come among them.

But there were others who were determined to learn from the West, even if only to use that knowledge to defeat the foreigner. Their slogan was *kaikoku jōi:* "open the country to drive out the barbarians." The learning process continued. In 1857 the *bakufu* opened an "Institute for the Investigation of Barbarian Books" near Edo Castle. Not only the *bakufu* but also some of the domains sent men on study trips abroad; in the case of the *han* this was often done illegally. The process of adopting Western technology, begun as we have seen even before Perry's arrival, was accelerated. An indication of the people's receptivity to the new knowledge is provided by the popularity of the writings of Fukuzawa Yukichi (1835–1901), who went abroad twice in the early sixties and published seven books prior to the Restoration, beginning with *Conditions in the West (Seiyō jijō)*, the first volume of which appeared in 1866 and promptly sold 150,000 copies. Another 100,000 copies were sold in pirated editions. These works, written in a simple style (easy enough for Fukuzawa's housemaid to read), were filled with detailed descriptions of Western institutions and life: hospitals and schools, tax systems and museums, climate and clothes, cutlery, and beds and chamberpots. Fukuzawa went on to become a leading Meiji intellectual, but the turbulent years just prior to the Restoration were dangerous for men of his outlook.

In contrast to men like Yoshida Shōin, others hoped for a reconciliation of the court and *bakufu*, and there were some who still hoped the *bakufu* could transform itself and take the lead in creating a more modern state. These issues, at work during the sixties, were finally buried in the Restoration.

Last Years of the Shogunate: 1860–1867

After the assassination of Ii Naosuke in 1860 the *bakufu* leadership tried compromise. An effort was made to effect a "union of the court and military" that was confirmed by the shogun's marriage to the emperor's sister. In return for affirming the emperor's primacy, the *bakufu* obtained assent for its foreign policy. It also sought to win daimyo support by relaxing the old requirements for attendance at Edo. However, this policy ran into the opposition of Kyoto loyalists, activists of the *sonnō jōi* persuasion, samurai, and voluntary *rōnin* who had escaped the bonds of feudal discipline by requesting to leave their lords' service. Psychologically this was not difficult, since their loyalty to their lords had become bureaucratized and since they now felt the claims of a higher loyalty to the throne. Men of extremist dedication, ready to sacrifice their lives for the cause, terrorized the streets of Kyoto in the early sixties and made the capital unsafe for moderates.

Foreigners, too, were subject to attack. The opening of the ports had been followed by a marked rise in the price of rice, causing great economic distress. Xenophobia, that is, intense patriotism coupled with hatred of foreigners, was reinforced by economic hardship caused by the Westerners. Several foreigners were assassinated by fervent samurai in 1859, and in 1861 Townsend Harris's Dutch interpreter was cut down, and the British legation in Edo was attacked. In 1862 a British merchant lost his life at the hands of Satsuma samurai. When the British were unable to obtain satisfaction from the *bakufu*, they took matters into their own hands. In August 1863 they bombarded Kagoshima, the Satsuma capital, in order to force punishment of the guilty and payment of an indemnity.

A similar incident involving Chōshū took place in the summer of 1863. By that time extremists had won control of the court and with Chōshū backing had forced the shogun to accept June 25, 1863, as the date for the expulsion of the barbarians. The *bakufu*, caught between intransigent foreigners and the insistent court, interpreted the agreement to mean that negotiations for the closing of the ports would begin on that day, but Chōshū and the loyalists interpreted it more literally. When Chōshū guns began firing on foreign ships in the Straits of Shimonoseki, the foreign ships fired back. First American warships came to shell the fortifications; then French ships landed parties which destroyed the fort and ammunition. Still Chōshū persisted in firing on foreign vessels, until in September 1864 a combined British, French, Dutch, and American fleet demolished the forts and forced Chōshū to come to terms. These losses, plus a defeat inflicted on Chōshū adherents by a Satsuma-Aizu force in Kyoto in August 1864, stimulated Chōshū to overhaul its military forces. It had already undertaken to purchase Western arms and ships. Now peasant militia were organized, and mixed rifle units were formed—staffed by commoners and samurai, a radical departure from Tokugawa practice and from the basic principles of Tokugawa society. One of these units was commanded by Itō Hirobumi, recently returned from study in England.

Satsuma's response to defeat, although not as radical as Chōshū's, was similar in its appreciation of the superiority of Western weapons. With British help the domain began acquiring Western ships, forming the nucleus of what was to become the Imperial Japanese Navy. The British supported Satsuma partly because they were disillusioned with the *bakufu* and partly because the French were supporting the shogunate with arms hoping to lay the foundations for future influence in a reconstituted shogunate. By now many *bakufu* officials appreciated the need for institutional change as well as modernization. During the closing years of the Tokugawa, the issue was no longer one of preserving the old system but of who would take the lead in building the new. In Chōshū and Satsuma too there was now less talk about "expelling the barbarians" and more about "enriching the country and strengthening the army," at least among the leaders.

The politics of these years were even more than usually full of complications and intrigues, and as long as Chōshū and Satsuma remained on opposite sides the situation remained fluid. Traditionally unfriendly to each other, competing for power in Kyoto, and differing in their policy recommendations, they were nevertheless unified in their opposition to a restoration of Tokugawa power. There were two wars against Chōshū. In the first, 1864–65, a large *bakufu* force with men from many domains defeated Chōshū. This in turn set off a civil war in Chōshū from which the revolutionaries with their mixed rifle regiments emerged victors. This led to a second *bakufu* war against Chōshū, but before this second war began, in 1866, Satsuma and Chōshū made a secret alliance. When war did come, Satsuma and some other powerful *han* remained on the sidelines. Chōshū, although outnumbered, defeated the *bakufu*.

After this defeat by a single *han*, the *bakufu* (under the direction of Tokugawa Yoshinobu, who inherited the position of shogun in 1866) tried to save what it could. There were attempts to work out a daimyo coalition and calls for imperial restoration. In November the shogun accepted a proposal that he resign in favor of a council of daimyo under the emperor. According to this arrangement he was to retain his lands and as the most powerful lord in Japan serve as prime minister. However, this was unacceptable to the *sonnō* advocates in Satsuma and Chōshū and to the restorationists at court, including the court noble Iwakura Tomomi (1825–83), a master politician. On January 3, 1868, forces from Satsuma and other *han* seized the palace and proclaimed the restoration. The shogunate was destroyed. Tokugawa lands were confiscated, and the shogun himself was reduced to the status of an ordinary daimyo. A short civil war ensued. There was fighting in Edo and in northern Honshū but no real contest. Last to surrender was the *bakufu* navy in May 1869.

Formation of a New Government (Meiji Restoration)

The men who overthrew the Tokugawa in January 1868 did not subscribe to any clear and well-defined program. There was general agreement on the abolition of the shogunate and "restoration" of the emperor, but this meant no more than that the emperor should once again be at the center of the political system, functioning as the source of legitimacy and providing a sense of continuity. It definitely did not mean that actual power should be given to the sixteen-year-old Meiji Emperor (1852–1912; r. 1867–1912),* nor did it necessarily imply the destruction of feudalism, for there were those who envisioned the restoration in terms of a new feudal system headed by the emperor. On the other hand, Japanese scholars had long been aware that the Chinese system provided a bureaucratic alternative to feudalism. This, very likely, eased the shift to bureaucratic centralization.

The new leaders did not always see eye to eye, but they did share certain qualities: they were all of similar age (35–43) and rank, and came from the victorious *han* or the court aristocracy, although the *han* coalition was soon broadened to include men from Tosa and Hizen. The three most eminent leaders in the early years of the restoration were Ōkubo Toshimichi (1830–78), Kido Kōin (1833–77), and Saigō Takamori (1827–77). Both Ōkubo and Kido had risen to leadership in their own domains (Satsuma and Chōshū), through their influence in the domain's bureaucratic establishment and among the loyalist activists. Of the two, Ōkubo was the stronger personality, disciplined, formal, and somewhat intimidating; completely dedicated to the nation; cautious, and practical. Kido was more lively but also more volatile, less self-confident but more concerned than Ōkubo with strengthening the popular base of the government. But he was just as devoted to building a strong state.

Ōkubo's was the single strongest voice in government during 1873–78. One of his initial tasks was to retain the cooperation of Saigō, the military leader of the Satsuma forces which had joined with Chōshū to overthrow the Tokugawa. Saigō was a man of imposing physique and great physical strength. He was known for his outstanding courage, and possessed many of the traditional warrior virtues, such as generosity and contempt for money. More conservative than the others, he was devoted to Satsuma and its samurai but worked with the others at least until 1873. They were united in their conviction that the country must be strengthened to resist the West.

---

* His name was Mutsuhito, but, as in the case of the emperors of Qing China, it is customary to refer to him and to his successors by the designation given to their reign periods (era names, *nengo*, Chinese *nianhao*).

For the sake of national self-preservation the leaders were prepared to enact vast changes, but it took time to plan and carry these out, and indeed, to consolidate their own power in a land where, as Kido complained, "we are surrounded on four sides by little *bakufu.*"[7] To insure that the emperor would not become a focus of opposition to reform, Ōkubo argued that he should be moved to Edo, renamed Tokyo (Eastern Capital) in September 1868. This took place the following year when the emperor moved into the shogun's former castle, which was finally, after much debate, renamed the "imperial palace" in 1871.

The Charter

Even before the move, in April 1868 while the emperor was still in Kyoto, a Charter Oath was issued in his name to provide a general if vague statement of purpose for the new regime. It consisted of five articles:

1. An assembly widely convoked shall be established and all matters of state shall be decided by public discussion.
2. All classes high and low shall unite in vigorously promoting the economy and welfare of the nation.
3. All civil and military officials and the common people as well shall be allowed to fulfill their aspirations, so that there may be no discontent among them.
4. Base customs of former times shall be abandoned and all actions shall conform to the principles of international justice.
5. Knowledge shall be sought throughout the world and thus shall be strengthened the foundation of the Imperial polity.[8]

Although the government was reorganized to provide for an assembly in keeping with the first article, power remained with the original leadership, and the attempt to implement this provision was soon abandoned. In contrast, the end of seclusion, the acceptance of international law, and the openness to foreign ideas conveyed by the last two articles did take place. Symbolic of this shift was the audience granted representatives of the foreign powers by the emperor in Kyoto just a month before the Charter Oath was issued. The document itself was drafted by two men familiar with Western thought; it was then revised by Kido. The ramifications of the Charter Oath were far from clear, but the last article, to seek for knowledge "throughout the world," was taken very seriously. Furthermore, the entire document illustrates the gulf between Japanese and Chinese leaders at this time. No Chinese government would have issued such a document in an attempt to gain political strength.

Dismantling Feudalism

While the machinery of the central government underwent various reorganizations, the prime need was for the government to extend and consolidate its authority. Since the continued existence of the feudal domains was a major obstacle to this, the government leaders undertook the delicate but essential task of abolishing the *han*. In March 1869, Kido and Ōkubo were able to use their influence to induce the daimyo of Chōshū and Satsuma to return their domains to the emperor. They were joined in this act by the lords of Tosa and Hizen, and many others followed suit, anxious to be in the good graces of the new government and expecting to be appointed governors of their former domains, which they were. The real blow came in 1871 when, in the name of national unity, the domains were completely abolished and the whole country was reorganized into prefectures. This was made palatable to the daimyo by generous financial arrangements. The daimyo were allowed to retain a tenth of the former domain revenue as personal income while the government assumed responsibility for *han* debts and financial obligations. The daimyo were also assured continued high social standing and prestige. Finally, in 1884, they were elevated to the peerage.

By background and experience the new leadership was keenly sensitive to the importance of military power. Initially the new government was entirely dependent on forces from the supporting domains, but this would hardly do for a government truly national in scope. Accordingly the leaders set about forming a new army freed from local ties. Rejecting the views of Saigō, who envisioned a samurai army that would ensure the warrior class a brilliant and useful role in Japan's future, the leaders decided in 1872 to build their army on the basis of conscription. In January 1873, the new measure, largely the work of Yamagata Aritomo (1838–1922), "father of the Japanese Army," became law.

The restoration had a profound effect on the samurai. The new army, by eliminating distinctions between commoners and samurai, cut right to the heart of the status system. Anyone could become a warrior now. Other marks of samurai distinctiveness were eliminated or eroded. In 1870 commoners were allowed to acquire surnames and were released from previous occupational and residential restrictions. In 1871 the wearing of swords by samurai was made optional—five years later it was to be prohibited entirely.

The samurai's position was further undermined by the dismantling of feudalism. The abolition of the *han* threatened their economic position because the *han* had traditionally been the source of samurai stipends, and the burden of continuing stipend payments at the usual rate was more than the central government could afford. In addition, without the old domains, the samurai no longer had any social or political functions to perform. Accordingly, they were pensioned off. But in view of their number, the government could not afford to treat them as generously as it did the daimyo. At first samurai stipends were reduced on a sliding scale from half to a tenth of what they had been, then they were given the right to commute these into 20-year bonds (1873), and finally they were forced to accept the bonds (1876).

Reduction and commutation of samurai stipends was only one of the measures taken to establish the new government on a sound financial basis. In addition to monetary and banking reforms, a tax system was created (1873). These fiscal measures were largely the work of Ōkuma Shigenobu

(1838–1922), a man from Hizen who was to remain prominent in Meiji politics, and Itō Hirobumi (1841–1909) of Chōshū. The main source of government revenue was, as before, agriculture, but in place of the old percentage of the crop payable by the village to the daimyo, the tax was now collected by the government in money in accordance with the assessed value of the land. It was payable by the owner, and for this purpose ownership rights had to be clearly established. This was not done in favor of the absentee feudal interest long divorced from the land, nor did ownership pass equitably to all peasants. Instead, certificates were issued to the cultivators and wealthy villagers who had paid the tax during Tokugawa times. In this way tenancy was perpetuated, and since poor peasants were often unable to meet their taxes and thus were forced to mortgage their land, the rate of tenancy increased, rising from about 25 percent before the new system to about 40 percent twenty years later.

Disaffection and Opposition

The creation of a modern political, military, and fiscal system benefited the state but hurt some of the people. The peasantry was unhappy, not only about the land system but also about forced military service, and showed its displeasure by staging uprisings with increasing frequency from 1866 to 1873. Many of the large merchant houses that had developed symbiotic relationships with the *bakufu* or daimyo also suffered during these years, and some went bankrupt.

More serious for the regime was samurai discontent. The new government was itself led by former samurai, and for many men the new order meant a release from old restrictions and the opening of new opportunities. Since the samurai were the educated class with administrative experience, it was they who supplied the personnel for local and national government, provided officers for the army, teachers for the schools, and colonists for Hokkaidō. Casting aside tradition, some entered the world of business and finance. Yet there were many who did not make a successful transition, who were unable to respond positively to the new vocations now opened to them or to use their payments to establish themselves in new lines of endeavor. And among the leaders as well as the supporters of the Meiji government were men who firmly believed that its purpose was the restoration of the old, not the creation of the new. A split between conservatives and modernizers developed early in the Restoration and came to a head in 1873.

The Crisis of 1873

The crisis centered on the issue of going to war with Korea in order to force that country to open her doors to Japan. Those who advocated war, such as Saigō and the Tosa samurai Itagaki Taisuke (1836–1919), did so not only out of nationalist motives but also because they saw war as an occasion to provide employment for the samurai, an opportunity to give them a greater role in the new society, a means to preserve their military heritage. Saigō, a military leader with great charisma and devotion to the way of the warrior, asked to be sent to Korea as ambassador so that the Koreans, by killing him, would provide a cause for going to war.

A decision for war was made in the summer of 1873, in the absence of Ōkubo, Kido, and other important leaders who were abroad, in America and Europe. They were on a diplomatic and study mission headed by Iwakura Tonomi, the noble who had played a leading role at court in bringing about the Meiji Restoration. The purposes of the Iwakura mission were to convey the Meiji Emperor's respects to the heads of state of the treaty powers and build good will, to discuss subjects for later treaty revision, and to provide its distinguished members with an opportunity to observe and study the West at first hand. Its major accomplishment was in fulfilling the last mentioned objective, for the trip made a deep impression on the Japanese leaders who were exposed for the first time to the West and saw at first hand the evidence of Western strength. They returned home with a new realization of the magnitude of the task facing Japan in her quest for equality, and a new appreciation of the importance and complexity of modernization. They were convinced of the urgent priority of domestic change.

When the mission returned, Ōkubo led the opposition to the Korean venture on the grounds that Japan could not yet afford such an undertaking. Ōkubo, Kido, and Iwakura prevailed, with the support of many officials and the court. It was decided to abandon the Korean expedition and to concentrate on internal development. The decision split the government. Bitterly disappointed, the war advocates, including Saigō and Itagaki, resigned. In opposition they provided leadership for those who were disaffected by the new government and its policies, an opposition which would prove troublesome to those in power. But their departure left the government in the hands of a group of men unified by a commitment to modernization. Most prominent among them were Ōkubo, Itō, Ōkuma, and Iwakura.

By 1873 the Meiji government had survived the difficult period of initial consolidation. It had established the institutional foundations for the new state, had found a means of defense and national security, and with the resolution of the 1873 crisis, had charted the basic course of development at home and peace abroad that was to dominate Japanese policies during the next twenty years.

The Meaning of the Restoration

A major aspect of the Restoration was increased openness to the West. Signs of at least superficial Westernization were already in evidence in the early 1870s, when the gentlemen of fashion sported a foreign umbrella and watch and indulged in beef stew. Faddish Westernism was satirized in one of the best-sellers of the day, *Aguranabe (Idle Talks in the Sukiyaki House)* (1871–72) by Kanagaki Robun (1829–1904). Ōkubo ate bread and drank dark tea for breakfast and wore Western clothes even at home. In 1872 Western dress was made mandatory at court and other official functions. The Gregorian calendar was adopted the same year. After the Tokyo fire of 1872, the city's main avenue, the Ginza, was rebuilt under the supervision of an English architect. It boasted brick buildings, colonnades, and gas lamps (see Figure 8.4), but already in 1874 the widening contrast between the prosperous modern capital and the hinterland induced Fukuzawa Yukichi to warn:

> The purpose [of the government] seems to be to use the fruits of rural labor to make flowers for Tokyo. Steel bridges glisten in the capital, and horse-drawn carriages run on the streets, but in the country the wooden bridges are so rotten one cannot cross them. The cherry blossoms bloom in Kyōbashi [in Tokyo], but weeds grow in the country fields. Billows of smoke such as rise from city stoves do not rise from the farmer's furnace. . . . We must cease making Tokyo richer and concentrate on rural districts.[9]

Ideologically the main thrust was to use the old to justify the new. Accordingly, there was an effort to turn Japan into a Shinto state. In 1868 Shinto was proclaimed the basis for the government and a Department of Shinto was established with precedence over the other government departments. There was a drive to purify Shinto, to eliminate Buddhist influences that had steadily seeped into Shinto, and to make Shinto the only religion of Japan. This drive, however, ran into opposition from Buddhists and also conflicted

Figure 8.4   The Ginza, 1873.

with Western pressures for the legalization of Christianity. In 1872 the Department of Shinto was abolished, and in 1873 the old ban on Christianity was lifted.

The Restoration leaders opted for the new, and they were able to initiate far-reaching changes partly because they inherited from Tokugawa times a political system that reached much deeper and more effectively into society than did that of other Asian countries. Furthermore, they introduced the new in the name of the emperor, a symbol of continuity with the old. This made it easier for them to innovate but also assured the survival of old values and ideas. In the light of hindsight they appear in the dual role of preservers of tradition and initiators of East Asia's first cultural revolution.

In many essential ways the restoration was revolutionary: it destroyed the feudal system and created a centralized state; it eliminated the old class lines and legally opened all careers to all men; in all areas of human activity it prepared the way for the profound changes that during the next century were to transform the very countryside of Japan. But if it was a revolution, it was a revolution from above, an aristocratic revolution, to borrow a term from Thomas C. Smith.[10] Relatively peaceful, it was not the product of a mass movement nor of a radical social ideology, and it did not radically change the structure of village life or the mode of agricultural production. It eliminated the samurai as a legally defined, privileged class, but, led by men who were themselves samurai, did so gently and in terms samurai could understand. This did much to shape the future. As Gilbert Rozman put it:

> The ability to keep alive and to diffuse samurai ideals was clearly one aspect of the anomalous combination of traits observed in Japan since the earliest phase of its modernization: high degrees of social mobility combined with intense consciousness of social status; emphasis on achievement accompanied by a downgrading of individualism, and an entrepreneurial spirit combined with group orientation.

But he concludes: "In form, the samurai way prevailed, but in practice, the chōnin-led transformation continued its relentless course."[11]

NOTES

1. Marius B. Jansen, ed. *The Cambridge History of Japan*, Vol. 5: *The Nineteenth Century* (Cambridge: Cambridge Univ. Press, 1989), p. 60.

2. Ibid., p. 121.

3. Harold Bolitho in Ibid., p. 159.

4. Bob Tadashi Wakabayashi, *Anti-Foreignism and Western Learning in Early Modern Japan: The New Theses of 1825* (Cambridge: Harvard Univ. Press, 1986), p. 134.

5. Michiaki Kawakita, *Modern Currents in Japanese Art*, Heibonsha Survey of Japanese Art, Vol. 24, trans. Charles S. Terry (New York and Tokyo: Weatherhill/Heibonsha, 1974), p. 29.

6. Marius B. Jansen, ed., *Changing Japanese Attitudes Toward Modernization* (Princeton: Princeton Univ. Press, 1969), pp. 57–58; quoting van Gulik, "Kakkaron: A Japanese Echo of the Opium War," *Monumenta Serica* 4 (1939): 542–43.

7. Albert Craig and Donald Shively, eds., *Personality in Japanese History* (Berkeley and Los Angeles: Univ. of California Press, 1970), p. 297.

8. Ishii Ryosuke, *Japanese Legislation in the Meiji Era*, trans. William J. Chambliss (Tokyo: Pan-Pacific Press, 1958), p. 145. Frequently quoted, as in William G. Beasley, *The Meiji Restoration* (Stanford: Stanford Univ. Press, 1972), p. 325, or *The Cambridge History of Japan*, Vol. 5, p. 623.

9. Quoted by Mikiso Hane, *Peasants, Rebels, and Outcastes: The Underside of Modern Japan* (New York: Pantheon Books, 1982), p. 33.

10. See Thomas C. Smith, "Japan's Aristocratic Revolution," *Yale Review* 50 (Spring 1961): 370–83. Also see Marius B. Jansen, "The Meiji State: 1868–1912," in James B. Crowley, ed., *Modern East Asia: Essays in Interpretation* (New York: Harcourt Brace Jovanovich, 1970), pp. 95–121, which cites Smith on p. 103.

11. Gilbert Rozman in *The Cambridge History of Japan*, Vol. 5, p. 533.

9
The Emergence of Modern Japan: 1874–1894

九

近代日本〈出現

1868	1877	1889 1890	1894	1912
The Restoration	Satsuma Rebellion	Promulgation of the Constitution	Rescript on Education	
	M E I J I J A P A N		Start of the Sino-Japanese War	

D uring the last thirty years of the nineteenth century, the Western challenge to the rest of the globe became more intense, more formidable, and more complex. With continued progress in science and technology, the power of the economically advanced countries continued to grow while capitalism and nationalism fueled competition over the acquisition of colonies. As the area left for possible expansion diminished, the race gained momentum. In these thirty years Europeans expanded their colonial empires by over 10 million square miles, about a fifth of the world's land area, inhabited by nearly 150 million people, about 10 percent of the world's population. Much of this expansion took place in Africa, but new colonies were formed also in Southeast Asia. Northeast Asia came under imperialist pressure leading to the Sino-Japanese War of 1894–95 fought over Korea. Its victory in that war demonstrated that Japan had by that time become a participant in, rather than a victim of, the new imperialism.

The leading maritime power in the world continued to be Great Britain, which, as before, had the largest foreign commercial stake in China and Japan. Russia persisted in its overland expansion into and beyond Central Asia. Two other powers, France and the United States, maintained an interest in East Asian developments. In Europe, the emergence of Germany after the FrancoPrussian War (1870) provided a conservative alternative to England's liberal model for modernization. After the war the German Chancellor, Otto von Bismarck (1815–98), adopted a policy of encouraging France to compensate for her losses in Europe by building an overseas empire. This gave an impetus to France's ambitions in Southeast Asia that led to war between France and China in 1883–85. The world was becoming smaller, and, for the weak, more dangerous.

Relations between China and Japan during the twenty years discussed in this chapter began with a minor clash and ended with a war that had profound internal effects in both countries and changed the balance of power between them for the next half century. The minor clash occurred in 1874 when Japan sent an expedition to Taiwan ostensibly to punish aborigines who had killed some Okinawans shipwrecked on their shores. Its real purpose was to mollify those who resented the abandonment of the Korean expedition so earnestly advocated by Saigō and his friends. An expedition to Taiwan was a smaller and less dangerous undertaking. It was successful, and the result was that China was forced to pay an indemnity and to recognize Japanese sovereignty over the Ryūkū Islands, of which Okinawa is the largest. This ended the ties that the Ryūkyūs had maintained with China even while they were Satsuma vassals.

For Japan the years between the Restoration and the Sino-Japanese War were a period of conscious learning from the West in an effort to become a modern nation accepted as an equal by the powers of the world. It was a time of great changes: in government and politics, in the economy, in people's ideas, in education—a time of building national strength. These changes were neither smooth nor simple. In the intricate interplay of old and new, foreign and traditional, some old ways went the way of the samurai's sword and topknot, but others were retained and put to new uses. This process still continues today, but Japan's victory in 1895 marked the end of a crucial stage, for by then Japan had achieved many of its initial objectives: a centralized government, a modernizing economy, and sufficient military strength to warrant international respect.

Political Developments

Acting in the name of the emperor, a small oligarchy (group of leaders) dominated the government during the 1870s and 1880s, but not without opposition. Embittered samurai resorted to arms, first in an uprising in Hizen in 1874 and then, more seriously, in 1877 in Satsuma. The Satsuma Rebellion was led by Saigō Takamori, who had withdrawn from the government after the 1873 decision against the Korean expedition. The number of those who threw in their lot with the rebellion rose as high as 42,000. Its suppression strained the military resources of the Restoration government, but after half a year the rebellion was crushed. The Satsuma Rebellion was the last stand of the samurai. When the military situation became hopeless, Saigō killed himself in the approved warrior manner. His was a martyr's death for a lost cause. Saigō died under official condemnation as a traitor, but the Meiji government soon rehabilitated him, and government leaders joined in expressions of admiration and acclaim for the man who came to be regarded as *the* hero of the Restoration. Not only conservatives but representatives of the most diverse political persuasions praised the magnanimity of his spirit and transformed Saigō into a legendary hero, celebrated in poems and songs (including an army marching song), portrayed on stage and in an extensive literature, depicted in portraits and prints, even identified with the planet Mars.

Protest against the government continued, on occasion, to take a violent turn. Less than half a year after Saigō's death, some of his sympathizers assassinated Ōkubo Toshimichi, also from Satsuma, who had worked so hard and successfully to create the new Japanese state. There were other assassination attempts as well, both successful and unsuccessful. More important in the long run, however, was the formation of nonviolent political opposition, animated not only by objections to one or another aspect of the government's policies, but also in protest against the political domination exercised by a few men from Chōshū and Satsuma who had exclusive control over the centers of power. Basing their position on the first article of the 1868 Charter Oath, opposition leaders early in 1874 demanded the creation of an elected legislature. Prominent among them was Itagaki Taisuke, the Tosa leader who, like Saigō, had left the government in 1873 over the Korean issue. In Tosa and then elsewhere, antigovernment organizations voiced the discontent of local interests, demanding political rights, local self-government, and formation of a national assembly. The advocates of a constitution, and the leaders of what became known as the movement for popular rights, drew upon Western political theories for support. They argued also that the adoption of representative institutions would create greater unity between the people and the emperor. In their view a constitution was needed not in order to limit the emperor's powers but in order to control his advisers.

The men in power were not adverse to some kind of constitution as a necessary and even desirable component of modernization. By the end of 1878, Kido, Ōkubo, and Saigō were all dead. Of the older men only Iwakura remained important, and three younger men who had already contributed significantly to the Meiji state now gained major prominence: Itō Hirobumi and Yamagata Aritomo, both from Chōshū, and Ōkuma Shigenobu from Hizen. Yamagata was the creator of the new army while Itō took the lead in political modernization and Ōkuma served as Finance Minister. But there were tensions between Itō and Ōkuma. In 1881 the latter precipitated a break when he wrote a memorandum advocating the adoption of an English-style political system. His proposals that the majority party in parliament form the government, that the cabinet be responsible to parliament, and that the first elections be held in 1883 clashed with the conservative and gradualist views of his colleagues. First his proposals were rejected; then when he joined in public criticism of the government over its sale of a certain government project in Hokkaidō, Ōkuma was dismissed. At the same time the government announced that the emperor would grant a constitution to take effect in 1890.

Formation of Parties

In response Itagaki and his associates formed the Jiyūtō (Liberal party), and Ōkuma followed by organizing the Kaishintō (Progressive party). Both parties advocated constitutional government with meaningful powers exercised by a parliament, but they differed considerably in ideology and composition. The Jiyūtō, linked to Tosa, was influenced by the ideas of Rousseau and the French Revolution. It drew much of its support from rural areas, where peasants and landlords were unhappy that their taxes remained as high as they had been under the Tokugawa and resented bearing a heavier tax burden than that required of commerce and industry. Ōkuma's party (linked to Hizen) was, in contrast, more urban and more moderate, advocating

English-style liberalism. It had the backing of merchants and industrialists. Although they both opposed the government, the two parties fought each other energetically. At the same time the parties were troubled by internal factionalism; party splits were based on master-follower and patron-client relations rather than on differences in programs.

The organized opposition was further hampered by the need to operate under restrictive laws, including some promulgated to control political criticism before the parties were formed. Restrictive press laws enacted in 1875 and revised in 1877 gave the Home Minister power to suppress publications and provided fines or imprisonment for offenders. The 1880 Public Meeting Law placed all political meetings under police supervision. Included among those prohibited from attending such meetings were teachers and students. Nor were political associations allowed to recruit members or to combine or correspond with similar bodies. Finally the 1887 Peace Preservation Law increased the Home Minister's powers of censorship and gave the police authority to expel people from a given area: 570 were shortly removed from Tokyo in this fashion.

The Liberal party was hurt not only by differences among its leaders but even more by antagonism within its membership, including conflicts between tenants and landlords. It proved impossible to contain within one party both radicals who supported and even led peasant riots and the substantial landowners who were the objects of these attacks. In 1884 the party was dissolved. At the end of the same year Ōkuma and his followers left the Progressive party, although others stayed to keep it in existence. Criticism of the government continued, but this initial attempt to organize political parties turned out to have been premature.

The Meiji Constitution

While suppressing its critics, the government was also taking steps to increase its effectiveness. A system of centralized local administration was established that put an end to the Tokugawa tradition of local self-government. Villages and towns were now headed by officials appointed by the Home Ministry in Tokyo, which also controlled the police. In the late seventies (1878–80), local assemblies were created as sounding boards of public opinion, but their rights were limited to debate and their membership restricted to men of means. The details of bureaucratic procedure were worked out and a civil service system fashioned. A new code of criminal law was enacted, and work was begun on civil and commercial codes.

To prepare for the promised constitution-making, Itō spent a year and a half in Europe during 1882–83, mostly studying German theories and practices, for he and his fellow oligarchs already had a general idea of the kind of conservative constitution they wanted. After his return, a number of steps were taken in preparation for the constitution: a new peerage was created in 1884 composed of the old court nobility, ex-daimyo, and some members of the oligarchy; in 1885 a European-style cabinet was created with Itō as premier; and in 1888 the Privy Council was organized as the highest government advisory board.

In 1889 work on the constitution was completed, and it was promulgated as a "gift" from the emperor to his people. It remained in force until 1945. The emperor, "sacred and inviolable" father of the family state, was supreme. He had the power to declare war, conclude treaties, and command the army. He also had the right to open, recess, and dissolve the legislature; the power to veto the latter's decisions, and the right to issue his own ordinances. The ministers were responsible not to the legislature but to the emperor. The Diet, as the legislature was called, consisted of two houses, the House of Peers and the House of Representatives. The latter was elected by a constituency of tax-paying property owners amounting to about 450,000 men or 1.1 percent of the total population. The most consequential power of the Diet was the power of the purse, but, borrowing from the Prussian example, the constitution provided for automatic renewal of the previous year's budget whenever the Diet failed to pass a new budget. Only the emperor could take the initiative to revise the constitution.

The emperor was the final authority but he was also above politics, and the actual exercise of imperial authority was divided between the Privy Council, the cabinet, the Diet, and the general staff. Since the constitution failed to provide for coordination between these bodies, this was provided by the men who had been governing in the emperor's name all along. Gradually the practice developed of deciding on the selection of prime ministers and other major questions, by consulting the *genrō*, elder statesmen of great influence such as Itō and Yamagata, who talked things out in private. Obviously, this could work only as long as there were *genrō* to consult.

The framers of the constitution viewed government, like the emperor in whose name it functioned, as above the divisive and unedifying world of party politics. But the parties turned out to be stronger than the oligarchs had expected. In the first election of 1890 the reconstituted Liberal party (Jiyuto) won 130 seats, the Progressives (Kaishintō) led once again by Ōkuma won 47, and only 79 members favoring the government were elected. As a result of this growing party strength there was a stiff parliamentary battle over the budget in the first session of the Diet, which was resolved only after the premier, Yamagata, resorted to bribery and force. When the budget failed to pass the following year, the Diet was dissolved. During the subsequent elections (1892) the government used the police to discourage the opposition but failed to obtain a more tractable Diet. Another election was held in 1894, but the constitution worked no better. It was the war with China over Korea that broke the political deadlock of that year and provided temporary unity in the body politic. During the war the government enjoyed enthusiastic support at home. By that time Japan was quite different from what it had been twenty years earlier when the oligarchs rejected intervention in Korea. The political developments were just one dimension of the transformation of Japan.

Western Influences on Values and Ideas

Enthusiasm for aspects of Western science and technology went back, as we have seen, to Tokugawa proponents of "Dutch Learning," and from the very start of Meiji, there was a fashion for Western styles, including styles of dress. Representative of Japanese attitudes, the Meiji Emperor himself wore Western clothes and dressed his hair in the Western manner. See, for example, the emperor's portrait by Takahashi Yūichi (1828–94) shown in Figure 9.1.

Not only the subject, but also the artist was influenced by Western styles. Takahashi was very conscious of his precursors: he revered Shiba Kōkan. Like Shiba and his own teacher, the prominent Western-style painter Kawakami Tōgai (1827–81), Takahashi placed great value on realism in his works. Most of these, unlike the emperor's portrait, were still-life studies of familiar objects, and his most famous work is a realistic painting of a salmon. A major difference between Kawakami and Takahashi is that whereas the former saw Western art as no more than a necessary component of Western learning to be mastered for technical reasons, Takahashi also valued it as art.

Similarly men turned to the West in other fields, not only for practical reasons but because they were attracted by the intrinsic nature of Western achievements. Prominent among such men were the intellectuals who, in

Figure 9.1
Takahashi Yúichi,
*Portrait of the
Meiji Emperor.*
Oil, 1880.

1873, formed the Meirokusha, a prestigious society devoted to the study of all aspects of Western knowledge. These same men led what was known as the movement for "civilization and enlightenment" *(bummei kaika)*. A leading theorist of this movement was Fukuzawa Yukichi, whose books on the West were mentioned earlier.

"Civilization and Enlightenment"

In eighteenth-century Europe the intellectual movement known as the Enlightenment sought to put all traditional ideas and institutions to the test of reason. Impressed by the achievements of science as exemplified in the work of Sir Isaac Newton (1642–1727), such philosophers as Voltaire (1694–1778) and Diderot (1713–84) believed that reason could produce similar progress in solving human problems and that the main obstacles to truth and happiness were irrationality and superstition. Their greatest monument was the encyclopedia compiled by Diderot and his associates, a summation of the accomplishments of reason in all fields of human knowledge.

Japanese intellectuals like Fukuzawa Yukichi were strongly influenced by the heritage of the European Enlightenment, particularly the emphasis on reason as an instrument for achieving progress. Their faith in progress was also confirmed by such influential Western historians as H.T. Buckle (1821–62) and Francois Guizot (1787–1874). Indeed, the belief in progress remained a major nineteenth-century conviction even after the faith in reason had faded.

A corollary to this new concept of historical progress, in Japan as in the West, was a negative reevaluation of Chinese civilization, now seen as unchanging and therefore decadent. No longer did the Japanese look up to China as the land of classical civilization; on the contrary, China was now a negative model, and, as China's troubles continued, Japanese intellectuals tended to regard it with condescension as well as concern. Now the source of "enlightenment" was in the West.

One of Fukuzawa's prime goals in advancing the cause of "civilization and enlightenment" was to stimulate in Japan the development of an independent and responsible citizenry. "It would not be far from wrong," he once complained, "to say that Japan has a government but no people."[1] Tracing the lack of individual independence back to the traditional family, Fukuzawa advocated fundamental changes in that basic social institution. Ridiculing the ancient paragons of filial piety, he urged limitations on parental demands and authority. While he viewed the role of women in terms of family and home, Fukuzawa also, on occasion, recommended greater equality between the sexes, championed monogamy, argued that women should be educated and allowed to hold property, and compared the Japanese woman to a dwarfed ornamental tree, artificially stunted.

According to Fukuzawa, history was made by the people, not by a few great leaders, and he thought it wrong to place too much faith in government or to give the political authorities too much power. His view of the role of government resembled the concept of the minimal state held by early European liberals. Consistent with these ideas he did not enter government himself but disseminated his views in books and through a newspaper he founded. He also established what became Keiō University, a distinguished private university in Tokyo whose graduates played an important part in the world of business and industry.

In Fukuzawa's mind the independence of the people and the independence of the country were linked; indeed, the former was a prerequisite for the latter. This view was widely held among the proponents of "enlightenment." For instance, the translator of the best-seller *Self-Help* by Samuel Smiles, whose Japanese version was published in Tokyo in 1871, explained that Western nations were strong because they possessed the spirit of liberty. John Stuart Mill's *On Liberty* appeared in Japanese translation the same year; Rousseau's *The Social Contract* was published in installments during 1882–84. Fukuzawa, with his faith in progress, believed that the ultimate universal movement of history is in the direction of democracy and that individual liberty makes for national strength.

Natural Law

Fukuzawa's liberalism of the early seventies was based on the eighteenth-century Western concept of natural law, that is, that human affairs are governed by inherent concepts of right just as the physical world is governed by the laws of nature. This belief resembled the Neo-Confucian concept of *ri* ("principle") in linking the natural and human orders, but the European doctrine, unlike the Chinese, included the affirmation of innate human rights. It postulated an affirmative body of law stating the inherent rights of man in society, in whose name societies could overthrow unjust governments and establish new ones. It was to natural law that the American colonists appealed when they declared their independence in 1776, and that the French revolutionaries appealed to when they promulgated their Declaration of the Rights of Man in 1789.

Social Darwinism

The concept of natural law, however, was soon displaced by another more recent Western import: Social Darwinism. There were various versions of this doctrine, most notably those developed by the enormously influential Herbert Spencer (1820–1903), but all were based on the theory of evolution by natural selection presented in Darwin's famous *On the Origin of Species* (1859). Darwin held that over time the various forms of life adapt to changing natural conditions and to competition with each other, and that those which adapt best are most likely to survive. This theory was summarized by the catch phrase "survival of the fittest." Social Darwinism was the application of these doctrines to human history, explaining the rise and fall of nations, for example, in terms of competition, adaptation, and "survival of the fittest."

Social Darwinism seemed entirely apropos to the Japanese experience. It explained why China and Japan had been unable to resist the Western powers, but held out the promise that a nation did not have to accept permanent inferiority. Instead it justified Japanese efforts to develop national strength by mastering the learning and techniques of the West. It purported to have a "scientific" basis. And, unlike natural law with its moralistic overtones, it turned strength itself into a moral criterion, and it provided a justification for imperialism to support the expansionism of any ambitious state. Relations among nations could thus be viewed as one vast struggle for existence in which the fittest survived.

In the mid-seventies Fukuzawa first became skeptical of natural law, and then abandoned it. One effect was a loss of confidence in international law and a new view of international relations as an arena in which nations struggle for survival. Already in 1876 Fukuzawa remarked, "a few cannons are worth more than a hundred volumes of international law,"[2] By 1882 he was willing to accept even autocracy if it meant strengthening the nation. Furthermore, he favored imperialist expansion both to assure Japan's safety and to bring the benefits of "civilization" to neighboring countries such as Korea. Thus he welcomed the war when it came in 1894.

Fukuzawa found words of praise for some aspects of the Japanese tradition, including the samurai value of loyal service, but continued to look primarily to the West for his models and ideas. However, he avoided the extremes of Westernization. In early Meiji some thinkers allowed their enthusiasm to get the better of their judgment, and there were all kinds of extreme proposals for radical Westernization, including one to make English the national language. However, not all supporters of Western ways were genuine enthusiasts. Many desired to impress Westerners in order to be accepted as equals and to speed treaty revision. This was the motive behind a variety of movements, ranging from a drive to reform public morals to the revision of the legal code. It also accounts for one of the symbols of the era, the Rokumeikan, a hall completed in 1883 to accommodate mixed foreign and Japanese social gatherings. Designed by an English architect in the elaborate manner of the European Renaissance, it provided the setting for dinners, card parties, and fancy dress balls.

The Arts

In the arts, Western influence was both audible and visible. It affected the music taught in the schools and that performed in military bands. In painting, we have already noted the work of Takahashi, but the impact of the West was visible also in more traditional genres. Sometimes called the last of the major *ukiyo-e* artists was Kobayashi Kiyochika (1847–1915). He

Figure 9.2   Kobayashi Kiyochika, *Train at Night*. Woodcut print.

introduced Western light and shading into *ukiyo-e,* using the principles of Western perspective but retaining a traditional Japanese sense of color (see Figure 9.2).

Western styles of painting were advanced not only by foreign artists who taught in Japan but also by Japanese who studied abroad, particularly in France, and brought back new styles and ways of looking at the world. Kuroda Seiki (1866–1924) studied in France from 1884 to 1893, and it was there that he painted *Morning Toilet* (Figure 9.3), which caused a stir when exhibited in Tokyo in 1894 and created a storm of controversy when shown in more conservative Kyoto the following year. Japan had never had a tradition of painting the nude, and there were protests that Kuroda's painting was pornography, not art. But Kuroda won the battle and went on to become one of Japan's most influential Western-style painters.

The initial enthusiasm for Western art led to the neglect and even disdain of traditional art, which shocked the American Ernest Fenollosa (1853–1908) when he came to Japan in 1878 to teach at Tokyo University. Fenollosa did what he could to make the new generation of Westernized Japanese aware of the greatness of their artistic heritage. He, himself, was an admirer of the last of the masters of the Kanō school, Kano Hōgai (1828–88), and together with the younger Okakura Tenshin (1862–1913) sparked a revived interest in traditional styles.

Figure 9.3
Kuroda Seiki,
Morning Toilet.
Oil, 1893, 178.5
cm × 98 cm.

Conservatism and Nationalism

The reaction against the enthusiasm of the early Meiji Westernizers was not limited to the arts. Starting in the late eighties there was a tide of conservative thought. Many were attracted by the old formula "Eastern ethics; Western technology," a concept earlier advanced by Sakuma Shōzan.

Some feared that acceptance of a foreign culture was a step toward national decline and sought for ways to be both modern and Japanese, to adopt the universalist aspects of Western culture while retaining what was of value in their own particularist past. The educated and sensitive were especially troubled by the tensions inherent in a program of modernization under traditionalist auspices. Western scientific rationalism could, by questioning the founding myth, undermine the throne itself. In 1892 a Tokyo University professor was forced to resign after he wrote that Shinto was a "survival of a primitive form of worship."[3] That was sacrilege. Similarly, Western individualism, fostered by the policy of modernization, clashed with the old family values that, Fukuzawa notwithstanding, continued strong and remained in official favor.

Drawing on German thought, new, modern conservative voices affirmed Japanese uniqueness along with a belief in national progress, arguing that change should come about gradually, growing organically out of past traditions with emphasis not on the individual but on the state. There was talk about a national "essence," though little agreement on how it should be defined. Akira Iriye has drawn attention to the weakness in Japan of the liberal elements that Western nationalism inherited from its origins, when it "had been part of the democratic revolution in which national identity was sought less in a country's ethnic and historical uniqueness than in the belief that it embodied certain universal values such as freedom and human rights." Such a nationalism "could often be transformed into internationalism because a nation could envision a world order that embodied some of the universalistic principles that it exemplified itself."[4] Japanese particularism often took a benign form but was also prone to lead to cultural exceptionalism and political chauvinism even if Japanese nationalists were hardly unique in celebrating (and exaggerating) the uniqueness of their nation.

Some Japanese intellectuals, notably Okakura, soon went on to define a wider world role for Japan by emphasizing Japan's Asian roots. Thus, Okakura, in a book bearing the revealing title *The Ideals of the East* (1902), presented the nation's mission in terms of preserving an "Asian" cultural essence. Not only Japan's cultural place in the world but also its political mission remained key issues throughout modern times.

Education

Japanese intellectual and political leaders were quick to realize the importance of education in fashioning a new Japan capable of competing with the West. In this, as in other areas, they showed great interest in the practices and institutions of European countries and of the United States. For example, one of the members of the Iwakura Mission paid special attention to education and wrote fifteen volumes on the subject after his return home.

At the beginning of the Meiji period, Japan sent many students overseas to obtain the advanced training it could not provide at home. One-eighth of the Ministry of Education's first budget (1873) was designated for this purpose, and 250 students were sent abroad on government scholarships that year. Furthermore, many foreign instructors were brought to Japan to teach in various specialized schools. These, however, were temporary expedients to be used until Japan's own modern educational system was in operation. By the late 1880s the number of foreign instructors was down, and only some 50 to 80 students annually were being sent abroad by the government. A landmark in the history of higher education was the establishment of Tokyo University in 1877 with four faculties: physical science, law, literature, and medicine.

Considerable progress was made in building a complete educational system, yet actual accomplishments fell short of the ambitious plan drawn up in 1872. This called for 8 universities, 256 middle schools, and 53,760 elementary schools, but thirty years later, in 1902, there were only 2 universities, 222 middle schools, and 27,076 elementary schools. Similarly, the government had to retreat from its 1872 ordinance making four years of education compulsory for all children. Among the difficulties this program encountered were money problems (elementary education was locally financed), teacher shortages, and the reluctance of rural parents to send their children to school. However, by the time four years of compulsory education were reintroduced in 1900, the great majority of children who were supposed to be in school were in actual attendance, and in 1907 the government was able to increase the period to six years. By that time the teachers were predominantly graduates of Japanese Normal Schools (teacher training institutes, the first of which was established in Tokyo in 1872).

When the Ministry of Education was first established in 1871, the French system of highly centralized administration was adopted. Although local schools were locally financed, the ministry not only determined the general direction of education but prescribed textbooks, supervised teacher training, and generally controlled the curriculum of schools throughout the country. Government educational policy therefore was decisive in determining what was taught.

There was wide agreement among political leaders that an essential function of the educational system was to provide the people with the skills necessary for modernization. They realized that not only factories and businesses but also armies and navies require a certain level of literacy and a command of simple arithmetic among the rank and file, as well as higher education for managers and officers. Beyond that, the leaders recognized that schools foster values and looked to them to mold the Japanese people into a nation. On the question of specific moral content, however, there were intense disagreements reflecting different visions of Japan's future. In the seventies when enthusiasm for the West ran high, even elementary readers and moral texts were frequently translated from English and French for use in Japanese schools. But there were also critics who insisted that the schools should preserve traditional Confucian and Japanese values. Another influential position was opposed to both Western liberal values and to traditional ideals but looked to the schools to indoctrinate the populace with modern, nationalist values. An influential proponent of this last position was Mori Arinori (1847–89), Minister of Education from 1885 until he was assassinated by a nationalist fanatic in 1889.

Although Mori had a strong hand in shaping the educational system, the most important Meiji pronouncement on the subject was drafted under the influence of the emperor's Confucian Lecturer. This was the Rescript on Education, which was issued in 1890. For half a century it remained the basic statement of the purpose of education, memorized by generations of Japanese school children. It begins by attributing "the glory of the fundamental character of Our Empire" to the Imperial Ancestors who "deeply and firmly implanted virtue" and calls upon His Majesty's subjects to observe the usual Confucian virtues beginning with filiality toward their parents, enjoins them to "pursue learning and cultivate arts" for the sake of intellectual and moral development, and "to advance public good and promote common interests." Furthermore, "should emergency arise, offer yourselves courageously to the State, and thus guard and maintain the prosperity of Our Imperial Throne coeval with heaven and earth."[5] In this document, Confucianism is identified with the throne (no mention is made of its foreign origins), and a premium is placed on patriotic service to the state and the throne. These values were further drummed into school children in compulsory ethics classes. Education was to serve both to prepare Japan for the future and to preserve elements of the past, or rather, to prepare Japan for the future in the name of the past.

Meanwhile the religious orientation of the state had also been settled. In 1882 Shinto was divided into Shrine Shinto and Sect Shinto. Most Shinto shrines, including the most prominent such as Ise and Izumo, came under Shrine Shinto and were now transformed into state institutions supposedly patriotic rather than religious in character, operating on a higher plane than the merely "religious" bodies such as the various forms of Buddhism, Christianity (legalized in 1873), and Sect Shinto. This formula permitted the government to identify itself with the Shinto tradition from which was derived the mystique of the emperor, source of its own authority, while at the same time meeting the demands for religious tolerance voiced by Japanese reformers and Western nations.

Modernizing the Economy

In the twenty years that followed consolidation of the Meiji regime, Japan laid the foundations for a modern industrial economy. The nation was still primarily agrarian, but Western experience had shown that capital accumulated through the sale of surplus agricultural production, and labor obtained through the migration of surplus rural population to the cities, were necessary conditions for industrial development. Both conditions existed in Meiji Japan.

Japanese agriculture had become more efficient due to the introduction of new seed strains, new fertilizers, and new methods of cultivation. New land for farming was being opened, especially in Hokkaidō. New applications of science to agriculture were being tried at experimental stations and agricultural colleges. In consequence, during the fourteen years preceding the Sino-Japanese War, rice yields increased by 30 percent and other crops showed comparable gains; per capita rice consumption increased. Agriculture was further stimulated by the development of a substantial export market for silk and tea, and a growing domestic demand for cotton. Thus trade also helped generate capital needed for investment in manufacturing.

Increased agricultural production did not result in major changes for the cultivator, however. Village government and the organization of village labor remained largely the same. Rents remained high: it was not unusual for a peasant's rent to equal half his rice crop. Profits resulting from the commercialization of agriculture went to the landlord, who handled the sale, rather than to the tenant. Even the creation of factory jobs did little to relieve population pressure on the land. Much of the factory labor was performed by peasant girls sent to the city to supplement their families' farm incomes for a number of years before they were married. Housed in company dormitories and strictly supervised, they were an untrained but inexpensive work force. When times were bad and factory operations slowed down, they could be laid off and returned to their villages. It was a system advantageous to both the landlord and the industrialist.

In Western countries the industrial revolution had been largely carried out by private enterprise. In Japan, however, where it was government policy to modernize so as to catch up with the West, the government itself took the initiative. The Meiji regime invested heavily in the economic infrastructure, that is, those basic public services that must be in place before an industrial economy can grow: education, transportation, communications, and so forth. As previously mentioned, students were sent abroad at public expense, for example, to study Western technologies, and foreigners were brought to Japan to teach in their areas of expertise. A major investment was made in railroads. The first line was completed in 1872, running between Tokyo and Yokohama. By the mid-nineties there were 2,000 miles of track, much of it privately owned, for government initiative was followed by private investment once the feasibility, and especially the profitability, of railroads had been established. Transportation within cities too began to quicken as Kyoto in 1895 became the first Japanese city to have trolleys.

This sequence of state initiative followed by private development can also be observed in manufacturing. The government took the lead, for example, in establishing and operating cement works, plants manufacturing glass and tiles, textile mills (silk and cotton), shipyards, mines, and munition works. The government felt these industries were essential, but private interests were unwilling to risk their capital in untried ventures, with little prospect of profits in the near term. Thus, if such ventures were to be started, the government would have to start them and finance the initial period of operations. It did so.

The *Zaibatsu*

The expenditure of capital required for this effort, the payments due to samurai on their bonds, the costs of the Satsuma Rebellion, and an adverse balance of trade combined to create a government financial crisis. Rising inflation damaged the government's purchasing power and also hurt the samurai, whose income depended on the interest paid on their bonds. These problems came to a head in 1880. The government's response was mainly to cut back on expenditures, and, thereby, it gradually brought the situation under control. As part of this economy move, the government decided, late in 1880, to sell at public auction all its enterprises with the exception of the munitions plants. The buyers were usually men who were friendly with government leaders and recognized the long-term advantages of buying the factories, which were selling at bargain prices. These enterprises did not become profitable immediately, but when they did the result was that a small group of well-connected firms enjoyed a controlling position in the modern sector of the economy. These were the *zaibatsu*, huge financial and industrial combines.

The *zaibatsu* were usually organized by new entrepreneurs, for most of the old Tokugawa merchant houses were too set in their ways to make a successful transition into the new world of Meiji. The outstanding exception to this generalization was the house of Mitsui, originally established in Edo as a textile house and also enriched by its banking activities. When it became apparent that government initiatives were creating new economic opportunities in commerce and industry, Mitsui brought new men into the firm to take advantage of them. The new leadership was vigorous and capable, establishing first a bank and then a trading company. These institutions became important factors in Japan's foreign commerce; they also engaged in domestic transactions, profiting handsomely from handling army supply contracts during the Satsuma Rebellion. In 1881 Mitsui bought government coal mines, which ultimately contributed greatly to its wealth and power. By that time the traditional drapery business had been relegated to a sideline and delegated to a subordinate house.

A contrast to Mitsui is offered by the Mitsubishi *zaibatsu*, founded by Iwasaki Yatarō (1834–85), a former Tosa samurai bold and ruthless in the wars of commerce. Iwasaki developed a strong shipping business by obtaining government contracts, government subsidies, and for a time even government guarantee of its dividend payments. At one point the government lent the company ships, a loan that eventually became a gift. Mitsubishi also benefited greatly during the Formosan expedition of 1874 and again during the Satsuma Rebellion from doing government business. The firm grew strong enough to displace some of its foreign competitors, and around its shipping business it developed banking and insurance facilities and entered foreign trade. It also went into mining, and its acquisition of the government-established Nagasaki shipyard assured its future as the leader in shipbuilding and heavy industry, although Iwasaki did not live long enough to see the shipyard turn a profit. Iwasaki ruled the combine like a personal domain, but he also recruited an able managerial staff composed largely of graduates of Fukuzawa's Keiō University.

For Iwasaki personal ambition and patriotism were fused. As he conceived it, his mission was to compete with the great foreign shipping companies, and he was convinced that whatever benefited his company was also good for the nation. Not everyone, however, agreed with this assessment. For a time Iwasaki had to face the competition of a rival company, one of whose organizers was Shibusawa Eiichi (1840–1931), one of the great Meiji entrepreneurs and bankers, founder of the Tokyo Chamber of Commerce and Bankers' Association, a believer in joint-stock companies, in competition, and in business independence from government. Iwasaki won this battle, but Shibusawa remained enormously influential, not only because of his economic power but also because of his energetic advocacy of higher business standards and of the view that business could contribute most to the public good by remaining independent of government.

The success of such men as Iwasaki and Shibusawa should not obscure the fact that new ventures continued to entail risk. Not all new ventures were successful. For example, the attempt to introduce sheep raising into Japan was a failure. Initial attempts at organizing insurance companies were similarly ill-conceived, since they used rates and tables appropriate for European rather than Japanese conditions. But insurance companies were finally established, and altogether successes outnumbered failures.

One reason for the success of the *zaibatsu* and other new companies was their ability to attract capable and dedicated executives. Formerly, many capable members of the samurai class had refused to enter the business world because concern with money making was considered abhorrent. But this obstacle was largely overcome after the Restoration, not merely because the status of the samurai was changing, but because commercial and industrial development were required for the good of the state, and the member of a samurai family who helped build a strong bank, trading company, manufacturing industry, and so forth was rendering a service to the emperor and to Japan. Indeed, the government's initial sponsorship of many enterprises lent them some of the prestige of government service. The fact that many of the companies were created by men of samurai origins also helped make business socially acceptable.

The association of business with government also influenced business ideology in Japan. From the beginning, the ethos of modern Japanese business focused on its contributions to the Japanese nation, not on the laissez-faire notions of economic liberalism that prevailed in the West. The company did not exist only, or even primarily, to make a profit for its share-holders. Similarly, the internal organization of the business firm followed different lines in Japan; old values of group solidarity and mutual responsibility between the samurai and his lord were incorporated into the business structure to give participants in the venture a strong sense of company loyalty. It also helped to justify the government's influence on business and helped to account for the continued acceptance of policies that kept consumption low even as national income rose.

In discussing the *zaibatsu* and other modern firms it should not be supposed that large-scale trading, mining, and manufacturing represented the whole of Japanese business. On the contrary, many small-scale traditional establishments continued to function well past the early Meiji era. But the new firms did represent a major growth and change in economic activity, and signaled a change in Japanese perceptions of their role in international affairs as well. This was reflected in economic terms by the government's efforts to preserve economic independence, for example, by protecting home markets, conserving foreign exchange, and avoiding dependence on foreign capital so as to assure Japanese ownership of railways and other large-scale enterprises. It was reflected, also, in Japanese foreign policy, and especially in the modernization and deployment of the Japanese military.

The Military

Japanese military forces engaged in three major military operations in the twenty years following the Restoration: the Formosa expedition of 1874, the Satsuma Rebellion of 1877, and the Sino-Japanese War of 1894–95. The first two operations were fought primarily for domestic purposes, as the new Meiji government sought to consolidate its power. The Sino-Japanese War, on the other hand, was an outward-looking venture from the start, a test of strength with China on the Korean Peninsula. An even more striking difference, however, was the difference in the quality of Japanese military organization, armament, and tactical skill in 1874–77 and 1894.

The Formosa expedition of 1874 was far from brilliant. The landing was poorly executed, hygiene was so defective that disease took a great toll, and equipment had to be abandoned because it was unsuitable for use in a tropical climate. Similarly, the force that suppressed the Satsuma Rebellion did so because of its superiority in numbers and equipment rather than because of its military excellence.

To improve the quality of the army, a major reorganization was carried out in 1878 under the direction of Yamagata. A general staff was established along German lines, and Germany became the overall model for the army, which had previously been influenced by France. By strengthening the reserves, the military potential was greatly increased. During the ten or fifteen years before the Sino-Japanese War, generous military appropriations had enabled the army to acquire modern equipment, mostly manufactured in Japanese arsenals and plants, while the creation of a Staff College and improved training methods further strengthened the army and made it more modern. Like Yamagata, most of the lending generals were from Chōshū.

Naval modernization was similar to that of the army except that England was the model and continued to be a source from which some of the larger vessels were purchased. In 1894 the navy possessed 28 modern ships with a total displacement of 57,000 tons and also 24 torpedo boats. Most important, Japan had the facilities to maintain, repair, and arm its fleet. From the start most of the naval leadership came from Satsuma.

The military is a good example of the way in which the various facets of modernization were intertwined and supported each other, for the armed forces both benefited and contributed to the process. Not only did they stimulate new industries, ranging from armaments to tin cans, but it was also in the army that the rural conscript was for the first time exposed to a wider and more modern world. Indeed, when conscription was first introduced, many men from backward districts were quite bewildered by the accouterments of modern life. There are reports that some bowed in reverence to the stove in their barracks, taking it for some kind of god. For many men, the army provided the first introduction to shoes. Before the spread of education, some men learned to read and write in the army. All were exposed to the new values of nationalism and loyalty to the emperor. Most also learned to smoke (cigarettes were first reported in 1877) and to drink (native beverages and also excellent Japanese beer, first brewed in the 1870s), and they had their first experience with the modern city. Soldiers also enjoyed a better diet, receiving more meat than the average Japanese. But discipline was very harsh, and draft dodging was prevalent: in 1889 almost one-tenth of those eligible avoided conscription. Nevertheless, the vast majority did serve.

In this and other ways life was changing for that majority, but, compared to later, it was changing very slowly. There were changes in style, such as glass replacing paper inside the house or the use of Western umbrellas outside, but as Susan B. Hanley has shown, the essential consumption patterns and basic components of the material culture of the Japanese people basically remained traditional and stable.[6]

Korea and the Sino-Japanese War of 1894–1895

In the nineteenth century Korea was sorely troubled by internal problems and external pressures. The Yi dynasty (1392–1910), then in its fifth century, was in serious decline. Korea's peasantry suffered from "a skewered or concentrated pattern of landholding; small average per capita holdings; high rates of tenancy; a regressive tax structure; false registration of taxable land; extortion and illegal charges and gratuities at tax collection time; and usury, especially official usury in the management of the grain loan system."[7] There was a serious uprising in the North in 1811. In 1833 there were rice riots in Seoul. And in 1862 there were rebellions in the South.

During the years 1864 to 1873, there was a last attempt to save the situation by means of a traditional program of reform initiated by the regent, or Taewŏngun (Grand Prince, 1821–98), who was the father of the king. The reform program proved strong enough to provoke a reaction but was not sufficiently drastic, even in conception, to transform Korea into a strong and viable state capable of dealing with the dangers of the modern world.

That world was gradually closing in on Korea. During the first two-thirds of the century a number of incidents occurred involving Western ships and foreign demands. Korea's initial policy was to resist all attempts to "open" the country by referring those seeking to establish diplomatic relations back to Beijing. This policy was successful as long as it was directed at countries for whom Korea was of peripheral concern, but this had never been the case for Japan. Japan, therefore, was the most insistent of the powers trying to pry Korea loose from the Chinese orbit. In 1876 Japan forced Korea to sign a treaty establishing diplomatic relations and providing for the opening of three ports to trade. The treaty also stipulated that Korea was now "independent," but this did not settle matters since China still considered Korea a tributary. Insurrections in Seoul in 1882 and 1884 led to increased Chinese and Japanese involvement in Korea, including military involvement, always on opposing sides. But outright war was averted by talks between Itō Hirobumi and Li Hongzhang (Li Hung-chang), which led to a formal agreement between China and Japan to withdraw their forces and inform each other if either decided in the future that it was necessary to send in troops.

During the next years the Chinese Resident in Korea was Yuan Shikai (Yüan Shih-k'ai, 1859–1916), a protégé of Li Hongzhang, originally sent to Korea to train Korean troops. Yuan successfully executed Li's policy of vigorous assertion of Chinese control, dominating the court, effecting a partial union of Korean and Chinese commercial customs, and setting up a telegraph service and a merchant route between Korea and China.

Conflicting ambitions in Korea made war between China and Japan highly probable; the catalyst was the Tonghak Rebellion. Tonghak, literally "Eastern Learning," was a religion founded by Ch'oe Si-hyong (1824–64). In content it consisted of an amalgam of Chinese, Buddhist, and native Korean religious ideas and practices. This religious organization took on a political dimension, serving as a vehicle for expressions of discontent with a regime in decay, and for agitation against government corruption and foreign encroachments. Finally outlawed, it was involved in considerable rioting in 1893, which turned to rebellion the following year when Korea was struck by famine. When the Korean government requested Chinese assistance, Li Hongzhang responded by sending 1,500 men and informing the Japanese, whose troops were already on the way. The rebellion was quickly suppressed, but it proved easier to send than to remove the troops.

When Japanese soldiers entered Seoul, broke into the palace, and kidnapped the king and queen, Li responded by sending more troops and war was inevitable. It was a war that everyone, except the Japanese, expected China to win, but all parties were stunned when Japan defeated China on sea and on land. The triumph of Japan's army, which rapidly made its way north through Korea, crossed the Yalu River into Manchuria, and captured Port Arthur on the Liaodong Peninsula, was matched by the victory Japan's naval forces won over the Chinese at sea. Begun in July 1894, the war was all over by March of 1895. In retrospect the reasons for the outcome are easy to see: Japan was better equipped, better led, and more united than China.

The Treaty of Shimonoseki (April 1895)

The war was terminated by the Treaty of Shimonoseki. China relinquished all claims to a special role in Korea and recognized that country as an independent state (although its troubles were far from over). In addition, China paid Japan an indemnity and ceded it Taiwan and the Pescadores, thus starting the formation of the Japanese empire. A further indication that the Japanese had now joined the ranks of the imperialist nations was the extension to Japan of most-favored-nation status, along with the opening of seven additional Chinese ports. Japan was also to receive the Liaodong Peninsula but, after diplomatic intervention by Russia, Germany, and France, had to settle for an additional indemnity instead.

Essentially Japan went to war to counter Chinese dominance in Korea. The motivations of Japan's leaders included alarm over the prospect of a weak Korea open to Western (particularly Russian) aggression as well as more positive empire-building sentiments. Many believed that bringing the peninsula under Japanese influence would foster needed reforms in a reactionary country, and there were Koreans who shared this view. As it turned out, the war did not assure Japanese security, let alone Korean progress. But it did signal the beginning of the Japanese Empire. It did not resolve the tensions created during the preceding years, but it did usher in a new phase of Japan's modern history. And it marked an unprecedented shift in the East Asian balance of power, a shift from China to Japan that was to continue until Japan's defeat in the Second World War.

NOTES

1. Quoted in Carmen Blacker, *The Japanese Enlightenment: A Study of the Writings of Fukuzawa Yukichi* (London: Cambridge Univ. Press, 1964), p. 111.
2. Ibid., p. 128.
3. Quoted in Kenneth Pyle, *The New Generation in Meiji Japan: Problems in Cultural Identity, 1885–95* (Stanford: Stanford Univ. Press, 1969), p. 124.
4. Akira Iriye in Marius Jansen, *The Cambridge History of Japan*, Vol. 5: p. 754.
5. "Rescript on Education," in David John Lu, *Sources of Japanese History* (New York: McGraw-Hill, 1974), 2: 70–71.
6. Susan B. Hanley, "The Material Culture: Stability in Transition" in Marius B. Jansen and Gilbert Rozman, eds. *Japan in Transition: From Tokugawa to Meiji* (Princeton: Princeton Univ. Press, 1986), pp. 467–69 and *passim*.
7. James B. Palais, *Politics and Policy in Traditional Korea* (Cambridge: Harvard Univ. Press, 1975), p. 63.

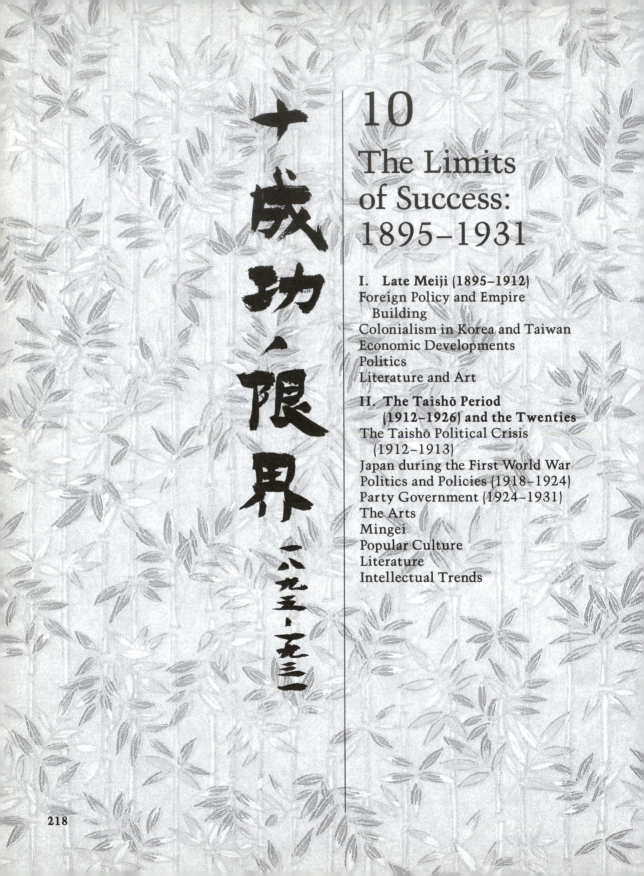

十成功・限界 一八九五・一九三一

10
The Limits of Success: 1895–1931

During the eventful years between the founding of empire in 1895 and the advent of militarism in 1931, Japan increasingly became part of the modern world in her own way. In many ways it was a success story, but later history was to show that it also harbored a potential for disaster. The death of the Meiji emperor in July 1912 was not as momentous an event as the fall of China's last traditional dynasty the year before, but it did mark something of a watershed. People at the time felt that the passing of the emperor who had presided over Japan's transformation for over forty years signified the end of an era, a judgment in which many modern scholars have concurred. This chapter is divided accordingly.

PART I.   LATE MEIJI (1895–1912)

Japan could take great pride in her victory over China in war and her increase in international status, but this did not bring stability either at home or abroad. For one thing, achieving full status as a world power proved no easy task in a world dominated by Western superpowers. For another, expansionism begot expansionism as each new acquisition increased what were perceived to be the security requirements of the empire in a process without foreseeable limits. At least as important as the logic of imperialism was its passion.

Foreign Policy and Empire Building

From the very beginning, the foreign policy goals of the Meiji leaders had been to achieve national security and equality of national status. But how were security and equality to be defined, and how were they to be attained?

A highly influential view of what constituted Japanese security was that of Yamagata Aritomo, architect of Japan's modern army, and an important political figure in or out of office. Yamagata was not a fanatical imperialist, but he was a hard-headed, realistic nationalist. The army's German advisor argued that Korea was the key to Japan's security, and Yamagata concurred in this analysis. In 1890 Yamagata propounded the thesis that Japan must not only defend its "line of sovereignty" but secure its "line of interest," which ran through Korea.

219

At the same time the Japanese navy was heavily influenced by the ideas of Admiral Mahan, an American advocate of the importance of sea power. From the navy's point of view, Japanese security demanded Japanese naval domination of the surrounding seas. The acquisition of Taiwan as a result of the Sino-Japanese War gratified the navy as a major step in this direction, but the army was very unhappy at having to give up the strategic Liaodong Peninsula. Typically, colonies were valued first of all for their strategic importance even as they were "the ultimate status symbol." As elsewhere, other considerations also entered in, but an authority on the subject has concluded "no colonial empire of modern times was as clearly shaped by strategic considerations."[1]

Equality was as elusive a concept as security, but everyone agreed that at a minimum it required the elimination of extraterritoriality and the restoration of tariff autonomy. Already in the 1870s work began on revision of the law codes to bring them into line with Western practices, so that the powers would no longer have reason to insist on maintaining jurisdiction over their own subjects. Even before the lengthy process of revising the codes had been completed, there was strong and vociferous public demand for an end to extraterritoriality. One result was that in 1886 the government was forced to back down from a compromise it had negotiated providing for mixed courts under Japanese and foreign judges. Appreciation of the intensity of public pressure was one of the factors that induced the British, in 1894 shortly before the start of the Sino-Japanese War, to relinquish extraterritoriality when the new legal codes came into effect (1899). Other countries followed suit. In return, foreign merchants were no longer limited to the treaty ports. These treaties also secured tariff autonomy, and in 1911 Japan regained full control over her customs duties.

By that time, Japan, under the most-favored-nation clause of the Treaty of Shimonoseki, was enjoying extraterritorial rights in China and benefiting from China's lack of tariff autonomy. As a result Japan's exports to China increased not only numerically but also in terms of the proportion of her total exports that went to China. This rose from less than 10 percent prior to 1894 to 25 percent by the First World War. A commercial treaty negotiated with China in 1896 gave Japan the right to establish factories in the treaty ports, spurring her investments in China.

During the Late Meiji period, imperialism was a cause for national pride in the colonizing countries of the West, and in Japan, too, the acquisition of overseas colonies and interests was hailed as a sign of national fulfillment. Conversely, there was a sense of great public disappointment and outrage when French, German, and Russian intervention forced Japan to give up the Liaodong Peninsula. The government's reaction to this setback was to follow a prudent foreign policy while increasing military spending.

Accordingly, Japan exercised careful restraint during the Boxer Rebellion (1900). However, this stance was not emulated by Japan's chief rival in Northeast Asia, Czarist Russia, which had demonstrated its intent to become a major power in the area by undertaking the construction of the great Trans-Siberian Railway (1891–1903). In 1896 Russia had obtained permission to run tracks across northern Manchuria directly to Vladivostok, and the Boxer Rebellion was used to entrench Russian interests in Manchuria. Russia's lease of Port Arthur on the Liaodong Peninsula gave it a much needed warm water port, but it also grated on the Japanese, who had so recently been denied the peninsula. Nor did Russia refrain from interfering in Korea, where it allied itself to conservative opponents of Japanese-backed reformers. Agreements reached in 1896, 1897, and 1898 kept this rivalry from exploding into war, but the Russian moves in Manchuria furthered Japanese apprehension about Russian ambitions in Northeast Asia.

Japan was not the only nation concerned over Russian expansion in East Asia. Great Britain, which had not joined in the Triple Intervention following the Sino-Japanese War, had long been alarmed over Russian expansion in Central Asia and was also apprehensive over Russia's plans for China. In 1902 Britain cast aside its policy of "splendid isolation" to enter into an alliance with Japan. Great Britain now recognized Japan's special interests in Korea, and each nation recognized the other's interests in China. Furthermore, Great Britain and Japan agreed that each would remain neutral in the event the other fought a war against a single enemy in East Asia and would come to the other's assistance if either were attacked by two powers at once. This meant that in the event of a war between Japan and Russia, Britain would enter on the Japanese side if France or Germany supported Russia. Japan would not have to face a European coalition alone. Aside from strengthening Japan's hand vis-à-vis Russia, this alliance with the foremost world power gave Japan new prestige and confidence. At the same time, Russia showed every intention of wishing to maintain and expand its position in East Asia.

The conflicting imperialist ambitions of Russia and Japan led to the Russo-Japanese War of 1904–05, fought both on land (mostly in Manchuria) and at sea. For both belligerents the cost was heavy, but the victories went to Japan. Despite some hard fighting, Russian troops were driven back on land; while in two separate naval actions the Japanese destroyed virtually the entire Russian navy. The naval war was spectacular. Japan attacked the Russian Pacific fleet at Port Arthur, just before the declaration of war. Russia's Baltic fleet then embarked on an 18,000-mile trip, sailing all the way around Africa because Britain refused passage through the Suez Canal. Its destination was Vladivostok, but it was demolished by the Japanese navy in a decisive battle in the Tsushima Straits, which run between Japan and Korea. Only 4 of the 35 Russian ships reached Vladivostok.

In Russia these defeats had fateful consequences. The discredited government of the Czar, long the object of terrorist attacks, now faced full-scale rebellion. The Revolution of 1905 was a precursor of the Revolution of 1917, which overthrew the regime. For their part the Japanese, although victorious, were thoroughly exhausted. It was essential that the war be brought to a close. Thus both sides were happy to respond affirmatively to an offer from the United States to mediate their disputes, and a peace conference was subsequently held in Portsmouth, New Hampshire.

In the resulting treaty, Japan gained recognition of its supremacy in Korea, the transfer of Russian interests in Manchuria (the railway and the leasehold on the Liaodong Peninsula), and cession of the southern half of Sakhalin Island (north of Hokkaidō). Going into the negotiations, Japan had demanded all of Sakhalin and also a war indemnity, but Russia successfully resisted these demands, much to the anger of the Japanese public, which, not informed of their country's inability to continue the war, expected more of the settlement. At home the treaty was greeted by riots. Elsewhere in Asia people were impressed by this first victory of a non-Western nation over a European power.

One immediate result of Japan's victory over Russia was economic expansion in Manchuria where the semiofficial South Manchurian Railway Company was soon engaged in shipping, public utilities, and mining, as well as railroading. From the start the Japanese government held half of the company's shares and appointed its officers. Although private Japanese firms also entered Manchuria, it has been calculated that in 1914, 79 percent of all Japanese investments in Manchuria were in the South Manchurian Railway. Furthermore, 69 percent of all Japanese investments in China prior to the First World War were in Manchuria. The remainder was largely concentrated in Shanghai.

Colonialism in Korea and Taiwan

Japan's victory over Russia determined the next forty years of Korean history. In 1906 Itō Hirobumi was sent to Korea as Resident General with wide powers over the Korean government, but in 1909 he was assassinated by a Korean nationalist, and in the following year Japan annexed Korea outright. Korea was then placed under the control of a governor-general, always a military man, although after 1919 a civilian could legally have been appointed to this post.

Like other imperialist powers, Japan governed its colonies for the benefit of the homeland. In both Taiwan and Korea, Japan's policies were designed to control the local population and to exploit the local resources through selective modernization. Japanese rule over Taiwan and Korea, accordingly, shared certain characteristics: in both cases the police were prominent, and dissent was repressed; transportation and communications networks were developed; the landholding system was remodeled, agricultural production encouraged and increased turning Taiwan and Korea into "agricultural appendages."[2] While rice production increased, so much was shipped to Japan that local rice consumption by Koreans and Taiwanese actually decreased. Furthermore, until the 1930s, industries that were potential competitors for Japanese firms, were actively discouraged. In both colonies, public health was improved, leading to population growth; basic education was fostered, emphasizing Japanese studies and spreading use of the Japanese language in a policy of partial assimilation. Grounded in a conviction of racial superiority, it was intended to turn colonials into loyal subjects without giving them the benefits accorded Japanese citizens. In sum, too many of the benefits of modernization went to the Japanese who dominated the colonial administrative machinery and operated the large colonial enterprises.

There were discussions about incorporating these colonies into metropolitan Japan, making the subject peoples citizens, but there were no plans for eventual independence.

There were also enormous differences between the two colonies—differences extending beyond such obvious factors as climate (Taiwan is suitable for sugar plantations, Korea is not) or Korea's more strategic geographic location. From the beginning, Japanese rule over Taiwan, while vigorous and firm, was not as harsh as that over Korea. There were, no doubt, numerous reasons for this, but important among them was the difference in historical background between Taiwan and Korea. When Japan assumed control over Taiwan after the Treaty of Shimonoseki, it encountered only sporadic resistance, for the island had only recently been fully incorporated into the political and cultural life of the mainland; even though its residents were almost all Chinese (about 3 million Chinese as compared to about 120,000 aborigines), they were as yet uninfluenced by modern nationalism and lacked a deep-rooted tradition of local cultural and political independence.

Korea, by contrast, boasted a culture older than that of Japan and a tradition of fierce independence. It also contained an old hereditary elite resentful of Japanese intrusion, and after 1895, a small but dedicated group of nationalists. Although the leadership against the Japanese takeover was traditional in composition and organization, violence was widespread. Japanese retaliation (by burning villages and committing other acts of terror) enflamed it even more. Between August 1907 and June 1911, the Japanese recorded 2,852 clashes involving 141,815 insurgents. Until 1919 Japanese rule remained totally uncompromising. Beginning March 1 of that year, there were massive nationalist demonstrations appealing, as did those in Beijing (Peking) on May 4, to the Wilsonian doctrine of national self-determination. The protests spread throughout Korea and before it was over some 2 million people participated. The Japanese repression was ferocious. In the twenties, the colonial administration was partially relaxed, but this was followed by further severity in the thirties.

Under Japanese rule the average Korean suffered economically. The land survey conducted between 1911 and 1918 favored large landholders. Tenancy increased. The largest landholder in Korea came to be the Oriental Development Company, a semigovernment corporation originally chartered in 1908 with the intent of opening new lands for Japanese immigrant farmers. When that plan proved unrealistic, the company bought up Korean-worked paddy fields instead. This was a development consistent with Korea's role as a supplier of inexpensive rice for Japan. After the First World War, the Japanese greatly expanded rice production in Korea, but there was still not enough for both Japanese and Koreans who had to include more barley and millet in their diets. In the twenties and thirties a beginning was made in industrial development, especially in the north, which was suitable for hydroelectric plants.

As demonstrated by the 1919 protest, the Japanese built up a vast reservoir of ill will in Korea, and there were nationalists in exile yearning for an end to Japanese rule. Others, however, acquiesced and/or cooperated, and both Taiwan and Korea continued to contribute to the Japanese sense of national accomplishment as well as to the Japanese economy.

Economic Developments

War against China in the 1890s, and against Russia during the following decade, stimulated the Japanese domestic economy. Both wars were followed by an outburst of nationalist sentiment that gave a strong boost to heavy industry (for example, the Yawata Steel Works, established in 1897) and to armaments, including shipbuilding. After 1906, Japan produced ships comparable in size and quality to any in the world. Japanese technology continued to progress and advances were made in new fields such as electrical engineering. Light industry, particularly textiles, continued to flourish and remained predominant in the modern sector. The single most important item of export, accounting for nearly half the total, was in partly finished goods, especially silk. (Because of superior quality control, Japanese silk exports overtook those of China.) Trade figures revealing an increasing emphasis on the import of raw materials and the export of manufactured goods are indicative of economic change, and in 1912 the industrial sector accounted for 36 percent of GNP (gross national product). Other statistics indicate increases in labor productivity and in urbanization, opening up a widening gulf between the city and the country. The government, guided by pragmatic conservative reformers, sponsored a program of rural cooperatives which were established by an act of the Diet in 1899. Through cooperatives which helped with credit, marketing, and production combined with intense propaganda, the government hoped to avoid the class conflict found in Western countries.

Meanwhile not everyone in the industrial sector benefited from economic development. Those working in the numerous small traditional establishments experienced little change in their living conditions. Especially harsh were the working and living conditions of those who labored in the factories and shops. These were comparable to those in Western countries at a comparably early stage of industrialization. During the first decade of the twentieth century, 60 percent of the work force was still female. An act promulgated in 1900 outlawed strikes, but when conditions became too bad, male workers, for whom a factory job was not an interlude prior to marriage but a lifelong occupation, rebelled, sometimes violently. Thus in 1909, three infantry companies were required to quell violence in the Ashio Copper Mines. Another labor action that made a deep impression was the streetcar strike in Tokyo in 1911.

Conservative reformers, mindful of the social legislation of Bismarckian Germany, insisted very early on that the government had the responsibility to ensure a balance between capital and labor, although the first factory laws were not passed until 1911. Efforts to improve the lot of women and children working in the factories also made headway only slowly. Not until

1916 did a law take effect giving them some protection, such as limiting their working day to eleven hours.

The distress of the workers was also of great concern to radical intellectuals. Beginning in the early nineties, there was a small radical movement composed of Christian socialists and anarchists. They exhibited great courage in opposing the war with Russia. Even after the war had begun, they held antiwar rallies in the Tokyo YMCA. However, barred by the government from forming a political party and facing government repression, they were unable to expand their influence beyond the world of intellectuals and college students. In 1911, twelve of their leaders were convicted, on very flimsy evidence, of plotting the death of the emperor, and were executed.

Among the main beneficiaries of economic growth were the huge industrial-financial combines (zaibatsu), which retained their close ties with government. The dominant political party during this period, the Seiyūkai (Association of Friends of Constitutional Government), also had a stake in economic development, since projects for railway and harbor development were a major means by which it won regional support and built up its political power.

Politics

During the Sino-Japanese War the oligarchs and the party-controlled Diet were united in pursuit of common national aims, but after the war the political struggles resumed. The oligarchs, enjoying the prerogatives of genrō ("elder statesmen"), advised the emperor on all important matters. They tended to see themselves as guardians of the general public good in contrast to the private interests represented by the parties and to stress the need for unity in face of a hostile world. As participants in the fashioning of the new state and architects of its major institutions, they enjoyed great prestige as well as the support of their protégés and associates in that process. The party politicians, on the other hand, resented the genrō's tendency to perpetuate their power and to limit political decision making to a small group of hand-picked insiders. Their main weapon against a prime minister who defied them was that under the constitution only the Diet could authorize increases in the budget.

Complicating the political situation but also making for compromise rather than confrontation were divisions within both the oligarchy and the party leadership. Among the former, Yamagata, a disciplined, rather austere military man, was committed to "transcendental government," dedicated to emperor and nation and above political partisanship. His main genrō rival was Itō, a more flexible conservative, the man who had supervised the writing of the constitution. Itō was more willing than Yamagata to compromise with the party forces.

Similarly not all Diet members were adamantly opposed to collaborating with the genrō. Some lost their enthusiasm for opposing a government that could dissolve the Diet and thereby subject them to costly reelection campaigns. Also, the oligarchs could—and did—trade office for support. Accommodation had its appeal to both sides, but initially it was an uneasy accommodation; there were four dissolutions of the Diet between 1895 and 1900.

Another political factor was the influence of the military. As stipulated in the constitution, the chief of the general staff reported directly to the emperor concerning command matters, thus bypassing the Minister of War and the cabinet. In 1900 the military's power was further strengthened when Yamagata obtained imperial ordinances specifying that only officers on active duty could serve as Minister of the Army or Minister of the Navy. This in effect gave the military veto power over any cabinet, for it could break a cabinet simply by ordering the army or navy minister to resign. However, control over funds for army expansion remained in the hands of the lower house.

Up to 1901 the oligarchs themselves served as prime minister, but after that date Yamagata's protégé Katsura Tarō (1847–1913) and Itō's protégé, Saionji Kimmochi (1849–1940) alternated as prime minister for the remainder of the Meiji period. Katsura, like Yamagata, was a general from Chōshū; Saionji was a court noble with liberal views but little inclination to political leadership.

Katsura and Saionji were able to govern because they had the cooperation of the Seiyūkai, a party founded in 1900 by Itō who saw this as the way to obtain assured support in the Diet. In 1903 Itō turned the presidency of the party over to Saionji, but the real organizing force within the party was Hara Kei (1856–1921), an ex-bureaucrat who became the leading party politician of his generation. Hara greatly strengthened the party by building support within the bureaucracy during his first term as Home Minister (1906–08) and also used his power to appoint energetic partymen as prefectural governors. He further linked the party to the provinces and provided it with local roots by freely resorting to the pork barrel to build up a constituency among the local men of means who formed the limited electorate.

The financial and business community, including the *zaibatsu*, was interested in maintaining a political atmosphere favorable to itself, and political leaders for their part welcomed business support. Thus Itō, when he organized the Seiyūkai, obtained the support of Shibusawa Eiichi and other prominent business leaders, although many remained aloof. The head of Mitsui was so intent on establishing his firm's independence from government that he even discontinued the practice of extending loans to Itō without collateral. However, the trend was toward closer association between the *zaibatsu* and politics, as exemplified by the close relationship between Mitsubishi and Katsura after 1908. During Katsura's second ministry (1908–11), his chief economic advisor was the head of the Mitsubishi Bank.

The relative strength of the participants in the political process did not remain unchanged. The *genrō* enjoyed great influence as long as they remained active, but theirs was a personal not an institutional power, and it tended to diminish with time. As the participants in the original Restoration diminished in number, the power of the oligarchs to orchestrate politics decreased. Katsura as prime minister did not always follow Yamagata's advice.

Furthermore, the *genrō* lost an important source of support when a new generation of bureaucrats came to the fore. These new officials did not owe their positions to *genrō* patronage, for after 1885 entrance to and promotion in the bureaucracy were determined by examinations. As servants of the emperor, the bureaucracy enjoyed high prestige and considerable influence.

Political compromise eroded much of the idealism found in the early movement for people's rights, but the Seiyūkai prospered. Indeed its strength in the Diet alarmed the party's opponents in that body, but this opposition was divided and diverse. It included not only those who opposed the Seiyūkai's compromise on principle, but also small and shifting groups of independents, and a series of "loyalist" parties that habitually supported the cabinet.

Decision making was complicated, and government policies were determined by the interaction of various power centers, none of which could rule alone. The system functioned as long as there were sufficient funds to finance the military's and the Seiyūkai's highest priority projects, and as long as none of the participants felt their essential interests threatened. When that ceased to be the case, it brought on the Taishō political crisis.

Literature and Art

Early Meiji literature had largely continued Tokugawa traditions, but during the Late Meiji a modern literature developed under the influence of Western literature and literary theories. The beginning of the modern Japanese novel can be traced to Tsubouchi Shōyō (1859–1935), a translator of Shakespeare and an advocate of realism, that is, the view that literature should portray actual life. In his *The Essence of the Novel* (1885) Tsubouchi argued for the adoption of realism in place of the earlier didacticism or literature written solely for entertainment. Futabatei Shimei (1864–1909) then wrote the realistic novel, *Drifting Cloud* (1887–89), a psychological study of a rather ordinary man, told not in the customary literary style but in more colloquial form.

Following the introduction of realism, two other Western literary theories became particularly influential: romanticism, with its emphasis on the expression of feelings, and naturalism, which aimed at treating man with scientific detachment as advocated by the French writer Émile Zola. Although in Europe naturalism was hostile to romanticism, this was not necessarily the case in Japan, where Shimazaki Tōson (1873–1943) won fame both for his romantic poetry and for a naturalistic novel, *The Broken Commandment* (1906). This novel was an account of a member of the pariah class (*burakumin*, see Chapter 7) who tries to keep the pledge he made to his father never to reveal that he was born into this group (which was still the object of social discrimination and contempt even though not subject to any legal restrictions).

Two writers of the Late Meiji era stand out in particular, producing works of lasting literary merit that transcended their age, even as they reflected its concerns: Mori Ōgai (1862–1922) and Natsume Sōseki (1867–1916). Ōgai identified with his family's samurai heritage while Sōseki was proud of being a son of plebian Edo. Their writings differed in substance and style, but both men, though deeply influenced by the West, achieved greatness by drawing on their own Japanese heritage.

Both spent time abroad. Ōgai was sent by the army to study medicine in Germany and after returning to Japan had a distinguished career as an army surgeon, rising in 1907 to the post of surgeon-general. He was both a modern intellectual profoundly influenced by his time in Europe and a samurai-style army officer: it was not an easy life, but it gave rise to major achievements.

Admired for the masculine, restrained style of his original works, he was also a prolific and excellent translator. Among his finest translations are his renderings of Goethe, including the full *Faust*, and of Shakespeare, which he translated from the German. He also translated modern German poetry, with the result that more modern German verse was available in Japanese translation than in English. Furthermore, he introduced German aesthetic philosophy to Japan and also had an influence on the development of modern Japanese theater: the performance of his translation of an Ibsen play in 1908 was one of the major cultural events of the Late Meiji.

Ōgai's first story, *Maihime* ("The Dancing Girl," 1890) recounts the doomed romance between a Japanese student sent by his government to Germany and a German girl named Alice. It became a precursor of the many "I novels," thinly disguised autobiographical works, which became one of the standard genres of modern Japanese fiction, although it also owes something to the old tradition of literary diaries.

After his initial romantic period, Ōgai went on to write works of increasing psychological insight and philosophical depth. He also turned increasingly to Japanese themes, as in his novel *The Wild Goose*. Ōgai was greatly moved when his friend General Nogi (1849–1912), hero of the Russo-Japanese War, followed the Meiji Emperor into death by committing ritual suicide along with his wife. After the event Ōgai published painstakingly researched accounts of samurai. One late work particularly acclaimed in Japan is his *Chibu Chūsai*, an account of a late Tokugawa physician with whom Ōgai identified.

Natsume Sōseki studied in England, where a meager government stipend forced him to live in poverty, and he had virtually no friends. Later he described himself as having been "as lonely as a stray dog in a pack of wolves."[3] Both this experience of loneliness and the extensive reading he did while in England were reflected in his subsequent work. Sōseki returned from Europe to teach English literature at Tokyo Imperial University, before resigning this position to devote himself wholly to writing. He was acclaimed not only for his fiction but also for poetry in Chinese, haiku, and literary criticism. He once described his mind as half-Japanese and half-Western, and his early novels reflect English influence, particularly that of Meredith, but in his mature work the Japanese element predominates.

In his early novels *I Am a Cat* (1905) and *Botchan* (1906), Sōseki presents slices of Meiji life portrayed with affectionate good humor. Also in 1906, in a mere week, he wrote a remarkable painterly and diarylike book, *The Grass Pillow*, also translated as *The Three Cornered World*, for "an artist is a person who lives in the triangle which remains after the angle which we may call common sense has been removed from this four-cornered world."[4] The main theme of Sōseki's mature works is human isolation, studied in characters given to deep introspection. Like Ōgai, Sōseki was deeply moved by the death of the Meiji Emperor and General Nogi's suicide, which entered into *Kokoro* (1914), a novel concerning the relationship between a young man and his mentor, called "Sensei" ("master" or "teacher"). In the novel Sōseki links Sensei's personal tragedy and his suicide in 1912 to the death of the emperor and the general, and the larger tragedy of the passing of a generation and with it of the old ethical values, for Sensei perceives that he has become an anachronism.

Painters, like writers, were grouped in several schools. The disciples of Okakura Tenshin, for example, continued to avoid the extremes of formalistic traditionalism and imitative modernism, while seeking a middle ground that would be both modern and Japanese. One member of this school was Yokoyama Taikan (1868–1958). His screen, shown in Figure 10.1, depicts a perennial favorite of Chinese and Japanese scholars, the poet Tao Qian (T'ao Ch'ien, 365–427), whose blend of regret and relief at withdrawal from public life continued to strike a responsive chord in the complicated world of the twentieth century.

Figure 10.1   Yokoyama Taikan, *Tao Qian*. Detail from one of a pair of six-fold screens, *Master Five Willows*. Color on paper, 1912, 169.4 cm × 361.2 cm. Tokyo National Museum.

Among the artists working in purely European styles was Kuroda Seiki, whose nude had so shocked Kyoto in the nineties. He continued to paint in a Western manner and had many students. At the time of his death in 1924, he had come to be "the Grand Old Man of Western painting in Japan."[5] Some attempts at rendering Japanese themes in Western style produced paintings that are little more than historical curiosities, but in other cases there was a happier result. The painting by Sakaki Teitoku (1858–1939) shown in Figure 10.2 was executed in oil around 1910. While the young men blow traditional bamboo flutes, two young women play violins.

Western influence on the visual arts was often direct and immediate. For instance, the noted Japanese artist Umehara Ryūzaburō (1888–1986) studied in France during the Late Meiji, met Renoir in 1909, and became his favorite pupil. The strongest influence on Japanese sculpture during this period was Rodin, who enjoyed a great vogue in Japan, especially after a major exhibition of his work in Tokyo in 1912. The Japanese continued to be informed, enthusiastic, and sensitive patrons of the visual arts.

There was also an interest in modernizing music. The Meiji government early on sponsored Western military music, and in 1879 the Ministry of Education agreed to a proposal made by Izawa Shūji (1851–1917) to combine Japanese and Western music in the schools. Izawa had studied vocal physiology in the United States and persuaded the Ministry of Education to bring Luther Whiting Mason (1828–96) from Boston to Japan to help develop songs for use in the elementary schools. The first of the song books to be completed (1881) consisted half of Western songs supplied with Japanese words ("Auld Lang Syne," for example, was turned into a song about fireflies) and half of Japanese pieces harmonized in the Western manner.

Figure 10.2   Sakaki Teitoku, *Concert Using Japanese and Western Instruments.* Oil, 1910. Takakiyu Mitsui Collection.

Meiji popular music was more freely eclectic than that taught in the schools. During the last decade of the nineteenth century and the beginning of the twentieth, Japanese composers began working with the forms of classical Western music (sonatas, cantatas, and so forth), and thanks to the efforts of the Tokyo School of Music good performers were available on the piano and violin, as well as on the koto and other traditional instruments also taught at the school. Actually, performers made greater progress than composers. The important compositions were still to come. Furthermore, as William P. Malm has suggested, "the training of generations of Japanese youth to harmonically oriented music has created a series of mental blocks which shut out the special musical potentialities of traditional styles."[6] The rediscovery of the latter, and their creative employment in original compositions, did not take place until after the Second World War.

PART II.   THE TAISHŌ PERIOD (1912–1926) AND THE TWENTIES

The Meiji Emperor was succeeded, in 1912, by the Taishō Emperor (r. 1912–26). There was a sense of unease in the country as it faced social and economic change. It mourned the old emperor, who had given his people a sense of continuity even as he presided over the transformation of the country.

The Taishō Political Crisis (1912–1913)

A political crisis arose when Japan's financial condition forced a cutback in government spending and brought two major interest groups into conflict. The dominant political party, the Seiyūkai, was determined to save its domestic spending program—in part because its political support depended on it, while the army, anxious to build two new divisions, pressed for increased military spending.

Although the Seiyūkai won support at the polls, Prime Minister Saionji was forced out of office in December 1912, when the army ordered the Minister of the Army to resign his post. While the genrō deliberated and sought for a successor to Saionji, a number of politicians, journalists, and businessmen organized a movement "to protect constitutional government," which led to mass demonstrations reminiscent of those greeting news of the Portsmouth Treaty in 1905. Called on to form a government once more, Katsura was no longer willing to compromise with the Seiyūkai, but he failed in an attempt to weld his bureaucratic followers and opposition politicians into a party strong enough to defeat the Seiyūkai. When the Seiyūkai threatened a vote of no confidence in the Diet, Katsura tried to save the situation by obtaining an imperial order forcing the Seiyūkai to give up its planned no-confidence motion. This was a stratagem employed previously by embattled prime ministers, but it did not work this time, for the Seiyūkai turned down the order. One consequence of Katsura's failure was to discredit such use of an imperial order, with the result that it was never attempted again. The crisis ended with Katsura's resignation. The parties, supported by a vociferous press and public opinion, had for the first time overthrown a cabinet. It was a notable victory.

Katsura died in 1913, but the coalition he had created held together under the leadership of Katō Tataaki (1859–1926) as Japan headed in the direction of a two-party system. Katō's background included graduation from Tokyo Imperial University, service in Mitsubishi, and a career in the Foreign Office capped by an appointment as Foreign Minister at the age of 40. He enjoyed a financial advantage from his marriage into the family that controlled Mitsubishi. A capable and determined man, he was personally reserved. But this was no handicap, for there was no need for party leaders like Katō or Hara to cultivate mass support. The power of a party leader depended on his strength *within* his party, although this was influenced by the party's success at the polls.

The emergence of a strong second party meant that from now on the Seiyūkai faced a rival for control of the lower house. The parties represented a cross section of skills and resources needed to make participation in government viable. As Arthur E. Tiedemann observes, "Each party had associated with it the three essential ingredients for achieving political power: professional politicians to do the nitty-gritty of day-to-day party management; former bureaucrats who had the administrative talents required to form a viable alternative government acceptable to the *genrō*; and businessmen who could supply the funds and influence essential to successful election campaigns."[7] Thus Japan came to be governed by a two-party system that lasted until 1932.

Although the Taishō political crisis confirmed the importance of the Diet and of the parties, they were not the only power center. Again there were compromises: not until Hara became prime minister in 1918 did the top government post go to a man who had made his career as a party politician. Meanwhile, there were three intervening prime ministers: Admiral Yamamoto Gombei (1913–14) a military bureaucrat from Satsuma whose government was brought down by a scandal in naval procurement; the septuagenarian Ōkuma Shigenobu (1914–16), who was committed to destroying the Seiyūkai but failed; and Terauchi Masatake (1916–18), a Chōshū general who had been governor-general of Korea and was backed by Yamagata. It was the Ōkuma and Terauchi governments that guided Japan during the First World War.

Japan during the First World War

When the Western powers became immersed in the struggle that was to bring an end to Europe's predominance in the world, new opportunities were opened for the expansion of the Japanese empire and industry.

In August 1914, Japan declared war on Germany and within three months proceeded to seize German holdings in Shandong and the German islands in the Pacific. In January 1915 the Ōkuma government presented the Twenty-

One Demands to China. Japan obtained additional rights on the continent but at the cost of stirring up strong Chinese resentment. A prominent critic of this policy was the pro-German Yamagata, who wanted an understanding with China in order to prepare for the war he anticipated against the West.

Much larger and more costly than Japan's military effort against Germany during the First World War was the country's effort against the Russians (1918–22). The Russian Revolution of 1917 had taken Russia out of the war and created disorder in Russia's East Asian territories. In Japan there was considerable disagreement over how to take advantage of a situation further complicated by the presence of Czech troops who were fighting their way out of Russia and were determined to continue the war against Germany. By mid-summer 1918, Japan controlled the eastern portion of the Trans-Siberian Railway and had seized Vladivostok. The United States then changed its earlier opposition to intervention, although President Wilson envisioned only a limited military operation. The Japanese, however, sent 75,000 troops, three times more than those sent by the Allies (United States, Britain, France, and Canada). In the light of Soviet victories and the absence of a viable alternative, the United States withdrew its forces in January 1919 and the other Allies soon did the same. This left only the Japanese, who continued their efforts in the vain hope of at least keeping the U.S.S.R. from controlling eastern Siberia.

Japan was able to pay for such a costly undertaking largely because of the great economic boom it experienced during the First World War, when there was an unprecedented demand for its industrial products and a withdrawal of the European competition. Old industries expanded and new ones grew up as exports surged. Japan earned enough foreign exchange to change its status from a debtor to a creditor nation. But while some prospered, others suffered. The sudden economic expansion produced inflation and workers' wages, as well as the income of men in traditional occupations such as fishing, failed to keep pace. Especially serious was the increase in the price of rice, which rose until people could no longer afford this most basic food. In August 1918, rice riots erupted in cities, towns, and villages all over Japan. Even as Japanese troops were setting off for Siberia other soldiers were firing on hungry people rioting at home. The bitter irony was not lost on Japanese radicals. The immediate effect of the turbulence was to bring down the Terauchi government. When the genrō met to choose a new prime minister, they settled on the Seiyūkai leader Hara Kei.

Politics and Policies (1918–1924)

Hara Kei had spent his career building up the Seiyūkai in preparation for the day of party rule, but when he finally attained the prime ministership he was too set in his ways to embark on significant new policies or to devise meaningful changes in the structure of government. The changes he initiated from 1918 until he was assassinated by a demented fanatic in November 1921 were minor, and his concerns tended to remain partisan. Democratic intellectuals, the leaders of labor and farmer unions, and students were disillusioned when the government turned a deaf ear to their demands for universal suffrage, and instead passed an election law that retained a tax qualification for voting and reconstructed local electoral districts to favor the Seiyūkai. Abuse of office, financial scandals, and actions prompted by narrow partisanship had damaged the public image of the parties for years, and the record of the first party prime minister did nothing to alter this. Liberals who had placed their hopes in parliamentary reform either became cynical or looked elsewhere, while the public at large was apathetic.

In foreign affairs Hara's prime ministership began with the peace conference at Versailles, where Japan failed to obtain a declaration of racial equality but did gain acquiescence to its claims in China and the Pacific. His government then adopted a policy of cooperation with the United States, the only possible source for capital badly needed by Japanese industry facing difficult adjustments after peace brought an end to wartime prosperity. The first product of the new policy was the Washington Conference of 1921–22, in which Japan's alliance with Britain was replaced by a Four Power Pact signed by France, Great Britain, Japan, and the United States. The conference also produced an agreement to limit construction of capital ships (that is, large warships) by the signatories, so as to maintain the existing balance of naval power. Under this agreement Japan promised to build no more than three capital ships for every five built by the United States and five built by Great Britain. In addition, Japan agreed to a Nine Power Treaty in February 1922, in which she acceded to the American Open Door Policy. Then, in October 1922, Japan agreed to withdraw from Siberia.

Also in the same month Japan reached an agreement with China where nationalist sentiment had turned bitterly anti-Japanese when the powers in the Treaty of Versailles (1919) ending the First World War had failed to block Japanese ambitions to succeed the Germans in Shandong even though China, too, had entered the war on the allied side and sent labor battalions to France. At Versailles Japan had agreed, in substance, to the restoration of Chinese sovereignty in Shandong, provided that it retained economic rights there. This was now officially agreed upon. The situation in China itself, however, remained highly unstable. While technically a republican government in Beijing presided over the country's affairs, actual power was fragmented among regional strongmen (warlords) who dominated the areas under their control largely through military means. In their struggles to enlarge and/or protect their holdings, they constantly entered into and betrayed alliances with each other and did not always resist the temptation to intrigue with foreign powers. A case in point was Zhang Zuolin (Chang Tso-lin), warlord of Manchuria, who had the support of the Japanese army.

A general policy of getting along with the United States and conciliating China was followed by Shidehara Kijūrō when he served as foreign minister from 1924 to 1927 and again from 1929 to December 1931. The policy's purpose was to avert another anti-Japanese outburst and costly boycotts of Japanese goods, in order to permit continuing Japanese economic expansion. After 1914 Japanese investments in China accelerated. By 1931 over 80 percent of Japan's total foreign investments were in China, where they accounted for 35.1 percent of all foreign investments in that country.* In 1930, 63 percent of Japanese investments in China were in Manchuria and another 25 percent in Shanghai, where Japanese engaged in trade, banking, and textile manufacturing. They were especially prominent in the latter: in 1930 Japanese owned 39.6 percent of the Chinese textile industry (calculated in spindles). They were also a very major factor in China's iron industry, with interests in Hankou and Manchuria.

Hara was initially succeeded by his finance minister, but this man lacked Hara's political skills and stayed in office only until June 1922. Three nonparty prime ministers followed, two were admirals (Katō Tomasaburō and Yamamoto Gombei) and one a bureaucrat (Kiyoura Keigo) who organized his cabinet entirely from the House of Peers but resigned when faced with a three-party coalition in control of the Diet. The leader of the strongest of these parties, the Kenseikai (Constitutional Government Association, established 1916) was Katō Tataaki, who had last served as foreign minister under Ōkuma during the war. He was now called upon to form a new government.

The most momentous event of the years between Hara and Katō was geological, not political: in September 1923 the Tokyo-Yokohama area was devastated by a severe earthquake followed by a conflagration, which came close to leveling the area. The red sky was visible all night from a hundred miles away. Around 100,000 people lost their lives. As so often in a disaster, the earthquake and fires brought out the best and the worst in the population. While some courageously and selflessly helped their fellows, others joined in hysterical mobs rampaging through the city killing Koreans. The police reacted to the emergency by rounding up socialists, anarchists, and Communists as a "security measure," and there were cases of police torture and killing.

Party Government (1924–1931)

The increase in the power of the parties which peaked during the twenties signified a shift in the balance of power rather than a systemic reordering of power centers. It was the power of the parties that induced Tanaka Giichi, a general from Chōshū much favored by Yamagata, to accept the presidency of the Seiyūkai in 1925. But the party's choice also confirmed the willingness of the parties to work within the existing parameters and highlighted the continued prestige and influence of the army even during the peaceful twenties.

The main accomplishments of party government came during the two years Katō was prime minister (1924–26). Foremost among them was the passage of a "universal" suffrage act, which gave the vote to all males 25 and

* Great Britain accounted for 36.7 percent of foreign investments in China, but this represented only 5 to 6 percent of all British overseas investments. Other countries accounting for over 5 percent of foreign investments in China were: U.S.S.R., 8.4; United States, 6.1; France, 5.9.

over. To still the fears of conservatives apprehensive over the possible spread of radical ideas, a Peace Preservation Law was also passed. This made it a crime to advocate change in the national political structure or to urge the abolition of private property. The Katō government never invoked the law, but it was available to later, less liberal regimes.

Katō also tried to reform the House of Peers (changing its composition and reducing its powers) but succeeded in making only minor changes. His government was more successful in introducing moderate social reforms, including the legalization of labor unions, the establishment of standards for factory conditions, the setting up of procedures for mediating labor disputes, and the provision of health insurance for workers. There was, however, no similar program to alleviate the problems of the rural poor.

Katō soon became embroiled in difficult political negotiations with other parties and the House of Peers among others. When Katō died in 1926, he had not transformed Japanese politics, but he did leave a record of accomplishment that might, under different circumstances, have served as a basis for building a strong system of party rule. That this did not happen is partly the result of the kinds of problems Japan had to face during the five years following Katō's death, but it also reflects the weaknesses of the parties themselves. Even the increased suffrage was a mixed blessing, for the larger electorate made election campaigns more expensive, so that politicians were more open to corruption.

From 1927 to 1929 the government was in the hands of Tanaka Giichi, a general from Chōshū who had entered politics and had been elected president of the Seiyūkai in 1925. In foreign policy Tanaka departed from Shidehara's conciliatory approach. In 1927 the Guomindang (Nationalist Party, Kuomintang) led by Chiang Kai-shek conducted a military expedition to unify China. Under political pressure at home, Tanaka sent an army brigade to Shandong claiming they were needed to protect Japanese lives and property. Clashes with Chinese soldiers ensued. Still more ominous was the assassination, in June 1928, of Zhang Zuolin by a group of Japanese army officers who did not think him sufficiently pliant and hoped their action would pave the way for the seizure of Manchuria. This did not happen. Instead Manchuria was brought under the new Chinese government by Zhang's son, and Tanaka had to recognize the Guomindang regime in Nanjing as the government of China. The Tanaka government itself collapsed when he incurred the displeasure of the Shōwa Emperor (r. 1925–89) and court by failing to obtain from the army suitable punishment for Zhang's murderers. This was one of the rare instances in which the emperor personally intervened in a political decision. The episode was also a harbinger of future unilateral army action, but first, party government had one more chance.

In 1929, Hamaguchi Ōsachi became prime minister, and in 1930 his party, the Minseitō, product of a merger of the Kenseitō and another party, won the election. Shidehara once again became foreign minister and resumed his policy of reconciliation with China and cooperation with Britain and the United States, as signified in the London Naval Treaty of 1930, which included provisions for a 10:10:7 ratio for other than capital ships. Ratification of the treaty was obtained only after heated debate and the forced resignation of the naval chief of staff. It generated much anger and bitterness among the military and members of patriotic societies, such as the young man who shot the prime minister in November 1930. Hamaguchi never recovered from his wounds, but he did not resign until April 1931. From April until December 1931, the Minseitō cabinet continued under Wakatsuki Reijirō (1866–1949), who earlier had served as Katō's home minister and as prime minister from January 1926 to April 1927. Wakatsuki was an experienced politician, but during 1931 the government lost control over the army.

The restlessness of the military was not Hamaguchi's only problem. During most of the twenties, Japan was beset by persistent economic difficulties, including an unfavorable balance of payments, failure of employment opportunities to increase fast enough to keep up with population growth, and a sharp decline in the price of rice, which helped consumers but hurt farmers. The giant *zaibatsu* profited from new technology, the economics of large-scale management, and the failure of weaker firms, but times were hard on small operators. In 1921 a dramatic dockyard strike in Kobe resulted in an eight-hour day, which was extended to other heavy industries, but by and large the union movement progressed only slowly. The same was true of unions of tenants, many of whom now worked for landlords who had moved to the city. Carol Gluck aptly summed up the situation when she characterized Japan as being in "a hiatus between a traditional agrarian paternalism that was disintegrating and a modern industrial paternalism that was still in its formative stages. The landlords were no longer offering succor to distressed tenants, and the companies were not yet acting in a paternalistic role on any significant scale."[8]

To solve the balance of payments problem, there were at various times during the decade calls for the government to cut expenses and follow a policy of retrenchment in order to reduce the cost of Japanese goods and improve their competitive position in international trade. This was the policy followed by Hamaguchi, who also strengthened the yen by returning to the gold standard. Unfortunately, he initiated this program just as the world depression was getting under way and persisted in it despite great economic dislocations and suffering. From 1925 to 1930 the real income of farmers declined by about a third. The poorest were, as always, the hardest hit. As in earlier periods of famine, there were cases of peasants eating bark and digging for roots or maintaining life by selling daughters into brothels.

The government's economic failure undermined the prestige of the political parties, which even in normal times had not enjoyed much public esteem. No mass movement arose directed against them, but there was also little in their record to inspire people to man the barricades in their defense. Their enemies included those dissatisfied not only with their policies and politics but with just about every facet of twenties liberalism and internationalism.

The Arts

Internationalism was represented not only in politics but also in the arts. Tokyo was not far behind Paris or London in experimenting with the latest styles and techniques. Indeed it sometimes led the other capitals, as when in 1922 Frank Lloyd Wright built the Imperial Hotel in Tokyo, a break with Japan's own version of the European Art Nouveau. The American architect, himself influenced by the Japanese tradition, was not the only stimulating visitor from abroad during the Taishō and early Shōwa years. Japanese scientists, for example, could converse with Einstein on his visit to their country in 1919, and music lovers enjoyed concerts by eminent foreign performers: both Kreisler and Heifetz gave concerts in Tokyo in 1923. Bach, Mozart, and Beethoven were becoming as much a part of the musical life of Japan as of any other country, foreshadowing the time when, after the Second World War, the Japanese were acknowledged as the pioneers in teaching young children to play the violin and also became the world's foremost manufacturers of pianos.

A grand piano dominates the four-panel screen (see Figure 10.3) painted in 1926 by Nakamura Daizaburō (1898–1947), which is representative of the followers of the Okakura school. Not only the traditional dress of the young woman playing by the light of an electric lamp but the technique and aesthetics of the painting recall the earliest Japanese art rather than contemporary Western styles. Conversely there were Japanese artists who, like Xu Beihong (Hsü Pei-hung) in China, depicted traditional subjects in Western

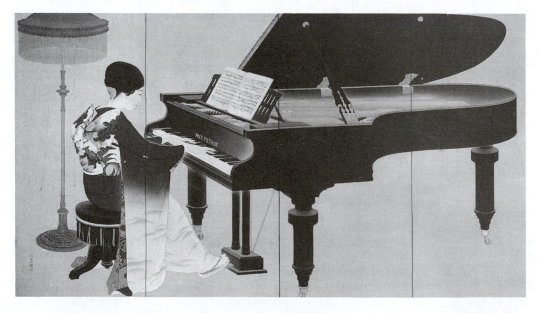

Figure 10.3   Nakamura Daizaburō, *At the Piano*. Four-fold screen, color on silk, 1926, 164.5 cm × 302 cm. Kyoto Municipal Museum of Art.

style, but the most successful modernists were modern in both subject and technique.

A major influence for modernism was the *White Birch (Shirakaba)* journal, which was published from 1910 to 1923 and was edited by a group of humanistic writers, including most notably Shiga Naoya (1883–1971). In contrast to the school of naturalism, the *White Birch* group was dedicated to exploration of the inner self, the pursuit of deeper personal understanding and self-expression, as in the "I novel" or in individualistic art. International in their orientation, seeking to become "children of the world" (their expression), they introduced a host of European writers, published articles on the work and theories of such artists as Van Gogh, Cézanne, and Rodin, and sponsored art exhibits.

Much of the art produced during this period was merely imitative, but one artist who was able to go beyond imitation to develop his own style was Umehara Ryūzaburō, whom we have already encountered as a disciple of Renoir. However, his work also owes something to the Japanese tradition he absorbed while still a child in Kyoto, where he became thoroughly familiar with the styles of Sōtatsu and Korin as still practiced in his family's silk kimono business. The secret of his lively coloring lay in his use of semitransparent gold paint which allowed the color beneath to shine through. A prolific and long-lived artist, he is illustrated here by a work of his old age, painted when he was on his third visit to the French Riviera (see Figure 10.4).

Figure 10.4   Umehara Ryūzaburō, *Cannes.* Oil, 1956, 32.5 cm × 49.5 cm.

Figure 10.5   Tōgō Seiji,
Saltimbanques. Oil,
1926, 114 cm × 71 cm.
Tokyo National Museum
of Modern Art.

European pointillism, cubism, futurism, dadaism, surrealism, and so on, all had their impact on the Japanese avant-garde, here represented by a painting dated 1926 (see Figure 10.5). Tōgō Seiji (1897–1978), was in Europe at the time and was influenced by French and Italian futurism and dadaism, but here exhibits an inclination toward cubism. The title, *Saltimbanques*, is French for "traveling showmen." It is a cheerfully decorative picture, modern in style and subject matter. And it would take a very keen eye, not to speak of considerable imagination, to detect a particularly Japanese element. The painter works in a medium which, for better or worse, is not bound to any particular national tradition, in contrast to the writer whose very language is linked to his historical culture.

Mingei

Many trends converged in the "folk craft" or "folk arts" movement promoted by Yanagi Muneyoshi (or Sōetsu, 1889–1961) who coined the term *mingei* in 1926. His deep belief in the creative genius of the people was in tune with Taishō democracy while his rejection of machine mass production and devotion to the strong, honest beauty created by the anonymous craftsmen working together to create objects for daily use are reminiscent of John Ruskin (1819–1900) and William Morris (1834–1896), founder of the Late Victorian Arts and Crafts Movement. Yanagi, like Morris, championed the dignity of the craftsman and linked the aesthetic beauty of folk art to the ethical qualities under which it was produced. His attempt, in 1927, to establish a commune for *mingei* artists failed, but he succeeded in inspiring a new appreciation for traditional woodcarving, household wares, tableware, woven and dyed cloth, and all kinds of articles made of bamboo, straw, handmade paper, wood (including furniture and traditional buildings), metal, and leather. The list goes on and on to include virtually all the products of traditional workmanship. Such works have now found a home in museums such as the Japan Folk Art Museum in Tokyo (1936). They continue to be displayed, studied, enjoyed, and celebrated today.

Yanagi's interest in folk culture was shared by Yanagida Kunio (1875–1962), Japan's foremost scholar of folklore. The massive survey of folklore he directed in the thirties laid the foundations for a whole field of studies. Yanagida's interest in the expressive side and Yanagi's concern for material culture complemented each other.

Yanagi, however, went beyond preserving and studying the folk craft (his preferred translation of *mingei*) of the past. He also strove to further the production of *mingei* as a living force. Foremost among his associates in the *mingei* movement were four potters: Tomimoto Kenkichi (1886–1963), the Englishman, Bernard Leach (1887–1979), Kawai Kanjirō (1890–1966), and Hamada Shōji (1894–1978). Others worked in other media such as textiles. Among the woodcut artists influenced by Yanagi was Munakata Shikō (see below, p. 294).

Popular Culture

Neither the flow of influence from abroad nor the appreciation of traditional crafts was restricted to the sophisticated or wealthy. After the war there was a wave of Western influence on the pattern of life, affecting people's diet, housing, and dress, particularly in the great cities, where there was a boom in bread consumption, the wearing of Western dress in public became prevalent, and it became the fashion to include at least one Western-style room in a house.

On the Ginza the "modern boy" (*mobo*) and "modern girl" (*moga*) appeared, dressed and coiffured in the very latest styles imported from overseas. They might be on their way to the movies, for film was now coming into its own, throwing off the shackles of the theatrical heritage that had dominated the early years of Japanese film making, when the narrator was as important as the pictures and female roles were played by men. Although there was always an audience for films filled with melodrama and sword action, others dealt with the problems and joys of daily life. It was in the twenties that the foundations were laid for the great achievements to come in Japanese films.

There was also a great increase in sports activity, not least of which was baseball, although the formation of professional teams had to wait until the thirties. Another new sport was golf, including, in that crowded land, "baby" or miniature golf. After golf or tennis, one could relax in a café or a fellow could practice the latest steps with a taxi dancer at the Florida or another dance hall. The old demi-monde dominated by the geisha, a world so fondly chronicled by Nagai Kafū (1879–1959), was on the decline, and modern mass culture was in the ascendancy.

Although centered on the cities, the new popular culture was rapidly diffused now that even the remotest village was accessible by train and car, not to speak of the radio, which was introduced in 1925. Furthermore, mass circulation magazines, some directed at a general audience, others written especially for women or young people, turned out huge printings catering to the unquenchable thirst of the Japanese public for reading matter.

Literature

Among the still active older writers whose reputations were established during the Late Meiji was Shimazaki Tōson, who after *The Broken Commandment* had turned to autobiographical writings published, as was so often the case, serially in magazines. Another master of the autobiographical form was Shiga Naoya, already mentioned as a member of the *White Birch* group, which rejected the pessimism of the naturalists. In the hands of the many lesser writers, the detailed examination of everyday life was apt to produce tedium rather than insight, but there was always a public for such works.

A highly gifted writer who rejected the autobiographical mode was Akutagawa Ryūnosuke (1892–1927), author of some 150 short stories between 1917 and 1927. Many of these are modern psychological reinterpretations of old tales such as can be found in the *Tales from the Uji Collection.* In the West he is probably best known for "Rashomon," a tale in which the story of a murder and rape is told from the viewpoint of three protagonists and a witness. This story inspired one of the finest films of Kurosawa Akira, released in 1950. Akutagawa's carefully crafted stories are frequently eerie, but they are saved from being merely macabre by the keenness of his psychological portrayals. Pessimistic, given to self-doubt, and distressed at the changing world about him, he committed suicide in 1927 citing "a vague unease."

In poetry as in art some dedicated themselves to new experiments, while others continued working with the old forms. In the nineteenth century, Shiki Masaoka (1867–1902), known primarily as a haiku poet, made notable contributions toward revitalizing traditional poetry, and many *tanka* and haiku continued to be written and published in every decade of the twentieth century. Others, however, looked to the West for models of poetry for a modern age. Some even employed the Roman alphabet *(rōmaji).* Foreign influence did not necessarily produce timeless verse; one poet proclaimed, "My sorrow wears the thin garb of one-sided love."[9]

The most admired master of free verse was Hagiwara Sakutarō (1886–1942), who employed the colloquial language to compose poems intensely personal both in their music and in their symbolism. The following is from a collection entitled *Howling at the Moon (Tsuki no hoeru*, 1917):

> *Bamboos*
>
> Out of the shimmering earth
> The bamboos grow, the green
> Bamboos; and there, below,
> Their growing roots grow lean
> As thinlier they grow
> Until their tiny tails,
> A glitter of hairlets make
> Veined meshes, flimsy veils
> Incredible a-quake
>
> Out of the frozen earth
> The bamboos grow, the tough
> Intent bamboos that flow
> Sky-tall with an almost rough
> Interior rage to grow.
> To grow. In hardening frost
> Their knots swell hard with ooze.
> To grow. The blue sky crosses
> With growth, with green bamboos.[10]

A major prose writer was Tanizaki Junichirō (1886–1965), who began with a fascination with the West but gradually returned to the Japanese heritage. His artistic journey was paralleled by his physical move from Tokyo to Kyoto after the great earthquake of 1923. In 1929 he published *Some Prefer Nettles*, a title taken from a line in a poem by Yuan Mei, "some insects eat sugar, some prefer nettles."[11] The protagonist in this novel is unhappily married to a "stridently" modern wife. He finds comfort in the arms of a Eurasian prostitute, symbolic of the West, but, as the novel unfolds, he is increasingly attracted to a traditional Kyoto beauty representing the old culture of Japan. Some of Tanizaki's best work still lay in the future, including his masterpiece, *The Makioka Sisters*, which was written during the Second World War. One theme in this long, panoramic novel is the contrast between two of the sisters, one traditional in appearance and mentality, the other modern. Tanizaki's devotion to tradition also led him to translate *The Tale of Genji* into modern Japanese. An identification with tradition was also to characterize the work of Kawabata Yasunari (1899–1972), but during the twenties this famous writer was just at the beginning of his brilliant literary career.

Intellectual Trends

Japanese students of philosophy were for many years under strong German influence, predominantly that of Kant and Hegel and their later elaborators.

After the war, along with German idealism, the phenomenalism of Husserl and Heidegger and the vitalism of Bergson and Eucken also attracted a Japanese audience. Outstanding among the philosophers who digested Western philosophy and assimilated it into their own original work was Nishida Kitarō (1870–1945), strongly steeped in Buddhism and best known for his philosophy of transcendent nothingness. Other theorists exploring subjects as seemingly far apart as aesthetics and politics grappled with the relationship between the universal principles valid everywhere and accessible to the intellect, and the particularist values imbedded in the unique culture of Japan, which must be apprehended by direct experience. In theoretical as in literary writings, the emphasis tended to be on the latter.

Nishida is said never to have discussed politics in his many years as a professor of philosophy at Kyoto University, but some of the most influential thinkers of the time were also important political theorists. Most widely read were Minobe Tatsukichi (1873–1948) and Yoshino Sakuzō (1878–1933), both deeply versed in German thought. Minobe was a legal scholar who followed his teacher at Heidelberg, Georg Jellinek, in making a distinction between sovereignty, which belongs to the whole state, and the power to rule, which is supervised by the emperor. In this sense, the emperor becomes the "highest organ" of the state, limited by the other components of the state and by the constitution. The constitution, furthermore, in Japan as elsewhere (according to Minobe) allows, and indeed requires, continuing change in the direction of increasing rationality, responsible government, and popular participation. Minobe's work gained wide currency, and his book was the most frequently assigned text in courses on constitutional law. In 1932 he was appointed to the House of Peers.

Yoshino did not obtain such Establishment approval, but his many articles were widely read. A Christian populist and a democrat, he was a philosophical idealist who argued for democracy as an absolute rather than on utilitarian or pragmatic grounds. He also held an idealistic view of the nation and rejected any suggestion that democracy was incompatible with the Japanese tradition: "Those who argue that democracy is not compatible with the national spirit believe in the anachronistic and erroneous notion that the Emperor and people are mutually exclusive of each other."[12] Democracy would fulfill, not diminish, the emperor's role.

The postwar world also witnessed a revival of interest in anarchism and socialism, suppressed in 1911, and Japanese intellectuals were drawn to Marxist ideals even as they were impressed by the Russian Revolution. After a brief period of political activity, Yoshino returned to academic life, but more radical intellectuals continued to seek political involvement. This some could find in the labor movement, but the labor parties formed after passage of the universal suffrage act suffered from an excess of factionalism and a lack of mass participation. This was also true of the Japanese Communist party, which was dominated by intellectuals. Some of these Marxists were people of great personal stature, but none was able to create a Marxism suitable to the particular conditions of Japan, nor did any have theoretical influence on international Marxism. Also more important for its program than for its literary accomplishment was a proletarian literary movement exemplified by such novels as *The Cannery Boat* (1929) by Kobayashi Takiji (1903–33), in which the workers revolt against a brutal captain. Even though much of this literature was propagandistic, it did serve to make the reader and writer more sensitive to social conditions, thereby opening up new terrain for Japanese literature.

These years also saw the beginning of a feminist movement, which campaigned for women's rights, particularly the right to vote, at a time when they were minors under the law and were completely excluded from the political process. Despite the efforts of several organizations and some dedicated leaders, change in this area was very slow.

While leftists were dissatisfied with what they considered the slow pace of progress in Japan, there had long been others who deplored the ills of modernity. Some idealogues, conscious of the hardships suffered by the countryside, condemned the life and values of the cities and called for a return to virtuous agrarianism. Among the most severe critics of the parties and *zaibatsu* was Kita Ikki (1883–1937), who combined advocacy of imperialistic assertiveness abroad with a call for egalitarianism at home to bring emperor and people together. Unhappy with Japan's political organization as well as her stance in the world, he looked not to the electorate or mass popular movements for salvation, but placed his faith in change from above enacted by a few dedicated men. Accordingly, his ideas found a friendly reception in small societies of superpatriots and among young army officers who saw themselves as continuing in the tradition of the *rōnin* who had selflessly terrorized Kyoto during the closing days of the Tokugawa; he also found more recent exemplars among post-Edo "patriots," including the ex-samurai who after Saigō's death had founded the Genyōsha (Black Ocean Society, 1881) in Fukuoka (Northern Kyūshū) and the related Kokuryūkai (Amur River Society, also translated Black Dragon Society, 1901), one dedicated to expansion in Korea, the other concentrating on Manchuria, both employing intimidation and assassination among their techniques.

The story of the attempts made by these men to effect a "Shōwa Restoration" belongs in the thirties, but Kita Ikki's most influential book was written in 1919. The seeds planted in one decade bore fruit in the next. The rejection in the thirties of party government and the general internationalism that had prevailed in the twenties revealed that these had as yet shallow roots. Whether they would have flourished in a gentler international climate remains an open question.

NOTES

1. Mark R. Peattie in Ramon H. Myers and Peattie, eds., *The Japanese Colonial Empire, 1895–1945* (Princeton: Princeton Univ. Press, 1984), p. 8. See p. 10 for colonies as "the ultimate symbol."
2. Samuel Ho in Ibid, pp. 348ff.

3. Quoted in Sōseki Natsume, *Ten Nights of Dream—Hearing Things—The Heredity of Taste*, trans. Aiko Itō and Graeme Wilson (Rutland, Vt. and Tokyo: Charles E. Tuttle, 1974), p. 12.

4. Natsume Sōseki, *The Three Cornered World*, trans. Alan Turney (Chicago: Henry Regnery, 1965), p. iii.

5. Shuji Takashina and J. Thomas Rimer, with Gerald D. Bolas, *Paris in Japan: The Japanese Encounter with European Painting* (St. Louis: The Washington Univ. Press, 1987), p. 105.

6. William P. Malm, "The Modern Music of Meiji Japan," in Donald H. Shively, ed., *Tradition and Modernization in Japanese Culture* (Princeton: Princeton Univ. Press, 1971), p. 300.

7. Arthur E. Tiedemann, "Big Business and Politics in Prewar Japan," in James W. Morley, ed., *Dilemmas of Growth in Prewar Japan* (Princeton: Princeton Univ. Press, 1971), pp. 278–79.

8. Carol Gluck, *Japan's Modern Myths* (Princeton: Princeton Univ. Press, 1985), p. 282.

9. Quoted in Donald Keene, ed., *Modern Japanese Literature: An Anthology* (New York: Grove Press, 1956), p. 20.

10. Hagiwara Sakutarō, *Face at the Bottom of the World and Other Poems*, trans. Graeme Wilson (Rutland, Vt. and Tokyo: Charles E. Tuttle, 1969), p. 51.

11. Arthur Waley, *Yüan Mei, Eighteenth Century Chinese Poet* (New York: Grove Press, 1956), p. 150.

12. Tetsuo Najita, "Some Reflections on Idealism in the Political Thought of Yoshino Sakuzō," in Bernard Silberman and H. D. Harootunian, eds., *Japan in Crisis: Essays on Taishō Democracy* (Princeton: Princeton Univ. Press, 1974), p. 40.

11
Militarism and War

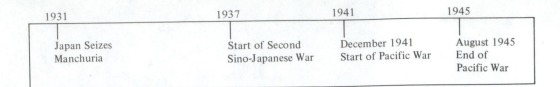

1931	1937	1941	1945
Japan Seizes Manchuria	Start of Second Sino-Japanese War	December 1941 Start of Pacific War	August 1945 End of Pacific War

*F*or much of the world the 1930s were bleak and somber years. In the capitalist nations of the West, the Great Depression ushered in an economic crisis that deepened the rifts in society and threatened existing institutions. In the Soviet Union, struggling to catch up with the West economically, the decade was marred by the brutalities of forced collectivization and Stalin's purge trials. To many people desperate for vigorous action, dictatorship of one kind or another seemed the most effective way of pulling a nation together, and it was not in Italy and Germany alone that fascism was viewed as a non-Communist means to achieve national unity and greatness. The crisis of Western democracy was not lost on observers in East Asia, where traditions of liberal constitutionalism were shallow at best.

During most of the decade those nations that preserved democratic government were preoccupied with domestic problems and the strongest, the United States, was committed to a policy of isolationism. International statesmanship was at a low ebb; national leaders gave only lip service to the principles of collective security embodied in the League of Nations. There was no credible external deterrent to keep Japan from expanding its empire, at China's expense. The future of Nationalist China and Imperial Japan became fatally intertwined when Japan seized Manchuria in 1931. This not only marked a turning point for those directly involved but also revealed the weakness of the League of Nations whose condemnation of Japan was not followed by meaningful sanctions. Those throughout the world who had relied on the community of nations to provide collective security had been proved wrong. The League emerged from the episode badly damaged.

The Manchurian Incident and Its Aftermath

Party government as it developed in the 1920s derived its legitimacy from the emperor, but there were those in Japan who believed that it was failing its sacred trust. In the name of the emperor, the enemies of constitutional government criticized the political manipulations of the Diet leaders, their ties with business, and the lackluster conduct of foreign affairs—especially the policy of accommodation with the West and conciliation of China, exemplified by the Washington Conference of 1921–22. These sentiments animated the members of various patriotic organizations in Japan. They also prevailed in the army, which considered itself an independent agent of the imperial will and resented cuts made in its budget during the twenties. In the army, dissatisfaction with the political ethos and government policies was thus combined with resentment against restrictions imposed by a civilian government and a sense of a separate mission for which the army was responsible to the emperor alone.

Among the most vehement critics of party government were radical egalitarians like Kita Ikki, who favored nationalizing industry, and radical agrarians like Gondo Seikyo (1868–1937), who would have abolished industry altogether and returned Japan to rural simplicity. Although their visions of the future might differ, such men agreed on two things: that the existing government obtruded on the imperial will and must be swept away, and that Japan had a divine mission overseas.

Such ideas formed the rallying point for small societies of extremists given to direct action. Some, like the Cherry Society, which planned an unsuccessful military coup in Tokyo in March 1931, were composed entirely of army officers, none higher in rank than lieutenant colonel. Indeed, the army was a major source of extreme right-wing patriotic discontent. When the government lost control of the army, the gates to imperialist adventurism were flung open.

The assassination of the Manchurian warlord Zhang Zuolin (Chang Tso-lin) in 1928 was the work of men such as these. They hoped that Zhang's murder would lead to a war in which this vast, strategically important and potentially wealthy area would be conquered for Japan. The attempt failed, but the extremists were not discouraged. Indeed, another attempt in this direction appealed to the superpatriots, not only because it might gain Manchuria, but also because it would strengthen their support in the army, increase the army's power and popularity at home, and undermine the government by political parties they so detested. For these champions of a "Shōwa Restoration" felt that party government was a betrayal of the divine emperor, whom they regarded as the very embodiment of Japan's "national polity" (kokutai), a term which became an "incantatory symbol,"[1] all the more powerful for being rather vague.

The shift of attention to Manchuria was also consistent with the ideas of more analytical army men, like Ishiwara Kanji (or Ishihara, 1886–1949), who worked out the plan of attack. He and other students of World War I wanted Japan to control the economic resources of Manchuria as a step toward the attainment of the economic independence required for waging total war. Many officers, concerned with the possibility of war with the Soviet Union, were also mindful of Manchuria's strategic value.

In the fall of 1931 the time seemed ripe, for China was hampered by floods in the Yangzi Valley and the Western powers were neutralized by the depression. The seizure was masterminded by Ishiwara and other officers serving with the Japanese Army on the Liaodong Peninsula. It was these officers, none with a rank higher than colonel, who fabricated an excuse for hostilities: a supposed Chinese attempt to sabotage the South Manchuria Railway Company. And they saw to it that the fighting continued until the army controlled the entire area. Although certain high army officials in Tokyo very likely knew of the plot, it was carried out without the knowledge, let alone the authorization, of the civilian government in Tokyo, which, once informed, tried to halt the operations but found itself powerless to do so. An attempted military coup in Tokyo in October did not immediately topple the government but did succeed in intimidating civilian political leaders. The Wakatsuki government, divided and helpless, resigned in December. It was followed by a Seiyūkai government under Inukai Ki (1855–1932), which for another half year tried to maintain a semblance of party control.

Events moved swiftly on the continent and at home. In Manchuria the army consolidated its hold and established a puppet state, which early in 1932 declared its independence from China. Manchukuo, as it was known, was placed under the titular rule of Puyi who, as an infant, had been the last emperor of China, but it was actually the army's domain. Meanwhile the fighting had spread to China proper; for six strenuous weeks, Japanese and Chinese fought around Shanghai until a truce was finally arranged. Japanese efforts to make a general settlement with China and obtain recognition of Manchukuo were rebuffed and condemned by the League of Nations from which Japan withdrew in March 1933.

A truce was concluded in May 1933 after the Japanese had crossed the Great Wall that spring. The temporary accord left Japanese troops in control of the area north of the Great Wall and provided for a demilitarized zone whose boundaries were marked by the railway line running between Beijing, Tianjin, and Tanggu, but it did not prevent the Japanese from setting up a puppet regime in that area nor from exerting continuous pressure on North China. In December 1935, Japanese army officers failed in their plans to engineer a North Chinese puppet regime, but that there was no common ground for real peace became crystal clear when full-scale war broke out in the summer of 1937. In the meantime, in Manchuria, and now also in Korea, the Japanese concentrated on the development of heavy industry, building up an industrial base on the continent under army control.

Japanese Domestic Politics and the Road to War

At home, 1932 was also an eventful year as members of the patriotic societies continued to implement their schemes by assassinating prominent men, including the head of the house of Mitsui. On May 15 they raided the Tokyo power station, a bank, Seiyūkai headquarters, and the official residence of the prime minister. They assassinated Inukai in his home.

When the men responsible for the May 15 incident were brought to trial, they were treated with great respect. They were allowed to expound their doctrines for days at a time and given a national podium from which to proclaim the selflessness of their patriotic motives. In this way they largely succeeded in creating for themselves an image of martyrdom that won considerable public support. The light sentences that were meted out after the trials were at last completed further discouraged those who hoped for a return to civilian rule. Instead, power shifted away from the political parties and into the hands of civilian bureaucrats and especially the military. In 1936 the leftist Social Mass Party managed to win half a million votes. The following year that party's total climbed to 900,000 votes, and it captured 37 seats in the lower house of the Diet. In that same election the Seiyūkai and Minseitō together polled some 7 million votes, giving them 354 out of a total of 466 seats. But their showing in the polls was to little avail. The parties were too weak to control the military. Those who wished to preserve constitutional government chose to compromise with the military establishment in the hope of averting a complete overthrow of the existing order, as envisioned by the military extremists.

Efforts to achieve political stabilization through a national union government in which all the power centers were represented were fostered by Saionji, the last of the *genrō* who also hoped to protect the throne from involvement in politics. But these met with only partial and temporary success. The next two cabinets, in office from May 1932 to March 1936, did include party men but were headed by admirals, who were considered more moderate than certain potential prime ministers from the army.

A prime source of continued instability were the divisions within each of the power centers. It was not only the political parties and the interests they represented that competed against each other: within the bureaucracies there was rivalry between ministries as well as disagreement between conservative officials and technocrats who envisioned radical restructuring of state and society.

The military too was divided. Not only did the army and navy frequently clash, but the breakdown in discipline evident in the actions in Manchuria and the violence at home, reflected disunity in the army itself. The lines of army factionalism were very complex: for example, there was a division between those who had studied at the Central War College and those who had attended officers' training school. However, two main groups stood out. The more extreme faction, led by Generals Araki Sadao (1877–1966) and Mazaki Jinzaburō (1876–1956), was known as the *kōdōha* or "Imperial Way faction," since it emphasized the imperial mystique and advocated an ill-defined doctrine of direct imperial rule. Like the radical civilian theorists of the right, it opposed existing political and economic institutions and sought a moral and spiritual transformation which would assure a glorious future for both army and country. In contrast the *tōseiha*, or "Control faction," led by General Nagata Tetsuzan (1884–1935), the leading proponent of total war, and including Ishiwara as well as Tōjō Hideki, gave priority to the long-range buildup of the economy and the transformation of Japan into a modern military state.

For a few years after late 1931, the advantage lay with the Imperial Way faction, but it suffered a setback in 1935 when General Mazaki was dismissed from his post as director-general of military education. A lieutenant colonel retaliated by assassinating General Nagata, and the Control faction reacted to this by arresting the officer and laying plans for the transfer of other firebrands to Manchuria. The lieutenant colonel's trial was still in progress when, on February 26, 1936, a group of junior *kōdōha* officers, commanding over a thousand men, seized the center of the capital and killed a number of prominent leaders, although some of their intended victims managed to elude them, including Admiral Okada Keisuke (1868–1952), the prime minister, who escaped by a fluke (his brother-in-law, who looked like Okada, was killed instead). The young officers hoped that their action would bring down the old system and that generals Araki and Mazaki would take the lead in restructuring the state, but these senior generals remained aloof. As in 1928, the emperor intervened, and the navy responded to the crisis with vigor. On the third day of the insurrection, the rebels surrendered. This time the leaders were tried rapidly and in secret. One of those who perished at the hands of a firing squad was Kita Ikki, who had not participated in the mutiny but was too closely associated with the young officers and their movement to escape punishment.

The elimination of the Imperial Way faction actually increased the army's power in government, since it could now threaten a second mutiny if it did not get its way, but the army still had to take into consideration the wishes of other components of the power elite. However, a substantial increase in the military budget for the army and navy did occur. Furthermore, Japan withdrew from the naval limitation agreement. This opened the possibility that it might have to confront the combined might of the Western powers and the U.S.S.R. The army's strategic planners thought primarily in terms of a war with the latter, thus providing a strong inducement for Japan to sign an anti-Cominterm Pact with Germany in December 1936.

Domestically there ensued an intensification of propaganda and indoctrination, coupled with a continuation of repression directed at the radical left and also victimizing those whose ardor for emperor and national polity (kokutai) was deemed insufficient. The most notorious case took place in 1935 when Minobe, the distinguished legal theorist, was charged with demeaning the emperor by considering him merely "the highest organ of the state." Minobe defended himself with spirit but was forced to resign from the House of Peers. Even then, in 1936 while living in seclusion, the old man suffered an attempt on his life which left him wounded. By that time his books had been banned. Censorship increased in severity, and expressions of intense national chauvinism filled the media.

The abandonment of the gold standard and the military buildup enabled Japan to recover from the depth of the Depression, but agriculture remained depressed and small firms benefited much less than did the zaibatsu.

War with China

The international situation was very problematic. The great powers refused to recognize Manchukuo or agree that Japan was entitled to an Asian version of the Monroe doctrine. Nor was anyone able to devise a formula regarding China acceptable both to the Chinese government and the Japanese army which, after its conquest of Manchuria, was steadily moving into "autonomous zones" in North China. Until the summer of 1937, the

Japanese pressure was primarily economic and political, but there was the danger that an unplanned military incident might escalate into a major war. This became more likely after December 1937 when Chiang Kai-shek was kidnapped in Xian by Manchurian forces who insisted on fighting the Japanese rather than Chinese Communists.

Matters came to a head in July 1937 when there was a clash between Chinese and Japanese soldiers on the Marco Polo bridge outside of Beijing and the Chinese refused Japanese demands for further concessions. The conflict rapidly expanded into large-scale fighting. By the end of July the Japanese were in possession of Beijing and Tianjin, and in August Japanese forces attacked Shanghai, where Chiang used some of his best German-trained troops in three months of bloody fighting, with heavy casualties. After Shanghai came Nanjing, which fell in December, followed by the notorious "Rape of Nanjing." Japanese soldiers went on a rampage, terrorized the inhabitants, killing and raping, burning and looting. When, after seven weeks, it was all over, at least 52,000 people were dead. The Japanese acquired a reputation for terrible cruelty, which stiffened the Chinese determination to resist.

Japan's prime minister at this time was Prince Konoe Fumimaro (1891–1945), a descendant of the Fujiwaras and protégé of Saionji. He was to hold office from June 1937 to January 1939 and from July 1940 to July 1941. Japanese policy making continued to be a very complicated process. The general staff, for example, did not share the optimism of the armies in the field, yet the government continued to expand the war, encouraged by a string of victories. As the war escalated so did the Japanese government's aims and rhetoric. What had begun as a search for a pro-Japanese North China turned into a holy crusade against the West and Communism. Unable to obtain Chinese recognition of Manchukuo, the Konoe government in 1938 declared Chiang's regime illegitimate and vowed to destroy it. Japanese troops continued their advance, taking Canton in October, Wuhan in December. Chiang still showed no inclination to submit. In November Konoe proclaimed Japan's determination to establish a "New Order in East Asia" to include Japan, Manchukuo, and China in a political, economic, and cultural union, a bastion against (Western) imperialism and against Soviet Communism. Those who did not see the light were to be brought to their senses by force.

In the summer of 1937 Japanese plans had called for a three-month campaign by three divisions at a cost of 100 million yen to destroy the main Chinese force and take possession of key areas while waiting for Chiang to ask for peace, but by the following spring they were preparing orders for 20 divisions and had appropriated over 2.5 billion yen with no end in sight. This occurred in the face of Chinese determination to resist at all cost. Following a strategy of "trading space for time," the Chinese Nationalist government moved its capital to Chongqing in Sichuan where it was joined by many refugees (see Figure 11.1). There Chiang held on gamely.

In 1940, when it became obvious that the Chinese would not bow to their demands, the Japanese set up their own puppet regime in Nanjing, headed by Wang Jingwei (Wang Ching-wei), erstwhile leader of the left wing of the

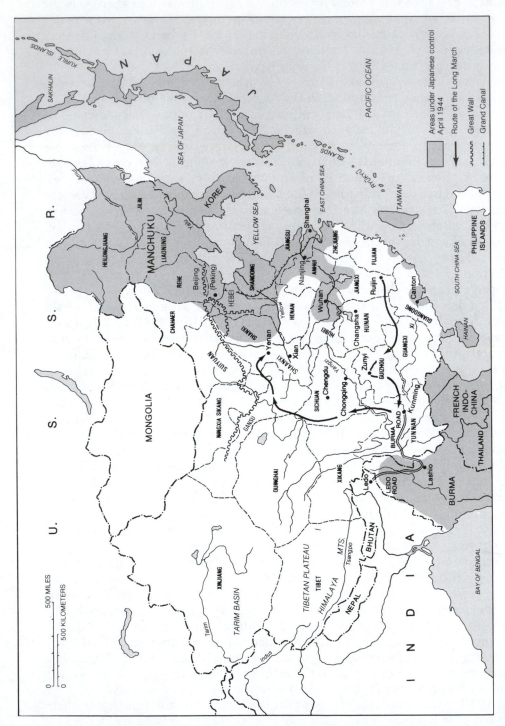

Figure 11.1 China, 1930–Spring 1944 (For Japan's maximum occupation of China, see Figure 11.4.)

Guomindang. This however, did little to reduce the role of the Japanese army in China, which, instead of enjoying the anticipated rapid victory, became bogged down in patrolling the best it could a vast area inhabited by resentful people (see Figure 11.2).

At home in Japan, wartime controls were imposed and a Central Planning Board was instituted, but the *zaibatsu* retained major economic powers. Unless a settlement with China was reached soon, the military expenses would exceed the capacity of the consumer industries and drain the export sector needed to earn the foreign exchange required for attaining the self-sufficiency sought by the believers in the doctrine of total war. That precisely such a total war would come before Japan was ready became increasingly plausible. At each step there were some leaders who wanted to hold back Japan's military advance, but the expansionists prevailed.

Expansion of the War into a Pacific War

The U.S.S.R. remained a major military and foreign policy concern for Japan throughout the thirties. During 1937–40 there were three military confrontations along Russia's frontier with Korea and Manchukuo. These operations, which increased in scale, involved the deployment of armor, artillery, and aircraft. The Japanese fought well, but the Soviets proved much more than a

Figure 11.2 *Refugees Crowding onto Trains Bound for Guilin,* woodcut by Cai Dizhi.

match. The last and most severe conflict cost Japan 18,000 men and resulted in an armistice.

In the grand arena of global politics, Japan was caught off guard diplomatically when Germany, without any warning, came to terms with the Soviet Union in August 1939. Japan was therefore neutral when the Second World War began in Europe shortly afterward. However, the dramatic success of the German blitzkrieg strengthened the hands of those in Tokyo who agreed with War Minister Tōjō that Japan should take advantage of the situation and "not miss the bus." In September 1939, Konoe signed the Tripartite Pact forming an alliance with Germany and Italy. Hindsight reveals that this marked a major turning point on the road to disaster.

The Germans again surprised the Japanese in June 1941 when Hitler invaded Russia. While some army men maintained that Japan should join the attack on the U.S.S.R., the navy wanted to advance into the oil and mineral rich south. As Alvin D. Coox pointed out, many army leaders saw this as a way out of the China impasse, "apparently convinced that the best way to climb out of a hole was to widen it."[2] Officially, Japan's mission was now expanded into the creation of a "Greater East Asian Co-Prosperity Sphere," but the underlying perception was that without the resources of Southeast Asia, Japan would never attain economic security.

Konoe hoped that, armed with the Tripartite Pact, he would be able to reach his aims without going to war with the United States, but the American government was becoming increasingly alarmed over Japanese expansion. When in the summer of 1941 Japan moved troops into southern Indo-China, the United States, Britain, and Holland (then in control of the East Indies, modern Indonesia) retaliated by applying the economic sanctions they had withheld in 1931. An embargo on scrap iron was serious but the crucial product cut off from Japan was oil.

America and Japan were on a collision course. To quote Michael Barnhart, "The Japanese Empire was determined to retain the rights and privileges it considered necessary for its economic and political security. The United States thought these rights and privileges contrary to its own deeply held principles and to the survival of what were now in effect its allies in the struggle against global aggression."[3] The United States was determined that Japan should withdraw from China as well as Indo-China. For Japan this would have meant a reversal of the policy pursued in China since 1931 and the relinquishing of the vision of Japanese primacy in East Asia. Dependent on oil and rubber from Southeast Asia, the Japanese were in no position to carry on protracted negotiations. Their choice was to fight or retreat. It is a bitter irony that Japan now prepared to go to war to attain the self-sufficiency that its proponents of total war had once considered a precondition for war.

When it became clear to Konoe that the situation had reached an impasse, he resigned, to be followed by General Tōjō Hideki (1884–1948), prime minister from October 1941 to July 1944 (see Figure 11.3). When last-minute negotiations proved fruitless, the Japanese decided on war as the least unpalatable alternative. It began on December 7, 1941, with a surprise

Figure 11.3   General Tōjō.

attack on Pearl Harbor, in Hawaii, which destroyed 7 American battleships and 120 aircraft, and left 2,400 dead.

Japan at War

Well before Pearl Harbor, the effects of the continued war in China were felt by the Japanese people as militarization and authoritarianism increased at home. The National General Mobilization Law of 1938 strengthened the prime minister at the expense of the Diet, and the government began to place the economy on a war basis, with rationing, economic controls, and resource allocations. However, those who wanted to turn Japan into a radically restructured national defense state did not get their way and getting the various centers of economic and political power to pull together remained a problem to the end.

In October 1940, the political parties were merged into the Imperial Rule Assistance Association, which, however, did not become a mass popular party along the lines of European fascism but served primarily as a vehicle for the dissemination of propaganda throughout Japan. Similarly labor unions were combined into a single patriotic organization. Great pressures were exerted to bring educational institutions and the public communications media into line so that the whole of Japan would speak with one collective voice. To effect the "spiritual mobilization" of the country, the government tried to purge Western influence from Japanese life. Not only were foreign liberal ideas banned, but such elements of popular culture as permanent waves and jazz, so popular during the twenties, were now suppressed. Efforts were made to remove Western loan words from the language, and the people were bombarded with exhortations to observe traditional values and revere the divine emperor. To mobilize the public down to the ward level, the people were formed into small neighborhood organizations.

Economically the war entailed a greater role for government not only in industry and commerce but also in agriculture. As Ann Waswo has shown, during the war "in purely economic terms and in terms of local political influence, ordinary farmers made significant gains."[4] The war years were hard on rural landlords, already hurt by the Depression, while ordinary tenant farmers benefitted from measures to control inflation such as the imposition of rent control of 1939, as well as government efforts to increase production by allocating fertilizer. In the last years of the war, it paid much larger bonuses to farm operators than to noncultivating landlords. As ever, war proved a potent catalyst for change.

Before the war was over the people were to suffer a great deal, but at first the war went spectacularly well for Japan. By the middle of 1942 Japan controlled the Philippines, Malaya, Burma, and the East Indies, and was assured of the cooperation of friendly regimes in Indo-China (controlled by Vichy France) and in Thailand. However, Japan's attempt to win over the population of the conquered areas by encouraging their native religious traditions, exploiting their resentment against Western imperialism, and teaching them the Japanese language was more than offset by Japan's own imperialistic exploitation, by the harshness of its rule, and by the cruelty of its soldiers, brutalized by the treatment meted out to them in the Japanese army. The slogan "Asia for the Asians" did not disguise the realities of what Mark R. Peattie has characterized as a "mutant colonialism." In his words, "the tightening demands on the energies, loyalties, and resources of Japan's colonial peoples by a nation at war with much of Asia and most of the West transmogrified an authoritarian but recognizably 'Western' colonial system into an empire of the lash, a totalitarian imperium, that dragged along its peoples as it staggered toward defeat."[5]

Things were particularly bad in Korea. The Japanese relentlessly stamped out Korean nationalism, sending its leaders into prison, exile, or underground activities. In the late thirties the Japanese expanded their suppression of political nationalism into an attack on Korean cultural identity. In line with a policy of total forced cultural assimilation, they stopped Korean language instruction in all secondary schools in 1938, and soon elementary schools followed suit. No longer could Korean children learn their own language in school; the use of Japanese was mandatory. In 1940 the Korean press was closed down. The Japanese made strong efforts to propagate the official State Shinto. To help the war effort they first launched a movement of voluntary conscription. Then, in 1943, military service became compulsory. At the same time, the Koreans had to bear the hardships and deprivations of war.

In China the Japanese forces ended up concentrated in the cities and guarding their lines of supply, but they did not have the manpower to patrol rural areas constantly and effectively. Instead, in the areas nominally under Japanese control, the Chinese Communists skillfully mobilized the peasant resistance. At best, people in occupied China went about their daily affairs as well as they could, but Japanese arrogance alienated countless Chinese. Humane behavior on the part of some individual Japanese was overshadowed by acts of cruelty that evoked Chinese hatred and resistance. Most notorious was the "kill all, burn all, destroy all" campaign carried out by the Japanese in 1941 and 1942 in parts of North China in retaliation for a Chinese Communist offensive. Implemented literally, the Japanese did hurt the Chinese Communists badly, but they also helped turn apolitical peasants into determined fighters. Furthermore, to the south, the Japanese puppet regime of Wang Jingwei was too obviously controlled by the Japanese army ever to gain credibility, let alone popular support. Throughout the war, China was a major drain on the Japanese military, but its strategic importance was greatly reduced when the Allies adopted a grand strategy that gave it secondary priority.

In June 1942 Japan was checked at the battle of Midway (see Figure 11.4). The Americans, taking advantage of advance knowledge of Japanese movements obtained from breaking the Japanese secret code, destroyed many Japanese planes and sank four Japanese aircraft carriers while losing only one of their own. The use of aircraft carriers and the extensive deployment of submarines, which took a tremendous toll of vital Japanese shipping, were two of the factors contributing to Japan's ultimate defeat. Another was the island-hopping strategy whereby the American forces seized islands selectively for use as bases for further advances, bypassing others with their Japanese forces intact but out of action. The closer the American forces came to the Japanese homeland, the easier it was for them to bomb Japan itself. Such raids were aimed not only at military and industrial installations, but also at economic targets and population centers. Incendiary bombs were dropped in order to sap the morale of the people, who by the last years of the war, were suffering from scarcities of all kinds, including food and other daily necessities, many of which were available only on the black market. The last year of the war was especially terrible; on one night in March 1945, some 100,000 people died as the result of a firebomb raid on Tokyo, and a similar raid in May devastated another large part of Japan's capital city. Short of resources, and with its cities in ruins, Japan during the last months of the war was reduced to desperate measures, such as the use of flying bombs directed by suicide pilots, called kamikaze after the "divine wind" that once had saved the land from the Mongols.

While internal propaganda persisted until the end in urging the people to ever greater efforts, it was clear to some political leaders that Japan could not win. After the fall of Saipan, largest of the Mariana Islands, General Tōjō was forced out of office in July 1944, but there was no change either in

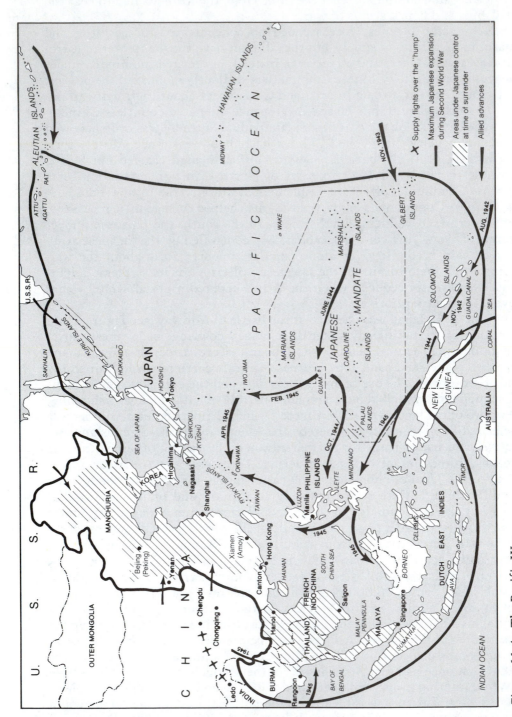

Figure 11.4 The Pacific War.

the fortunes of war or in policy under his successor General Koiso Kuniaki (1880–1950). Koiso remained in office until April 1945, when he was succeeded by Admiral Suzuki Kantarō (1867–1948). Some civilian leaders sent out peace feelers to the Allies, but their efforts were hampered by the noncooperation of the Soviet Union, anxious to have the war continue long enough to allow it to participate, and by the demand issued at Potsdam in July 1945, insisting on Japan's unconditional surrender. The demand for unconditional surrender reflected the Allied belief that it had been a mistake to allow the First World War to end in an armistice rather than in a full capitulation. The Allies felt that the armistice had permitted Hitler to claim that Germany had been "betrayed" into defeat, not beaten on the field of battle, and that he had been able to use this emotionally charged argument to generate the popular support that brought the Nazi party to power. Determined not to commit a similar mistake in the Second World War, the Allies demanded an unconditional surrender. But the insistence on an unconditional surrender actually stiffened Japanese resistance because it left the fate of the emperor in doubt, and this was impossible for the Japanese to accept.

The end came in August 1945. On August 6 the United States dropped an atomic bomb on Hiroshima (see Figure 11.5) in southwestern Honshū, razing over 80 percent of the buildings and leaving some 200,000 people dead

Figure 11.5   Hiroshima. Through the vault over the Memorial Cenotaph for the Atomic Bomb Victims can be seen the Atomic Bomb Memorial Dome. The steel skeleton of the dome and the gutted building (formerly the city's Industrial Promotion Hall) have been left standing unaltered, in witness to the tragedy.

or injured and countless others to continue their lives under the specter of radiation sickness. This holocaust added a new chapter to the horrors of war.

Two days later, on August 8, the U.S.S.R. entered the war, and the next day the United States dropped a second atomic bomb, this time on Nagasaki. Twice during these fateful days a government deadlock was broken by the personal intervention of the emperor, each time in favor of peace. Even after the final decision for peace, diehards tried to continue the war by a last resort to violence in the tradition of the terrorists who had first helped steer Japan toward militarism and war. They set fire to the homes of the prime minister and president of the privy council and invaded the imperial palace in search of the recording of the emperor's peace message, but they failed. When all was lost, several leaders, including the war minister, committed ritual suicide.

On August 15, the imperial recording was broadcast over the radio, and throughout Japan the people, for the first time, heard the voice of their emperor. In the formal language appropriate to his elevated status, he informed them that the war was lost. This is how Ōe Kenzaburō, ten years old at the time, recollects the impact of the broadcast:

> The adults sat around their radios and cried. The children gathered outside in the dusty road and whispered their bewilderment. We were most confused and disappointed by the fact that the Emperor had spoken in a *human* voice, no different from any adult's. None of us understood what he was saying, but we had all heard his voice. One of my friends could even imitate it cleverly. Laughing, we surrounded him—a twelve year old in grimy shorts who spoke with the Emperor's voice. A minute later we felt afraid. We looked at one another; no one spoke. How could we believe that an august presence of such awful power had become an ordinary human voice on a designated summer day?[6]

Japan and East Asia at the End of the War

Defeat brought an end to the half century during which Japan was the dominant military and political power in East Asia. It marked the dissolution of the Japanese Empire, for Japan was made to relinquish not only Manchuria and other areas seized since 1931, but all gains since 1895. It thus opened a new phase in the history of Taiwan and Korea. The defeat of Japan also initiated a new phase in the history of South and Southeast Asia, where former colonies resisted the return of Western colonial masters. Here, as generally in the world, the end of the war marked the beginning of the end of colonialism. However, the demise of the Japanese empire left a heritage of suspicion and distrust, especially intense among the Korean and Chinese people.

The impact of defeat on Japan was far-reaching. At the time, within Japan itself as well as abroad, it was perceived as marking a sharp break with the past, for it thoroughly discredited the militarists and all they stood for. As so often in the study of history, the perspective afforded by another half a century reveals that many old patterns survived after all, even as significant changes took hold. But that would seem the case equally for any of history's "turning points."

It took further warfare to determine the future of the rest of East Asia. Until 1949 China was still a subject of contention between forces locked in civil war. The end of the great war brought no peace to that long-suffering country. Nor would it permit a peaceful determination of the future of Korea and Vietnam.

On the broad international scene, the war left the United States and the Soviet Union as the two giant powers who maintained a presence in East Asia and had the capacity to influence events in that part of the world. And Hiroshima and Nagasaki had demonstrated just how dangerous a place that world could be.

NOTES

1. The term "incantatory symbol" comes from Masao Maruyama, in Ivan Morris, ed., *Thought and Behavior in Modern Japanese Politics*, Expanded edition (New York: Oxford Univ. Press, 1969), p. 376.
2. Alvin D. Coox in Peter Duus, ed. *The Cambridge History of Japan*, Vol. 6: *The Twentieth Century*. (Cambridge: Cambridge Univ. Press, 1988), p. 324.
3. Michael A. Barnhart, *Japan Prepares for Total War: The Search for Economic Security, 1919–1941* (Ithaca: Cornell Univ. Press, 1987), p. 234.
4. Ann Waswo in *The Cambridge History of Japan*, Vol. 6, p. 104.
5. Mark R. Peattie in Ibid., p. 269. For "mutant colonialism," see p. 270.
6. Ōe Kenzaburō, *A Personal Matter*, trans. John Nathan (New York: Grove Press, 1968), pp. vii–viii.

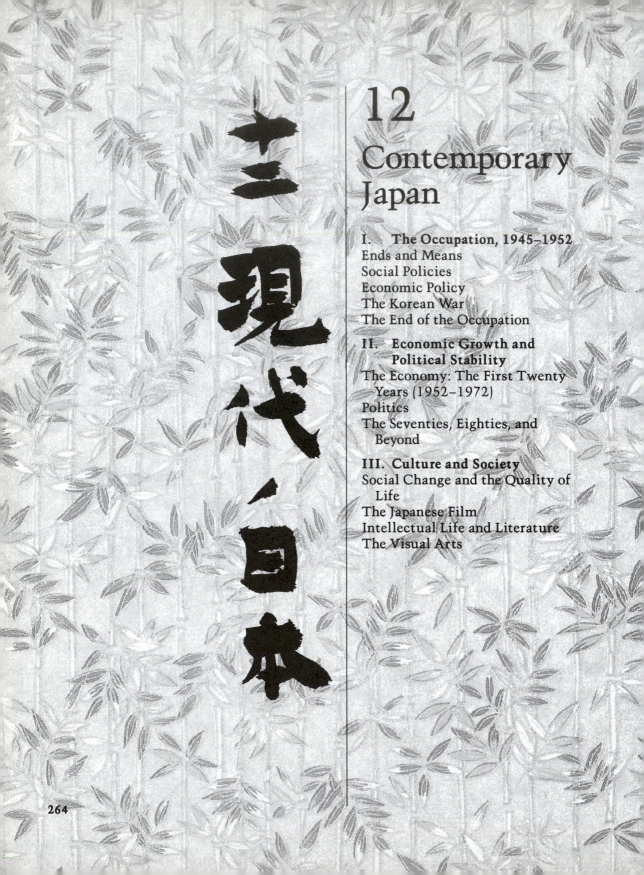

12
Contemporary Japan

1952 - Termination of the Occupation	**1968** - Kawataba Awarded Nobel Prize
1954 - Resignation of Prime Minister Yoshida	**1971** - Floating of the Dollar
1955 - Formation of the Liberal	**1972** - Visit of Prime Minister Tanaka to Beijing
Democratic Party (LDP)	**1976** - Lockheed Scandal
1956 - Admission of Japan to the United Nations	**1980** - Automobile Production Exceeds That of U.S.
1960 - Demonstrations against Continuation of	**1989** - Death of Shōwa Emperor
U.S.-Japan Mutual Security Treaty	Recruit Scandal

Throughout East Asia, the Second World War was followed by a period of change unprecedented in its rapidity and scope, affecting the direction of civilization, economic systems and social structure, and the very rhythm of the lives of millions of people. Two wars fought in Korea and Vietnam present grim proof that change did not always come peacefully nor without outside interference.

In China, Korea, and Japan the basic parameters of postwar history were decided during the years immediately following the Second World War. The triumph of the Chinese Communists, the war in Korea, and the remolding of Japan under the Occupation all fell into those years. This is not the case with the history of Vietnam, but since it too developed out of problems left unsettled by the Second World War, it is also discussed in this chapter.

The Second World War destroyed the Japanese Empire, confirmed the eclipse of the Western European powers begun by the First World War, and hastened the end of the old colonialism. In Asia the greatest of the empires, that of Britain, was dismantled as India and Burma attained independence (1947) followed by the Malayan Peninsula (1957) leaving only Hong Kong as a Crown Colony scheduled to revert to Chinese rule in 1997. However, the Dutch in Indonesia and, especially, the French in Indo-China did not yield as gracefully as did the British. Meanwhile only two world powers, the United States and the Soviet Union, had the resources to exercise major influence over events in East Asia. During the immediate postwar years they developed a bitter Cold War rivalry that, despite an occasional thaw, remained the prime fact of international relations.

PART I. THE OCCUPATION, 1945–1952

The war left Japan in ruins, its cities largely destroyed, the economy wrecked. The devastation extended also to the psyche of the Japanese people, for whom the known world had ended in a cataclysm of destruction. Unprepared for defeat, they could not turn to their own history for guidance, for never before in historic times had their country been occupied by a foreign victor. They had no inkling of what the future held in store. The whole nation now found itself in a psychological position not unlike that of the rare Japanese soldier who during the war, despite his best efforts and contrary to all expectation, found himself an American prisoner. Such men, their old orientations and expectations shattered, were usually most cooperative toward their former enemies, and the Japanese people too were disposed to cooperate with the Occupation authorities. In both cases, decent treatment of the defeated also helped. Thus, when defeat came, the Japanese evacuated many women to the countryside and even the government ordered its female employees out of town. It is not difficult to imagine people's relief when such measures turned out to have been unnecessary.

Ends and Means

In theory the Occupation was placed under the authority of the Far Eastern Commission, which sat in Washington and whose members included representatives of all the countries that had fought Japan, but actual control was in American hands. The Japanese government continued to function but did so according to the directives and suggestions of the Occupation authorities who were responsible to the American government. At the head of the Occupation was General MacArthur, Supreme Commander for the Allied Powers (SCAP). Despite the reference to Allies in the title and the presence of some British and Commonwealth officials, the Occupation was essentially American. In MacArthur it had a leader who won easy credibility, a commanding figure, confident in his sense of historical mission, a military man who commanded respect and exuded confidence. Despite the popular image of MacArthur as a "blueeyed shogun,"[1] and his undoubted influence, he did not dictate specific policies. These were fashioned in a complex process in which Washington, the occupation bureaucracy, and the Japanese participated, and which reflected divisions within as well as between these entities.

Among the initial and pressing tasks of the Occupation was the disarming of the Japanese military and the provision of relief to prevent famine. The widespread destruction of capital goods and industrial plants, a soil starved for lack of fertilizers, the loss of the natural resources from the former empire and of the entire mercantile fleet, and the need to provide for six million Japanese expatriates and refugees from overseas threatened economic catastrophe. In this situation, suffering was unavoidable. By supplying food and medical supplies, the Occupation authorities helped to avert the worst. But it was not until around 1947 that the United States, in the light of the emerging Cold War, became seriously concerned with rebuilding the Japanese economy, particularly Japanese industrial strength.

The basic long-term policy of the Occupation was to demilitarize Japan and turn the country into a peaceful and democratic state; or, we might say, "a peaceful because democratic state," reflecting the optimistic American belief that the one equaled the other. The American conviction of the righteousness of their political values, as well as confidence in the problem-solving powers of American "know-how," was an important ingredient in the history of the Occupation.

Demilitarization entailed the dismantling of the military establishment and a purge from positions of political and economic leadership of those most closely associated with the establishment that had led the country to war. Individuals charged with wartime brutality were placed on trial. At the top, twenty-eight leaders were charged with responsibility for the war and were brought to trial before an international tribunal in Tokyo, which sat from May 1946 to April 1948. When the sentences were handed down in November 1948, seven leaders were condemned to die. Foremost among them was Tōjō, the rather colorless general who had headed Japan's wartime government. His role during the war had been more like a chairman of the board than a dictator, but wartime propaganda had cast him as a Japanese Hitler, and it was as such that he was tried and condemned. The lengthy judicial proceedings produced voluminous records but never attained the legal clarity nor the moral authority achieved by the trial of Nazi leaders at Nuremberg.

In the end, the number purged came to around 200,000 with about half in the military. However, most of these men were later reinstated, and some became very prominent. If it was the military elite who lost the most, the decision of the Occupation to operate through, rather than replace, the

Figure 12.1
General Douglas
MacArthur and the
Emperor of Japan.

existing government made for a high level of continuity within the bureaucracy. This contributed to the continuing importance of the bureaucracy even after a new constitution placed government on a new footing.

The emperor was not charged with war crimes, but his person was subjected to a process of demythification. He was required to substitute a more open life-style (akin to that of the British monarch, for example) for the secluded and ritualized existence traditionally led by Japanese emperors. An example of the demythification process was the emperor's unprecedented visit to MacArthur at his headquarters. The resulting photograph (Figure 12.1) showing the stiffly formal emperor standing next to the open-shirted general caused considerable shock and dismay throughout Japan. In his New Year's message of 1946 the emperor publicly and explicitly denied his divinity, and under the new constitution he became a symbol of the nation.

This constitution, which went into effect in May 1947, was practically dictated by the Occupation. It stipulated that sovereignty belongs to the people, placed the highest political authority in the hands of the Diet (to which the executive was now made responsible), and established an independent judiciary. Another noteworthy set of political changes were those decreasing the power of the central government, particularly the Home Ministry, and fostering local self-government. Accompanying these structural changes were provisions for universal suffrage and human rights, including the equality of women. A unique feature was the renunciation of war that became Article IX of the constitution. This stipulates, "The Japanese people forever renounce war as a sovereign right of the nation and the threat or use of force as a means of settling international disputes" and goes on to say, "land, sea, and air forces, as well as other war potential, will never be maintained."[2] In this way the authors of the constitution hoped to incorporate peacefulness into the very framework of the new Japanese state.

Social Policies

The authorities at SCAP headquarters knew that Japan could not be turned into a democracy simply by changing the political system. Consequently they tried to change Japanese society itself and to do so in the relatively short time allotted to them. Since many American officials lacked previous study or experience in Japan and high military officials could be quite narrow in their outlook, there was a tendency to rely excessively on American prototypes without taking into sufficient account Japan's own experience and situation.

An example of limited success was the reform of the educational system. This was restructured to conform to the American sequence of elementary school, junior high school, high school, and college. The Japanese were forced to eliminate their old technical schools and special higher schools, which previously covered the eleventh to thirteenth years of education and prepared students for university study. Under the old system, only the student elite had access to a university education, but under the new, all students were to be given equal educational opportunities through high school. In an effort to expand opportunities for higher education, many of the old technical and higher schools were upgraded to become universities. But these new universities were not of a quality comparable to the old established schools like Tokyo University. Competition for admission to this and other prestigious universities remained brutal. Students found themselves embroiled in a veritable "examination hell."

In order to reform the content of education, the Occupation abolished the old ethics courses and purged textbooks fostering militaristic and authoritarian values. Its attack on these old values was rather successful, especially since they had been already largely discredited by defeat. Similarly, language reform found ready acceptance: the list of standard characters, many of them simplified, issued by the cabinet in 1946 (1,850 tōyō kanji) required only minor modifications and additions when revised in 1981 (the current system of 1,945 jōyō kanji).

The Occupation was rather less successful in its attempts to create a positive sense of individual civic responsibility and citizenship. Social change entails a transformation of values and thus naturally takes longer than institutional change but changes in the legal system can encourage social change. Among the Occupation's notable efforts in this area were measures to enhance the status of women and limit the powers and privileges of the family's male head. The new constitution stated explicitly, "Marriage shall be based upon the mutual consent of both sexes, and it shall be maintained through mutual cooperation, with equal rights of husband and wife as a basis."[3] The presence of many thousands of Americans in their country also gave the Japanese an unusual opportunity to observe foreign mores. It may have encouraged them to become somewhat more relaxed toward authority and also stimulated a measure of cosmopolitanism.

Economic Policy

It was generally recognized that the desired political and social changes demanded an economic foundation, and the authorities set about restructuring the Japanese economy. Most successful in this respect was the program of land reform. This prohibited absentee landlordism and restricted the amount of land a resident landowner could hold to a maximum of 7 1/2 acres to work himself and another 2 1/2 acres to rent out (except in Hokkaidō where the average farm is 12 1/2 acres because the climate precludes intensive rice cultivation). Anything in excess had to be sold to the government, which resold it to former tenants. There was provision for compensation for the landlords, but inflation made this meaningless. The old inequity in the countryside was eliminated. In terms of productivity too, the land policy was a success, for the agrarian sector was the first to recover.

In the urban industrial sector, the Occupation tried to eliminate or at least to reduce the concentrations of economic power, which Americans viewed as a major component of Japanese authoritarianism. One policy was to foster labor unions. The constitution guaranteed "the right of workers to organize and to bargain and act collectively."[4] As intended, a vigorous union movement developed, but contrary to American wishes, the Japanese unions did not, like the American AFL and CIO, limit themselves to economic demands. Much like European unions, they were political in orientation, developing into labor arms of the Socialist and Communist parties. In February 1947, the Occupation banned a planned general strike and thereafter was less friendly toward the unions. Laws prohibiting public employees from striking followed.

On the management and ownership side, the Occupation did break up the old holding companies and purged the old *zaibatsu* families from positions of economic leadership. Contrary to initial expectations, however, this did not lead to genuine decentralization. Where old systems were broken up, new and equally pervasive patterns of trade and finance developed, bearing a marked resemblance to the old. Furthermore, a plan to break up operating companies petered out: of 1,200 companies initially considered, only 28 were, in the end, broken up. Economic power and decision making remained concentrated. The reasons for this are instructive for understanding the accomplishments and failures of the Occupation as a whole, for they include both a Japanese and an American component.

On the Japanese side, strong support for land reform contrasted with a marked lack of enthusiasm for American-style trust busting. Few shared the American faith in the ultimate benefits of maximum competition. Instead, the feeling was that Japanese companies needed to be large in order to compete in the international market. Radicals and conservatives disagreed about ownership and control, not about the structure of industry and commerce.

Decentralization of the economy also faltered because it was abandoned in line with a shift in American policy already signaled by the ban on the 1947 general strike. In an atmosphere of mounting Cold War tension and in line with what is frequently called the "reverse course," economic and strategic considerations came to prevail. Increasingly, the United States saw Japan, called by the Secretary of State "the workshop of Asia," as a potentially valuable and much-needed ally after the victory of the Chinese Communists in 1949. On the advice of Joseph Dodge, a Detroit banker sent out by Washington on a study mission, the value of the yen was set at 360 to the dollar, low even then, to encourage exports by making Japanese goods inexpensive abroad and to promote frugality at home. Not only labor and economic policies were affected by the policy shift. Communists were purged (1949–50), and others who had earlier been purged were allowed to reemerge in public life. Since an armed ally, capable at least of self-defense, would be more valuable than one unarmed, the United States also had second thoughts about Japan's renunciation of military force.

The Occupation also had unplanned side effects, including the influx of foreign culture. Intellectuals eager to catch up with the recent Western developments devoured translations of Western books, and popular culture was equally open to foreign influence. In some respects the scene resembled that after the First World War, and it is well to remember that it did not take the Occupation to introduce the Japanese to baseball and jazz. However, this time change went deeper, and there was to be no radical turning away such as took place in the thirties. Japan remained at peace, but it could not but be affected when warfare broke out in neighboring Korea.

The Korean War

The Second World War left Korea divided at the 38th parallel with a Communist state in the north and an American-backed regime in the south. Increasing international tensions between the United States and the Soviet Union as well as bitter hostility between the governments of the two Koreas reduced the chances for unification by negotiation. Both the Communist state in the north and the anti-Communist government in the south harbored the ambition to rule over the entire country. These ambitions erupted into war in June 1950, when North Korea attacked the south.

The period of intense fighting can be divided into three main phases, each with its own subdivisions. First, from June to September 1950, the North Koreans were on the offensive, pushing the South Korean and American forces back until they established a defense perimeter around Pusan from which they could not be dislodged. The second phase began with MacArthur's amphibious landing at Inchon in September, which led to the recapture of Seoul and then to an offensive intended to unify Korea by force. Then, in November, the Chinese, alarmed by the American advance to the Yalu River, and having had their warnings ignored, sent massive "volunteer" armies into Korea. These succeeded in regaining the north but were unable to win control over the south. This became clear in late May 1951, and in July of that year truce talks began. Earlier, in April, President Truman had dismissed General MacArthur, thereby making it clear that America would not extend the war beyond Korea. His dismissal of the eminent and popular general also demonstrated the American system of civil control over the military, a demonstration that had considerable impact in Japan.

Casualties in this war were heavy on both sides. They included over 800,000 Koreans (approximately 520,000 North Koreans and 300,000 South Koreans) and probably as many or more Chinese soldiers. The southern forces were sanctioned by the United Nations and fought under a United Nations command, but approximately half of the ground troops in addition to most of the air and naval forces were supplied by the United States, which suffered 142,000 casualties. South Korea supplied two-fifths of the remaining United Nations troops, and thirteen other countries combined to make up the remainder. The truce talks dragged on for two years until an armistice was signed in July 1953. Although marred by incidents, this armistice still remains in effect today.

For Japan the war brought profitable orders for equipment and supplies, a procurement boom that gave a substantial boost to a still faltering economy. Even after the war, orders to supply American troops and bases continued to benefit the Japanese economy. Under American encouragement, Japan also created a paramilitary force of 75,000, a first step toward limited rearmament. A basic pattern of internal economic growth and dependence on the United States for ultimate military protection was set. For decades Japan continued to take its foreign policy cues from the United States.

During the years after the Korean War, both China and Japan were able to concentrate on domestic development, although this always took place within the parameters of the Cold War. The two leading countries of East Asia, of course, remained keenly aware of each other, but they had little to do with each other. Kept apart by Japan's alliance with the United States, oriented toward contrasting models of social and economic development, influenced by different ideologies, they interacted only sporadically and then in a limited way.

The End of the Occupation

The ending of the Occupation—broached by MacArthur as early as 1947—was delayed largely because of Soviet opposition. Although the Occupation continued, by the time MacArthur took command in Korea in July 1950, its work was practically complete. The next two years were little more than a holding operation awaiting the conclusion of peace. This was finally accomplished with the signing of a peace treaty in San Francisco in September 1951, which was ratified the following April and accompanied by a defense treaty that provided for American bases in Japan and Okinawa. The U.S.S.R. was not a party to the San Francisco treaty. Formal diplomatic relations were established in 1956, but the Soviet Union and Japan could not agree on the disposition of four small islands and never signed a peace treaty to conclude World War II.

Assessments of the Occupation must naturally take into account later history since so many institutions and practices of contemporary Japan are rooted in this period. Inevitably there are both those who feel the Occupation went too far and, more numerous in Japan and elsewhere, those who deplore the "reverse course" taken in response to the Cold War and the persistence of certain traditional institutions and patterns. One such is the role of bureaucracy. The relationship between government and business is another. By definition the dominance of conservative political leadership implies continuity with the past.

What does seem clear is that the Occupation did bring about major changes but that it was most successful in areas where there were Japanese precedents and substantial support. This was true of much of the political program, the land reform, and the advocacy of liberal values. Representative institutions, after all, went back to the nineteenth century, and demands for land reform, for equality, and opposition to authoritarianism all predate the rise of militarism. The movement for women's rights had begun in the 1910s.

Thus, despite misconceptions and mistakes and despite the contradiction inherent in a plan to foster democracy by command, much of what the

Occupation attempted did actually take hold. For example, the constitution continues in effect.

PART II. ECONOMIC GROWTH AND POLITICAL STABILITY

After regaining its independence in 1952, Japan went on to achieve such phenomenal economic growth that by the 1970s it had become one of the world's industrial giants, and by the 1980s people in the United States and Britain were turning to Japan for lessons in industrial management. This economic growth was part of a broader transformation that had a profound effect on every aspect of Japanese life as the forces of modernity relentlessly tested old values and ideas, traditional forms of social organization, long-accepted patterns of life, and previously unquestioned beliefs. Like other peoples, the Japanese faced the continuing challenge of working out a satisfactory blend of new and old. In the eighties and beyond, even as Japan's own contribution to what is new in the world was increasing, the juxtaposition and interweaving of old and new in Japan itself continued to make it a fascinating and unique land.

The Economy: The First Twenty Years (1952–1972)

The Japanese economy made tremendous gains during the Korean War, largely through producing goods and services needed to support the United Nations' war effort there. By 1953, economic production had practically returned to pre-Second World War levels, although the country's trade volume was still only half of what it had been previously. After 1954, the economic surge continued, transforming recovery into growth. The annual GNP (gross national product—the total goods and services produced by a nation) rose an average of roughly 9 percent per year from 1954 to 1961, followed by an even higher rate (over 11 percent) during the 1960s. GNP figures are admittedly very rough indices, but they are useful for measuring broad trends in national economic activity, and for comparing the performance of national economies.

Not only did Japan's industrial output increase in quantity, it also changed qualitatively, as old industries were transformed and new ones developed. During the fifties, with government support, great strides were made in heavy industry—despite the fact that Japan lacks raw materials and is poor in energy resources. For example, by building manufacturing plants in port cities, which provided the advantage of low-cost ocean transport, and through the sophisticated application of modern technologies, Japan was able to become the world's leading shipbuilder and the third largest producer of iron and steel (after the United States and the Soviet Union). With heavy industry well established, Japan then concentrated on such high-technology fields as electronics and developed a host of strong modern industries. Cars and television sets, computers and cameras, watches and even pianos—it is difficult to think of a major branch of consumer technology in which Japan has failed to excel.

Some of these products were built by new companies, such as Sony or Honda, founded by entrepreneurs who took advantage of the opportunities offered by postwar economic dislocation to build up new enterprises from scratch. Other ambitious men reorganized or rejuvenated older companies, often importing technology by buying rights to foreign patents. In the dominant position in the economy, however, familiar old names reappeared, including Mitsui, the world's oldest major firm, as well as Mitsubishi, Sumitomo, and others.

The names were old, but they now designated a new kind of enterprise grouping *(keiretsu)* rather than the family-centered *zaibatsu* of the prewar period. Each group included financial institutions (a bank, insurance company, and so forth), a real estate firm, and a cluster of companies engaged in every conceivable line of business, where its main competitor was most likely a member of a rival group. The activities of the various member firms of each group were coordinated in periodic meetings of their presidents in presidents' clubs. Interlocking directorships, mutual stock holdings, and internal loans further held the organizations together, although more loosely than in the old *zaibatsu*. However, the *keiretsu*, now grouped around a central bank, continued to grow in size and strength until in the mid-seventies a study by Japan's Fair Trade Commission found that the six major groupings, composed of a total of 175 core companies, held 21.9 percent of all the capital in Japan and had a controlling interest in another 3,095 corporations that held 26.1 percent of the nation's capital. To this must be added their substantial investments in other companies that they influence without controlling.

Among the member firms of these enterprise groupings the most spectacular were trading companies *(shōsha)* that conducted their business not only at home but all over the world: exporting and importing, transporting and storing, financing and organizing a host of multifarious projects—an airport in Kenya, a large commercial farm on Sumatra, a petrochemical industry for Iran, or copper mining in Zaire. One of the greatest assets of these companies is their command of information gathered from throughout the world. Thus the Mitsui trading company has computers in Tokyo, New York, and London that exchange information automatically and are connected with Mitsui offices throughout the world to form an information-gathering network more extensive than that of any other private organization and larger than those operated by most governments. Furthermore, Mitsui, Mitsubishi, and the others have their own research organizations analyzing information, charting future trends, and drawing up plans to provide for future project recommendations. Their experts are engaged in city planning, energy research, research into the world's oceans and other major investigations that are likely to influence the future lives of people all over the world.

Japanese companies provided varied services and facilities for their employees, including company dormitories for the unmarried. There were company athletic teams and a host of recreational activities, such as organized outings to mountain retreats. These were intended to foster not only the health and well-being of the employees but also to strengthen feelings of group solidarity and identification with the sponsoring firm, which used them to convey an image of paternalistic solicitude. It was, of course, in the companies' interest to keep alive as long as possible the old values that had assured Meiji enterprises as well as Tokugawa merchant houses of the loyal devotion of their servants. Yet, it is important not to exaggerate their effectiveness nor to overemphasize the traditional aspects of Japanese labor relations, for company extras increasingly became matters not of traditionalistic paternalism but rather of contractual rights subject to collective bargaining, like fringe benefits in other countries.

Other signs indicated that, gradually, non-work-related activities and relationships were gaining in importance in the workers' lives, even as industry's quest for economic efficiency was weakening the nexus of personal relationships that had long prevailed at work. At the same time, managerial personnel continued to receive intensive training and indoctrination in order to imbue them with company ways and spirit. Thus at Toyota, Japan's leading automobile manufacturer, white-collar men are given an entire year of training, including a month in a company camp. Recruitment patterns centered on certain universities, ties between men entering a company in the same year, an emphasis on longevity in promotions, the practice of extensive consultation, and a strong preference for decision by consensus all helped foster management solidarity.

For the most part, Japanese companies, especially the large modern concerns, retained the loyalty of their employees, who were made to feel that what was best for the company was also best for Japan. This business ideology gained credence from management's practice of plowing earnings back into the firm so that it could continue to grow and hopefully surpass its rivals. Since that rather than any increase in payouts to stockholders was the company's objective, management was long able to persuade workers to moderate their demands for wage increases and fringe benefits. Naturally, the threat of foreign competition was also used to good effect, and for many years Japanese companies enjoyed a lower labor bill and greater labor peace than many of their competitors in Europe and America. The threat of foreign competition helped to motivate employees to work harder at a time when the quest for increased GNP gave Japan a sense of national purpose even as it promised an improved standard of living for the people.

Japan's concentration on economic development was epitomized in the widely proclaimed and acclaimed "income-doubling" policy of Ikeda Hayato (1899–1965, prime minister 1960–64) that provided for the doubling of per capita production in ten years. Politicians and the very capable and prestigious bureaucrats who staffed the ministries helped to orchestrate economic growth. Because of popular sentiment, constitutional constraints, and the country's reliance on the American "nuclear umbrella," Japan was freed from the burden of supporting a large and costly military establishment. Funds and energies were thus released for economic development.

The government fostered growth not only by establishing a political climate favorable to economic expansion and by adopting appropriate fiscal and monetary policies but also by setting production targets, assigning priorities, and generally orchestrating the economy. At the center of the government's economic apparatus were the Finance Ministry and the Ministry of International Trade and Industry (MITI). The importance of the latter reflects the crucial role of foreign trade in Japan's economy and the determination of the government to oversee the country's economic as well as political relations with other countries. By deploying foreign exchange allocations, manipulating quotas, and establishing barriers protecting native capital from foreign competition, the government could channel the flow of investment funds according to its priorities. It could also extend or deny tax privileges. It thus had at its disposal a variety of weapons to bring recalcitrant firms into line if persuasion and/or pressures failed. Generally, however, it preferred to rely on discussion and to act as much as possible on the basis of a shared government-business consensus.

Such a consensus was possible because government and business shared common aims, and government support was a major asset for firms engaged in international competition. It was facilitated by business concentration and also by ties between government and the business community. Some of these ties were personal, for the men at the top in the private sector and those heading the influential and prestigious government ministries tended to share similar backgrounds (both included a high proportion of Tokyo University graduates). Some of the ties were ideological, since Japan was ruled during these years by conservatives. And some of the links were financial, for elections were costly and business constituted a major source of funds for conservative politicians.

Politics

Under the Occupation, electoral politics was reintroduced, and political parties representing a broad range of ideas and a variety of interests battled for votes. The Diet again became the central arena for national politics. The general trend favored conservatives.

The leading political personality to emerge during the Occupation was Yoshida Shigeru (1878–1967), a former diplomat who had opposed the military leadership in Japan during the thirties. Yoshida dominated Japanese politics for the better part of a decade, serving as prime minister in 1946–47, and again from 1948 to 1954. A coalition of conservatives and socialists of various shades of radicalism held power briefly in 1947–48, but it was unable to create a viable government, partly because of divisions within its own ranks, and partly because of Occupation hostility toward socialism. Upon reassuming the prime ministership, Yoshida called a new election. Held in 1949, it provided his Liberal party with an absolute majority. He remained in office until he was forced to resign in 1954 in the wake of a scandal involving the shipping industry.

In foreign affairs Yoshida's policy was pro-American and anti-Communist. In 1951 he signed the San Francisco peace treaty for Japan, officially terminating the state of belligerency between Japan and the United States. In domestic affairs Yoshida was a conservative. His policies favored business and economic development. In 1950 he received permission from the Occupation to form a National Police Reserve of 75,000 men, a paramilitary force that assumed responsibility for internal security, thus releasing American troops for duty in Korea. In 1953 this was expanded to form the Self-Defense Forces, but Yoshida resisted enlargement of the SDF.

Ever since the resumption of party politics under the Occupation there had been rival conservative parties, and Yoshida as prime minister had his conservative critics. However, the main opposition to Yoshida's policies came from the Socialists, who in 1951 divided into left- and right-wing parties. In 1955, after Yoshida's downfall, they reunited in their quest for political power, but again split into two parties in 1959. In the elections of 1955 the conservative Democratic party won a plurality of seats in the Diet but required the cooperation of the Liberal party to govern. Negotiations between the two parties led to their merger in November 1955 to form the Liberal Democratic party (LDP), which continues to this day.

Since 1955 the LDP has been opposed by the two Socialist parties (Japan Socialist party and the Democratic Socialist party), by the "Clean Government party" (Kōmeitō, formed in 1964, first ran candidates for the lower house in 1967), by the Communist party, and by independent politicians. This opposition was too divided to constitute a serious alternative to conservative rule, but it was sufficient to prevent the LDP from gaining the two-thirds majority in the Diet needed for revising the constitution. Some conservatives, concerned about Japan's security, favored the revocation of Article IX so as to enable Japan to acquire her own military power. In the light of a dangerous world and in response to American urgings, the Self-Defense Forces were expanded to include well-equipped naval and air arms and the defense budget continued to increase. However, Japan continued to forego offensive weapons or capabilities, and total defense expenditures remained limited to approximately 1 percent of GNP.

Once the LDP was entrenched in power, the party's internal politics had a decisive influence on Japanese politics and government. Dominating the internal dynamics of the LDP, and thus determining the composition of Japan's government and influencing its policies, has been the interplay of political factions. These are formal, recognized political groupings built around a leader, usually a man with prospects of becoming a prime minister. From his faction a member derives political as well as financial support in his election campaigns and backing in his attempts to gain high government or party office. In return he owes his faction leader political support, especially during the complicated political maneuvering that determines the party presidency and thus Japan's prime ministership. In keeping with this system, the men who have presided over Japan's government have generally been seasoned politicians skilled in the art of assembling votes and working out combinations rather than leaders with wide voter appeal.

What has counted has been skill in political manipulation, not popular charisma.

This kind of factionalism was not a new phenomenon in Japanese politics. The LDP's origin as an association of independently based politicians also helps to account for the strength of the factions. Also helping to perpetuate it was Japan's system of multimember election districts. In these districts there were frequently more conservative candidates than could reasonably expect to win election. For example, in a five-member district, there might be four LDP candidates with only three likely to win. In such cases, the conservative politicians would be backed by rival factions within the LDP.

The power of the factions set limits on the prime minister's authority. Factionalism also weakened the party itself, which remained weak, particularly at the grass-roots level where each politician cultivated his own local support organization composed of various groups within his constituency. This local political machine was kept oiled by the politician's ability to further the interests of the community by obtaining public works and other special interest legislation, by his support for various community activities, and by his personal assistance to constituents. In seeking to fulfill these expectations, politicians found the political clout of their faction and a purse kept full by friendly interests to be obvious assets. Although some politicians were solidly entrenched, there were enough shifts in political fortunes on both the local and the national level to provide for political interest. More importantly, the system retained the flexibility to adjust policies to changing circumstances and weather all challenges.

For the opposition parties of the left these were years of frustration. The two Socialist parties were closely associated with labor, each linked to one of the labor confederations. They depended on organized labor for votes, and labor leaders figured prominently in their leadership. Many of their Diet members also came from a labor background. Ideologically the Socialists ran the gamut from Maoist radicals calling for revolution to moderate reformists. During the fifties the Communist party was very weak, but it picked up strength in the late sixties after adopting pragmatic policies. However, even had they been able to unite, the three leftist parties lacked the strength to topple the LDP regime.

Domestically the opposition parties viewed with special alarm LDP measures that seemed to represent a retreat from Occupation reforms and a return to the past. These included measures to recentralize the police and education functions and to give Tokyo greater control over local government. Socialist fears of LDP intentions may have been exaggerated, but they were fortified by the prominence in the conservative leadership of men who had held cabinet offices in the thirties and had been purged from politics by the Occupation authorities.

The left was adamantly opposed to government moves to recreate a military establishment and did what it could to block or at least delay the expansion of the Self-Defense Forces. They also objected to the government's consistently pro-American foreign policy, protested against the continued presence of American bases, and protested against American nuclear weapons and tests.

Unrestrained by expectations of forming a government themselves, the Socialist parties did not conduct themselves like a loyal opposition but engaged in bitter struggles, including boycotts of the Diet and physical disruptions of Diet proceedings leading to police intervention. The LDP for its part did not refrain, on issues it considered important, from using its majority to ram legislation through the Diet with little regard for the niceties of parliamentary procedure let alone any attempt to conduct a genuine exchange of views.

Political animosity reached its greatest intensity in 1960 over the issue of renewing the Security Treaty with the United States, first signed in 1952 along with the peace treaty. Opponents of the renewal were not limited to advocates of revolutionary ideologies. Many felt that instead of providing for Japanese security it endangered Japan, threatening to involve the country in American wars. The specter of nuclear war was particularly terrifying to a people who had experienced the holocausts at Hiroshima and Nagasaki. The Socialists mustered impressive support for their opposition to the renegotiated treaty. Union workers, housewives, students, professors, and members of diverse organizations took to the streets in mass demonstrations in which millions of people participated. There was also a one-day general strike. All this activity did not block ratification or enactment of the treaty, but it did lead to the resignation of Prime Minister Kishi (1896–1987, prime minister 1957–60) who had rammed the treaty through the Diet in what many thought was an undemocratic manner. Kishi's own background as a former bureaucrat and member of Tōjō's cabinet suggested the extent to which the old establishment had survived.

After the 1960 confrontation, politics simmered down to less violent exchanges as the success of Japan's economic development became apparent. Ikeda's ten-year plan to double per capita GNP was actually achieved in only seven years. Ikeda was succeeded by Satō Eisaku, Kishi's younger brother, who continued in office from 1964 to 1972, longer than any other prime minister since the promulgation of the Meiji Constitution. During the Satō years, the government continued to work closely with the business community and to follow the American lead on major policy issues. In 1970 the Security Treaty was renewed with little trouble.

In 1964 the political scene was complicated by the appearance of the new Clean Government party formed by the Sōka Gakkai (Value Creation Society), a religious sect. As implied by its name, the party program opposed corruption, but it was vague on other issues. After obtaining 10.9 percent of the vote in the 1969 election, it declined to 8.5 percent in 1972. The LDP for its part aroused little enthusiasm and was particularly weak in the cities. Before 1967 its candidates had received over 50 percent of the vote, but in the election of that year its percentage declined to 48.8 percent. The trend continued slowly downward until it bottomed in 1976 at 41.8 percent. But even then, it remained by far the largest vote getter and also benefitted from an electoral system that favored rural areas.

The Seventies, Eighties, and Beyond

During the seventies and eighties there were no sharp breaks with the preceding decades, but there were signs of longer-term changes as well as a series of short-term economic and political shocks. The latter began in 1971 when the United States, Japan's largest trading partner, placed a 10 percent surcharge on imports and effectively devalued the dollar by floating it, that is, by allowing the international monetary market to determine its value vis-à-vis the yen and other currencies rather than maintaining a fixed rate of exchange. Both these American actions were aimed at reducing, if not eliminating, a mounting U.S. trade and payment deficit in its dealings with Japan, but they proved ineffective.

A political blow followed these economic acts when, still in the same year, Washington announced the impending visit of President Nixon to China, an act on which Japan was not consulted and which undercut Prime Minister Satō, who, primarily to please Washington, had been following the unpopular policy of maintaining the fiction that the Nationalist regime on Taiwan was the government of China.

Other shocks followed. The Arab oil boycott in 1973 reminded Japan of her dependence on imported energy and was followed by a quadrupling of the price of this vital import. As a result there was a substantial decline in GNP, and during 1974–76 Japan suffered a severe recession.

However, the system demonstrated remarkable resilience in surmounting these crises. An outstanding example was the rescuing of Mazda faced with a crisis comparable to that of Chrysler in the United States. It was accomplished through the cooperation of government-backed financial interests, management, workers, dealers, suppliers, and the local community that offered a "lesson in managing interdependence" and led two American experts to conclude, "Relatively low interest rates, MITI bureaucrats, trade barriers, and the like are, no doubt, important factors in a comparative history of economic growth, but only managers and workers build cars and other products. And their capacity to pull together in a crisis is a crucial measure of a society's strength."[5]

In the later seventies and eighties Japan's emphasis on high technology led to a decrease in dependence on imported raw materials. By 1984 Japan had reduced its use of imported raw material per unit of manufacture to 60 percent less than it had been twenty years earlier. This change also positioned Japan to compete with the emergent economies of such neighbors as Korea and Taiwan. In line with this policy, special encouragement was given electronics, telecommunications, ceramics, biochemicals, and machine tools. In these ways the economy continued to sustain a population which by 1985 had reached 121 million, up from 65 million in 1930 and about four times the number of inhabitants of Japan at the time of the Meiji Restoration.

As elsewhere, the move away from "smoke-stack industries" hurt the labor movement by reducing the number of its members. Furthermore, the great majority of people considered themselves middle class.

Growth of GNP declined to the level of other fully developed countries, but Japan's trade imbalance, especially with the United States, posed a continuing problem. Expectations to the contrary, it was not solved by the rising value of the yen which did, however, facilitate Japanese investment in the United States. One business response to new conditions was the transformation of Japanese companies into multinationals. Increasingly, Japanese concerns became involved in manufacturing as well as trading overseas. These operations generally were successful on the factory floor, but it proved more difficult to internationalize management or "localize" the "transplants." In many cases Japanese companies were resented for reserving the best jobs for those at home, for building factories far from the troubled, job-hungry cities, for favoring their *keiretsu* partners, and generally taking advantage of opportunities abroad denied to foreign companies at home. Foreign managers enjoyed job security, but they were isolated from the informal communication networks out of which corporate decisions frequently emerged.

In politics as in economics, the system proved highly resilient. Early in 1976, the Lockheed scandal ("Japan's Watergate") shook the political world as it was revealed that millions of dollars of the American company's funds had been used to corrupt the highest Japanese government officials. Among those indicted was Tanaka Kakuei, prime minister 1972–74, who was found guilty in a 1983 decision that was upheld in 1987.

Predictions that the LDP would decline to the point of losing its ability to form a government proved false. It did reach a low of 41.8 percent of the popular vote in 1976 but made a strong comeback in 1980. In 1986 it won 49.6 percent of the vote entitling it to 300 seats, the highest number in the party's history. Not only the party but its internal factional structure remained essentially the same. Tanaka, despite the Lockheed scandal, continued to control his faction until he suffered a stroke in 1985.

The leading political figure in the eighties was Nakasone Yasuhiro (1918–   ), who as prime minister during 1982–87 brought a new style of vigorous leadership and national assertiveness into the office. Prosperity, self-confidence, and American pressure combined to induce the government in 1986 to exceed in the 1987 military budget the 1 percent GNP cap on defense spending. Though the increase was modest, this did have symbolic significance. It was also in 1986 that the Socialist Party in an attempt to become more mainstream dropped its long-standing opposition to the Self-Defense Forces based on Article IX of the constitution. Its new position, that the Self-Defense Forces were "unconstitutional but legal," showed just how troublesome an issue this remained for the largest opposition party.

Nakasone also cooperated with the United States to reduce the trade surplus by emphasizing domestic spending, cooperating on monetary policy, and trying to open Japanese markets to more imported goods. The last of these, however, was difficult in face of powerful, deeply entrenched domestic interests and business patterns. Farmers and construction companies were just two examples of major domestic constituencies on which many LDP leaders had long depended. At the time Nakasone left office, the trade imbalance was more acute than ever, but expectations were that the rise of the yen and decline of the dollar would do much to correct the situation. The flow of Japanese capital into the United States was just one indication that what had once been Japanese dependence on the United States was now a mutual interdependence that linked the economies as well as the stock markets of the two countries. Adjustment to this new situation was difficult and did not always bring out the best in either the Japanese or the American side.

Nakasone was succeeded as prime minister by Takeshita Noboru (1924–   ), a more conventional politician who had served in the Satō, Tanaka, and Nakasone cabinets and who headed the Tanaka faction after 1985. In keeping with a general trend in the capitalist world, Japan divested itself of the government railway in 1987 and also sold its shares in the National Telegraph and Telephone Company and in Japan Air Lines. However the Takeshita administration lasted less than two full years (Nov. 1987–June 1989). Takeshita himself resigned under a cloud arising out of revelations that the head of the Recruit group of companies had attempted to buy influence by giving large amounts in shares and money to leading politicians and bureaucrats. Though not personally charged, the men close to both Takeshita and Nakasone were implicated.

The death of the emperor in January 1989 had little immediate political effect, and it is too early to determine what effect, if any, the release of new documentation will have on his reputation or that of the throne. Most Japanese seemed happy with the personality of the new, more accessible emperor, the first to have married a commoner.

In July 1989 the LDP, burdened by scandal, by its identification with a very unpopular sales tax, and by unsuitable leadership, lost its majority in the upper house. The main beneficiaries were the Socialists, led by Doi Takako (1928–   ), the first woman to become a real force in Japanese politics. The role of the female vote in the elections was also reflected in the inclusion of two women in the cabinet formed by Kaifu Toshiki (1931–   ) in August. However, the Socialists were unable to follow through, and the LDP rallied. In February 1990 the LDP won 272 of the 512 seats in the lower house. Kaifu's new cabinet was all male. After the Socialists did very poorly in the local elections in the spring of 1991, Doi resigned from the leadership as the party took stock.

The LDP continued to dominate politics. Kaifu was publicly committed to electoral reform, but in October 1991 was replaced by Miyazawa Kichi (1919–   ), who had resigned as Finance Minister in 1988 when his office was tainted by the Recruit scandal. He was thus not implicated in a series of scandals involving big brokerage firms and big money that broke in 1991 and forced another Finance Minister out. Miyazawa's own background as an insider, his indebtedness to the Takeshita faction, and the reemergence of Nakasone as a "senior advisor" lead some observers to see his assumption of the leadership as a return to the old ways and others to wonder what it would take to induce change.

In foreign affairs Japan continued to maintain a relatively low profile for a country with such economic power. In 1972 Japan had the satisfaction afforded by the return of Okinawa by the United States. It then became more active in the international economic realm as a major source of funding for international agencies and for special projects, including the War in the Persian Gulf (1991). This war certainly served as a reminder of Japan's dependence on world trade.

Closer to home, after Prime Minister Tanaka's visit to Beijing in 1972, Japan had recognized the Peoples' Republic of China. Economic ties developed apace, disrupted only briefly by the Chinese government's bloody suppression of student protestors in 1989. Symbolizing the desire for good relations on both sides was Prime Minister Kaifu's visit to Beijing in August 1991, the first by a major head of state since the student uprising in 1989. Meanwhile, closer relations with Russia and The Commonwealth of Independent States awaited resolution of the territorial issues left over from the Second World War.

From the seventies on there were moves to increase trade with and investments in Southeast Asian countries. These have borne generous fruit, but trade with the developed countries of the Atlantic Community, especially the United States, remained crucial. Despite increased domestic spending and concessions made in "structural impediments" talks begun in 1989, the trade imbalance continued to bedevil Japanese-American relations and to tempt publicists in both countries to bash the other.

PART III. CULTURE AND SOCIETY

During the second half of the twentieth century, Japanese culture and society underwent changes every bit as profound as those of any period in its history. In some respects these changes brought Japan closer to the patterns experienced in other developing countries, and there is hardly a mode of dress, a style of music, or a social or political movement which did not attract at least a modest following in Japan. But Japan remained Japan.

Social Change and the Quality of Life

Economic growth brought with it an unprecedented degree of affluence and well-being. The very physiognomy of the Japanese people was affected as an improved diet produced a new generation taller and healthier than their parents. As the nineties began, the Japanese people had the world's highest rate of life expectancy. People now ate more fish and meat, although the proportion remained modest by American standards. Dairy products became a staple of the daily diet. Changing tastes were reflected in a steadily rising consumption of wheat at the expense of rice, which, thanks to the government's price support policy, was in overabundance. While traditional cuisines continued to flourish so did Western foods and beverages. Japan became a nation of coffee as well as tea drinkers. During the seventies, the influx of Western foods continued apace as the arch of McDonald's hamburgers spread from Tokyo's Ginza to less likely places, where it was soon joined by the figure of Colonel Sanders inviting passersby to partake of Kentucky Fired Chicken, and Mr. Donut and Dairy Queen did their part to propagate popular fast-food culture American style.

Changes in dress were equally dramatic. In the eighties blue jeans became the universal dress of the young and pants were worn in public by women of all ages as a matter of course. Conversely, the kimono was reserved for special occasions. In other respects too, particularly in the practice of the old crafts, traditional elegance gave way to modern practicality.

Japan became a nation of Western-style consumers. The washing machine, vacuum cleaner, and refrigerator of the fifties were soon joined by the television set and the air-conditioner, with the video-recorder and microwave following in the eighties. Meanwhile, the worsening traffic jams that clogged Japan's roads demonstrated that many a family had realized its dream of owning a private automobile. Thus a solid domestic market supported Japan's major consumer-export industries.

Ownership of the new products was not confined to the cities, for the countryside also participated in the general prosperity. This was partly because the economic boom produced a labor shortage, so that wage scales were set and plant locations determined in such a way as to draw rural manpower into the factories. At the same time, as already noted, agricultural production nevertheless increased. Another source of rural well-being was the LDP's policies, including the support of rice that the government purchased from farmers at several times the price current in the international market. Thus the stark economic distinction between city and country, which had existed in prewar years, was eliminated. At the same time, the spread of television accelerated the process, begun by radio, of diffusing the culture of the cities to the countryside. However, despite the omnipresence of the television set, the Japanese remained the world's most avid consumers of newspapers, magazines, and comic books and supported more bookstores per capita than any other country in the world.

Japan also enjoyed an excellent public transportation system, including the bullet trains which by the mid-seventies connected Tokyo and Northern Kyūshū, whisking passengers past Japan's greatest mountain at 125 miles per hour (see Figure 12.2). Since then, the system has been extended to northern Honshū and there is more to come. Within the cities, public transport is frequent, punctual, and efficient, although in Tokyo's rush hour ("crush hour" would be more appropriate) "pushers" are needed to cram the people quickly into the overflowing subways.

Public transportation, communication, and security were excellent early on, but government was at first slow to respond to the rising threat of

Figure 12.2   The bullet train passing Mt. Fuji.

pollution. Only after Tokyo became enshrouded in a semiperpetual screen of smog did the government take action. In Mie prefecture asthma was linked to pollution while in Toyama a river caused cadmium poisoning. Most notorious was the "Minamata Disease" (1953) caused by people eating fish contaminated by methyl mercury discharged by a fertilizer plant in Kyūshū. Government measures taken in the seventies did noticeably ameliorate the problem, but the quality of air and water remains a matter of concern. Furthermore, there was also visual pollution as Japan's long industrial area, running along its Pacific coast, became one of the most ugly to be found anywhere. While the Japanese people continued to cherish nature in miniature, lovingly tending tiny gardens on the most unlikely bits of land, Japan's leaders, in their rush to modernize, sacrificed much of the natural beauty that had once been Japan's beloved heritage. As the nineties began, environmentalists expressed concern not only over the situation at home, but also called attention to the destruction Japanese companies were inflicting on the tropical forests of Borneo and other lands. If the aims of Japanese environmentalists were similar to those elsewhere, the same was true of the power of the forces arrayed against them.

A serious social and economic problem was the constantly escalating price of land and housing in Japan's large cities. Young married people, despite their modern wish for independence, found themselves forced to live with their in-laws because they could not afford separate establishments. Others were crowded into tiny apartments in drab and monotonous buildings made of reinforced concrete. Raising a family in such confined quarters was no easy task. Although the small apartments reduced women's household chores, releasing time for other activities, the residents of such buildings were slow to develop a sense of community, since they regarded these quarters as temporary expedients marking a stage of their lives and careers soon to be surmounted. This outlook was not unreasonable, since in Japan promotion, particularly in the early career stages, was generally by seniority.

The absence of grandparents in the new housing was but one of the factors making for discontinuity between the generations. Such discontinuity was not unique to Japan, for in other countries too, rapid changes during the postwar years created a "generation gap." Indeed, the presence of this phenomenon in Japan can itself be regarded as one more sign of Japan's modernity. However, in Japan the gap was particularly severe. Not only did the younger people grow up in a society that had suddenly become very different from that of their parents, but a whole generation of leaders had been thoroughly discredited and the old values blamed for leading the nation to catastrophe. Included were many of the old values that long had helped to provide Japanese society with its cohesiveness.

New life-styles and values appeared in the factories as young workers preferred to spend their leisure time manipulating pachinko (vertical pinball) machines, playing video games, or listening to rock music rather than going on company outings, and their valuation of skill over length of service, although very much in tune with the new technology, set them apart from their elders. Furthermore, they tended to regard the factory not so much as a second home but merely as a place of work. The number of hours they would have to spend there was also steadily decreasing by the beginning of the nineties, and a survey conducted in 1990 revealed that workers were more interested in obtaining more leisure than in higher pay.

Meanwhile, those fortunate enough to survive a brutal entrance examination system found themselves admitted to universities oriented largely to research and graduate work. Ostensibly paternalistic, the universities demonstrated their supposed concern for the youngest members of the academic community by virtually guaranteeing graduation to all matriculants. Neglected after having worked so hard for university entrance, the students expressed their discontent in radical political activities. Their dissatisfaction helped fuel widespread demonstrations and disruptions in the later sixties, their protest directed against both national and university policies. In this again, Japanese young people were, of course, not alone, and, as elsewhere, the pendulum swung back to greater conservatism in the seventies and eighties.

The general loosening of traditional patterns and values presented contemporary Japanese with a wide range of choice but within what remained, by and large, a closely knit society. For example, young people increasingly insisted on making their own selection of a spouse, and they were now always consulted before a marriage was arranged. Nevertheless, even in love marriages, most young people still asked their employer or teacher to serve as an official matchmaker. A surprisingly large number of others continued to leave the initiative to their parents. Under the postwar legal system, wives as well as husbands could now initiate divorce proceedings; however, the divorce rate remained low.

Gradually more careers were opened to women and their employment grew steadily, but most wives remained content with their traditional roles, which gave them a predominant influence over their children and firmly established the home as their field of authority. Although submissive to their husbands in public, most wives controlled the family budget and ran the household. Many treated their husbands as they would an older, somewhat difficult, and rather special child. They accepted their exclusion from much of their husbands' social lives, which the husbands spent largely in the company of their fellow workers. Like their Tokugawa predecessors, wives also tolerated visits to bars and overlooked occasional frolics with female playmates as long as nothing serious developed and their husbands continued to look after their families.

However, as in all periods of social change, there were some who suffered because change was too rapid and others for whom it was too slow. Among the former were old people bewildered and distressed by the whirl about them. One of the strengths of the old society had always been the dignity and security afforded to the aged, but now cramped quarters and new ideas ate away at old values and threatened traditional comforts. These were people who found that the social rules had changed just when it came to be their turn to reap the rewards the system offered to those who played by the rules. While the erosion of respect for the aged diminished the traditional attractions of longevity, forced retirement at an early age (usually 55) and the devaluation of savings because of continual inflation deprived the old of a sense of economic security. Most families did manage to take care of the elderly one way or another. Most old people were not shunted off into nursing homes or set up in special retirement communities, but the social arrangements made for the elderly by their children were often grudging and poisoned by resentment. Niwa Fumio's short story "The Hateful Age" (1947), a revolting portrait of senile selfishness, was an early expression of the new attitude.

At the other end of the spectrum were those who felt that change was coming too slowly, such as the young and middle-aged adults who felt constrained to maintain and live with their parents. They felt stifled rather than supported by a social system that still expected the individual to be subordinate to the group, whether it be family or company. They also balked at conforming to a social hierarchy that had lost much of its theoretical support. The discontented were a disparate group. They included women who wanted to make a career of work and found themselves discriminated against and artists and intellectuals seeking to fill the vacuum left by the passing of the old values with something more solid than consumerism and the race for increased GNP. This discontent was frequently shared by students and by radicals impatient for a more egalitarian society. Meanwhile, some of the young men who had no prospects for university study vented their frustrations by joining motorcycle gangs. However, most of the disaffected worked out a *modus vivendi* for themselves, and many, especially among the young, gradually came to terms with society.

The great majority of the population, however, neither mourned the passing of the old nor were impatient for the arrival of the new. Appreciative of the increase in material wealth, they were nevertheless unsure of the future. Many turned to new religious sects, seeking to satisfy their spiritual hunger and to cure a psychological malaise brought on by the loss of community entailed by moving from traditional village to modern city. Attracting the largest membership was Sōka Gakkai, which we have already encountered as the sponsor of the Clean Government party. Doctrinally based on Nichiren Buddhism, it denounced all other faiths and insisted that its members proselytize relentlessly. One of the obligations of the faithful was a pilgrimage to the head temple at the foot of Mt. Fuji, where an average of 10,000 people a day came to pay their homage. By passing a series of examinations, the faithful could rise in an academic-like hierarchy of ranks. For the devoted members, the sect provided not only spiritual community but a sense of personal worth and of belonging to a large, integrated, purposeful group.

Others found it more difficult to find new certainties, however, for the world offered a bewildering range of choices.

The Japanese Film

If, as is often said, the film is the characteristic art form of the twentieth century, then the worldwide acclaim accorded Japanese films is but one more indication of Japan's full participation in the culture of this century. All Japanese films were by no means masterpieces: Japanese film companies were second to none in turning out ephemeral entertainments—samurai movies that were the artistic equivalents of American westerns, lachrymose melodramas with torrents of tears intended to induce a similar flow in the audience, horror and monster films, and, in the seventies and eighties, a wave of erotica with little artistic or social value but much sexual action. Such films, reflecting social stereotypes and people's daydreams, are of considerable interest to psychologists and social scientists, but it is important to remember that the stereotypes they contain—the self-sacrificing but self-centered mother, the wife finding herself, daughters in various degrees of revolt—are never simple mirror images of society. The more ambitious and truly fine films also reflected the times and the society, but, beyond that, they provided new insights into the Japanese and the human reality. And they did this while drawing an enthusiastic mass audience as had the kabuki and *bunraku* (puppet theater) in their day.

The major films were the creations of fine actors, sensitive cameramen, and above all great directors. While some fine directors were remarkably versatile, the most outstanding were able to use the medium to create their own personal styles, conveying their own personal visions. If they had anything in common, it was a superb visual sense employed to create an atmosphere. Some may be said to have used the camera to paint their vision on the screen. Many are best viewed as one would view a painting—with a contemplative eye.

Exercising classic restraint in his insistence on a strict economy of means (empty spaces, simple objects, minimal plot) and avoiding anything superficial or artificially clever was Ozu Yasujirō (1903–63), whose traditionalism also extended to his subject matter, for he was the filmmaker par excellence of the Japanese family. Describing the effect and tone of Ozu's films, Donald Richie has used the old term, *mono no aware*, first encountered in our discussion of *The Tale of Genji*. Richie went on to say that Ozu's "emphasis on effect rather than cause, emotion rather than intellect" and "his ability to metamorphose Japanese aesthetics into terms and images visible on film" made Ozu "the most Japanese of all directors."[6]

Other directors did not take as positive a view of Japan's social tradition and the old values. For example, in *Harakiri (Seppuku*, 1962), directed by Kobayashi Masaki, the hero sets out to avenge his son who had been forced to commit an unimaginably painful *seppuku* (ritual suicide) using a sword with a bamboo blade, but in the end the whole system is revealed as founded on hypocrisy. Or there is *Night Drum (Yoru no Tsuzumi*, 1958), directed by Imai Tadashi, in which a samurai kills the wife he loves and thereby deprives his own life of meaning, because this is what society demanded. Such vivid and moving historical films were among the triumphs of the postwar cinema, a part of a continuing and sometimes bitter dialogue with a still living past.

Outstanding as a truly great director is Kurosawa Akira (1910–   ), who, while remaining Japanese in his aesthetic and historical vocabulary, displays a concern for truly universal themes. Thus his world-famous *Rashomon* (1950) suggests the relativity of all truth through a demonstration of the power of human subjectivity and self-interest. In *Ikiru* (1952) the viewer is taken through a Faust-like quest for meaning in life. The main character, a petty bureaucrat dying of cancer, in the end finds fulfillment in one meaningful social act—surmounting endless red tape and bureaucratic obstructionism, he gets a small park built. Kurosawa's mastery of large scenes with vast casts as well as his versatility and continued creative vigor was apparent in such late films as *Dreams, Dreams* (1990), *Rhapsody in August* (1991) and *Ran* (1985), an imaginative metamorphosis of *King Lear* into sixteenth-century Japan. It, like the earlier *Seven Samurai* (1954), is one of those rare films in which powerful and sensitive acting, beautiful visual composition and realistic detail, story line and structure, friction and harmony, violence and stillness, blend into a major artistic statement, a masterpiece.

Despite Kurosawa and a few others, there were signs in the eighties that the great age of Japanese film was over. Increasingly Japanese studios churned out films of violence and pornography. Refreshing exceptions were the comic films of Itami Juzo (1933–   ) (*The Funeral* {1984}, *Tampopo* {1986}, *A Taxing Woman* {1987}).

Intellectual Life and Literature

After the war Japan rejoined the international intellectual community, participated in scientific and scholarly meetings at home and abroad, and increasingly contributed to specialized disciplines in important ways. Many Japanese scholars became conversant with a foreign language, usually English, and all had access to a broad and steady stream of translations.

Writings addressing broader human or philosophical issues, published in journals of opinion as well as books, have attracted less attention abroad than have the works of the filmmaker or novelist. One reason, no doubt, is the language barrier. Another may be that much, whether or not Marxist in general orientation, was derivative. Also, many Japanese intellectuals, like their American counterparts, applied their energies to studying their own society and to addressing their own countrymen. Notably fascinating but problematical has been the literature of exceptionalism (Nihonjinron) that burgeoned in the seventies and continued to fuel a growing sense of self-confidence and assertiveness. The literature which focused on Japanese uniqueness included the highly respected and stimulating work of such scholars as the psychiatrist Doi Takeo and the sociologist Nakane Chie (see Suggested Readings). Lesser scholars, however, expounded on and frequently took pride in the uniqueness of just about every aspect of Japanese behavior, institutions, and/or climatic and racial characteristics. Japan's increasing cosmopolitanism did not prevent the persistence of insularity.

What it meant to be Japanese was also one of the themes explored in postwar fiction. After the war older novelists published manuscripts they could not release during the war, while new writers appeared to sound new themes. An outstanding example of the former is the long novel by Tanizaki translated as *The Makioka Sisters*.

In 1947 Kawabata published the last installment of *Snow Country*. Previous segments of the novel had been published in various journals over the course of the preceding twelve years, each part appearing as though it might be the conclusion, as though each part were a stanza in a *renga* (linked verse) rather than a building block for a novel. Characteristically Kawabata's novels sacrifice structure and plot for the sake of naturalness and poetry. *A Thousand Cranes* (1948) and *The Sound of the Mountain* (1951) followed, each imbued with the author's visual sensibility and with his concern for beauty and sadness, inseparable as ever in Japanese literature, and evoking what one critic termed a "vibrant silence."[7] The essential Japaneseness of Kawabata's method and vision was clearly demonstrated in his Nobel Prize acceptance speech (1968). Translated as *Japan, the Beautiful, and Myself*, it is an evocation of the Japanese tradition, a string of poems and images held together by a shared perception of beauty and truth.

Women writers had reappeared toward the turn of the century, but were particularly prominent after the war. As Donald Keene pointed out, "At no time since the Heian period had women figured so prominently in the literary world."[8] Appropriately enough, one of the most distinguished among them, Enchi Fumiko (1905–86) translated *The Tale of Genji* into modern Japanese (1972–73). She also wrote realistic novels such as *Waiting Years* (1957) as well as the subtle and imaginative *Masks* (1958), both available in English.

A brilliant, prolific, versatile, and uneven writer was Mishima Yukio (1925–70) who, in a series of well-constructed novels, developed his ideas on such universal themes as the relationship between art and life, warrior and poet, and the nature of beauty. One of his most compelling novels was *The Temple of the Golden Pavilion* (1956). Based on the actual burning down of the Golden Pavilion (Kinkakuji, see p. 103) in postwar Kyoto, it includes powerful psychological and philosophical explorations. A noted dramatist and critic as well as novelist, Mishima's work defies summarization. And it went beyond literature, for he tried to mold his life and his body as he did his art. Wishing to be both athlete and artist, he took up body building and succeeded in developing a strong torso (but on spindly legs). Seeking to achieve a unity of knowledge and action as in the philosophy of Wang Yangming whom he admired, Mishima's culminating act was a public *seppuku* committed after the completion of his final work, a tetrology entitled *The Sea of Fertility*. His ritual suicide was both a protest against what he perceived as contemporary Japanese decadence and an act fulfilling his life's work.

A productive writer also well-known abroad is Endō Shūsaku (1923–   ), who in a series of brilliant novels grappled with the tensions between his Catholic faith and his Japanese heritage to arrive at a vision of the compassionate Christ. Just as Endō contributed to modern Christian as well as Japanese literature, Abe Kōbō (1924–   ) has an international reputation as an existentialist. He is perhaps best known for his novel *Woman in the Dunes* (1962), subsequently made into a film. In this work as well as later novels such as *Face of Another* (1964), *The Boxman* (1973), and *The Ark Sakura* (1984), and in such plays as *Friends* (1967), Abe explored some of the themes and predicaments besetting the contemporary human condition. Although one of these themes is the search for identity (and for Abe this includes identification with place and community), he did not, like Mishima and others, draw on his specifically Japanese heritage but set out to make artistic statements valid for his time rather than only or even primarily for his place.

The search for identity and for roots also infuses the work of Ōe Kenzaburō (1935–   ), two of whose novels, *A Personal Matter* (1964) and *The Silent Cry* (1967) have been translated into English. Insight into psychological complexities of modern people, including the sources of violence, a concern for social morality, a strong personal symbolism, and his grapplings with basic problems of existence in the second half of the twentieth century mark him as a major writer and one who speaks to the central problems of his age. The publication in 1990 of his *Jinsei no Shinseki* (Pariete de la Vida) attests to his continuing productivity.

Working a different vein was Inoue Yasushi (1907–91) many of whose novels were set in China, including his last, *Confucius* (1989) in which the sage, seen through the eyes of a disciple, is treated with great respect. Less well-known abroad is Maruya Saiichi (1925–   ), an entertaining writer, serious but funny, whose *Singular Rebellion* (1972) provides a delightful, comic window into the times. More recently "young writers demonstrate that Hollywood, Madison Avenue, and rock and roll have generated a global reservoir of images, icons, and modern myths."[9] Many of the younger writers are female. Who will rise to prominence or what the nineties will bring is impossible to predict, but Noguichi Takehiko seems right on target in describing the literary scene of the first year of the decade: "But the imbalance from sensory overload and intellectual floundering together produce a surprisingly creative chaos."[10]

Creative chaos was also congenial to some commentators who found the deconstructionism of Jacques Derrida or the post-modernism of Jean-Francois Lyotard, fitting for "post-industrial" society, although there were also those who argued that, for better or worse, Japan had never been "modern." It will not do to attempt to define "postmodernism" since it entails a rejection of the very act of definition, along with any single point of view or method. In Japan as in the West, we will have to await post-postmodernism to gain perspective, but it has clearly had a forceful impact on architecture, rejecting the functionalism of modernism as sterile, and stimulating a host of experiments in Japan as in the West.

The Visual Arts

Not only Japanese films but also the work of Japanese painters, potters, and architects won international recognition for their contributions to the world of art. As in the prewar years, some artists found their inspiration in, and took their cues from, the latest trends, so that Japan had its practitioners of abstract expressionism, action painting, pop art, and the various other international art movements that at their best reflected the search for a style appropriate to a bewildering age and at their worst degenerated into fads. The cacophony of the art scene may be suggested by the disjointed ears in Figure 12.3. What are they listening to? No doubt their metallic color is appropriate for the age of the machine. Do they symbolize modern (Japanese?) people? Are they all that is left of humankind—disembodied ears?

More in keeping with the Japanese aesthetic tradition was the work of artists who strove to create beauty without attempting to convey a symbolic message. Japanese potters, both innovators and traditionalists, continued to blend shapes, textures, and colors to create works worthy of the great tradition to which they are heirs.

An area of major artistic achievement was the modern woodcut. Unlike the earlier *ukiyo-e* artists, those who now worked in this medium took responsibility for the entire process of print making. They did their own cutting and printing, although they might have students assist them in the more routine aspects of the process. Among the finest was Munakata Shikō (1903–75), a gifted painter as well as print artist, whose style was influenced by traditional Japanese folk art, but who also developed new techniques. One was to

Figure 12.3   Miki
Tomio (1937–1978)
Ear 201. Bronze,
1965, 41.4
cm × 34.7 cm.

add color to his prints by hand, applying color on the back of the print and
letting it seep through the paper to create gentle, diffused coloring. This
helped Munakata create a general decorative effect. Munakata's concern with
decoration is well illustrated by his rendition of the clothing in *Lady in Chinese Costume,* shown in Figure 12.4. The lines marking the folds in the cloth
and suggesting its ornamentation are repeated in the remainder of the print,
giving it its rhythm. Strong black areas and lines contrast pleasingly with soft
blues and browns.

A similar love for the decorative is evidenced by Munakata's frequent use
of written characters for ornamentation. In subject matter his work ranges
from the religious to the sensuous and the whimsical (for example, a nude
with the artist's eyeglasses resting on her belly). In tone his art is positive
and life-affirming—there is no echo here of the agony of the century. There
are strong hints of Persia and India, but in the vigor of his lines, his gentle
eroticism, and the decorative qualities of his art, Munakata resembles
Matisse while his coloring is also reminiscent of Chagall.

Figure 12.4   Munakata
Shikō, *Lady in Chinese
Costume.* Woodcut,
1946, 45.5 cm × 32.6 cm.

Perhaps no art is as revealing of society as is architecture. Although many
opportunities for architectural excellence were missed in the rush of postwar reconstruction and some of Japan's industrial centers are among the
ugliest cities in the world, there were also new buildings of great distinction. The achievements of Tange Kenzō (1913–   ), designer of the Hall
Dedicated to Peace at Hiroshima, were recognized internationally when he
received the Pritzger Prize (1987), architecture's most coveted award. His
work can be seen not only in his own country, where the Swimming Pool and
Sports Center he designed for the 1964 Tokyo Olympics is one of the most
famous, but also in Europe, North Africa, the Middle East, and the Arts Complex in Minneapolis (1970–74). In addition to designing superb buildings,
Tange also involved himself deeply in urban planning.

Among the most creative of Tange's students is Isozaki Arata (1931–   ).
Postmodernist in seeking a "shifting, revolving, flickering style" rather
than a "lucid, coherent institutional style" for his Tsukuba Science Center,
Isozaki is also an internationalist who could write, "the Katsura Palace, the
Parthenon, the Capitoline piazza, and so on all live in a time and place
equidistant from us. Anything occurring in the history of architecture—

Figure 12.5   Art Tower Mito. Mito Ibaragi. 1986–1990. 100 m high.

even the history of the world—is open to quotation."[11] Such quotation yields new and complex meaning. But often Isozaki does not quote, and some of his most successful buildings employ solid geometric forms as in his Museum of Contemporary Art in Los Angeles. Illustrated here (see Figure 12.5) is the tower for his arts center in Mito, which, although located in a place once famous for historiography, does not refer to anything except itself.

The diversity of modern Japanese architecture (good and bad) is far too great for any single building possibly to be representative of the art, let alone the society at this moment in time. But architecture can, among other things, be fun. The example of Japanese "pop architecture" in Figure 12.6 was built to house an exhibit on coffee for an exposition celebrating the completion of an artificial island in Kobe. Later, it was turned into a permanent coffee museum and given a more dignified but conventional exterior. Perhaps the cup ranneth over and the joke wore off—humor may be as ephemeral as beauty. Still, it is a splendid museum housing fine exhibits on the history, the preparation, and the consumption of coffee and also providing facilities for study and a "Training Room" for coffee makers. It is an effective reminder that Japan is a world leader in coffee appreciation, for its many and varied coffee houses are justly famous, and it is the major importer of the choicest South American beans. By extension this building may evoke all that is modern and international in Japan. Further, if this

Figure 12.6   Coffee Pavilion, Port-pia Exposition, Kobe 1981. Takenaka Construction Firm. Height 25 m. Diameter, ca. 22 m.

gargantuan cup seems out of keeping with the tradition of the Japanese tea house, perhaps there is yet something traditional in the celebration of coffee. It is admittedly premature to speak of a "way of coffee" or a "coffee ceremony" to set alongside those of tea, but that day may come. Meanwhile, coffee has found a home in Japan. Essentially it is a serious beverage befitting hard workers and diligent students, but it can also be taken lightly and for pleasure.

NOTES

1. Carol Gluck in Warren I. Cohen, ed., *New Frontiers in American-East Asian Relations* (New York: Columbia Univ. Press, 1983), p. 144.

2. Article IX of the Constitution. A convenient source is David John Lu, *Sources of Japanese History* (New York: McGraw-Hill, 1975), 2:193–97.

3. Article XXIV of the Constitution. Lu, 2:195.

4. Article XXVIII of the Constitution. Lu, 2:195.

5. Richard Pascale and Thomas P. Rohlen, "The Mazda Turnaround," *The Journal of Japanese Studies* 9, No. 2 (Dec. 1983), p. 263.

6. Donald Richie, *Japanese Cinema* (New York: Doubleday, 1971), p. 70.

7. Masao Miyoshi, *Accomplices of Silence: The Modern Japanese Novel* (Berkeley: The Univ. of California Press, 1974), p. 120.

8. Donald Keene, *Dawn to the West: Japanese Literature in the Modern Era* (New York: Holt, Rinehart, and Winston, 1984), p. 1162.

9. Jay McInerney, introduction to Helen Mitsios, ed., *New Japanese Voices: The Best Contemporary Fiction from Japan* (New York: The Atlantic Monthly Press, 1991).

10. Noguchi Takehiko, "A Survey of Literature in 1990," *Japanese Literature Today* 16 (March 1991), p. 4.

11. Isozaki Arata in Masao Miyoshi and H.D. Harootunian, eds., *Postmodernism and Japan* (Durham: Duke Univ. Press, 1989), pp. 57 and 59.

Suggestions for Further Reading

The literature in English on the history and civilizations of Japan is so extensive that careful selection is imperative for student and researcher alike. The effort here has been to suggest books that are broad enough to serve as introductions to their topics, that incorporate sound and recent scholarship, that make for good reading, and that in their totality reflect a variety of approaches. This listing gives special attention to sources of well-researched bibliography. When such sources are up-to-date and readily available, additional readings are generally not given. Please also note that the length of individual subsections depends in part on the availability of a good recent source for further readings—not on the intrinsic importance of a topic nor on the current state of research. Therefore, there may be fewer items given for a well-researched topic on which there is a recent bibliographical essay or other source of readings than for a topic on which less work has been done but for which there exists no good bibliography. Textbooks, collections of classroom readings, and translations of modern literature are not included. Years given are dates of first publication.

Reference Works

Frank J. Shulman, *Japan*, Vol. 103 of the *World Bibliography Series* (Oxford: Clio Press, 1990) is a highly recommended annotated bibliography covering a wide range of subjects. *The Bibliography of Asian Studies* published annually by the association for Asian Studies, Inc. is a basic resource. Also see John W. Dower, *Japanese History and Culture from Ancient to Modern Times: Seven Basic Bibliographies* (1986). *The Kodansha Encyclopedia of Japan* (1983) is a generally useful reference work.

General Works and Surveys

A basic resource is *The Cambridge History of Japan* of which four (out of five) volumes were published between 1989 and 1991. In general, the essays in these volumes offer a reliable account of the state of the field and provide bibliography for further study. However, inevitably there is some unevenness

299

in coverage, in the quality of writing, and in the amount of background knowledge expected from the reader.

Considering the explosion of knowledge, the age of monumental all-inclusive syntheses seems past (and only teachers of survey courses and textbook writers are left to dare a general overview). It therefore seems unlikely that anyone soon will emulate Sir George Sansom's *History of Japan*, 3 vols. (1958–63). Although out-of-date, it can still be read with profit and *pleasure*.

General Works on Culture, Literature, the Arts, Thought, and Religion

H. Paul Varley, *Japanese Culture: A Short History*, exp. ed. (1977) is a fine general survey. A valuable book on the visual arts is Robert T. Paine and Alexander Soper, *The Art and Architecture of Japan* (1955). Sherman E. Lee, *A History of Far Eastern Art*, rev. ed. (1973) is helpful in putting Japanese art (especially Buddhist art) into an Asian perspective. Other fine books on art include the volumes in the *Heibonsha Survey of Japanese Art* (1972–75) and *The Japanese Arts Library* (Kodansha, 1976–   ).

The Princeton Companion to Traditional Japanese Literature (1985), Earl Miner et al., eds. is highly regarded. Also see Thomas J. Rimer, *A Reader's Guide to Japanese Literature* (1988). Donald Keene, *The Pleasure of Japanese Literature* (1988) is itself a pleasure. For a Japanese view of Japanese literature, see the monumental work by Jin'ichi Konishi, *A History of Japanese Literature* (1984, 1986), trans. Aileen Gatten et al. (5 vols. projected). Donald Keene's delightful *Anthology of Japanese Literature* (1955) can be supplemented by Helen Craig McCullough's *Classical Japanese Prose: An Anthology* (1990). On drama, see Benito Ortolani, *The Japanese Theater: From Shamanistic Ritual to Contemporary Pluralism.* (Leiden: Brill, 1990). For a stimulating, sophisticated study, see David Pollack, *The Fracture of Meaning: Japan's Synthesis of China from the Eighth through the Eighteenth Centuries* (1986).

East Asian Civilizations: A Dialogue in Five Stages (1988) by Wm. Theodore de Bary is a masterful summation that concludes by pointing to the need for both East Asia and the West to catch up with each other. Gilbert Rozman, ed., *The East Asian Region: Confucian Heritage and Its Modern Adaptation* (1991) contains stimulating essays treating Japanese Confucian tradition in comparative perspective. H. Byron Earhart, *Japanese Religion: Unity and Diversity* (1974) is an excellent introduction. For a fuller treatment of the subject, see Joseph M. Kitagawa, *Religion in Japanese History* (1966). Heinz Bechert and Richard Gombrich, *The World of Buddhism* (1984) is a well-illustrated introduction. Two well-regarded books on Buddhist thought are Paul Williams, *Mahayana Buddhism: The Doctrinal Foundations* (1989) and Roger J. Corless, *The Vision of Buddhism: The Space Under the Tree* (1989). Wm. Theodore de Bary, ed., *The Buddhist*

Tradition in India, China, and Japan (1972) is a useful anthology. There are good up-to-date entries on many topics in Mircea Eliade, ed., *The Encyclopedia of Religion*, 16 vols. (1987).

PART I. BEGINNINGS AND FOUNDATIONS

Windows on the Japanese Past: Studies in Archaeology and Prehistory (1986), edited by Richard J. Pearson, is a collection of demanding essays on major issues. A good book on the marvelous figures that decorated the outside of Japan's great tombs is Fumio Miki, *Haniwa: The Clay Sculpture of Proto-historic Japan* (1960), English adaption by Roy A. Miller. For Shinto and general works on Buddhism, see the bibliographies in the books listed above. For Japan's oldest anthology of poetry, see Hideo Levy, trans., *The Ten Thousand Leaves: A Translation of the Man'yoshu, Japan's Premier Anthology of Classical Poetry* (1981) and the review essay by Edwin A. Cranston, *The Journal of Japanese Studies* 9, No. 1 (1983): 97–138. For other translations and discussions, see the *Princeton Companion*.

PART II. ARISTOCRATS, MONKS, AND SAMURAI

Institutional history from the Heian period to the mid-sixteenth century is particularly well-represented in the *Cambridge History of Japan*, Vol. 3, edited by Kozo Yamamura. It can be supplemented by the numerous books written and edited by John Hall and Jeffrey Mass. On politics, also see Cameron Hurst III, *Insei: Abdicated Sovereigns in the Politics of Early Heian Japan* (1976). William W. Farris, *Population, Disease and Land in Early Japan, 645–900* (1985) presents findings and ideas which merit the attention of all students of early Japan. Robert Borgen, *Sugawara no Michizane and the Early Heian Court* (1986) is important for both political and cultural history. Two books by Paul Varley are recommended for the political history of the fourteenth and fifteenth centuries: *Imperial Restoration in Medieval Japan* (1971) and *The Onin War* (1967).

Heian literature is well-represented in translations (see the *Princeton Companion*), and there is a growing literature on *The Tale of Genji* in English. A useful introduction to Japan's greatest novel is Richard Bowring, *Murasaki Shikibu, The Tale of Genji* (1988). A delightful, well-written book is Ivan Morris, *The World of the Shining Prince: Court Life in Ancient Japan* (1964).

William R. LaFleur, *The Karma of Words: Buddhism and the Literary Arts in Medieval Japan* (1983) includes an excellent discussion of Buddhism as well as literary analysis and a provocative thesis. Daigan and Alicia Matsunaga, *Foundations of Japanese Buddhism* 2 vols. (1976) provide a detailed account of Japanese Buddhism. James Dobbins, *Jodo Shinshu: Shin Buddhism in Medieval Japan* (1989) deals with a subject central to Kamakura religious history.

There is a vast literature on Zen. The standard work on its history is Heinrich Doumoulin, *Zen Buddhism: A History: Japan*, 2nd ed. (1989). The most scholarly translation of a key Chinese text is Philip P. Yampolski, *The Platform Sutra of the Sixth Patriarch: The Text of the Tun-huang Manuscript* (1967). For an excellent philosophical study, see T. P. Kasulis, *Zen Action-Zen Person* (1981). Recommended with enthusiasm is Jan Fontain and Money L. Hickman, *Zen Painting and Calligraphy* (1970), a catalog of an exhibition of both Chinese and Japanese works. For other works on the arts, see the appropriate volumes in "The Arts of Japan" and "Heibonsha" series. Paul Varley and Kumakura Isao, eds., *Tea in Japan: Essays on the History of Chanoyu* (1989) is recommended on this subject.

The heroes of an age reveal much about its values: see Helen Craig McCullough, trans., *Yoshitsune—A Fifteenth Century Japanese Chronicle* (1971). Among McCullough's numerous contributions to our understanding of traditional Japanese literature is her recent translation of *The Tale of the Heike* (1988) which includes a discussion of this work as literature. Also appearing too late for inclusion in the *Princeton Companion* is Thomas B. Hare, *Zeami's Style: The Noh Plays of Zeami Motokiyo* (1986). *Japan in the Muromachi Age* (1977), John W. Hall and Toyoda Takeshi, eds., includes essays on cultural as well as social-political topics.

PART III. LATE TRADITIONAL JAPAN

The Cambridge History, Vol. 4, edited by John W. Hall is a major resource. For the sixteenth century, see George Ellison and Bardwell Smith, eds., *Warlords, Artists, and Commoners* (1981). A brilliant and well-formulated interpretation of the Tokugawa political system is provided by Harold Bolitho, *Treasures Among Men: The Fudai Daimyo in Tokugawa Japan* (1974). Readers would also do well to consult Conrad Totman, *Politics in the Tokugawa Bakufu, 1600–1843* (1967).

An excellent introduction to the initial contacts between modern Europe and East Asia is provided by George Sansom, *The Western World and Japan* (1950). A well-written, informative account is C. R. Boxer, *The Christian Century in Japan* (1951). Also see Michael Cooper, S. J., *They Came to Japan—An Anthology of European Reports on Japan, 1543–1640* (1965), and George Ellison, *Deus Destroyed: The Image of Christianity in Early Modern Japan* (1973). For foreign relations under the Tokugawa, see Ronald P. Toby, *State and Diplomacy in Early Modern Japan* (1984).

Politics and Confucianism are examined in Kate W. Nakai, *Shogunal Politics: Arai Hakuseki and the Premises of Tokugawa Rule* (1988). Also see John W. Hall, *Tanuma Okitsugu, 1719–1788, Forerunner of Modern Japan* (1968), and John W. Hall and Marius Jansen, eds., *Studies in the Institutional History of Early Modern Japan* (1968). A splendid study of Tokugawa economic history is Thomas C. Smith, *The Agrarian Origins of Modern Japan* (1959). The same author's essays have been collected under the title, *Native Sources of Japanese Industrialization, 1750–1920* (1988). Also see

Susan B. Hanly and Kozo Yamamura, *Economic and Demographic Change in Preindustrial Japan, 1600–1868* (1977), as well as Ann B. Jannetta, *Epidemics and Mortality in Early Modern Japan* (1987). For some pertinent reflections on society and technology, see Noel Perrin, *Giving up the Gun: Japan's Reversion to the Sword, 1543–1879* (1979).

Recent years have seen increased attention given to Tokugawa intellectual history. For Confucianism, see Peter Nosco, ed., *Confucianism and Tokugawa Culture* (1984), Herman Ooms, *Tokugawa Ideology, Early Constructs, 1570–1680* (1985) and Mary Evelyn Tucker, *Moral and Spiritual Cultivation in Japanese Neo-Confucianism: The Life and Thought of Kaibara Ekken (1630–1714)* (1989). For the intellectual history of the merchant class, see the important book by Tetsuo Najita, *Visions of Virtue in Tokugawa Japan: The Kaitokudō Merchant Academy of Osaka* (1987). A good place to begin studying nativism is Peter Nosco, *Remembering Paradise: Nativism and Nostalgia in Eighteenth-Century Japan* (1990). A delightful book on "Dutch Learning" is Donald Keene, *The Japanese Discovery of Europe, 1720–1830* (1969). Keene is also author of the masterful survey, *World Within Walls: Japanese Literature of the Pre-modern Era, 1600–1867* (1976).

Ronald P. Dore, *Education in Tokugawa Japan* (1965) is a major study of a major topic. The lively culture of the Tokugawa is depicted in a number of scholarly and entertaining books. A good place to begin is Howard Hibbett, *The Floating World in Japanese Fiction* (1960). For Bashō, Saikaku, Chikamatsu and other writers, see Keene's survey and the *Princeton Companion*. Recommended on the art of the woodcut is Richard Lane, *Masters of the Japanese Print—Their World and Their Work* (1962). For individual artists, see the volumes in the *Masterworks of Ukiyo-e* series (Kodansha International, 1968–   ). There are other worthy books on Tokugawa art, popular and aristocratic. One such is *Hokusai: One Hundred Views of Mt. Fuji*, introduction and commentaries by Henry D. Smith II (1988). A window on life in Edo in late Tokugawa is Edwin McClellan, *Woman in the Crested Kimono: The Life of Shibue Io and Her Family Drawn from Mori Ogai's "Shibue Chusai"* (1985). A book that stands out is Elise Grilli's superb *The Art of the Japanese Screen* (1970), a truly beautiful book.

PART IV. MODERN JAPAN

The last two volumes of the *Cambridge History*, Vols. 5 and 6, edited respectively by Marius Jansen and Peter Duus deal with the nineteenth and twentieth centuries. Tessa Morris-Suzuki, *A History of Japanese Economic Thought* (London 1989) provides a clear and balanced brief survey of its topic from the Tokugawa to the present. Similarly broad in scope are the essays of Thomas C. Smith collected under the title, *Japanese Industrialization, 1750–1920* (1988). Donald H. Shively, ed., *Personality in Japanese History* (1971) spans the last two centuries. A specialized book dealing with the same time span is Conrad Totman, *The Origins of Japan's Modern Forests* (1985) which analyzes and documents a case of successful reforestation and poses a basic question: "What level of human disaster must overtake a society before it is moved to confront its problems?" (p. 58)

Two books analyzing Japan's relations with the outside world during the entire modern period are: Akira Iriye, ed., *The Chinese and Japanese: Essays in Political and Cultural Interactions* (1980) and Warren I. Cohen, ed., *New Frontiers in American East Asian Relations* (1983).

Economic history is treated at length in *The Cambridge History*. For the history of individual companies, readers should note the ongoing *History of Japanese Business and Industries Series* (Harvard Univ. Press). On the values and ideas during the formative period of modern capitalism, see Byron K. Marshall, *Capitalism and Nationalism in Prewar Japan: The Ideology of the Business Elite, 1868–1941* (1967), and Earl Kinmoth, *The Self-made Man in Meiji Japanese Thought* (1981). Mikio Hane, *Peasants, Rebels, and Outcasts: The Underside of Modern Japan* (1982) calls attention to those who did not benefit by "modernization." See also E. Patricia Tsurumi, *Factory Girls: Women in the Thread Mills of Meiji Japan* (1990). Andrew Gordon, *The Evolution of Labor Relations in Japanese Heavy Industry, 1853–1955* (1985), the same author's *Labor and Imperial Democracy in Prewar Japan* (1991), and Sheldon Garon, *The State and Labor in Modern Japan* (1987) are major studies of crucial issues. On agriculture, see Penelope Francks, *Technology and Agriculture Development in Pre-War Japan* (1984).

For Meiji political history, the following are still useful: George Akita, *Foundations of Constitutional Government in Modern Japan* (1967), Nobutaka Ike, *The Beginnings of Political Democracy in Japan* (1950), and Joseph Pittau, *Political Thought in Early Meiji Japan, 1868–1889* (1967). A study of a major Meiji statesman is provided in Roger F. Hackett, *Yamagata Aritomo in the Rise of Modern Japan, 1838–1922* (1971). For Japanese and Western historians' evaluations of Meiji statesmen, see the survey conducted by Richard T. Chang, *Historians and Meiji Statesmen* (University of Florida Social Science Monograph, No. 41, 1975). An important institutional development is examined in Robert M. Spaulding, Jr., *Imperial Japan's Higher Civil Service Examinations* (1967). The schooling of the men who succeeded into positions of leadership in the world of business and letters is described and analyzed in Donald T. Roden, *Schooldays in Imperial Japan: A Study in the Culture of the Student Elite* (1981).

A good way to begin studying Meiji intellectual history is by examining the life and ideas of Fukuzawa Yukichi. His *An Encouragement of Learning* (1969), trans. David A. Dilworth and Umeyo Hirano, is a collection of essays written in the 1870s. Also well worth reading is his *Autobiography* (1966), trans. Eiichi Kiyooka. Important secondary studies are Carmen Blacker, *The Japanese Enlightenment: A Study of the Writings of Fukuzawa Yukichi* (1964), and an article by Albert Craig in *Political Development in Modern Japan* (1968), ed. Robert E. Ward. Also see William R. Braisted, trans. and ed., *Meiroku Zasshi: Journal of the Japanese Enlightenment* (1975). Two other valuable books on intellectual history are Kenneth B. Pyle, *The New Generation in Meiji Japan: Problems of Cultural Identity, 1885–1895* (1969), and Irwin Scheiner, *Christian Converts and Social*

Protest in Meiji Japan (1970). For intellectual and social history in a different perspective, see Sharon Sievers, *Flowers in Salt: The Beginnings of Feminist Consciousness in Modern Japan* (1983). This might well be read in conjunction with Gail L. Bernstein, ed., *Recreating Japanese Women, 1600–1945* (1991).

Carol Gluck, *Japan's Modern Myths: Ideology in the Late Meiji Period* (1985) is a brilliant, nuanced study that goes beyond intellectual history to explore a wide range of sources.

W. G. Beasley, *Japanese Imperialism, 1894–1945* (1987), is a thoughtful scholarly synthesis. Two of a projected three-volume study of the Japanese empire have appeared to date: *The Japanese Empire, 1895–1945* (1984) edited by Raymond Myers and Mark R. Peattie (1984) and *Japan's Informal Empire in China, 1895–1937*, ed. by Peter Duus, Myers, and Peattie (1989). Surveys of foreign policy are provided by James W. Morely, *Japan's Foreign Policy, 1868–1941: A Research Guide* (1974), and Ian Nish, ed., *Japanese Foreign Policy, 1869–1942* (1977). A detailed study is Francis Hilary Conroy, *The Japanese Seizure of Korea, 1868–1910* (1960). Indispensable for an understanding of Korea itself, and a fine starting point for anyone interested in modern Korean history, is the excellent book by James B. Palais, *Politics and Policy in Traditional Korea, 1864–1876* (1975).

On the Russo-Japanese War, see Shumpei Okamoto, *The Japanese Oligarchy and the Russo-Japanese War* (1971), and John A. White, *The Diplomacy of the Russo-Japanese War* (1964). Also see Richard Neu, *The Uncertain Friendship: Theodore Roosevelt and Japan, 1906–1909* (1967). I. H. Nish has written two books on Anglo-Japanese relations: *The Anglo-Japanese Alliance: The Diplomacy of Two Island Empires 1894–1907* (1966) and *Alliance in Decline: A Study in Anglo-Japanese Relations 1908–23* (1972).

Late Meiji politics is analyzed by Tetsuo Najita in *Hara Kei in the Politics of Compromise, 1905–1915* (1967). The best study on the political system as it evolved during the next decade is Peter Duus, *Party Rivalry and Political Change in Taishō Japan* (1968). A valuable and stimulating collection of essays is Bernard S. Silberman and H. D. Harootunian, eds., *Japan in Crisis: Essays on Taishō Democracy* (1974). A book rich in detail is George O. Totten III, *The Social Democratic Movement in Prewar Japan* (1966). An indispensable book for the student of Marxism in East Asia is Gail L. Bernstein, *Japanese Marxist: A Portrait of Kawakami Hajime, 1879–1946* (1976). A strong recent addition to the literature is Miriam R. Silverberg, *Changing Song: The Marxist Manifesto of Nakano Shigeharu* (1991). For a very different kind of radical, see Thomas A. Stanley, *Osugi Sakae, Anarchist in Taishō Japan* (1982). Two good books on foreign policy are James W. Morley, *The Japanese Thrust into Siberia, 1918* (1957), and Akira Iriye, *After Imperialism: The Search for a New Order in East Asia, 1921–31* (1965).

Thomas J. Rimer, ed., *Culture and Identity: Japanese Intellectuals during the Interwar Years* (1990) is the best book in its field. Maruyama Masao, a distinguished Japanese intellectual historian, has written a number of perceptive essays in Japanese ultranationalism, published as *Thought and Behavior in Japanese Politics* (1963), ed. Ivan Morris. The thinking and politics of a key military man are examined by Mark R. Peattie, *Ishiwara Kanji and Japan's Confrontation with the West* (1975). A distinguished political analysis of the thirties is provided by Gordon M. Berger, *Parties Out of Power in Japan: 1931–1941* (1977). A major stream of opposition to urbanization and capitalism is traced and analyzed in Thomas R. Havens, *Farm and Nation in Modern Japan: Agrarian Nationalism, 1870–1940* (1974). On the official ideology prevailing in the thirties, see R. K. Hall, ed., *Kokutai no Hongi: Cardinal Principles of the National Entity of Japan* (1949). The essays in James W. Morley and Donald H. Shively, eds., *Dilemmas of Growth in Prewar Japan* (1967) deal primarily with the thirties. A key incident is studied in Ben-Ami Shillony, *Revolt in Japan: The Young Officers and the February 26, 1936 Incident* (1973).

Akira Iriye, *The Origins of the Second World War in Asia and the Pacific* (1987), provides a masterful overview of Japanese diplomatic history. Also recommended are Robert Butow, *Tōjō and the Coming of the War* (1961); James B. Crowley, *Japan's Quest for Autonomy: National Security and Foreign Policy, 1930–38* (1966); and Michael A. Barnhart, *Japan Prepares for Total War: The Search for Economic Security, 1919–1941* (1987). More specialized studies include Sadako Ogata, *Defiance in Manchuria: The Making of Japanese Foreign Policy, 1931–32* (1964); James W. Morley, ed., *Deterrent Diplomacy, Japan, Germany, and the U.S.S.R., 1935–1940* (1976), and Dorothy Borg, *The United States and the Far Eastern Crisis of 1933–1938* (1964). On the Japanese military, see Ernest L. Presseisen, *Before Aggression: Europeans Prepare the Japanese Army* (1965), Saburō Hayashi in collaboration with Alvin D. Coox, *Kōgun: The Japanese Army in the Pacific War* (1959), and Paul S. Dull, *A Battle History of the Japanese Navy* (1978). Additional perspectives are provided by Akira Iriye, *Power and Culture: The Japanese-American War, 1941–1945* (1981) and John W. Dower, *War Without Mercy: Race and Power in the Pacific War* (1985).

The Pacific War began with Pearl Harbor and ended with the atomic bomb. Both events have been written about at length and remain foci of scholarly controversies. On Pearl Harbor, see Dorothy Borg and Shumpei Okamoto, eds., *Pearl Harbor as History* (1973), and Gordon Prange, *Pearl Harbor: The Verdict of History* (1985). For a writer, particularly an American, to deal with Hiroshima demands unusual sensitivity: the classic account is John Hersey, *Hiroshima* (1946). For the American decision to use the bomb, see Martin J. Sherwin, *A World Destroyed: Hiroshima and the Origins of the Arms Race* (1975, 1987). For Japanese responses, see Kyoko Selden and Mark Selden, eds., *The Atomic Bomb: Voices from Hiroshima and Nagasaki* (1989) and its bibliography. A famous novel on the bomb is *Black Rain* (1965) by Ibuse Masuji. Also see Ōe Kenzaburō, *Hiroshima Notes* (1981) and the book he edited, *The Crazy Iris and Other Stories of the Atomic Aftermath* (1984).

Donald Keene, *Dawn to the West* is a comprehensive and authoritative account of modern Japanese literature from the Meiji period until the present with an extensive bibliography. A fine book that approaches modern Japanese literature through its historical roots is J. Thomas Rimer, *Modern*

Japanese Fiction and Its Traditions (1978). On poetry, see Makoto Ueda, *Modern Japanese Poets and the Nature of Literature* (1983).

There is a rich critical literature on individual modern authors including: Paul Anderer, *Other Worlds: Arishima Takeo and the Bounds of Modern Japanese Fiction* (1984), Phyllis I. Lyons, *The Saga of Dazai Osamu: A Critical Study with Translations* (1985), Alan Wolfe, *Suicidal Narrative in Modern Japan: The Case of Dazai Osamu* (1990), John Whittier Treat, *Pools of Water, Pillars of Fire: The Literature of Ibuse Masuji* (1988), Michiko N. Wilson, *The Marginal World of Ōe Kenzaburō* (1986).

A useful overview of Japanese philosophy is provided by Gino K. Piovesena, *Recent Japanese Philosophical Thought: 1862–1962, A Survey*, revised ed. (1968); and for a statement by a major modern philosopher, see *Fundamental Problems of Philosophy* (Nishida Kitarō's *Tetsugaku no kompon mondai*) (1970), trans. David A. Dilworth. There is no general survey in English of the period's visual arts, but the following are helpful: Michiaki Kawakita, *Modern Currents in Japanese Art* (Heibonsha Survey of Japanese Art, Vol. 24, 1974); *Arts of Japan*, Vol. 6, *Meiji Western Painting by Minoru Harada* (1964); and the excellent exhibition catalog, *Paris in Japan: The Japanese Encounter with European Painting* (1987), by Shuji Takashima and J. Thomas Rimer. For this and other arts, including music, see also Donald H. Shively, ed., *Tradition and Modernization in Japanese Culture* (1971).

Contemporary Japan

There is fine discussion of the historiography of the Occupation of Japan by Carol Gluck in Warren Cohen's *New Frontiers* (see the first paragraph under Section V). Theodore Cohen, *Remaking Japan—The American Occupation as New Deal* (1987), is the most recent addition to the ever-growing corpus of scholarship on the Occupation.

The Japanese economy has been quite extensively studied. Good books include Hugh Patrick, ed., with the assistance of Larry Meisner, *Japanese Industrialization and Its Social Consequences* (1976), and Hugh Patrick and Henry Rosovsky, eds., *Asia's New Giant: How the Japanese Economy Works* (1976), consisting of papers described by a reviewer as ranging in style "from semi-Galbraithian sparkle to semi-dissertation ponderosity" (see *Journal of Japanese Studies* 3 [Winter 1977]:166). Also see Chalmers Johnson, *MITI and the Japanese Miracle: The Growth of Industrial Policy, 1925–1975* (1985), and especially Ronald Dore, *Taking Japan Seriously: A Confucian Perspective on Leading Economic Issues* (1987). For the transformation of village Japan, see the same author's *Shinohata: A Portrait of a Japanese Village* (1978). Another very informative study is Robert E. Cole, *Japanese Blue Collar: Changing Traditions* (1971). In the eighties and nineties a number of books of high journalism appeared warning Americans of the competition they faced from Japanese companies. One of the best by a veteran journalist is David Haberstam, *The Reckoning* (1986) which focuses on a comparison between Nissan and Ford. Also see *Japan in The Passing Lane* by Satoshi Kamata (1982). One of the more interesting and informative recent analyses of Japanese politics is Karel Van Wolferen, *The Enigma of Japanese Power* (1990).

Nathan Thayer, *How the Conservatives Rule Japan* (1960) is a cogent analysis of the system of local support organizations. Also see Gerald L. Curtis, *Election Campaigning Japanese Style* (1971) and *The Japanese Way of Politics* (1988). For a blow by blow analysis of the LDP'S response to various challenges, informed by recent theory and scholarship, see Kent E. Calder, *Crisis and Compensation: Public Policy and Political Stability in Japan, 1949–1986* (1988).

Much has been written on contemporary Japanese culture and society. For a recent discussion of some salient aspects as well as methodology, see Yoshio Sugimoto and Ross E. Mouer, eds., *Constructs for Understanding Japan* (1989). Theodore C. Bestor, *Neighborhood Tokyo* (1989) is a worthy sequel to Ronald P. Dore, *City Life in Japan: A Study of a Tokyo Ward* (1958). A book with implications beyond Japan is David Plath, *Long Engagements: Maturity in Modern Japan* (1980). Plath is also the editor of *Work and Life Course in Japan* (1983). Much attention has been paid in recent years to education, on which see James J. Shields, ed., *Japanese Schooling: Patterns of Socialization, Equality, and Political Control* (1989).

Shunsuke Tsurumi, *A Cultural History of Postwar Japan 1945–1980* (London: Kegan Paul, 1987) is unsystematic but contains interesting information on popular culture. Donald Richie and Joseph I. Anderson, *The Japanese Film: Art and Industry* (1982), is recommended as is Richie's *The Films of Akira Kurosawa* (1984). The serious student will want to consult Beverly B. Bueher, *Japanese Films: A Filmography and Commentary, 1921–1990.* (Jefferson, NC: McFarland & Co., 1990.)

For Japanese self-perceptions, see Ross Mouer and Y. Sugimoto, *Images of Japanese Society: A Study in the Social Construction of Reality* (1986). For a taste of postmodernism as well as some insights, see Masao Miyoshi and H. D. Harootunian, eds., *Postmodernism and Japan* (1989). Also see Botond Bogner, *The New Japanese Architecture* (1990), and Jackie Kerstenbaum, ed., *Emerging Japanese Architects of the 1990s* (1990).

Copyrights and Acknowledgments

For permission to use copyrighted material reprinted in this book, the author is grateful to the following publishers and copyright holders:

COLUMBIA UNIVERSITY PRESS   For five lines of poetry from *Sources of Japanese Tradition*, compiled by Ryusaku Tsunoda, Wm. Theodore De Bary, and Donald Keene, © 1958, Columbia University Press, New York. Used by permission of the publisher.

DOUBLEDAY   From *An Introduction to Haiku* by Harold G. Henderson, © 1958 by Harold G. Henderson. Used by permission of Doubleday, a division of Bantam Doubleday Dell Publishing Group, Inc.

UNIVERSITY OF MICHIGAN MUSEUM OF ART   For a poem by Bashō from *The Poet Painters: Buson and His Followers* by Calvin L. French, exhibition catalog published by the University of Michigan Museum of Art, 1974.

STANFORD UNIVERSITY PRESS   For a poem by Ono no Komachi, a poem by Saigyo, a poem by Fujiwara Teika, a poem by Lady Jusami Chikaku, and an excerpt from "On Seeing the Body of a Man Laying Among the Stones on the Island of Samine in Sanuki Province" by Kakinomoto Hitomaro, all reprinted from *An Introduction to Japanese Court Poetry*, with translations by the author and Robert Brower, by Earl Miner, with the permission of the publishers, Stanford University Press. © 1968 by the Board of Trustees of the Leland Stanford Junior University; and for figures reprinted from *Japan: A Short Cultural History* by G. B. Sansom, with the permission of the publishers, Stanford University Press © 1941, 1943, 1952 by G. B. Sansom.

CHARLES E. TUTTLE, CO., INC.   For a poem by Ariwara no Narihira from *The Tales of Ise*, translated H. Jay Harris; and for "Bamboos" by Hagiwara Sakutarō, from *Face at the Bottom of the World and Other Poems*, translated by Graeme Wilson. All reprinted by permission of Charles E. Tuttle Co., Inc. of Tokyo, Japan.

Illustrations

p. xi, Magnum/Steven McCurry

p. 8, Osaka University

p. 8, Osaka University

p. 9, Tohoku University

p. 11, Katherine Young

p. 14, Lore Schirokauer

p. 29, Japanese National Tourist Organization

p. 36, Japanese Information Center, Consulate General of Japan, New York

p. 37, Katherine Young

p. 39, Sakamoto Photo Research Laboratory

p. 40, (top) Lore Schirokauer
   (bottom) Robert Treat Paine and Alexander Soper, *The Art and Architecture of Japan* (Pelican History of Art, 2nd rev. ed., 1974). Reprinted by permission of Penguin Books Ltd.

p. 40, Shankia Photo Library

p. 61, Lore Schirokauer

p. 65, Lore Schirokauer

p. 66, Muroji Publishers

p. 67, Sakamoto Photo Research Laboratory

p. 68, National Commission for Protection of Cultural Properties of Japan

p. 69, Sakamoto Photo Research Laboratory

p. 70, National Commission for Protection of Cultural Properties of Japan

p. 71, Lore Schirokauer

p. 86, Katherine Young

p. 87, Katherine Young

p. 88, National Commission for Protection of Cultural Properties of Japan

p. 91, (top left) Robert Treat Paine and Alexander Soper, *The Art and Architecture of Japan,* (Pelican History of Art, 2nd rev. ed., 1974). Reprinted by permission of Penguin Books Ltd.
(top right) Lore Schirokauer

p. 91, (bottom left) Lore Schirokauer
(bottom right) Robert Treat Paine and Alexander Soper, *The Art and Architecture of Japan,* (Pelican History of Art, 2nd rev. ed., 1974). Reprinted by permission of Penguin Books Ltd.

p. 92, Shankinko Photo Library

p. 109, Lore Schirokauer

p. 109, Lore Schirokauer

p. 111, 1988 Kyoto National Museum. All rights reserved.

p. 125, Lore Schirokauer

p. 126, Imperial Household Collection (photo from Zauho Press)

p. 127, Hakone Art Museum, Japan

p. 136, Courtesy of Namban Bunkakan, Osaka

p. 139, Reprinted with permission from Charles E. Tuttle & Co.

p. 150, 1988 Kyoto National Museum. All rights reserved.

p. 151, National Treasures Kenninji (photo from Zauho Press)

p. 152, Nezu Museum, Tokyo (photo from Zauho Press)

p. 154, Collection of W. Boller

p. 155, By permission of The Fine Arts Museum of San Francisco, Achenbach Foundation for Graphic Arts purchase

p. 159, The University of Michigan Museum of Art, Margaret Watson Parker Art collection

p. 160, Asia Society

p. 161, Sakamoto Photo Research Laboratory

p. 171, Lore Schirokauer

p. 181, Library of Congress, "Yokohama-e" Prints, Chadbourne Collection

p. 182, Peabody Museum of Salem (photo by Mark Sexton)

p. 202, Collection of the Imperial Household, Tokyo

p. 206, Courtesy of Robert Muller

p. 230, Takakiyu Mitsui collection (photo from Zauho Press)

p. 239, Sakamoto Photo Research Laboratory

p. 255, From *The Gates of Heavenly Peace: The Chinese and Their Revolution, 1895–1980,* 1981 by Jonathan D. Spence (Viking Penguin, Inc.).

p. 261, Wide World Photos

p. 267, Wide World Photos

p. 293, Minami Gallery, Tokyo

p. 295, Arata Isozaki & Associates (photo by Yasuhiros Ishimoto)

p. 296, Lore Schirokauer

Index

Page numbers in italics refer to illustrations.

Novels. *See* Literature
Nuclear weapons, 279

Occupation of Japan. *See* Japan, Occupied
Oda Nobunaga, 120–121, 134–135
Ōe Kenzaburō, 291
Ōgai [Mori], 228
Ogata Kōrin, 151–152, *152*
Ogyū Sorai, 162–163, 165–166
Oil boycott, 280
Okada Keisuke, 252
Okakura Tenshin, 206, 208, 229
Okinawa, 272, 283
Ōkubo Toshimichi, 188–190, 192–193, 198, 199
Ōkuma Shigenobu, 190–191, 199, 200, 232
On Liberty (Mill), 204
Ōnin War, 102, 107, 114
Ono no Komachi, 63
Opium War, 180
Oriental Development Company, 223
Osaka, 146, 156, 176
Osaka Bay, 5
Osaka Castle, *xi*, 123, 124, 125, 128
Ōshio Heihachirō, 175
Ozu Yasujirō, 289

Paine, Robert, 36
Painting: in Ashikaga Shogunate, 100–101, *100*, 110–112, *111*; in Azuchi-Momoyama epoch, 125–128, *126–127*; Buddhist painting in Japanese temples, 36–37, *39*; in Heian period, 67–71, *67–70*; in Kamakura period, 90–92; in Late Meiji period, 229–230, *229–230*; "literati painting," 158; in Meiji period, 202, *202*, 205–206, *206–207*; in Taishō period, 238–240, *238–240*; in Tokugawa Shogunate, 150–152
Paleolithic Period, 5
Pariahs, 146–147, 227
Patriarchs of the Three Creeds (Josetsu), 104–105, *104*
Pearson, Richard, 7
Peasants: in Korea, 215; and Meiji Restoration, 191; in Taishō period, 237; in Tokugawa Shogunate, 144–145, 175; and Toyotomi Hideyoshi, 121, 123; uprisings of, 114, 175, 191. *See also* Feudalism
Peattie, Mark R., 258
Perfumes, 56
Perry, Matthew C., 180–183, *181*, 184, 185
Persian Gulf War, 283
Personal Matter (Ōe), 291
Pescadores, 216
Philippines, 136–137
Phoenix Pavilion (Byōdōin), 71–72, *71*
Pietism, during Heian period, 61–62
Pillow Book (Sei), 55–56, 101
Pimiko, 12–13
Pine Grove (Hasegawa), 127–128, *127*
Piracy, 80, 123
Poetry: in Ashikaga Shogunate, 100, 110; free verse, 242–243; from Germany, 228; haiku,

152, 157–158, 160, 228, 242; in Heian period, 62–63; in Kamakura period, 93–94; in Nara period, 33–34; in Taishō period, 242–243; in Tokugawa Shogunate, 152, 157–158
Political parties: factionalism in, 277–278; in Late Meiji period, 225; in Meiji period, 199–200; in 1930s, 250–251; in 1952–1972, 277–280; in 1970s–1980s, 282; in Occupation of Japan, 276–277; in Taishō period, 232, 235–237; in World War II, 257. *See also* names of specific parties
Politics: in Late Meiji period, 225–227; in Meiji period, 198–200; in 1952–1972, 276–280; in 1970s–1980s, 280–283; during Occupation of Japan, 276–277; in Taishō period, 231–232, 233–235; after World War I, 233–235
Pollution, 285
Polygamy, 16
Portsmouth Treaty, 221–222, 231
Portugal: in East Asia, 130, *131*, 132; expulsion from Japan, 138; introduction of firearms to Japan, 115, 121
Pottery: in Azuchi-Momoyama epoch, 127–128; of Jomon Culture, 7–8, *8*; and *mingei* (folk arts) movement, 241; in Tokugawa Shogunate, 150; in Tomb Period, *1*, 12; of Yayoi Culture, 9–10, *9*
Print making, 153–154, 158–159, 205–206, 292–293
Puppet theater, 148, 155–156
Pure Land sect, 82–83
Puyi, 250

Quality of life, 283–288

Railroads, 211, 220–221, 222, 233, 284
Raku ware, 127, *128*, 150
Ran, 289
Rashomon, 289
Records of Rites, 23–24, 162
Recruit scandal, 282
Religion: Buddhism, 11, 17, 25–30, *28*, *29*; Christianity's legalization, 194, 210; Confucianism, 21–24, 25, 144, 145, 147; female shamans in Tomb Period, 12–13; Heart Learning (Shingaku), 149; Jesuit missionaries, 132–137; in Jomon Culture, 8; Neo-Confucianism, 174, 179, 204; Nichiren, 83–84; Pure Land sect, 82–83; Shingon Buddhism, 59–61; Shinto, 13–15, *14*, 30, 32, 41, 59, 60, 86–87, 166–167, 178, 179, 193–194, 207; Sōka Gakkai, 84, 279, 288; Tendai Buddhism, during Heinan period, 57–59; Tokugawa Confucianism, 162, 164–166; Tonghak, 216; True Pure Land Buddhism, 82–83, 114; Zen, 84–86, *86*. *See also* Temples
Renga, 110, 290
Rennyo, 83
Renoir, Pierre-Auguste, 230
Rhapsody in August, 289